W9-CIE-970

THE GREATNESS THAT WAS BABYLON

Other titles in the Great Civilizations Series:

CARTHAGE
Gilbert Charles Picard and Colette Picard

THE WONDER THAT WAS INDIA, VOL. I
A. L. Basham

THE WONDER THAT WAS INDIA, VOL. II
S. A. A. Rizvi

PRE-OTTOMAN TURKEY
Claude Cahen

THE VIKING ACHIEVEMENT
P. G. Foote and D. M. Wilson

THE SPLENDOUR THAT WAS EGYPT
Margaret A. Murray

THE GLORY THAT WAS GREECE
J. C. Stobart

THE GRANDEUR THAT WAS ROME
J. C. Stobart

THE MAJESTY THAT WAS ISLAM
Montgomery W. Watt

THE MIGHT THAT WAS ASSYRIA
H. W. F. Saggs

THE NORMAN ACHIEVEMENT
Richard F. Cassady

The Greatness that was BABYLON

A Survey of the Ancient Civilization of the Tigris–Euphrates Valley

Fully revised and updated

H. W. F. SAGGS

SIDGWICK & JACKSON
London

Original edition first published in Great Britain in 1962
by Sidgwick & Jackson Limited
Second edition published in 1988

ISBN 0-283-99623-4

Photoset by Rowland Phototypesetting Limited
Bury St Edmunds, Suffolk
Printed in Hong Kong
for Sidgwick & Jackson Limited
1 Tavistock Chambers, Bloomsbury Way
London WC1A 2SG

To the memory of my grandfather,
WILLIAM GEORGE SAGGS,
Gamekeeper and Farmer

Contents

List of Illustrations

BETWEEN PAGES 74 AND 75

BETWEEN PAGES 170 AND 171

LIST OF ILLUSTRATIONS

BETWEEN PAGES 266 AND 267

BETWEEN PAGES 362 AND 363

ACKNOWLEDGEMENTS

The sources of the plates are as follows:

Courtesy of the Trustees of the British Museum: plates 2B, 5, 7, 8B, 9A, 9B, 10, 11B, 12, 18A, 20, 21A, 22, 23, 24, 25, 26A, 26B,

26C, 27A, 27B, 28, 29, 30, 31, 32, 33A, 33B, 34, 35, 36, 38, 39, 40, 41, 42, 43A, 43B, 44A, 44B, 45, 46A, 46B, 47, 48, 49, 50A, 50B, 51A, 51C, 52, 53, 54A, 54B, 55, 56A, 56B, 58A, 60A, 60B, 62, 63

Courtesy of Penguin Books Ltd.: plates 1, 2A, 6, 8A, 16B, 17, 19, 51B

Courtesy of Joan Saggs: plate 4B

Courtesy of Monsieur le Conservateur du Musée du Louvre: plates 11A, 18B, 58B, 61A, 61B

Courtesy of the Oriental Institute, University of Chicago: plates 13A, 13B, 15A

Courtesy of the Department of Antiquities of the Republic of Iraq, and Professor D. J. Wiseman: plate 14

Courtesy of the University Museum of the University of Pennsylvania: plate 15B

Courtesy of the Mansell Collection: plates 16B, 21B, 64

Courtesy of the Berlin Museum, and Professor D. J. Wiseman: plate 37

Courtesy of Dr. O. R. Gurney and the late Profesor D. S. Rice: plate 57A

Courtesy of Monsieur le Conservateur du Musée des Beaux-Arts, Dijon: plate 57B

Courtesy of Harvard University Press: plate 59

Author's photographs: plates 3A, 3B, 4A, 16A

List of Line Illustrations in Text

List of Maps

From the Foreword to the First Edition

THERE is in English, so far as I am aware, no book which gives an up-to-date account of the civilization of Babylonia and Assyria as a whole. In this work I have attempted to make good this deficiency. . . . No previous knowledge of the subject is assumed beyond such biblical knowledge as any reader interested in the broader aspects of human history may reasonably be expected to possess.

It is hardly necessary to point out that in an introduction to such a vast field of human activity, much of interest and importance has had to be omitted or dealt with cursorily. . . . Thus Mesopotamian art . . . is limited to a few pages, whilst the fascinating history of Mesopotamian excavation has been omitted altogether in view of the many excellent popular accounts of the subject from A. H. Layard's *Nineveh and its Remains* (1849) to M. E. L. Mallowan's *Twenty-five years of Mesopotamian Discovery* (1956). . . .

The translations are, except where otherwise indicated, my own renderings of the original text into (I hope) English which accords with modern idiomatic usage. Restored words or passages about which there can be no doubt are not specially marked. Round brackets within translations denote words implied but not verbally represented in the original, whilst square brackets enclose an explanatory remark; bracketed question-marks indicate an element of doubt in the translation of the words concerned.

Biblical quotations are mostly from the Revised Version. . . .

H. W. F. SAGGS
Epiphany, 1962

Foreword to the Second Edition

RESEARCH and teaching over the quarter of a century since the first edition have modified my views on some aspects of Babylonian civilization. The same period has brought much new information. In the present revision I have attempted to take account of these factors, whilst retaining the framework of the original edition. I have also reduced the attention paid to Assyria, in view of the detailed treatment now available in my *The Might that was Assyria* (1984).

My professional colleagues will doubtless notice that there is new material published in the last two or three years, or the last twenty years, to which I make no reference. But to incorporate all new evidence would have required two large supplementary volumes rather than a revision, and since my terms of reference were to make the book more succinct rather than to enlarge it, I have introduced only such new material as seemed to me to give the general reader a sharper picture of Babylonian civilization. I hope he or she will find it as interesting as I do.

For biblical quotations in this edition I have used the Authorized Version wherever it is sufficiently accurate, and otherwise the Revised Standard Edition, the only modern translation which does anything like justice to the poetic beauty of the original Hebrew text of the Old Testament.

H. W. F. Saggs
Long Melford, *Epiphany*, 1987

Note on Transliteration of Cuneiform

The signs used in cuneiform writing include

(i) logograms (ideograms): signs denoting a whole word. A given logogram may, according to context, be read as either Sumerian or Akkadian, with different values.
(ii) syllograms: signs denoting a syllable. A syllogram may have several different values, and there may be several syllograms with the same value.
(iii) phonetic complements: syllograms used to remove ambiguity about the pronunciation of a logogram with more than one value.
(iv) determinatives: signs placed before or after a logogram to show the class of thing to which it belonged, e.g. 'land', 'city', 'deity'.

Assyriologists have devised conventions for the transliteration and transcription of cuneiform texts. (Transliteration represents syllables actually used; transcription accurately renders the form intended. E.g., *i-na-di-na-ku-um* is a transliteration, and *inaddinakkum* is a transcription of the same word.) The main conventions are these:

(i) lower-case roman type (often widely spaced) is used for Sumerian.
(ii) lower-case italic type is used for Akkadian.
(iii) upper-case roman type is used for any sign of which the value in the context is in doubt.

To distinguish in transliteration between syllograms with the same value, the following conventions are used. The sign deemed the most common to represent a given syllable (although it may not be the most common at all periods) is written with no accent or subscript number, e.g., *du*. The next most common is transliterated as *dú* (or du_2). There then follow in sequence *dù* (or du_3), du_4, du_5, etc.

Transliterations of determinatives are often printed above the line, as, e.g. ^{mul}APIN.

These conventions, although essential in Assyriological research, are not necessarily followed at all points in the present book: in particular, Sumerian words are often written in italics, to conform to the normal practice for foreign words.

Some Semitic phonemes have no equivalent single symbols in the English alphabet. Where a completely accurate transcription is essential these are usually represented by ʾ (ʾaleph), ḥ, ḫ, ʿ (ʿayin), ṣ, š, ṭ, but in the present book, unless some point depends upon a technically exact transcription, ḥ and ḫ are generally represented by h (the latter sometimes by kh), ṣ and ṭ by s and t, and š by sh.

I

Prehistoric Background

Babylon in tradition

IN the ancient world, no city was more celebrated than Babylon. The Greeks knew it for its Hanging Gardens, one of the wonders of the world, and the Bible tells of its Tower of Babel, presumptuously built to reach the heavens. It was also the city of Nebuchadnezzar, the conqueror of the Jews. For the early Christians it was the archetypal wicked city, so that when divine inspiration impelled the author of Revelation to damn the metropolis of Rome for its wickedness, he used the more ancient capital as a code-name: 'BABYLON THE GREAT, THE MOTHER OF HARLOTS AND ABOMINATIONS OF THE EARTH' (17:5). Until this day Babylonian orgies remain a byword.

The city gave the name Babylonia to the country of which, in the second millennium BC, it became the capital. Babylonia was the southern half of what used to be called Mesopotamia and is now Iraq. More precisely, it was the region between and along the twin great rivers Euphrates and Tigris, from just north of the latitude of Baghdad, down to the Persian Gulf. In the third millennium BC, before it became Babylonia, its inhabitants knew this land as Sumer and Akkad; both these names, which denoted respectively the southern and northern halves of the country, occur in the Bible. Akkad, spelt Accad in most translations, is to be found in Genesis 10:10, although as the name of a city rather than of a country. Sumer, in the variant form Shinar, occurs in Genesis 11:2–3 as a plain where some of the earliest humans settled and began to make burnt brick, which they used in a building programme so ambitious that it brought down the wrath of God.

The Bible was right about Sumer. This was indeed the region where monumental building first began. It was also the place of origin of many other fundamental elements of human civilization.

Babylonia then and now

Anyone who visits south Iraq today may judge it an improbable region for the beginning of civilization. In many parts one sees for most of the year nothing but flat and – one might suppose – lifeless desert. Nowhere away from the rivers is a tree to be seen, and the only plants are low dust-covered shrubs, leafless and apparently dead. Except for insects and a few lizards, no animal life is visible.

But there are other sides to south Iraq. Through it run the Euphrates and the Tigris, making the land along their banks luxuriant with lush vegetation. Vast groves of date-palms, stretching mile upon mile, dominate this region. Here and there grow belts of poplars and willows. Where the soil is not under cultivation for food-crops, there burgeons a jungle of sedges, grasses, tamarisk and other brushwood species. And in the southernmost parts the contrast becomes greater still. Here the rivers have spread themselves to give vast stretches of fen and perennial marshlands, where the predominant vegetation consists of giant rushes towering fifteen feet or more above the water. Though it is not without patches of land, some extensive enough for sizeable villages, others no more than tiny islands formed of silted-up reed-beds big enough for a single reed-house, the predominant impression is of a world of water.

All three of these different terrains owe something to human intervention. Before man arrived on the scene and learned to

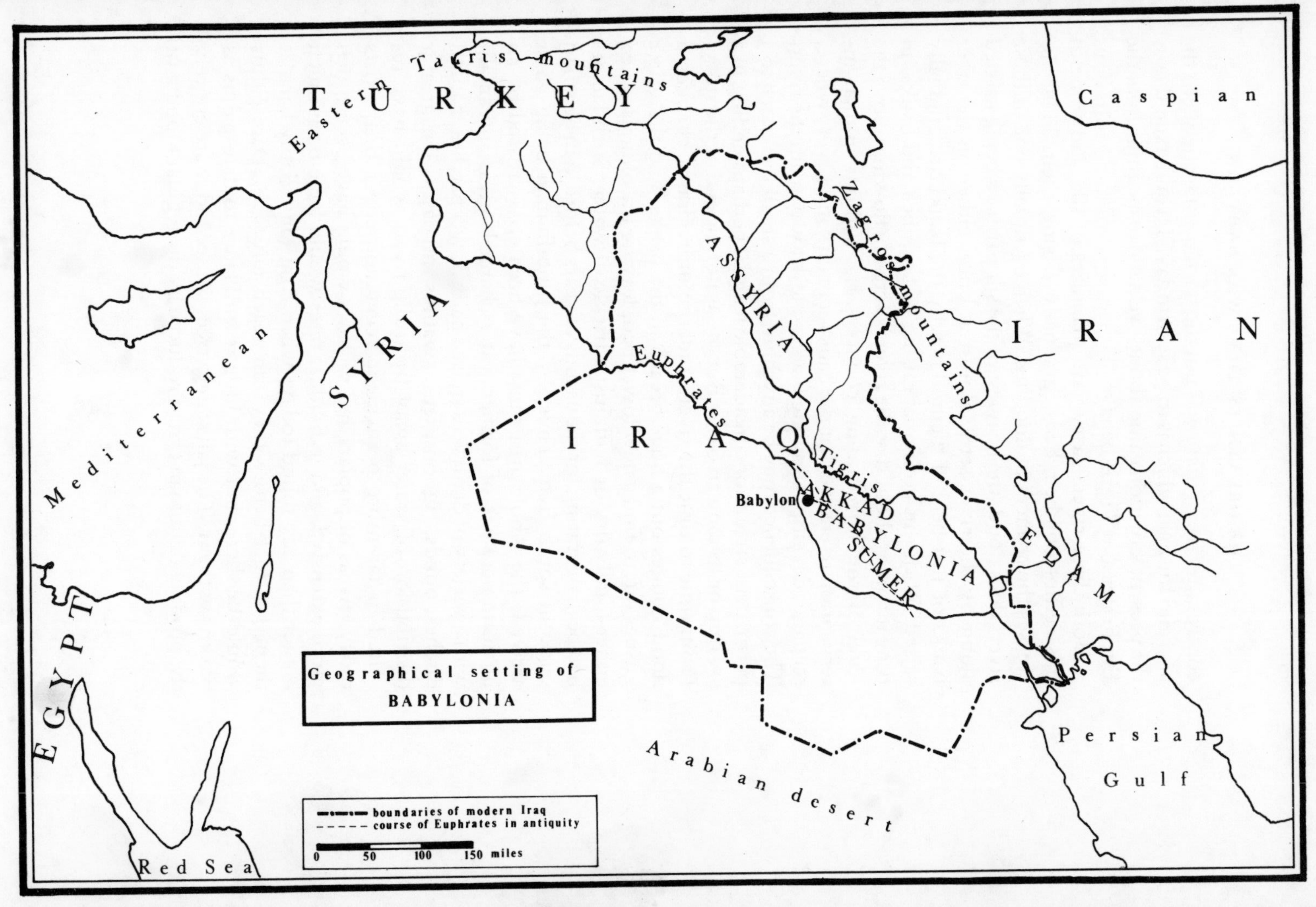

Geographical setting of BABYLONIA

control the rivers, there was not the stark contrast between the arid and the lush which is to be seen today. To understand how the present situation came about, we have to examine how the Euphrates and Tigris behave.

Both these rivers carry vast quantities of silt, and some of this settles on their beds, gradually raising them. This increases the chances of flooding. When eventually one of these rivers does flood, the heaviest of the silt particles being carried along by the river settle almost at once, either on the river banks or just behind them. Thereby the banks are gradually raised. With this continual raising of both bed and banks, in time it comes about that the river is actually flowing above the level of the surrounding countryside. Without human intervention to ensure that the banks remain sound everywhere, seepages develop, allowing water to leak away from the river. The consequence may be anything from a small wet patch to a permanent stream of considerable length, perhaps ending in a swamp or feeding an oasis. But this is not the end of the story. From time to time the rivers undergo more drastic changes; a flood gouges out a huge breach in the banks, and the water gushes out to find a new lower bed, leaving the old raised bed either totally dry or with just a trickle of water. Such factors had been operating for thousands of years before man began to settle in south Iraq. Thus, by the time human beings first arrived, the whole area must have been criss-crossed by an intricate network of former water channels great and small, with a variety of dry levees (raised banks), wet patches, natural ditches, ponds, lagoons, fens, swamps and oases. The greater distribution of water away from the rivers would have resulted in far more permanent vegetation cover than exists today. Areas of poplars and willows would have been much more extensive, and individual trees would have been much bigger than any found today, when Arabs invariably hack at them for fuel before they can reach any size. Date-palms would be there, but with little resemblance to date-palms as we know them. The tall stately trees we see today are entirely the product of human care, produced by the regular lopping of all side-shoots. Left to itself, the date-palm does not grow tall; instead, it spreads outwards by means of basal shoots (virtually suckers), forming a dense impenetrable thicket with leaves as broad as swords and almost as sharp.[1]

It was into this kind of environment that the earliest human arrivals in south Iraq came.

Early man in Mesopotamia

When man first came there is another matter. The earliest archaeological proof of human presence is only from a century or two before 5000 BC, but it cannot be ruled out that man was already there much earlier. Even today it would be possible for a human community to live in southernmost Iraq wholly by food-gathering; the marshes there still abound in fish, turtles, wild birds and wild boar, whilst besides the date-palm there are other edible plants native to the area, such as liquorice and a species of reed with a very toothsome root much like celery. Early man might well have lived in south Iraq without leaving traces recognizable by existing archaeological techniques. But this is speculation, and our present concrete evidence for human occupation in Babylonia begins with the stage at which man was already engaging in agriculture. To see how this came about, we have to go back to an earlier period and a different region.

Soon after 10,000 BC, man began a radical change in his way of life. Instead of relying wholly on hunting and food-collecting, he started to undertake the cultivation of crops, particularly cereals; he also started to domesticate animals. It was not, of course, necessarily the same group that initiated both these changes. Why man should have made such changes remains in dispute. It used to be thought that a deteriorating climate drove him to it, but it is now known that, on the contrary, the climate in the Near East was becoming wetter and warmer at this period.[2] More recently another hypothesis has been offered. It is suggested that man as a hunter and food-gatherer was so successful that finally the population began to outstrip the food supplies available by these techniques; in consequence, in order to obtain sufficient food for a fast-growing population, he was forced to turn to the more intensive uses of land which we know as agriculture and animal husbandry.[3] Whatever caused it, the change first happened in the region between Palestine and the Taurus and Zagros ranges, where wheat and barley grew wild (as indeed they still do), and where also were found the wild ancestors of dogs, goats, sheep and pigs. Cattle were probably first domesticated in eastern Europe, and the ass in north Africa.

The first animal to be domesticated was probably the dog, a tamed wolf, when it attached itself to human camps as an easy source of food. The domestication of goats and sheep, and later cattle, soon followed. This was probably not a sudden step. Over the millennia, hunters had learned to drive the wild flocks and herds to where they wanted them, and to restrict their range. Full domestication was simply an extension of this to bring the animals under closer control. Recognition of the possibility of cereal cultivation could have been a by-product of religious practices. Early man certainly harvested wild cereals, and what we know of primitive religion suggests that he would have offered some of the best of the crop at the shrine of his family gods. Germination of the grain scattered around shrines would have shown early man that it was possible, simply by dropping seed-corn on broken ground, to obtain a crop of cereals in the places most convenient to him.

These changes, often referred to as the Neolithic Revolution, were not sudden. It was certainly centuries, perhaps millennia, before animal-rearing and cereal-growing anywhere displaced hunting and gathering as the main source of food; as recently as the beginning of the nineteenth century AD there were still tribes in the forests of the Zagros southeast of Sulaimania who were reputed to cultivate nothing and to live wholly by food-gathering.[4] Even now in the most advanced societies, hunting and food-gathering remain as popular activities in the form of rabbiting, fishing and picking wild berries or mushrooms. But changes always have their adverse side, and although food production increased man's security, it also robbed him of some of his freedom. The Bible, that treasury of ancient wisdom, reflects this, in the tale of the expulsion of Adam and Eve from the Garden of Eden. Before the expulsion, God had told Adam, 'Of every tree of the garden you may freely eat' (Genesis 2:16): afterwards, Adam could only eat bread in the sweat of his brow. The changed economy also adversely affected the status of woman, for whereas formerly Eve had been Adam's full equal, now God told her: 'He [Adam] shall rule over you' (Genesis 3:16).

Accompanying these changes came a considerable increase in population. As families united in food production and defence against other groups like themselves, settlements grew into villages; and the consequent relative security of food supply brought leisure which permitted some measure of specialization. This particularly affected religious developments. From far back in the Old Stone Age man had practised religious rites; but now, as man began to live by agriculture, there arose a specialized social group concerned with the religious response of man to the pattern which the agricultural cycle imposed upon his life. In due course, this was to dominate the whole of Mesopotamian society, giving rise to a priesthood, great temples in honour of the gods, temple estates to support the cult, and an elaborate social and economic structure.

Increased control of natural resources loosened geographical constraints. Sheep, goats and cattle in controlled flocks and herds could be driven to wherever suitable grazing was found. Wherever there was land with adequate rainfall, wheat and barley could be sown with the prospect of a crop. And when the population had so abundantly increased that all the utilizable land around the original settlements in the hills had been taken up, some of the next generation could migrate to found new villages in the plains, on either side of the Zagros and Taurus ranges. Archaeologists can now trace the spread of these neolithic settlements over a wide region from Asia Minor to Iran. The remains of thousands of them are still to be seen scattered across Syria, Iraq, Iran and eastern Turkey, in the form of mounds known as *tell*, *tepe*, or *huyuk*, according to the local language.

The Neolithic Revolution brought other advances. Amongst these was the invention of pottery. Pottery can be significant to the archaeologist in several ways: it can show technical developments, such as the introduction of the potter's wheel; its designs can shed light on religious concepts; and above all it is a valuable tracer of cultural links. Because of human conservatism, related groups of peoples made their pottery by the same techniques, and the shapes, patterns and designs they used underwent modification only very slowly. In consequence, archaeologists can use prehistoric pottery for relative dating and for tracing relationships between settlements. Usually archaeologists name a type of pottery after the site at which it was first found. For example, after they had found a hitherto unknown type of pottery at a mound called Tell Hassuna (not far from Mosul), they subsequently gave the name *Hassuna* to any stratum anywhere where that sort of pottery was found. Pottery is not, of course, the only marker of successive prehistoric cultures (or 'assemblages', as archaeologists prefer to call them); there are others, such as household equipment and tools, the forms and materials of buildings, the presence or absence of metals, and evidence of trading connections. But it is the pottery which is the handiest tracer.

Prehistoric cultures of Mesopotamia

The principal prehistoric stages found in north Iraq, after humans had begun to settle on the Assyrian plains, are known as: *Hassuna*, beginning soon after 6000 BC;[5] *Samarra* (possibly an offshoot of *Hassuna*), around 5500 BC; and *Halaf*, from around 5500 BC to after 5000 BC. These cultures concern us here only in so far as they bear upon later developments in what became Babylonia. *Hassuna* settlements show that copper was beginning to be used in Iraq, even though only on a small scale. The *Samarra* stage is of great importance for another reason. Some of its sites – all near minor watercourses – are in a region where rainfall is inadequate for cereal-growing, and since cereals were certainly cultivated at these sites, the *Samarra* people must have begun to use irrigation. Since the great civilization of Sumer and Babylonia could never have arisen without irrigation, this was a vital development.

Halaf settlements show a distinct rise in the quality of life. A *Halaf* site named Arpachiyeh, a village near Nineveh (modern Mosul), shows such features as cobbled streets, considerable advances in copper-working, and houses equipped with efficient bread ovens. The pottery was decorated and of considerable beauty, and there were amulets and other *objets d'art* skilfully cut from stone. It may even have been the *Halaf* people who gave the world the wheel, if those archaeologists are correct who see a certain pattern on *Halaf* pottery as representing a wheeled chariot. *Halaf* sites were spread across more than 500 miles, from the southeastern coast of Turkey to Lake Van and northeastern Iraq – an extensive trading area.

It was not until 5000 BC, or a little before, that we meet the first settlements in Babylonia. These are known as *Ubaid*, after a small site in south Iraq, not far from the famous city of Ur of the Chaldees. Another small site, Abu Shahrein, about seven miles southwest of Ur, shows the earliest phase of *Ubaid*, formerly called *Eridu* after the ancient name of the city there. The most significant feature of *Ubaid* settlements was their extensive use of irrigation for grain production. This was a major advance in control of the environment. The *Samarra* people further north had begun it by channelling waters from streams along natural contours and small ditches to create a primitive canal system to supplement the rainfall, but to tackle either the Tigris or the Euphrates, two of the world's greatest rivers, was a task of a different magnitude. It is likely that the *Ubaid* people came to it gradually, first clearing and sowing areas that were kept moist by natural seepages, and then progressing to use leaks through the river banks to feed old silted-up natural channels easily adapted as primitive irrigation canals. But they would have encountered difficulties. Both the Tigris and the Euphrates can flood disastrously, just before harvest, at a time likely to devastate the crops. Or a small gap cut in the bank to give a usable head of water can rapidly grow to an uncontrollable torrent. In the course of developing their irrigation techniques, the *Ubaid* people learned how to limit such problems. Their first need was a large, well-organized labour force, for digging and clearing canals and for keeping the river banks sound: one of the earliest officials was the Canal Inspector. This shaped their social system, since it meant that people had to live in large units and be willing to accept centralized direction of their labour. In this we see in embryo the origin both of the city and of bureaucracy, two fundamental features of later Mesopotamian society. The size of settlements increased.

Irrigation had another social effect. Some land would be far more productive than other plots, according to how favourably it was placed for irrigation. Families settled on the best land would become more prosperous than others, with the consequent beginning of social stratification based on wealth.

The *Ubaid* pattern of life was very successful, and spread far beyond its area of origin in southernmost Mesopotamia. By 4000 BC there were settlements with *Ubaid*-type pottery across the whole region from the western coast of the Persian Gulf to north Syria – that is, as far as from London to the Russian border. Whether this spread was simply the result of extensive trading contacts or whether it involved actual colonization we do not know. Whichever it was, a factor in this spread must have been journeys in quest of the stone, metal ores and large timber of building quality lacking in south Iraq. The use of river transport by the *Ubaid* people is proved by the finding of a model boat of baked clay.

The *Ubaid* expansion represented the beginning of a unified way of life over the whole of Mesopotamia and some of the adjacent lands. But it remained essentially a society of peasants, living in villages. Houses were still of unbaked brick, and although stone was imported, it was used only for doorways, pavings, fireplaces and drains.

The Uruk period

The next cultural stage in southern Iraq, covering the half-millennium down to 3000 BC, introduced a revolutionary change, marked by six main features: (1) the rise of the city as an economic and social unit, a development from the clustering of population necessary to control and utilize the rivers; (2) the beginning of monumental architecture, with increasing use of stone; (3) the more widespread use of metals; (4) the beginning of an art tradition; (5) the introduction of the cylinder seal;[6] and, above all, (6) the invention of writing.

Archaeologists know this period as *Uruk*, so called because the ancient name of Warka, where it was first recognized, was Uruk, the Erech of Genesis 10:10. The term *Protoliterate* is also used for it. When the writing system reaches a stage at which we can read it, we find that the language used is what the scribes called 'the tongue of Sumer'; for this reason we refer to the language, the people and the civilization as Sumerian. However, we have no proof either that the first devisers of writing used it to represent Sumerian, or that the population group who were the first creators of cities already called themselves Sumerians.

Sumerian origins

Erech was one of the most important early centres of what we know as Sumerian civilization. The emergence of this civilization brings us up against the problem of what we mean by 'Sumerian'. Primarily the word refers to a language. But some people assume, or work from the unstated assumption, that Sumerian civilization was a civilization exclusively associated with a particular people who spoke this particular language. How far is this justified?

We know the Sumerian language only from ancient inscriptions, and these are often obscure in content and difficult to understand. Even those who know Sumerian best, understand it only about as well as a good school-leaver understands French. Sumerian has no obvious link with any other language, but since it is agglutinative in structure, as Turkish and Hungarian are, and probably tonal like Chinese, there have inevitably been attempts to relate it to one or other of these languages: none is convincing. It has also been compared, often quite unscientifically and equally fruitlessly, with scores of other languages, from Tibetan through Dravidian to the remoter languages of Africa, the Pacific and the American Indians.

Attempts at linking Sumerian to other languages have been based on the assumption that all languages must belong within a comparatively few families. This way of thinking stems from the fact that, for example, English, French, German, Russian, Armenian, Latin, Greek, Persian, Hindi, Sanscrit and other languages have so many features in common in their structure and vocabulary that it is a reasonable conclusion that they all developed from a single language or groups of related dialects far back in prehistoric times. A corresponding situation holds for the Semitic languages, Hebrew, Aramaic, Arabic, Akkadian (predominant in Babylonia after 2000 BC) and Ethiopic. By analogy, many researchers assume that somewhere there must be a language family into which Sumerian can be fitted, and that there must have been an original Sumerian homeland in or near that region. But is this a valid approach? A Hungarian scholar, G. Komoróczy, questions it. He shows that in ancient times there were other languages which it is impossible to attach to any known family, and that even today there remain 'loners' amongst living languages.[7] It may therefore be a false assumption that all known languages developed out of a much smaller number existing in prehistoric times.

Human beings in every respect like ourselves existed by 30,000 BC, living at first in communities likely to have been numbered at most in hundreds. Many of them could have been self-contained and isolated, with only rare contacts with other communities. In such circumstances, the twenty thousand years down to the Neolithic Revolution gave ample time for very many unrelated languages to develop. Population growth and increased contacts between communities would have brought the extinction of many minor languages, but many others could have remained. There is no reason why the peoples of each of the main cultural groups which left their mark upon prehistoric Mesopotamia – *Hassuna*, *Samarra*, *Halaf* and *Ubaid* – should not have spoken unrelated languages, possibly more than one in some of these groups.

The earliest intelligible writing from Mesopotamia proves that in the early third millennium not less than three languages were current there – Sumerian itself, the Semitic language Akkadian (evidenced by loan words in Sumerian), and at least one other. The proof of the last lies in the many ancient place-names which cannot be explained as either Semitic or Sumerian. Yet another language, known as Hurrian by modern scholars although the Sumerians seem to have called it Subarian, was widely represented in Mesopotamia well before the end of the third millennium, and may have been there all the time, although the predominant view is that the Hurrians were third-millennium immigrants from the north.

One hypothesis to explain this situation is that the non-Sumerian, non-Semitic place-names were in the language (or languages) of the original inhabitants – perhaps in archaeological terms the *Ubaid* people – and that the speakers of all the other languages had come in by immigration after 4000 BC. This is not to be rejected out of hand. The earliest speakers of Akkadian probably did enter Mesopotamia in that way. The geographical distribution of other Semitic languages in the ancient Near East points to a centre of diffusion somewhere between Syria and Arabia. Dialects in isolation gradually diverge, so that by comparing two languages of the same family we can estimate roughly how long since they separated. The divergence of Akkadian from the other Semitic languages known from 2000 BC onwards suggests that it had not separated from them earlier than about 4000 BC, making that the earliest date of Semitic immigration into Mesopotamia.

But a corresponding situation cannot be shown for other languages of ancient Mesopotamia. There remains the possibility that immigrants from the Zagros and Taurus foothills or Syria from 10,000 BC onwards included communities speaking many different unrelated languages, some of which – perhaps Sumerian and Hurrian amongst them – continued in use into historical times, to become the predominant language in a particular period and region.

Sumerians not a race

Language is therefore not conclusive for the origin of a people whom we could from their beginning call Sumerians. Let us look at other considerations. The first is race. This term properly means a group linked by inherited physical characteristics. To prove that the Sumerians constituted a race would require anthropologists to establish from skeletal remains that they were of a uniform physical type distinct from other peoples around them. But such proof is lacking and the case fails. There was no Sumerian race.

If not a race, were the Sumerians a distinct ethnic group, separated off from Semites? The criteria to define an ethnic group are that its members share a number of features which separate them from others. These usually include some or all of language, religion, burial customs, food, habits of dress, hairstyles, marriage customs and other sexual conventions, and attitude to ownership of land.

In the second half of the third millennium there began an immigration of a Semitic-speaking people – the nomadic *Martu*, that is, Amorites – who were quite certainly an ethnic group distinct from the existing inhabitants of the city-states, that is, units of territory where the social structure was based not on the tribe, but on the institutions of a central urban complex. The ethnic differences of these peoples were explicitly recognized at the time. The city-dwelling Mesopotamians were quick to point out the oddities of their way of life, calling them 'people of the highlands, who know no corn', 'who know no towns', 'who dig for truffles, who know not how to bend the knee, who eat raw meat, who in life know no house, and after death go unburied'.[8] Right down to the first millennium, Mesopotamians would comment on the odd hairdos and strange dress of foreign peoples. Silence on such matters between people speaking different languages in the city-states of the early third millennium must mean that they themselves were aware of no such ethnic distinctions.

Despite this, some scholars take religion as a marker of ethnic distinction between two groups in the city-states of the early third millennium. They start with the assumption that there was something called 'Sumerian religion', and a different set of concepts called 'Semitic religion'. Working from this premiss, they identify data related to deities with Sumerian names as part of Sumerian religion, and correspondingly with data related to gods bearing Semitic names. When this produces inconsistencies, they explain the anomalous items as due to the influence of one religion upon the other.

I do not accept the premiss underlying this approach. As I see it, the real situation is this. In third-millennium Mesopotamia a distinctive type of religion developed, appropriate to life in city-states within a particular social and ecological framework based on an irrigation economy. It had roots in prehistory, but it was the natural and social environment which gave it its particular characteristics. There was not a complete uniformity across all city-states, but such differences as there were arose not from language or 'racial' background but from local variations in natural environment. It is easy to see how environmental variations could give local differences in religion. For example, one city might have good meadowlands for cow-herding, whilst in another the terrain might be such that cultivation of the date-palm would predominate: inevitably, such differences would affect the forms of the gods worshipped and details of the cult. Sumerian was predominantly spoken in some cities and Akkadian in others, and if, of two cities with environmental differences, one happened to be in a Sumerian-speaking region whilst the citizens of the other mainly spoke Akkadian, the deities themselves might have names in different languages. But the differences of nomenclature and religious practice would derive solely from differences of environment; they would have no direct connection with the language group, and still less would they be a matter of different gene pools.

Other features which serve to mark off an ethnic group – food, habits of dress, treatment of the hair, sexual conventions, burial practices, land tenure – are still more dubious as support of a distinct ethnic group paralleling use of the Sumerian language, since, as we have already noted, the citizens of the Mesopotamian city-states were ready enough to comment on such differences in other peoples but saw none of this kind amongst themselves.

Were Sumerians immigrants?

Another argument that Sumerian-speakers were in origin a separate people who came into Mesopotamia from outside is based on traditions of links of Sumerian civilization with other regions. One tradition, transmitted through Greek, speaks of a fish-man, Oannes, who swam up the Persian Gulf, bringing with him the gifts of civilization. Is it legitimate to conclude that the Sumerians themselves thought their ancestors had migrated up the Persian Gulf? Sumerian myths link the gifts of civilization to Enki, the god of Wisdom, and Enki's city was Eridu,[9] which Sumerian tradition held to be the first of five cities which existed before the Flood. Now Eridu was the most southerly of all ancient Mesopotamian cities, lying on a lagoon running northwest from the Persian Gulf. Thus the Oannes tradition may simply reflect no more than the memory of a very early centre of civilization in Eridu, which because of its lagoon was considered to lie on the Persian Gulf. Sumerian literature seems to reflect another link with the Persian Gulf when it makes allusions to a golden age in a place known as Tilmun (or Dilmun), even older than Eridu. But this depends upon how we interpret the term 'Tilmun'. By soon after the middle of the third millennium, it denoted, as almost all Assyriologists agree, Bahrein in the Persian Gulf, possibly with neighbouring parts of Arabia. If it had always meant this, it could indeed indicate that the Sumerians thought of themselves as having come up the Persian Gulf with Bahrein as an earlier base. But there is another possibility. The application of place-names can change. Folk-memory may originally have used 'Tilmun' as a blanket term for the first settlements in south Mesopotamia, and the name may have become attached to a specific place in the Persian Gulf only when, after the middle of the third millennium, the memory of those earliest settlements grew so remote that it was felt that Tilmun must have been at the very edge of the known world.

Another region suggested for Sumerian origins is Iran or beyond. There are epics which indicate a close cultural relationship in the early third millennium between Sumer and places in or beyond the Zagros mountains; and pottery proves, from the *Ubaid* period onwards, a connection of Sumer with the part of southwest Iran now known as Khuzistan or Arabistan. There is also a writing system, early Elamite, related to the earliest writing in Sumer; this is attested as far away as Sialk near Isfahan in central Iran. But these connections could all be explained as the consequence of trading journeys by the peoples of Mesopotamia in quest of timber, metal ores and stone.

Another suggestion is that the Sumerians came from the Caucasus, and made their way into south Mesopotamia down the Euphrates. Some sites in northern Mesopotamia and east Syria show *Uruk* features, and those who see the Sumerian homeland in the Caucasus argue that these were established by the Sumerians on a southward migration. This theory would require the northern sites to represent earlier stages of *Uruk* than those in the south, and this lacks proof. Any settlements of *Uruk* type in north Mesopotamia or Syria are more likely to have been established from Sumer in connection with trade.

Some features of third-millennium Mesopotamian religion have been claimed as proof that the Sumerians were immigrants from somewhere mountainous. The most prominent religious buildings were great stepped temple-towers known as ziggurats, and it is argued that these must have been substitutes for real mountains of religious importance in an earlier homeland. But there is no proof in cuneiform texts that the Sumerians thought of ziggurats primarily as substitute mountains. A second point made is that there were deities in the Sumerian pantheon whose homes were in the mountains, but this again is not conclusive. Ancient religions often associated deities with mountains, but the basis of this was not that the worshippers came from a particular type of terrain; rather it was that mountains touched chords of religious awe. For example, in Israelite religion Mount Horeb (alias Sinai), Mount Carmel and Mount Zion were all important, but the biblical traditions do not link Israelite origins to a mountainous homeland. Although there are no mountains in south Iraq, the Zagros can be seen dimly in the distance from along much of the lower Tigris, and the sense of mystery which that sight arouses could well have given rise to the idea that it was there that some of the great deities had their dwellings.

Archaeological evidence on Sumerian origins is inconclusive. Some scholars see a definite break between the *Ubaid* and the *Uruk* periods, shown by new pottery shapes, the introduction of the potter's wheel and the more widespread use of metals. They also argue that the striking new features associated with *Uruk* culture are themselves evidence of a new population stratum. But others differ. They argue that the supposed cultural break between *Ubaid* and *Uruk* was not as definite as claimed, and point to an overlap between *Ubaid* and *Uruk* pottery at Warka. They interpret the new features of *Uruk* as development rather than an abrupt change, and argue that innovation can derive from other factors than new populations. One important piece of evidence comes from Abu Shahrein, the site of Eridu, the most ancient city of Sumer. Here a series of temples were rebuilt on the same site from the earliest phase of *Ubaid* into the Sumerian period, with no change in general plan. Such continuity points to the absence of the kind of upheaval which one might expect from a major Sumerian immigration. But this is not as conclusive as might appear: history offers many instances of incoming peoples taking over the religious institutions of their predecessors, and Sumerian immigrants might have preserved existing religious installations as they found them.

All the evidence from south Iraq in the first half of the third millennium points to a considerable cultural uniformity, which is totally against the idea that the population at that time contained several ethnically separate groups of distinct origin. Thus, if any new Sumerian-speakers did enter as late as the second half of the fourth millennium, they must have been quickly absorbed into the older and larger population. Our conclusion is that, whether or not Sumerian-speakers were recent immigrants, what we call Sumerian civilization was the creation of a group of peoples of diverse origin who in the late fourth and early third millennia coalesced into a society with a single social, political and religious system. They included people of different linguistic ancestry and background, but from the cultural viewpoint they were all Sumerians.

The beginnings of Sumerian civilization

Erech, represented by the site Warka, is the most important source for our knowledge of *Uruk* civilization. It began as two main settlements, whose names were retained in later temple areas as Kulaba and Eanna. By 3500 BC it had become a substantial town, and by 3000 BC it was a rapidly expanding city, with a population estimated at as much as 50,000. At the same time, many old *Ubaid* settlements, both in the surrounding area and as far away as coastal Saudi Arabia, ceased to be occupied; this suggests that over a wide area the population was moving into developing cities like Erech. This is as near as we come to direct evidence for prehistoric immigration into Mesopotamia, but it cannot be linked to any of the specific theories of Sumerian immigration, since this population shift was only out of old *Ubaid* settlements of the kind which had long existed within south Mesopotamia. Early in the third millennium a wall enclosing some 1,300 acres was built around Erech, presumably for defence in the event of conflict with other developing cities competing for natural resources.

The developments within Erech can be traced through successive archaeological strata. In excavation, it is most usual to number the strata from the top downwards, so that the lowest number denotes the latest period and the highest the earliest. At Warka, the earliest strata (XVIII to XV) represent *Ubaid* occupation: the later strata XIV to IV form a homogeneous group, and it is these that are usually known as *Uruk*.

At the beginning of the *Uruk* period the temples carried on the building traditions of the preceding *Ubaid*, but later they developed in size and magnificence, becoming striking features of the Mesopotamian landscape, visible to great distances across the flat Sumerian plain and proclaiming afar the wealth and splendour of the city god. Colour added to the impressive effect: by stratum VI the walls and columns of temples were decorated with clay nails, their heads painted red, white or black arranged in mosaic patterns (plate 2A).

Stratum IV of *Uruk* brings a development of the highest importance – the invention, or at least the first known use, of writing.[10] Writing arose not as the servant of religion (except indirectly), nor as a vehicle for transmission of history or fine literature, but simply in connection with the prosaic task of keeping accounts. In the earliest period of settlement most of the land was owned by extended families, but a share of it would be set aside for the maintenance of the community's shrine. The history of Christian and Buddhist monasteries illustrates the tendency of corporate religious institutions to become wealthy and powerful, and from simple beginnings the Mesopotamian temples quickly developed to control large estates and the labour of many people. These workers had to deliver their products, and in return received rations of the staple commodities of the period – corn, oil and wool. By the time the numbers of workers had grown from scores to thousands, administration would only be feasible if accounts were kept. The accounts began when officials took a handful of clay, moulded it in their palms, and used a reed to scratch on it simple pictures of objects as memoranda. Impressed marks were used for numerals. Hundreds of examples of this early writing have been found from stratum IV at Erech; some of these early tablets – round in the earliest stage, afterwards square or oblong – are so well preserved that the palm prints of the scribe are still clear. In many instances the pictographic origin of signs is quite clear; examples may be seen on page 22. But within these earliest examples of writing there are other signs which give no suggestion of an underlying picture. This difficulty led in the 1970s to a modified theory of the origin of writing.

The new theory is based on finds, dating from the ninth millennium onwards, at sites across the region from Egypt to Iran. The objects in question are groups of clay tokens, in such shapes as spheres, cones and rods, sometimes with inscribed lines; they are typically of the size of a small marble. The suggestion is that these tokens were used in a recording system to represent different types of sheep and goats or possibly different kinds of merchandise. It is argued that when the *Uruk* people first developed writing, they adopted for their signs, or some of them, two-dimensional forms of the old tokens, retaining their traditional meanings. This is a neat theory, but there is a serious objection to it: there are not more than two or three of the early *Uruk* writing signs which bear a really convincing resemblance to any of the tokens. One which does show a resemblance is the sign ⊕ which eventually developed into , meaning 'sheep'; this could be a two-dimensional representation of an old token which took the form of a sphere incised with two intersecting circles. But there is a difficulty here: we have no independent knowledge of what that token signified, and the only reason we have for thinking it meant 'sheep' is that it suggests the writing sign

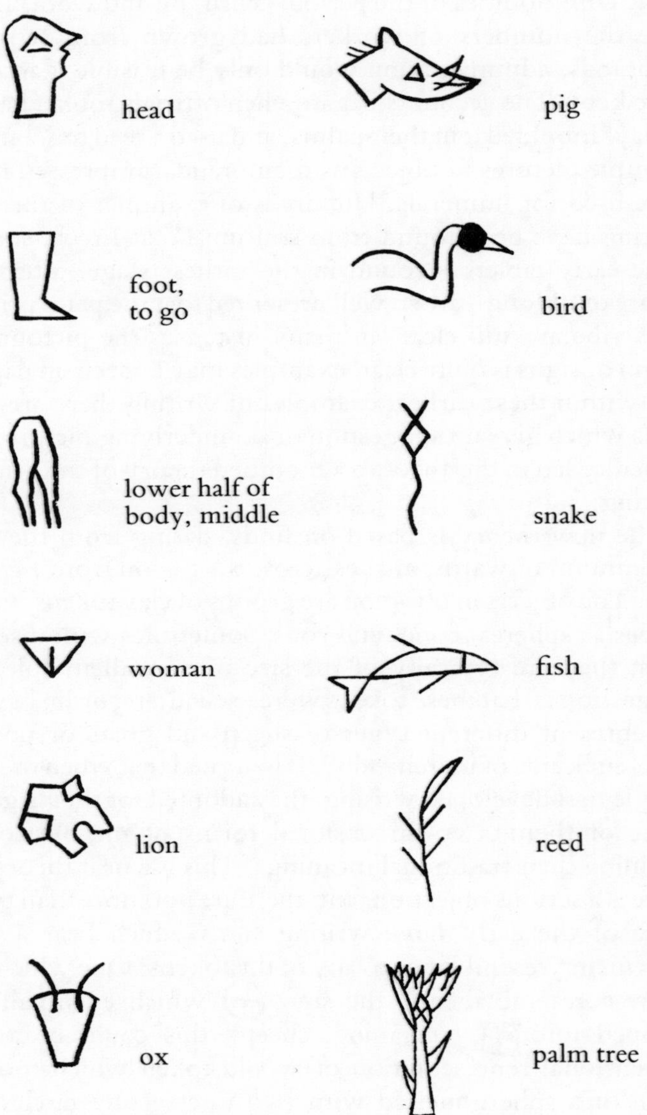

The earliest pictographs

which later had that meaning. That is to say, we are explaining the writing sign from the token and the token from the writing sign, so that the argument is circular. Our conclusion is that it still remains to be proved that the prehistoric token system played any part in the invention of the *Uruk* IV writing system.

Clay always remained the most common writing material of ancient Mesopotamian civilization; and the reed, the plant generally used as the stylus, was associated with the patron deity of the scribal art. Once clay has been kneaded, it will retain marks made on it for thousands of years, whether left in the raw state or baked into terracotta; except when deliberately smashed it is virtually indestructible. In consequence the soil of Iraq and neighbouring countries contains literally millions (at least half a million have already been excavated) of these inscribed lumps of clay spanning the whole period from about 3000 BC to the final extinction of this means of writing, just after the time of Christ.

Within a century or two of the first attested writing, the scribes came to alter their writing techniques. Instead of scratching lines on the clay, they began to make their signs by impressing marks with the apex of a reed of triangular cross-section. Also, because of the way in which they held the reed stylus relative to the clay tablet, the signs came to be written at ninety degrees to their natural position as pictographs. The consequences of these changes were twofold. Firstly, all curves disappeared, and the signs were all on their backs, so that they no longer portrayed their pictographic origin; secondly, all the signs came to consist of combinations of wedges. When writing has reached this stage it is called 'cuneiform' (meaning 'wedge-shaped'). The shape and size of cuneiform clay tablets vary considerably. Some of the early ones are more or less oval or round, like a flattened bun, but later they are almost always roughly rectangular, often with curved front and back (obverse and reverse), making them pillow-shaped. The dimensions range from no bigger than a matchbox to the size of a tabloid newspaper, although most commonly the tablet is small enough to be held in the hand. In its final form, cuneiform on clay tablets was always written from left to right. When the scribe continued from obverse to reverse, he normally turned the tablet on its bottom axis, not its side axis like a book. This had the result that the reverse was inscribed upside-down relative to the obverse. There are rare instances in which an inexperienced scribe turned the tablet on its side axis to continue on to the reverse.[11]

Innovation in architecture was another major feature of the *Uruk* period. This period saw the beginning of the ziggurat, the great stepped tower which dominated later Mesopotamian cities, the type of structure which has lived on in Jewish and Christian tradition as the 'tower of Babel' (Genesis 11:2–9). The prototype at Erech consisted of a high terrace about an acre in extent, built of trodden clay and unbaked bricks, with its corners orientated to the points of the compass, rising forty feet above the plain. Access to the top was by a stairway or ramp. On the terrace stood a temple, generally called the 'White Temple' (see plate 1), from the white plaster that covered it. This building consisted of a long rectangular chamber running northwest to southeast, with rooms opening off on the two long sides. The monotony of the exterior walls was broken by a series of vertical recesses, a form of ornamentation which was to become traditional in Mesopotamian temples. A temple of a similar plan and on a high terrace (in this case in two stages) occurs at the same period at Tell Uqair further north, whilst the celebrated ziggurat of Ur (see plate 3A) also appears to have had its origin in the *Uruk* period. We can obtain a fair idea of the appearance of such buildings from fragments of stone models found at Erech, and from the surviving foundations of the buildings themselves.

Religion of the Uruk *period*

It would give us a better insight into the motivation of the *Uruk* people if we knew more of their religion, but at present our knowledge is limited to little more than a few pointers from cylinder seals, reliefs and temples, helped out with inferences from more definite later information.

The cult at Erech was always dominated by the fertility goddess Inanna, a name which the Sumerians sometimes took as deriving from (N)in-an-a, meaning 'Lady of Heaven', although this may not be its genuine etymology. Her cult is represented on cylinder seals as early as the *Uruk* IV period, by scenes of worshippers bringing offerings to her symbol, originally a column made from a sheaf of tall reeds (*see fig. page 287*). There are indications that it was not until after 3000 BC that anthropomorphic conceptions of deity became predominant, and the use of this symbol may show that at this stage Inanna was not yet thought of as essentially in human form. But even if she was not yet perceived primarily in the form of a woman, she certainly represented the feminine principle upon which all life depended. In the historical period Inanna was associated with the fertility god later known as Dumuzi (Tammuz of Ezekiel 8:14; see pages 326f.), and seals of the *Uruk* III (*Jemdet Nasr*) period seem to represent the cult of a god of this type. A typical scene on a cylinder seal shows a figure in male human form holding vegetation in the shape of a rosette, which was a symbol associated with Inanna. He stands between two feeding rams, behind each of which is a further symbol of Inanna, in the form shown on page 287. The male figure is evidently the prototype of the Good Shepherd, which was one aspect of Dumuzi; but it is the feminine principle, in the form of the symbols of Inanna, which dominate the composition, enclosing and shielding the male figure to right and left. We note that anthropomorphism is coming in with the human form of this proto-Dumuzi, but it is not used to represent the major divine power, Inanna. (See also plate 11B.)

There are *Uruk* IV and *Jemdet Nasr* seals with scenes of monsters, such as lion-headed eagles or long-necked dragons, which reflect an attempt to represent, in non-anthropomorphic form, the sometimes terrifying supernatural powers which these people felt around them in their world.

The Inanna cult in the *Uruk* period is also seen in two carved alabaster vessels. One, a trough (see plate 9A), bears on its long side a relief depicting a building dominated by the symbols of Inanna, with a ram, a ewe and a lamb to right and left. The building is clearly a reed structure of a type still found today in the southern marshes of Iraq and was manifestly the temple of Inanna; the scene makes it clear that one of her main functions was the welfare of the flocks, and that she was vitally concerned in animal fertility.

The other alabaster vessel was a vase nearly three feet six inches high, with four bands of reliefs (see plate 8A). In the bottom band are stylized ears of corn and palm trees, and the band above it shows a line of sacrificial sheep. The next band up depicts naked personnel carrying containers of fruit and drinks, whilst the top band shows a cult procession, in which men bring offerings of animals and baskets of fruit to a female figure (a priestess?) standing in front of the symbols of Inanna. Behind those symbols is an enclosure with two human figures. Obviously the whole reflects a cult scene in which offerings were brought to the great goddess Inanna, in her role of concern for the fertility of animal and plant life. Later in third-millennium Mesopotamia there was an annual Sacred Marriage in which human participants enacted the sexual intercourse of the deities upon which fertility was supposed to depend. It is therefore possible that the two figures inside the enclosure on the top band are the bride and bridgegroom in the Sacred Marriage of the deities later known as Inanna and Dumuzi.

2

South Mesopotamia in the Third Millennium

AFTER the initial steps towards urban civilization, the third millennium saw a series of developments basic to most of the fundamental institutions and concepts of the mainstream of all later civilized life.

Erech was by no means the only city developing in the *Uruk* (*Protoliterate*) period. By 2900 BC there may have been as many as fifty substantial urban complexes in south Mesopotamia, of which perhaps about a dozen had already reached a stage of political and social development for which the term 'city-state' is appropriate. This development continued and saw its peak during the succeeding four hundred years. Typical of this period was the rise of dynasties ruling individual city-states or groupings of states; for this reason it is generally known as *Early Dynastic* (often abbreviated *E.D.*). Just after 2400 BC came the first successful attempt at creating an empire; this incorporated not only all city-states of south Mesopotamia but even extensive regions beyond, enduring for more than a century until it broke down under the pressure of its own internal stresses, coupled with foreign invasion. The final two centuries saw a brief return of independent city-states, culminating in another more compact empire, which in turn collapsed a few years before 2000 BC under the weight of immigrant Semites.

Chronology

The dating of events of the third millennium is subject to a margin of uncertainty which ranges from just over a century at the beginning of this period to just over half a century at its end. Some scholars avoid giving absolute dates which may subsequently prove to be inaccurate, by referring to periods rather than years BC. Several different nomenclatures are in use for this. The following table gives the main terms likely to be found, related to absolute dates (which are, of course, subject to the margin of error mentioned).

Commonest term		*Other terms*	*Absolute date*
Uruk IV		Protoliterate;	Before 3000 BC
Uruk III	*Jemdet Nasr*	Protohistoric	3000–2900 BC
Early Dynastic			2900–2370 BC
E.D. I			2900–2700 BC
E.D. II			2700–2600 BC
E.D. III			2600–2370 BC
Late *E.D.* III	*Fara*	Pre-Sargonic;	After 2500 BC
Agade		Akkadian; Sargonic	2371–2230 BC
Gutian		Dynasty of Gutium; Post-Akkadian	2230–2120?BC
III Ur		Third Dynasty of Ur; Neo-Sumerian Period	2113–2006 BC

For the third millennium BC, no less than for much of all later human history, a great part of our information about events comes from the records of conflicts between states. From as early as the *Uruk* IV period, we find trussed-up prisoners depicted in sculpture in the round and cylinder seals,[1] showing the occurrence of organized warfare, which implies war leaders. By the *Early Dynastic* period named kings or war leaders begin to appear: the earliest, in late *E.D.* I or early *E.D.* II, are shadowy figures, known only from king lists, epics or religious traditions, which remember them as superhuman, sometimes fully divine; but by *E.D.* III we meet rulers who are fixed firmly on the human plane by their own inscriptions or by mention in the inscriptions of their contemporaries. Although documentation is sparse and often of doubtful interpretation, at this stage we have fully entered history.

SOUTH MESOPOTAMIA IN THE THIRD MILLENNIUM

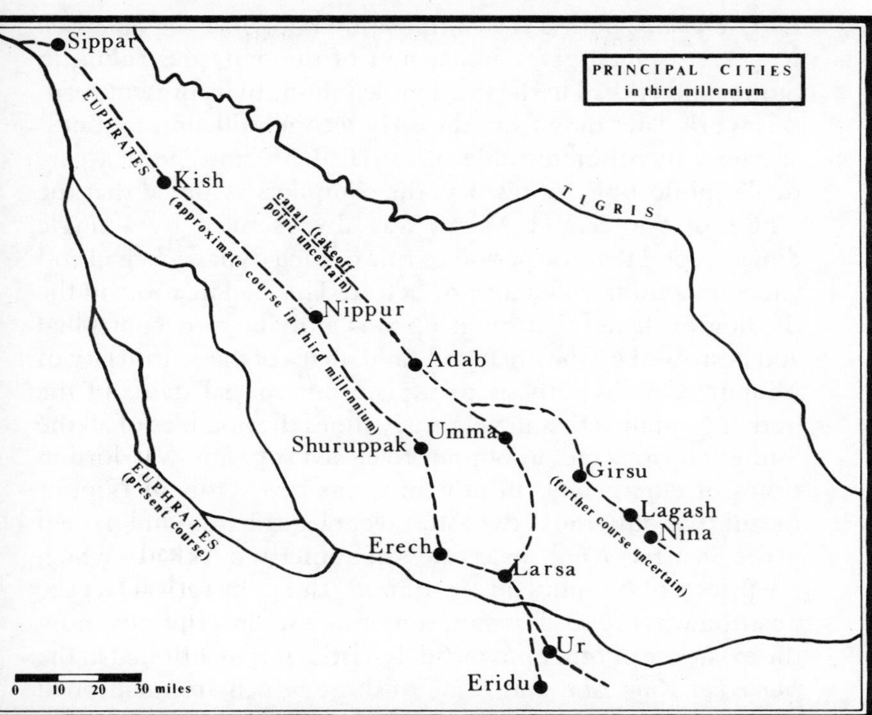

Written sources for history

For developments in the earliest part of the third millennium, Erech remains our principal source. We owe this situation to a school of poets which flourished there, creating a number of myths and epics which relieve us from total dependence upon records of war. Thorkild Jacobsen of Harvard has argued convincingly that the myths dealing with the exploits of gods, and epics concerned with human heroes, reflect human institutions at the time from which they derived,[2] perhaps 2900 BC for the myths (including some not from Erech) and between 2750 and 2600 BC for the epics.

A convenient starting-point for the interpretation of the

Early Dynastic period is a composition known as the *Sumerian King List*, which gives an account of the dynasties ruling in Sumer and Akkad in the third millennium. In its present form this work dates only from the early second millennium, but it certainly incorporates older material. Its form reflects a particular philosophy of history: the compilers assumed that the whole of Sumer and Akkad was always ruled by a single dynasty, and that the period of rule of each dynasty began and ended in a military victory or defeat. This had its roots in the theological belief that kingship was a divine gift, controlled and bestowed by the great god Enlil, deity of the central city of Nippur. One hypothesis to explain this special status of the god of Nippur is that in very early times the notables of all the Sumerian cities met in Nippur to elect a supreme war-lord in times of emergency. In human terms this status of Nippur meant that only those dynasties were legitimate – and named in the *Sumerian King List* as rulers of Sumer and Akkad – which the priests of Nippur had recognized. But in historical fact the position was not so clear-cut; contemporary inscriptions show the existence of other powerful dynasties not mentioned in the *Sumerian King List*; and some of those which are mentioned there certainly did not rule the whole of Sumer and Akkad.

The Sumerians, like the Israelites, had a tradition of a great Flood, but they held that their history began even earlier. Their *King List* knew of five cities – Eridu, Bad-tibira, Larak, Sippar and Shuruppak – so ancient that they existed before the Flood. The text begins:

> When kingship was let down from heaven, the kingship was in Eridu. In Eridu, Alulim was king and reigned for 28,800 years. Alalgar reigned for 36,000 years. 2 kings reigned for 64,800 years.
>
> I bring to an end (the ascendancy of) Eridu. Its kingship was carried to Bad-tibira . . .

The formula continues on the same pattern through the periods of rule of Bad-tibira and the other pre-diluvial cities. One of the supposed kings of Bad-tibira was 'divine Dumuzi, a shepherd', who reigned 36,000 years. The *King List* gives the same name but not the same epithet for a ruler of Erech; Dumuzi was also the name of a Sumerian fertility god (see pages 326f.) who occurs in the Bible as Tammuz (Ezekiel 8:14). The relationship between the kings and the god of the same name is probably that some very early ruler or rulers became identified with the fertility god by participation in the Sacred Marriage. The account of the pre-diluvial dynasties ends:

> Five cities were they. Eight kings reigned for 241,200 years. The Flood swept thereover.

The incredible lengths of reigns show the remoteness of these traditions.

With the Flood tradition linked in this way to particular cities, we are able to make a rough estimate of the date at which the Sumerians believed the Flood to have happened: they thought of it as after the time at which Eridu flourished and before the *King List*'s first post-diluvial dynasty – Kish – rose to prominence. Archaeology shows that there was no important occupation of Eridu after the *Uruk* period, and that it was virtually abandoned well before the *Early Dynastic* period; that is to say, the heyday of Eridu was past by about 3000 BC. Excavation has established that Kish did not become a major city until the *Jemdet Nasr* period (i.e. in the century after 3000 BC). This fixes the date at which Sumerian tradition placed the Flood as between 3000 and 2900 BC.

The *Sumerian King List* asserts that after the Flood kingship was once again 'let down from heaven', lighted first upon Kish, and then passed to Erech in the south. Clearly, tradition held that the main seat of civilization in the south, which in the beginning of history had been Eridu, after the Flood moved to Erech. This is amply borne out by the archaeological evidence about the very early decline of Eridu. There is also a myth which reflects the change of cultural centre. It concerns Inanna, the great goddess of Erech, telling how she paid a visit to her father Enki at his shrine in Eridu. There Enki fittingly entertained her, and drinking too freely of his own good wine, became filled with such generosity that he proceeded to heap gifts upon her. These gifts – more than a hundred of them – comprised the basic concepts of the Sumerian way of life (the Sumerian word is *me*) and included such things as kingship, priestly functions, justice, truth and falsehood, ritual prostitution, music, heroism, happiness and sadness, security, crafts such as leatherworking, carpentry, metalworking and smithery, scribal skill, wisdom and understanding, judgement and decision. Inanna loaded them all into a boat, and despite steps taken by the repentant Enki to try to intercept her and recover his gifts when his alcoholic liberality had worn off, managed to convey the precious objects safely to Erech. Thus did Erech become the centre of civilization.

Yet according to the *Sumerian King List*, Erech was not the first centre in terms of political power. That fell to Kish, recorded as the first dynasty after the Flood. Kish lay in Akkad, that is, north Babylonia, not far from the site of the later Babylon. The city has been excavated to virgin soil, and the earliest major phase of occupation was in the *Jemdet Nasr* period. A majority of the kings of the first dynasty of Kish bore Semitic names, but the *Sumerian King List* gives no indication that its compilers regarded the Kish dynasty as in any respect different from lines of kings with Sumerian names – a further indication that these people had no concept of distinct Sumerian and Akkadian (Semitic) ethnic groups.

Kish was indisputably the most important centre of north Babylonia in the *Early Dynastic* period: such was its traditional reputation as a centre of political power that later in the millennium, even when it was no longer an independent dynastic capital, its name was included in the title of any ruler who claimed dominion over the whole of Babylonia.

The last king of the first dynasty of Kish, as stated in the *Sumerian King List*, was Akka son of Enmebaragesi. After a reign of Akka given as 625 years, we are told

> Kish was smitten with weapons. Its kingship was carried to Eanna [i.e. Erech].

With this mention of the defeat of Akka, we link up indirectly with one of the epics from Erech.

From the Erech dynasty succeeding Kish, the *King List* gives twelve kings, of whom the second to fifth are:

> Enmerkar . . . *Lugal* of Erech, the one who built Erech;
> Divine Lugalbanda, a shepherd;
> Divine Dumuzi;
> Divine Gilgamesh (his father was a *lillu* [a semi-divine being]), the *En* of Kulaba.

Lugal in origin meant no more than 'great man' (literally 'Mister Big', from Sumerian *lú* 'man' and *gal* 'great'), but eventually came to denote 'king'. *En* was a Sumerian word which later meant 'lord', but originally it seems to have designated the person who acted as high priest or high priestess (the *En* could be a woman) to the city deity. Generally, cities with a goddess had a male *En* and vice versa, but there were exceptions. By *E.D.* II at latest, the *Lugal* and the *En* (when a man) were frequently the same person, as was the case with Enmerkar. The *Lugal-En* came to play the male role in a central religious ceremony of the Sumerian city known as the Sacred Marriage (see pages 330ff.), but there is dispute as to whether that belonged originally with the *Lugal* or with the *En*, when those roles were distinct.

Epics as history

Of nine Erech epics known, two concern Enmerkar, two centre on Lugalbanda but also involve Enmerkar, and the other five have Gilgamesh as their hero. It is one of the Gilgamesh epics – *Gilgamesh and Akka* – which links events in Kish and Erech. It begins:

> The messengers of Akka son of Enmebaragesi
> Came from Kish to Gilgamesh in Erech,
> The *En* Gilgamesh put the matter before the city Elders,
> Sought their opinion: . . .

Are we to submit to the house of Kish?
Shall we not smite it with weapons?

The Elders, probably the heads of families, met in assembly and advised submission. But

Gilgamesh, the *En* of Kulaba,
Who does heroic things for Inanna,
Took not the words of his city Elders to his heart.[3]

Instead he went to consult the men in their prime, of an age to bear arms. They in turn convened an assembly, but their decision was to resist Kish. A siege of Erech ensued, but ended when Gilgamesh appeared on the wall, striking the attackers with such terror that they lifted the siege.

This obviously illuminates the political institutions of the period concerned, probably *E.D.* II (the century after 2700 BC). The *En*, although war-lord, did not have absolute power; heads of families normally decided on matters of public policy, but in the last resort, in grave affairs threatening the state as a whole, the decision was remitted to the assembly of all adult male citizens. Thorkild Jacobsen introduced the term 'primitive democracy' for this social structure. He showed that some of the myths reflect the society of a still earlier stage, when women as well as men took part in decision-making – sometimes with a dominating role. At that time, all citizens – both male and female – came together to decide upon action when some emergency threatened. All citizens had the right to speak, but the opinions of some, particularly the older men, carried greater weight. Discussion continued until virtual unanimity was reached: there was no question of taking a majority vote. The final decision was formally announced by a small group called 'law-makers'. Anthropologists have found similar methods of decision-making in some primitive societies today.

Erech had a trading partnership with a distant city-state called Aratta which it is generally agreed was somewhere in

Iran, and three of the epic poems are related to this: they imply that to reach Aratta one had to go to Susa in southwest Iran, then on to Anshan at the southern end of the Zagros, and then across seven mountain ranges. One of the valuables obtained from Aratta was the semi-precious stone lapis lazuli, of which the nearest source known is Afghanistan; but that need not fix Aratta near Afghanistan, as it may only have been a transhipment centre. A proposed identification on the borders of Afghanistan, a thousand miles from Erech as the crow flies, would require the merchants of Erech to cross not only the specified seven mountain ranges but also a vast salt desert which a handbook on Persia describes as 'the most dangerous area of central Persia' and perhaps 'the hottest part of the earth'. Another theory places Aratta in Kerman province in south Iran, and there is a third view which sees it north of Kermanshah in Iranian Kurdestan, less than six hundred miles away via Susa, and half that in a straight line.

In the epic poem known as *Enmerkar and the Lord [En] of Aratta*, Enmerkar, the *En* of Erech, wished to build and beautify a shrine to his patroness the goddess Inanna, and sent to the ruler of Aratta demanding the sending of lapis lazuli and timber. In payment he dispatched to Aratta a donkey caravan laden with barley which the soil of Sumer so bountifully yielded: the appearance of the string of asses winding with their burdens through the mountains is aptly likened to a line of ants filing from their hole. But the *En* of Aratta, named Ensuhkeshdanna, as we know from another poem, claimed that he himself enjoyed a special relationship with Inanna, and the question of their religious privileges caused dissension between the two rulers. These poems thus reflect a tradition of a common religion and economy covering the region from the lower Euphrates to at least the other side of the Zagros. *Enmerkar and the Lord of Aratta* is not without threats of the use of military force, but they never happened: it was inconceivable that they should, as even at the nearest placing of the two city-states, attack by one upon the other was not a practical possibility. In practice, according to the epics, such disputes as arose were no more than verbal clashes, with, at the most, the employment of magic to favour one side or the other. As the epics are all written from the Erech point of view, Aratta always lost in the end.

What was the purpose of these epics? A look at the sort of material they contain may suggest an answer. They are not primarily concerned with historical narrative, but incorporate such other matter as riddles, folk-tales (see below), descriptions of travel in difficult terrain, and snippets of cultural history. As instances of the last item, one passage mentions that Enmerkar was the first to use writing on a clay tablet to supplement the verbal communication transmitted by the messenger,[4] and another, if I have interpreted it correctly, tells of an invention in chemical technology, concerned with making an artificial substitute for lapis lazuli.[5] These features suggest that the epics were composed not for any religious purpose, nor as historical records, but simply to be recited for entertainment. This sheds light on the sort of people the early Sumerians were: they enjoyed the intellectual challenge of riddles; they found a fascination in folk-tales, which often (as in an example in *Enmerkar and Ensuhkeshdanna*) have the theme of a pretentious person being outwitted by someone he thought his inferior; they liked to hear of foreign lands; and they liked to hear how advances in technology came about. The picture one gets is that these epics were devised by, and for the entertainment of, people with lively and enquiring minds.

Archaic writing

Another illustration of the creativeness of the third-millennium Sumerians is the way in which writing developed. Its use quickly passed beyond the humble beginnings for which it was devised, so that by the middle of the millennium it was being used for works of literature in the narrower sense.

There were no sudden breaks in the development of writing in the third millennium, but for convenience scholars divide it into periods. The principal find-places of texts earlier than the

Agade period are summarized below, in chronological sequence from oldest to latest: some scholars use the term 'archaic' for the writing on the earlier groups and 'Old Sumerian' for that of the Lagash texts onwards.

Name of find-place		
Modern	*Ancient*	*Archaeological period*
Warka	Erech (Uruk)	*Uruk*
Al-Uhaimir	Kish	*Jemdet Nasr* III
Jemdet Nasr	?	*Jemdet Nasr* III
Al Uqair	?	*Jemdet Nasr* III
Muqayyar	Ur	*E.D.* I
Fara	Shuruppak	*E.D.* III
Abu Salabikh	?	*E.D.* III
Nuffar	Nippur[6]	*E.D.* III
Bismaya	Adab	*E.D.* III
Tello	Girsu (part of city-state Lagash)	End of *E.D.* III
Mardikh	Ebla (in Syria)	Approx. Agade

Writing of the *Uruk* stage cannot be read, although some scholars believe that, on the basis of similarities of archaic signs with later Sumerian signs, they are able to identify various city-names and even to analyse some groups of texts as records of flocks of sheep and goats. But we do not know for certain what language was represented, though many assume it was already Sumerian. When we reach the *Jemdet Nasr* period, we are certain the language is Sumerian, if we accept the argument of the late Adam Falkenstein. Falkenstein's argument was in essence as follows.

In texts of the *Jemdet Nasr* period there is a group (several times repeated) of three signs, which we may represent by X–Y–Z. The two signs X–Y can be recognized, from their virtual identity with forms found in later Sumerian writing, as the name of a god, 'Lord Air', read in Sumerian as EN.LÍL. This in itself does not prove that the signs X–Y were read as Sumerian, since EN.LÍL could conceivably have been the way in which an earlier language represented that god's name, later taken over into Sumerian. Z, , is recognizably the picture of an arrow, but there are few if any contexts in which 'Lord-Air-arrow' would make sense. We must therefore look for a language which has another word with the same pronunciation as the word for 'arrow'. Sumerian is such a language. The pictogram we have called Z is unmistakably the source of the later Sumerian sign pronounced TI, and in Sumerian TI had two different meanings: (1) 'arrow', (2) 'life' or 'to live'. Reading the sign as TI, with its second sense, gives a meaningful phrase, since 'Enlil, give life!' represents a personal name of a type very common throughout Sumerian and Babylonian civilization. The group X–Y–Z is therefore to be read as Sumerian, EN.LÍL.TI, establishing that Sumerian was the language of texts of the *Jemdet Nasr* period.

Falkenstein's argument was challenged by A. A. Vaiman in 1976, on the grounds that the signs read as EN.LÍL.TI were really É.EN.TI.[7] Whichever view finally proves correct, the possibility should be borne in mind that even if Sumerian was written on some of the Jemdet Nasr texts, it may not have been the only language represented there. Indeed, even in the archaic texts from Fara, Abu Salabikh and Nippur, all later than those from Jemdet Nasr, there are some which are written differently from texts which can be read as Sumerian, giving the possibility that they were in a language other than Sumerian.[8]

The intelligible archaic texts from the *Jemdet Nasr* period onwards are of two main kinds, economic and literary. There are several categories of literary texts. The first group are those usually called 'school texts', although a principal authority on this period, R. D. Biggs, has proposed that this term should be abandoned as misleading. It suggests that such texts were student exercises, whereas many of them were certainly the work of expert scribes, since they contain a line saying 'So-and-so copied the tablet'. Their contents comprise lists of such things as professions, deities, kinds of fish, birds, animals, plants or names of cities, forming a kind of primitive lexicon.

But besides the 'school texts', there are literary works in the narrower sense. These include some proverbs; a composition generally known as *The Instructions of Shuruppak* (see page 385), which is a work of moral instruction taking the form of advice by a father to his son; hymns glorifying temples; some incantations; and several myths. Such texts show that well before the middle of the third millennium writing was already being applied far beyond the mere keeping of records for which it had originally been invented, and that creative literature began in the *E.D.* III period.

Yet the keeping of economic and administrative records had lost none of its importance, and texts of this kind give us a good deal of information about developments in the *E.D.* III period. For example, texts found at Fara (the site of the ancient city, Shuruppak, the home of the Babylonian counterpart of Noah), include palace records listing large numbers of personnel. In some categories the numbers appear far too high for an actual palace staff: there are, for instance, 144 cupbearers and 65 cooks. Because of this, it has been suggested that the documents actually concern personnel of military garrisons. This hypothesis is strengthened by the fact that these records also refer to the repair of war-chariots, and include lists of troops going to battle. If this interpretation is correct, it indicates that by 2500 BC, kings of some of the city-states had reached a position in which they could maintain standing garrisons in key cities.

Third-millennium city-states

We know of many Sumerian city-states in the middle of the third millennium, but the one about which we are best informed is Lagash. This city-state was based on three distinct urban centres, Lagash itself (now marked by the site Al-Hiba), Girsu (Tello) and Nina (Surghul),[9] which together, it is estimated, had a free population of about 100,000.[10] The region in which these sites lie still enjoys considerable agricultural prosperity today, by virtue of an efficient system of irrigation canals. In antiquity the principal canal there, known as the Luma-girnunta, ensured to the city-state of Lagash not only bountiful crops but also a thriving river-borne trade. Its first ruler known to us, Ur-nanshe, speaks of ships of Tilmun (Bahrein in the Persian Gulf) bringing timber to Lagash from foreign lands. The consequent economic and social stability provided conditions in which Ur-nanshe was able to found a dynasty which ruled in unbroken succession through six reigns for over a century.

Upon the same canal as Lagash lay another city-state, Umma, also a complex of several centres. Umma was so placed that it could interfere with the water-supply of Lagash, and this was a ready source of strife; in addition, the ownership of some of the irrigated land between the two city-states was in dispute. We have several documents recording the history (from the Lagash point of view) of the conflicts to which these circumstances gave rise. The longest inscription is on a monument known as the *Stele of the Vultures*, set up by Eannatum, third ruler of the dynasty. This monument, now in the Louvre, takes its name from the carrion birds it depicts fighting over the entrails of the slain after a decisive battle. In that battle, Eannatum, although himself shot by an arrow (as the accompanying inscription records), defeated the ruler of Umma and made him swear to pay rent for the land in dispute and neither to divert the irrigation canals nor to smash the boundary monuments.[11] A slightly later inscription on a clay cone of Eannatum's nephew, Entemena, gives the history of the conflict between the two states for several generations up to the time it was written.

It is easy to overstate the scale of the military conflict between these neighbouring city-states; indeed, the rulers of Lagash themselves set a precedent for so doing. Eannatum, for example, in the *Stele of the Vultures*, has his god promise him in a dream that the heaps of enemy corpses would be so vast as to reach the base of heaven.[12] But military technology was not yet available to make the achievement of such ambitions possible. The indications are that typically a 'war' involved no more than a period of increasing tension followed by a single military engagement lasting a few hours at most. The account of one such 'war', from the Lagash side, states as the climax of military success that although the ruler of Umma escaped he was killed in his own city, after abandoning sixty ass-teams whose crews were then slaughtered. These ass-teams would be drawing chariots used as mobile platforms from which an archer could shoot arrows; at the likely manning rate of one driver and one archer per team, this would amount to 120 battle casualties at the most. Allowing some discount for the almost universal exaggerations in such claims, we may say that a hundred dead would have been exceptionally heavy casualties in a 'war' between *E.D.* III Sumerian city-states. Figures given by Ur-nanshe suggest that military clashes during his reign typically resulted in casualties of well under ten.

These Lagash records refer back to still earlier events, and thereby tell us something of the wider aspects of *Early Dynastic* Sumerian political organization. They mention an ancient occasion of dispute, when a certain 'Me-salim, king of Kish' had arbitrated between the two city-states, arranging peace terms and setting up a boundary stone to demarcate their territories. Clearly, either both city-states formally accepted Me-salim as overlord, or he enjoyed such prestige that, although not overlord in title, he could effectively act in that capacity. This power of early kings of Kish to wield authority far beyond the borders of their own city-state eventually led to the title 'king of Kish' being adopted by any ruler who claimed overlordship of Sumer and Akkad, even if his primary territory was some city-state other than Kish.

Social structure in Early Dynastic city-states

It was formerly believed that in the *Early Dynastic* period all the land of the city belonged to the temple, and was administered by the *Ensi* (city ruler, governor) as the bailiff of the city deity. More recent research gives a very different picture. It is likely that in the original village settlements all land was community land, from which all families received an allotment according to their needs. Part of the land would also be set aside to maintain the shrine of the community's deity and the priests who served there. But in primitive societies, religious functionaries are in a position to exercise powerful sanctions, by their ability to manipulate divine decisions; and this would favour the temple priesthood acquiring disproportionately large allotments of land. Moreover, primitive people have a feeling that once something has been in the possession of a god, it has become sacral and must henceforth be set apart from ordinary use. In consequence, land once allotted to the deity would come to be thought of as distinct from the common pool of community land and thus separated off as the permanent property of the temple. There were also factors leading to other parts of the communal land coming into the permanent ownership of particular families. When plots were first allotted from the communal land, the more powerful families would ensure that they received the most favourable allocations, and once having taken all the best land they would be loath to let it go back into the general pool for a redistribution which could only be to their disadvantage; eventually it would be in the interests of all the most influential families to adopt as a legal principle that land was the hereditary property of the family currently holding it. Families could, and sometimes did, sell their land; in such an event a senior member, or group of members, would act for the whole.

A third possible owner of land was the state, in the form of the *Ensi* and his family. In the Sumerian view of things, the *Ensi* ruled because he was the human representative of the city god, and that status gave him the opportunity of taking over (not always without opposition) some of the temple lands to support his functions; thus, in some circumstances, some of what had been temple land became state land.

For the middle of the third millennium we know less about land in state or private tenure than about temple lands. Temple lands were of three categories: the first, known as 'the Lord's field', was used to supply the needs of the temple itself, including the cult. The second category was land allotted to labourers, administrators and artisans of the temple estate in return for the services they gave to the god. The remainder of the temple land was let out on a share-cropping basis, for which rent equivalent to one-third of the crop was paid, partly in silver and partly in kind.

As Lagash grew wealthy by trade, and the power of the ruler increased in consequence of the stable dynasty, it underwent economic and social changes which appeared to some sections of the population as abuses. The main complaints were two. Firstly, the *Ensi* was treating the temple lands and the god's possessions as his own property. Secondly, citizens were subject to excessive taxes: taxes were, for example, levied on cattle, fisheries, sheep-shearing, betrothal, divorce and burial. The economic developments also produced a class of rich men who used their wealth to oppress the poor; a rich man might make a poor man a loan and then foreclose at an inconvenient time. When the poor man proved unable to repay, the creditor would seize in settlement an animal or other goods of value far exceeding the amount owing.

Economic reforms

These economic problems, combined with a power struggle between the temple authorities and the city-state administration, brought an end to the Ur-nanshe dynasty. Thirteen years after the end of that dynasty, there came to power Uru-inimgina, who made a brave attempt to eradicate the abuses which had arisen. We have several inscriptions of his in which he records the abuses and lists his reforms, designed to protect the poor from victimization. Some abbreviated extracts follow:

> Formerly shepherds had to pay silver (to an official) for (the shearing of) the sheep. . . .
>
> The god's oxen ploughed the onion field of the *Ensi*, and the *Ensi*'s . . . fields were in the best fields of the god. . . .

When someone brought a dead man for burial, (the official) received 7 measures of beer and 420 loaves of bread. . . .

The houses and the fields of the *Ensi*, the houses and the fields of the *Ensi*'s women folk, were joined side by side. [This recalls the much later social condemnation of Isaiah 5:8: 'Woe unto them that join house to house, that lay field to field, till there be no place'.]

These were the practices of former times. But when the god Ningirsu . . . gave the kingship of Lagash to Uru-inim-gina, . . . he set up for him the divine decrees of former times.

He forbade the official to receive silver for (the shearing of) the sheep. . . .

He made Ningirsu king of the houses and the fields of the *Ensi*. He made the goddess Bau queen of the houses and the fields of the *Ensi*'s women folk.

When someone brought a dead man for burial, the fee was (reduced to) 3 measures of beer and 80 loaves of bread.

If a retainer has an ass which bears a good foal, and his patron says; 'I want to buy it', . . . if the retainer is unwilling to sell, the patron may not beat him.

However, Lagash was too far gone in decline: these reforms were not sufficient or soon enough to restore economic strength and stability, and Uru-inim-gina fell a victim to the perennial rivalry between Lagash and Umma. The latter was now closely tied to the powerful city-state of Erech, with whose support the king of Umma, Lugalzagesi, finally overthrew Uru-inim-gina shortly after 2400 BC.

The beginnings of imperialism

Lugalzagesi was an early imperialist. He embarked upon a policy of military conquest which ultimately brought all Sumer (not at first Akkad) under his control, with Erech as his capital. He also claimed to wield influence well outside Sumer, 'from the Lower Sea [the Persian Gulf] along the Tigris and Euphrates to the Upper Sea [the Mediterranean]', so that 'all rulers of Sumer and of independent countries bowed to his arbitration in Erech'. How far this claim accords with the truth is questionable. Probably it is an idealized picture, not necessarily fully according with political realities. None the less, it does indicate that in the twenty-fourth century BC an ideal was current of internal peace under a suzerain powerful enough to check all rivalry, and of external peace through a ruler of such influence that he was acceptable as an international arbitrator. Lugalzagesi's political expansion was not an entirely new phenomenon. Since the time of Akka of Kish there had been fleeting attempts at hegemony over wide areas; for example, during the reign of Ur-nanshe's second successor, Eannatum, the forces of Mari on the middle Euphrates had penetrated almost to Lagash, four hundred miles to the southeast. Lugalzagesi was aiming at a more permanent domination of Mesopotamia, which he seemed to achieve when he successfully attacked Kish, still the leading city in north Babylonia. The *Sumerian King List* tells us:

> Kish was smitten with weapons. Its kingship was taken away to Erech. In Erech Lugalzagesi became king and reigned for 25 years.

But Lugalzagesi himself was then overthrown:

> Erech was smitten with weapons; its kingship was taken away to Agade. In Agade Sharrum-kin, whose [father(?)] was a gardener, cupbearer of Ur-zababa [an earlier king of Kish], . . . became king and reigned for 56 years.

Sargon of Agade

The name Sharrum-kin, meaning 'the king is true', better known in the form Sargon, is Semitic. The latter word should properly only be used (as here) as a technical term for a language of a particular group, and where use is made in this book of such phrases as 'Semitic peoples', Semites', or the like, it is to be understood that this is a convenient shortening for 'peoples who spoke Semitic languages', without implying any ethnic presuppositions or theories about race.

There is an Arabic proverb which says: 'The desert is the cradle of the Arab, and Iraq his grave.' This recognizes the fact that throughout history successive waves of Semitic-speaking peoples have moved from the west into Mesopotamia, there to be assimilated into the existing population. We have already seen that Semitic speakers were one of the elements in ancient Mesopotamian civilization from its very beginnings, before 3000 BC, and that by 2900 BC the Semitic element was so prominent, at least in the north of what was to become Babylonia, that the *Sumerian King List* gives Semitic names for most of the rulers of the first dynasty of Kish. By 2600–2500 BC, tablets from Abu Salabikh, near Nippur in central Sumer, bear a large number of Semitic names, including the names of about half the scribes who wrote those tablets – in Sumerian. There is no evidence from the century or so before Sargon (reigned 2371–2316 BC) for anything in the nature of a Semitic 'invasion', and such Semites as did arrive during that time probably came in as individual families, settling in the Sumerian cities and rapidly adopting Sumerian culture and a loyalty to their adoptive city-state.

All that we know directly of Sargon's antecedents is what we are told in the *Sumerian King List* already quoted. This is supplemented by traditions in legends, of which the most important is preserved only in cuneiform copies of the first millennium BC, although in literary origin it probably goes back to the early second millennium. The legend is presented as though told by Sargon himself, and has been called a 'pseudo-biography'. It reads:

I am Sargon, the mighty king, the king of Agade.
My mother was a high-priestess. I do not know my father.
My paternal kin inhabit the mountains.
My town was Azupiranu, which lies on the bank of the Euphrates.
My mother conceived me and bore me in secret.
She put me in a reed basket, she made it watertight with pitch.
She left me to the river, from which I could not get away.
The river took me along; it brought me to Aqqi, a water-drawer.

Aqqi the water-drawer drew me up when he dipped his bucket in.
Aqqi the water-drawer brought me up as his son.
Aqqi the water-drawer put me to his garden work.
Through my garden work, Ishtar came to love me, and so
I exercised the kingship for fifty-five years.

This composition must have had some purpose. It may have been written to entertain with a story about an already famous hero, or to edify population groups who saw Sargon as their ancestor, or to boost a ruler who wished to present himself as in the mould of the great Sargon. Whatever the purpose was, it would not have been achieved unless its framework for Sargon conformed to existing traditions about him. The essential framework of the legend tells us this about Sargon. His father was unknown: this need not imply illegitimacy but only – since in Semitic society descent is defined by the male line, and the longer the more honourable – that his forebears were nobodies. But the legend then brushes aside the insignificance of Sargon's paternal descent by a theme that combines religious belief and folklore. His mother, it tells us, was an *Entu*, a high priestess. Now an *Entu* was from the cultic point of view the wife of the god and in human terms invariably of noble birth, and often a royal princess. The legend is saying obliquely that Sargon's birth was by no means insignificant: his mother may have passed on to him royal blood, perhaps even – from her relationship to the god – an element of divinity.

A legend glorifying an historical figure cannot disregard generally known facts, but it can reinterpret them in the way most favourable to the hero. Having explained that Sargon's birth was far more exalted than formerly supposed, it now turns to Aqqi, the water-drawer. The name means 'I poured out', and looks very much like a name invented as suitable for a water-drawer. Since the legend found it necessary to introduce such a foster-father to explain how it was that Sargon began as an irrigator and gardener, we must accept that historically Sargon actually was at some time an irrigator and gardener. The *Sumerian King List* confirms this by saying 'his father(?)

[word damaged and restored] was a gardener'. But the *King List* says in addition that he was cupbearer of a former king of Kish. Was he, though? In Akkadian the word for 'cupbearer' is *šaqû*, and a word with exactly the same spelling means 'irrigation worker'. But these two officials are not denoted by the same word in Sumerian. It looks as though the compiler of the *Sumerian King List*, writing in Sumerian, mistook an Akkadian tradition which said that Sargon was an irrigation official of Ur-zababa and wrongly rendered it to say that he was his cupbearer. Everything then ties up: Sargon was of insignificant descent, his people came from the middle Euphrates, he was brought up as an irrigator, and because he did this very successfully (which is what being loved by his goddess implies), when his family moved southeast into the territory of Kish he entered the royal service, becoming the senior administrator in charge of the irrigation system so vital in Babylonia. This would have involved him in organizing large bodies of men. After the downfall of the last king of Kish he used the administrative organization he had built up to develop his own authority, and, by installing himself at Agade, a deserted site on a branch of the Euphrates, he was able to create a power base without running up against vested interests within existing northern cities. With his tribal links, he was in a position to reinforce his new city with his kinsmen.

Agade is the usual but possibly inaccurate rendering of the name of the city which Sargon founded as his capital; the Semitic spelling is Akkad, which may have meant 'the ancestral town',[13] and this term became used not only for the city but also for north Babylonia as a whole. The city is still unidentified, although it was probably not far from its ultimate successor, Babylon. The *Sumerian King List* gives no hint of thinking that Sargon's succession supplanted a Sumerian dynasty by a different ethnic stock. Certainly Sargon himself did not reject the Sumerian cultural heritage. His first action after defeating Lugalzagesi was to display him as his prisoner before the great Sumerian god Enlil in his city, Nippur, in recognition of the theological principle that only Enlil at

Nippur could legitimate a king; and he explicitly claimed that it was Enlil who had given him victory. He named Sumerian deities in his titles, and his daughter not only bore a Sumerian name, but was high priestess (*En*) of the great Moon-god Nanna in the major Sumerian-speaking city of Ur.

The dynasty Sargon founded, though it endured for little more than a century, left a permanent imprint on Mesopotamian history. Sargon tells us that he won thirty-four battles, taking cities stretching from Ur in south Sumer to Ebla in north Syria; the latter (now Tell Mardikh) has been excavated since 1974, and the results show how far Sumerian culture had spread from its home region of south Mesopotamia. The finds included over 10,000 inscribed clay tablets of about the time of Sargon, obviously very heavily dependent upon the Sumerian writing system and Sumerian literary forms, although also using a West Semitic language distinct from the Semitic language, Akkadian, spoken in south Mesopotamia.

Sargon exercised a deliberate policy of centralization. He destroyed the walls of cities within south Mesopotamia, thereby depriving potential rebels of strongholds. However, he certainly did not engage in a vendetta against Sumerian influence, and he seems to have left many of the former governors in their posts, subject to transfer of allegiance to him; there is even some evidence that he reinstated the defeated Lugalzagesi as governor of his original city, Umma. It is true that Sargon says in an inscription that citizens of the city of Agade exercised government throughout south Mesopotamia, but this means no more than that as governorships fell vacant he filled them with his own townsmen.

International trade flourished under Sargon, and he claimed that his control reached from the Persian Gulf to the Mediterranean, the Cedar Forest (the Amanus) and the Silver Mountains (the Taurus). His influence may have extended even further to the northwest, to judge by traditions in later texts, which tell of an expedition he made to protect a Mesopotamian merchant colony deep in Asia Minor, probably not far from Kayseri in central Asiatic Turkey, some six hundred miles from Sargon's base as the crow flies, and far more by any practicable route. In the interests of trade, Sargon made his capital a major river-port, and he tells us that 'ships from Meluhha, Magan and Tilmun moored at the quay of Agade'. Tilmun was Bahrein, halfway down the Persian Gulf, Magan was somewhere not precisely identified in the region of the straits of Hormuz at the southern end of the Gulf, and Meluhha probably represented the contemporary Indus Valley civilization in what is now Pakistan, nearly two thousand miles by the sea route from Sargon's capital. From Turkey to Pakistan was a huge trading empire for the twenty-fourth century BC, the achievement of a man who began as an irrigator.

Equally remarkable with Sargon was his daughter, who bore the Sumerian name Enheduanna, and was the high priestess (*En*) of the Moon-god Nanna in Sumerian-speaking Ur in the south of Sumer. But, more importantly, she was the world's first poet known by name. She wrote – and in most cases signed with her colophon – a number of hymns in honour of the temples of Sumer and Akkad and of the goddess Inanna (Innin): some of these works are discussed later. We even have a picture of this lady, on an artefact from Ur.[14]

Sargon remained active throughout his long reign of fifty-five years and even as an old man was able to put down a rebellion. He was helped in this by maintaining a standing army, if that is the meaning of an inscription which says of Sargon that '5,400 soldiers ate in his presence daily'. Two of his sons, Rimush and Manishtusu, successively reigned after him. They also faced revolts, which must have been on a large scale, to judge by an inscription of Rimush which speaks of killing over twelve thousand men in a rebellion of Kazallu, a city in northern Babylonia. (It may be pointed out that Kazallu was as 'Semitic' as Agade itself, so that this rebellion was not a matter of Sumerians against Semites.) But these two rulers managed to maintain themselves and even to extend their empire eastwards into southwest Iran. Manishtusu may have died in a palace revolution.[15]

Naram-sin

The other major figure in the dynasty after Sargon was his third successor, his grandson Naram-sin (2291–2255 BC). He is frequently mentioned in later omens and proverbial sayings, usually very obscure, for example:

> The east wind is a wind of prosperity, the friend of the divine Naram-sin.

This presumably relates to a tradition about an ancient incident in some campaign by Naram-sin, but it is meaningless to us.

Some of Naram-sin's own inscriptions, and later ones about him, place the sign for 'god' before his name, and there are even inscriptions in which he receives the title 'the god of Agade'. Clearly, so great was his prestige that he was considered divine. Another title newly introduced by Naram-sin was 'king of the four regions', a claim for universal dominion. This was not a mere empty boast. A poetic composition of some centuries later extols the magnificence of Naram-sin's times, speaking of

> mighty elephants and apes, beasts from distant lands, jostling in the great square [of the capital].

This suggests trade relations with the Indus Valley civilization of Pakistan. According to his own inscriptions, Naram-sin inflicted a military defeat upon the king of Magan, a claim given credence by the finding of alabaster vases on which were carved the words 'booty of Magan'. This implies that Naram-sin controlled the length of the Persian Gulf, since Magan was somewhere at its southern end. In the northeast Naram-sin penetrated into what are now the Kurdish mountains, quelling the hill-tribes, and setting up a great relief, carved high in the face of the rock (see plate 16A). To guard the route into Asia Minor he built a great castle at Tell Brak in what is now eastern Syria, and another at Nineveh (Mosul); and a stele of his has been found as far north as Diyarbekr in Turkey.

Mesopotamian literary tradition gives a mixed judgement upon Naram-sin, treating him on the one hand as a great hero and on the other as an ill-fated ruler. The adverse side of his reign is reflected in a religious tradition which tells of the goddess Inanna deciding to abandon the capital, Agade. Also, his own inscriptions mention a general rebellion of the principal cities of Sumer and Akkad. This is emphatically not to be seen as a revolt of Sumerian cities against a Semitic dynasty, since the rebels contained both Sumerian-speaking and Semitic-speaking cities in alliance.[16]

A Sumerian text traces the origin of the evil fate which eventually befell the land. In its opening lines it describes the early splendour and wealth of Agade, to which came people from all quarters bearing their tribute. It was an impious deed of Naram-sin which brought this to an end. His offence was that he allowed his troops to sack and loot the *Ekur*, the temple of the great god Enlil in the holiest of Sumerian cities, Nippur. For this desecration, Enlil brought down upon the fertile lands a barbarous race from the hills, the Gutians. These savages disrupted communications and trade, broke down the irrigation system, and spread famine and death throughout the land. But not all of Sumer and Akkad had been guilty of offence, and to turn aside Enlil's wrath from the innocent cities of the land, eight of the senior gods undertook that Agade should itself be destroyed in requital for the violation of Nippur, and achieved the enduring desolation of Agade by a curse reminiscent of Isaiah's execration of Babylon some fifteen hundred years later (Isaiah 13:19–22).

In sober fact the consequences of Naram-sin's policies were not as sudden and catastrophic as the Sumerian poem suggests, and although Gutian raids on Mesopotamia may well have begun during his reign, it was not until the time of his son and successor Sharkalisharri (a name meaning 'King of all kings') that the central authority finally broke down.

Despite the traditions, the Gutians were only the beneficiaries and not the primary cause of the downfall of the Agade dynasty. The real cause was the pressures resulting from the very size of Naram-sin's empire and the conflicting interests of the many different peoples in it. Even in the nineteenth century AD, the Ottoman empire, with several centuries of administrative experience behind it, frequently found it impossible to maintain its authority over the whole of the same area, from the Mediterranean to the Persian Gulf.

The Gutians and after

A period of anarchy succeeded the Gutian invasion, laconically summarized in the *Sumerian King List* with the words: 'Who was king? Who was not king?' The *King List* names twenty-one so-called kings of the Gutian period, but the extremely short reigns attributed to them (about half were three years or less) makes it likely that they were tribal chiefs who held office in rotation. Later tradition remembered the Gutians as barbarians, which suggests a primitive social organization in which kingship may well not yet have existed. There are indications that later Gutian rulers were becoming assimilated to Mesopotamian culture; the names of some later kings are Semitic, and dedication inscriptions show that they had adopted the religious cults of the land.

The later peoples of Babylonia remembered the period of Gutian dominance with abhorrence, as a time of barbarism, when the gods were not respected, temples were plundered, and neither women nor children were spared. It was in the northern part of the land, Akkad, that the impact of the Gutians was felt most severely; in Sumer several of the old city-states, despite suffering material damage in the first wave of invasion, remained virtually autonomous. One of the cities which suffered least was Lagash. This city, destroyed by Lugalzagesi, had been rebuilt during the prosperous days of the Agade dynasty. It now had the opportunity to recover much of its earlier prominence, particularly since the destruction of Agade had removed its principal rival as a terminal for sea-borne trade up the Persian Gulf. Its *Ensis* were able to extend their authority beyond their own city-state, forming a new dynasty, known from their own inscriptions although unmentioned in the *Sumerian King List*. The best-known ruler of this dynasty is the fourth, Gudea, whose inscriptions give us much information about his activities. He claimed to be suzerain to Nippur and Erech, and even undertook a campaign to loot the Elamite city of Anshan in southwest Iran. But commerce was more important than conquests, and his inscriptions, although principally concerned with his piety in temple-building and the fulfilment of his duties to the gods, contain many references to trading expeditions. Once again the Persian Gulf trade flourished, for Gudea claimed that 'Magan, Meluhha, Gubi and Tilmun brought tribute; their ships came to Lagash with timber'. Stone, bitumen and gypsum were brought in shiploads for the building of the temple of Ningirsu, whilst other imported goods included diorite from Magan, cedarwood from the Lebanon, copper from Kimash (in western Iran) and gold from Hahu in Asia Minor.

The wealth channelled into Sumer through Lagash reinvigorated the whole country and brought the re-emergence of other independent city-states, so that by the time of Gudea's second successor, his grandson, some of these overshadowed Lagash. The ruler of Erech, Utu-hengal (2120–2114 BC) was able to overthrow the last of the Gutian rulers, for which he was duly recognized at Nippur as 'King of the Four Regions' (a title introduced by Naram-sin), and was included in the *Sumerian King List*. This marks the re-emergence of centralized government; subordinate city-states were ruled through governors, who recognized Utu-hengal as overlord.

The Third Dynasty of Ur

One such governor was Ur-nammu of Ur, who subsequently became an independent king (2113–2096 BC), and founded a dynasty known as the Third Dynasty of Ur (or III Ur), which endured for more than a century (2113–2006 BC). This was an empire more compact than that of Sargon of Agade, and shows Sumerian civilization in its most fully developed form.

It was a highly organized bureaucratic society, reflected in the fact that cuneiform tablets from this period, mainly administrative and economic in content, are represented in our museums to the number of well over a hundred thousand; the majority of these are still unpublished. Documentation became obsessive. Everything had to be documented, such as, on one tablet, an exact count of a certain kind of fish (2,740 of them) delivered as food for the temple dogs. Two sheep, dead from natural causes, were regarded as a matter requiring record. There were even documents recording that there was nothing to record.[17] But despite, or perhaps even because of, this extreme bureaucracy, it was a time of considerable material prosperity, as archaeology witnesses, in the form of widespread evidence of building activities. Ur-nammu himself, founder of the dynasty, built or rebuilt temples in many of the ancient cities, such as Erech, Lagash, Nippur and Eridu, but above all at his capital, Ur. Here, in honour of the Moon-god Nanna, he rebuilt the ziggurat, a great rectangular stepped tower in three stages, about 200 feet by 150 at the base and perhaps 70 feet or so high, with a shrine on top. This ziggurat, restored by later kings and finally uncovered from 1923 onwards by Sir Leonard Woolley, still stands as a monument to the piety of Ur-nammu (see plate 3A). Chance references on tablets of the period make possible some interesting calculations in connection with temple building. One temple, built at Umma in the reign of Ur-nammu's third successor Shu-sin, required at least seven years for its completion, although it was by no means the largest in Sumer. Nearly nine million large and seventeen million small bricks went into its construction. Since a tablet informs us that a brickmaker could produce eighty bricks a day, simple arithmetic shows that the mere making of the bricks for this temple would have occupied a thousand men for nearly a year.

In the interests of a thriving agriculture Ur-nammu dug many canals, and to promote trade he restored Ur's seaborne connection with Magan at the far end of the Persian Gulf. As a further achievement he claims to have re-established civil order and security, which had become notably absent wherever the Gutians had settled; the finding of fragments of laws promulgated by him (see pages 178f.) substantiate this claim.

Early empires in Mesopotamia faced the threat that local city-states might become centres of rebellion. The III Ur administrative system minimized this risk by reducing the status of *Ensis* from local dynasts to appointed governors; as such, they might be posted from one city to another if they threatened to acquire too much power through building up strong local ties. A corps of royal messengers kept the king informed of affairs within his cities, and he used diplomatic representatives to maintain relations with princes beyond the empire.

Ur-nammu's achievements made an enormous impact upon the people of Sumer, and we have a Sumerian text[18] reflecting the shock and horror occasioned by his premature death, apparently on the field of battle. It was felt that the great gods had cheated him:

> The god An altered his holy word,
> Enlil deceitfully perverted the fate he had decreed.

The text goes on to describe the grief of Ur-nammu's wife and his soldiers, when his body was brought to Ur for burial. On his arrival in the Underworld, he made gifts, appropriate to his exalted rank, to the leading deities there, and was treated as an equal by Gilgamesh, king of the Underworld, described as 'his beloved brother'. The Sumerian poet expresses the emotions of Ur-nammu when his realization of his fate hit him, telling of his longing for his city, Ur, which he had left unfinished, for his new palace, and for his wife and children; and he puts into his mouth a bitter tirade against the injustice of the gods, which must have mirrored a widespread incredulous shock at the death of the great and good Ur-nammu.

Shulgi of Ur

Ur-nammu was succeeded by his son Shulgi (2095–2048 BC), who in his long reign further increased the extent and splendour of the empire. His fame was so great that hymns were written in his honour, depicting him as a superman, and, indeed, more than that, an incarnate god. Qualities in every sphere of existence were attributed to him: he was of divine birth; he excelled all others in his command of the skills of writing and mathematics; he was faultless in reading omens; he was of incomparable bravery and military expertise; he was the greatest of hunters, who could kill a lion face to face and run down a gazelle; he was a masterly musician, as a splendid singer, a writer of incomparable hymns and songs and a man who could play, to the delight of those round him, every musical instrument, even the obsolete ones; and he was of such great piety that he had access to all the gods for the benefit of his people.[19] He even claimed, or allowed to be claimed on his behalf, that he had run from the city of Nippur to Ur and back – a total journey of over 200 miles – between sunrise and sunset on one day, despite a violent hailstorm; this would make him not only the first man in history who ever ran a four-minute mile, but a man who could repeat the achievement two hundred times non-stop!

How are we to explain this enormous reputation? The first thing to note is that, according to his own accounts, Shulgi founded, or at least re-endowed, in the great Sumerian cities of Ur and Nippur, two institutions called *edubba*. *Edubba* is Sumerian for 'tablet-house', and meant what today we might call a college of the humanities. The *edubba* was the place where scribes were trained, and where creative literary writing took place. Sumerian hymns were the product of the *edubba*, and so, in view of Shulgi's patronage, it is not surprising that hymns should be written in his honour. This is not a guess. One of the hymns, phrased as if spoken by Shulgi himself, expresses the wish that songs about him shall be in every mouth and never be forgotten. The scribe is urged to read them out to the illiterate professional singer, so that he may learn them and sing them in cult-places.[20]

We do not necessarily have to believe that Shulgi possessed all the qualities of strength, wisdom, expertise and courage claimed for him. As a human being he may have been – and, in view of the claims he made for his running, almost certainly was – no more than a megalomaniac who could not bear to be surpassed in anything. But the importance of these claims is that they give us an insight into Sumerian values. All the qualities attributed to Shulgi represented facets of what the Sumerians saw as the good and full and noble life.

The things of greatest significance to the people of Sumer were fertility, security, justice, destruction of peoples conceived as national enemies, and the prosperity resulting from trade. In the reign of Shulgi all these were achieved, and, whether with or without justification, Shulgi as figurehead claimed the credit for it.

Foremost of these concerns was fertility, in its widest sense. It was this factor which enabled Shulgi to claim actual divinity. As we have seen earlier, in the most ancient Sumerian cities there was a functionary known as the *En*, male where the city deity was a goddess and vice versa, who played the part of spouse to the deity in an annual Sacred Marriage. This was supposed to ensure to the city fertility of humans, animals and vegetation for the following year. There are differences of view about the exact details of the ceremony. Was the Sacred Marriage simply an act of sexual intercourse between two humans representing the city deity and his or her divine spouse, or did the *En* merely go symbolically to meet the deity? The answer is almost certainly that the details differed from city to city and from period to period, but it is certain that in Ur at the time of Ur-nammu and Shulgi the ruler himself took a sexual role in the ceremony.

One of the hymns refers to Shulgi being born in the temple, from, as one scholar interprets it, intercourse of the king with a high priestess,[21] and according to another, from a union between two deities. These two interpretations are not necessarily mutually exclusive, and both situations may be inherent in the Sumerian text. There is no reason why physical phenomena should preclude divine numina. For example, as a believing Anglican, whilst I accept that what I see in the Communion on the physical level is bread and wine, I believe that on the spiritual level I am partaking of the body and blood of Christ. In most religions, believers hold that ultimate reality is not bounded by what one can see and touch, and this will have applied to the ancient Sumerians as much as to us. Although they well knew that on the human level the persons taking part in the Sacred Marriage were a king and a high priestess, this did not preclude them from seeing it on the religious level as a union of deities: for them, during the ceremony a deity was immanent in each of the participants.

If, as Shulgi claimed, his conception was the consequence of a Sacred Marriage, he was by virtue of that indeed born of the gods and was himself a god. When he grew to manhood and himself became king, this sense of divinity would be reinforced, as year by year he was called upon to play the role of the spouse of a goddess in the Sacred Marriage. And so Shulgi formally assumed divinity, and had hymns and prayers written in his honour, to be passed on from generation to generation; more than twenty are known, from copies dating from four hundred years after his death.

Shulgi also promoted the other aspects of life valued by the Sumerians – security, good government, defence against enemies, and economic prosperity. He achieved defence and security against potentially troublesome peoples in the Zagros, by a combination of punitive expeditions and marriage alliances; and he brought under his control both Elam (southwest Iran) and Assyria as far as the mountains of Kurdistan,[22] to the benefit of trade. Like his father and successors, Shulgi also engaged in temple building, always a pointer to a sound economy, and a mass of cuneiform tablets of economic and administrative content bear witness to meticulous concern for sound government.

Amorite invaders

Two of Shulgi's sons, Amar-sin (2047–2039 BC) and Shu-sin (2038–2030 BC), successively followed him, after serving apprenticeships as city governors. During these reigns we have indications of a new wave of Semitic infiltration from the west. This time it took the form not of peaceful families of migrants but of armed incursions by whole tribes of peoples, known collectively as Amurru, a term which occurs in the Bible as Amorites. Despite the building of a huge defensive wall by Shu-sin, this was to spell the end of the empire; though it was not upon Shu-sin but upon his successor, Ibbi-sin (2029–2006 BC), that the disaster fell.

Ibbi-sin came to the throne whilst still a youth, and at first the administration continued as before. Taxes (in the form of cattle) flowed in from the various parts of the empire, and two Sumerian literary compositions from the beginning of Ibbi-sin's reign imply that calamity had not yet fallen upon the land. Then, gradually, legal and administrative documents from city after city are no longer dated by his year-formulae,[23] showing that the central authority was no longer recognized, and after Ibbi-sin's sixth year the various cities no longer made their normal deliveries of beasts for the offerings for Nanna, divine overlord of Ur. The date-formula for Ibbi-sin's sixth year mentions the repairing of the defences of the key cities of Nippur and Ur; clearly a major military threat was recognized.

We know the nature of the threat from a letter from a certain Ishbi-erra, a foreigner from Mari in the service of Ibbi-sin. He was himself destined to become a king, but at the time he wrote he was a senior administrator in north Babylonia, with the task of buying grain for the capital. He had been able, he told his royal master, to acquire some 10,000 tons on favourable terms before the price doubled. But he had to add the less welcome news that the Amurru were forcing their way into the country, taking the fortresses one by one, and that in consequence he was unable to forward the grain to Ur.

Ur relied largely on imported grain, and Ishbi-erra's inability to deliver his consignment put the capital in a desperate position; this is evident from Ibbi-sin's reply, in which he offered to pay double for the corn if only his official could get it through. This situation set off rampant inflation in the capital, so severe that in the seventh and eighth years of Ibbi-sin's reign barley and fish were selling, according to the account tablets, at fifty to sixty times the normal price. Doubtless the breakdown of communications caused by the Amorite invasion brought inflation and famine in many other cities of Sumer, and later omen literature refers to risings and rebellions.

The turning-point came after Ibbi-sin's seventh year. By then Nippur, the city of Enlil, the god who legitimated kingship over Sumer, no longer recognized him; this is shown by the disuse of his date-formulae there. With the support of Nippur lost, the divine mandate for Ibbi-sin's rule could now be considered at an end. By this time his effective empire consisted of little more than the city-state of Ur, although some governors elsewhere retained a personal allegiance to him, without being able to give any effective support. Amongst these loyalists was Ishbi-erra; not until the twelfth year of Ibbi-sin did he begin to issue his own date-formulae as ruler of Isin.

With the collapse of the central authority in Sumer and Akkad, the land faced a further menace, the ever-recurrent threat from peoples to the east, in the south of the Zagros. For several years before the end of Ibbi-sin's reign, there were raids from Elam, and in his twenty-fourth year the Elamites made a major attack on the land, in the course of which Ur was sacked and Ibbi-sin himself deported to Elam. So finally vanished the last relics of the Third Dynasty of Ur. At Ur itself an Elamite garrison remained in the ruins of the devastated capital, and was not finally expelled until Ishbi-erra was in a position to consolidate his kingdom.

3

The Coming of Babylon

THERE is a Sumerian composition known as *Lamentation over the Destruction of Ur*, written a generation or two after the event, which gives a graphic reflection of the destruction wrought by the Elamite invaders at the capital. Part of it reads:

> O Father Nanna [the Sumerian Moon-god, the god of Ur], that city was turned to ruins; the people groan. . . .
> Its walls were breached; the people groan. . . .
> Within all its streets, where people used to walk, corpses lay. . . .
> Mothers and fathers who did not flee their houses were destroyed by fire.
> Babes in arms were carried off by the waters like fish.[1]

It goes on to describe how even the temples were demolished by pickaxe and fire. But this was only in the capital itself, and even there restoration both of buildings and of institutions was being undertaken within a few years. Away from the capital city, the Elamite invasion would have been far less severely felt, and in south Mesopotamia as a whole the disappearance of the Third Dynasty of Ur brought no sudden break in the traditional way of life.

It is true that a number of changes now become apparent, but in the main these were the culmination of developments that had been under way for centuries. One feature which became very evident at this time was the growing prominence of new elements of population. Another change lay in the language predominantly used. Under the Third Dynasty of Ur the usual language for correspondence had been Sumerian; now it became largely replaced by the Semitic language, Akkadian. But it would be wrong to conclude from this that there had been something in the nature of a 'defeat' of Sumerian culture. In fact, Sumerian as a living tongue had been in decline for centuries, and by the end of the Third Dynasty of Ur the Sumerian used in letters may well have been written by scribes who knew it as a taught language rather than as their mother tongue. The widespread use of Akkadian in correspondence from the beginning of the second millennium reflects the fact that most people in Mesopotamia now spoke a Semitic language. But the Sumerian language, although no longer spoken, had by no means lost its prestige, and it remained important for scholarly and religious purposes as long as Babylonian civilization endured. Equally, Sumerian institutions and traditions were so strongly entrenched that they not only remained the basic elements in the culture of ancient Mesopotamia itself throughout its whole history, but also had influence on regions beyond, eventually as far away as Greece.

It is difficult to follow events at the beginning of the second millennium without some picture of the current political and ethnic structure of the Near East. During the third millennium the civilization which had started in south Mesopotamia had spread along the trade routes up the Euphrates into Syria, where major city-states such as Ebla developed; into Asia Minor; up the Tigris, where lay the major kingdom of Assyria, and then on as far as the Taurus and eastwards into the foothills of the Zagros; and also into southwest Iran, where there lived the Elamites with a culture which had been closely linked with Sumer from its beginning. Within Mesopotamia itself (taking that term in the widest sense to include all the territory in the basins of the Euphrates and Tigris and their tributaries), from at least the middle of the third millennium there had been, besides speakers of Sumerian and Akkadian, another ethnic group whom we know as the Hurrians, and in the city-states of Syria lived a population speaking a Semitic language distinct from Akkadian. The Zagros foothills to the east had long been the home of yet other ethnic groups, in addition to the Gutians whom we have already encountered there; and in Asia Minor at the beginning of the second millennium, new groups of peoples speaking Indo-European languages were moving in from the north.

The most important ethnic group to come into prominence in the second half of the third millennium BC was a people called at first Martu and afterwards Amurru, whose descendants we meet in the Bible as Amorites (Deuteronomy 20:17, etc.). They started moving out from the Syrian highlands between Palmyra and the Euphrates and settled in the lands around, from Palestine through Syria and along the Euphrates as far as south Mesopotamia. They spoke a language of the type we call West Semitic, different from the Semitic language, Akkadian, already used in Mesopotamia but akin to later Aramaic and Hebrew. These people had the primitive way of life of desert-dwellers and at first the settled inhabitants of Mesopotamia thought of them with amused contempt for their lack of the amenities and customs of civilization (see page 15). The first of them to reach Mesopotamia moved in as small peaceful groups, and quickly assimilated to settled life by taking service within the urban centres. West Semitic names in lists of temple personnel show that substantial numbers had already settled in this way during the Third Dynasty of Ur.

During the Third Dynasty of Ur the pressure of Amorite immigration increased. No longer was it a movement of isolated families; whole tribes were involved. Later III Ur rulers found it necessary to undertake military measures against them, and Shu-sin in 2034 BC built 'the Amorite wall' to keep them out. But this was a vain hope, and even before the sack of Ur there were chieftains of Amorite origin who, from a base in the service of the empire, had brought some city-states under their personal rule.

Because the records of the Third Dynasty of Ur are our main source for the crucial stage of Amorite immigration, we tend to look at the Amorite movements from the point of view of south Mesopotamia. But what was happening in south Mesopotamia was also happening all along the Euphrates and over in Syria; and in those places, also, Amorite chieftains were carving out kingdoms for themselves. This does not mean that the old way of life was being overturned. The Amorites did not simply come in straight from the wilds and change everything. Those who eventually had the greatest influence mostly began as immigrants who took service within the existing social and administrative framework of their adoptive city. In some cases which we can trace, it was several generations before a member of an immigrant Amorite family rose to prominence, and by that time such a person would be firmly committed to the institutions of Sumerian origin upon which settled life rested.

The centres which came under Amorite control did not exist in isolation. Most of them were along the Tigris and Euphrates and their tributaries, and routes along these rivers were the main arteries of trade; trade was the principal *raison d'être* for many of the cities taken over by Amorites, and trade was the indispensable link between them. There was a second feature which maintained links between Amorite rulers. They came from a nomadic background in which, as amongst the biblical Hebrews, long family ancestries were held in high esteem. We know that some at least of the Amorite leaders claimed lines of descent which linked them with each other, for we have the actual genealogies for two major Amorite rulers, which trace both kings back to the same ancestors.

The kingdoms of Isin and Larsa

Thus, at the final fall of the III Ur Dynasty, there were already many petty Amorite rulers, not only in south Mesopotamia, but also spread over the whole region from the borders of Elam to Syria. Their shared background ensured a large degree of cultural unity over the whole area. With the collapse of the central authority of what had been the III Ur empire, a power struggle ensued amongst such local petty kings. The first to achieve a temporary supremacy was Ishbi-erra of Isin, whom we encountered earlier as an administrator under the last king of Ur. After asserting his independence in Ibbi-sin's twelfth year (2017 BC), he was able within the next two or three years to extend his authority to Nippur, the city whose recognition was necessary if a king hoped to be recognized as a legitimate ruler in Sumer. Some years later, he demonstrated, by expelling the Elamite garrison which had been left on the ruins of Ur, that he was indeed the true successor of its former rulers, and he added to his claim by afterwards rebuilding the city. As a mark of the continuity between the former dynasty and his own, Ishbi-erra used the title 'king of Ur', even though he actually ruled from Isin further north. As yet another measure to stress continuity, additions were made to the old *Sumerian King List* during the Isin period, to tack on Isin as a legitimate Sumerian dynasty:

> Ur was smitten with weapons. Its kingship was taken away to Isin. In Isin Ishbi-erra became king and reigned for 33 years.

Ishbi-erra was succeeded in the direct line by four descendants. It was a time of regeneration: law and civil order were enforced, and internal and foreign trade restored. Literary compositions speak of Ishbi-erra's third successor, Ishme-dagan (1953–1935 BC), as a king who 'set law in the land', although at present the only laws known from this dynasty are those of his successor, Lipit-ishtar, of which fragments (see pages 179ff.) have been found at Nippur and Kish. Lipit-ishtar himself speaks of the 'freeing' of citizens of certain cities, which probably refers to social and economic reforms.

There was a second city-state which grew to prominence at this time. This was Larsa, in the south of Babylonia, on the Euphrates between Erech and Ur; it emerged as a definite rival to Isin under its king Gungunum (1932–1906 BC). One of

Gungunum's more important military feats was the capture of Ur; by this, he not only curtailed the authority of Isin in the south of the country, but also won control of the important Persian Gulf trade through that city. But there was no immediate major conflict between Isin and Larsa, for the unifying force of religious tradition overcame political fragmentation; even after Ur had fallen to Larsa, we find daughters of kings of Isin acting as high priestesses there, and one of the Isin kings made dedications in that city.

Successive kings of Larsa made gradual advances northwards. The main objective was probably to obtain control of canals, for Larsa rulers bestowed considerable attention upon the irrigation system. Gertrude Bell said of Iraq that 'he who holds the irrigation canals, holds the country', and the kings of Larsa seem to have been well aware of this truth. We have mention of many public works of this kind, some of them involving thousands of labourers; and we know from letters that kings of Larsa inspected irrigation projects in person.[2]

Gungunum's second successor was contemporary with the first stages in the rise of Babylon. This city was first mentioned at the end of the Agade dynasty, but as a place of little consequence, and it had never been a major city-state. Its name, probably originally Babil, of unknown meaning from an unknown language, was later proudly interpreted as Semitic Bab-ili, 'Gateway of the gods'.[3] In 1894 BC an Amorite leader, Sumu-abum, installed himself as king there, so initiating what we know as the First Dynasty of Babylon (1894–1595 BC). He occupied his fourteen-year reign (1894–1881 BC) in strengthening the fortifications of Babylon, and in gaining control of other north Babylonian cities by military or diplomatic means.

Larsa in the south of southern Mesopotamia, Babylon in the north, and the waning Isin in between, were by no means the only urban centres of significance at this time. The legacy of Sumerian civilization was far from being limited to south Mesopotamia. It had long before spread up the Tigris, eastwards along the Diyala, and up the Euphrates into Syria. In all these areas there were powerful kingdoms with an infrastructure of Sumerian institutions and now new dynasts of Amorite descent; the most important of these kingdoms were Assyria on the middle Tigris, Eshnunna along the Diyala, Mari on the middle Euphrates and in the Habur valley, Yamhad in the region of Aleppo in Syria, and Qatna (or Qatana) to the south of the last-named. These states were closely interlinked by ties of commerce, with all that that involved in terms of both competition and cooperation.

East of the Tigris, a certain Kudurmabuk, probably an Amorite chieftain although his name was Elamite, had established himself in the territory bordering on Elam in southwest Iran. When eventually the old Larsa dynasty was overthrown by invasion, Kudurmabuk moved in and set up his son, Warad-sin, upon the throne. Warad-sin reigned only briefly, and was succeeded by his brother Rim-sin (1822–1763 BC). Halfway through his long reign, in 1793 BC, Rim-sin conquered Isin, thereby making himself the sole ruler of middle and south Babylonia. It was just at this time that there came to the throne the sixth and greatest ruler of Babylon's First Dynasty, Hammurabi (1792–1750 BC). (The name was probably pronounced Khammurapiʿ, but it is convenient to continue to use the form of the name which has been current for most of this century. It may be this name, but not necessarily this person, which is the basis of 'Amraphel king of Shinar', said in Genesis 14:1 to have come into conflict with Abraham.)

Hammurabi of Babylon

Sumu-abum, founder of the kingdom of Babylon, had had four successors with reigns of steady consolidation, mainly marked by building works and the unspectacular but economically important digging of irrigation canals. In consequence Hammurabi succeeded to a well-established but still minor kingdom, no bigger than a small English county, with a radius of about fifty miles. His ultimate success, not only in creating a realm larger than modern Iraq but also in permanently reshap-

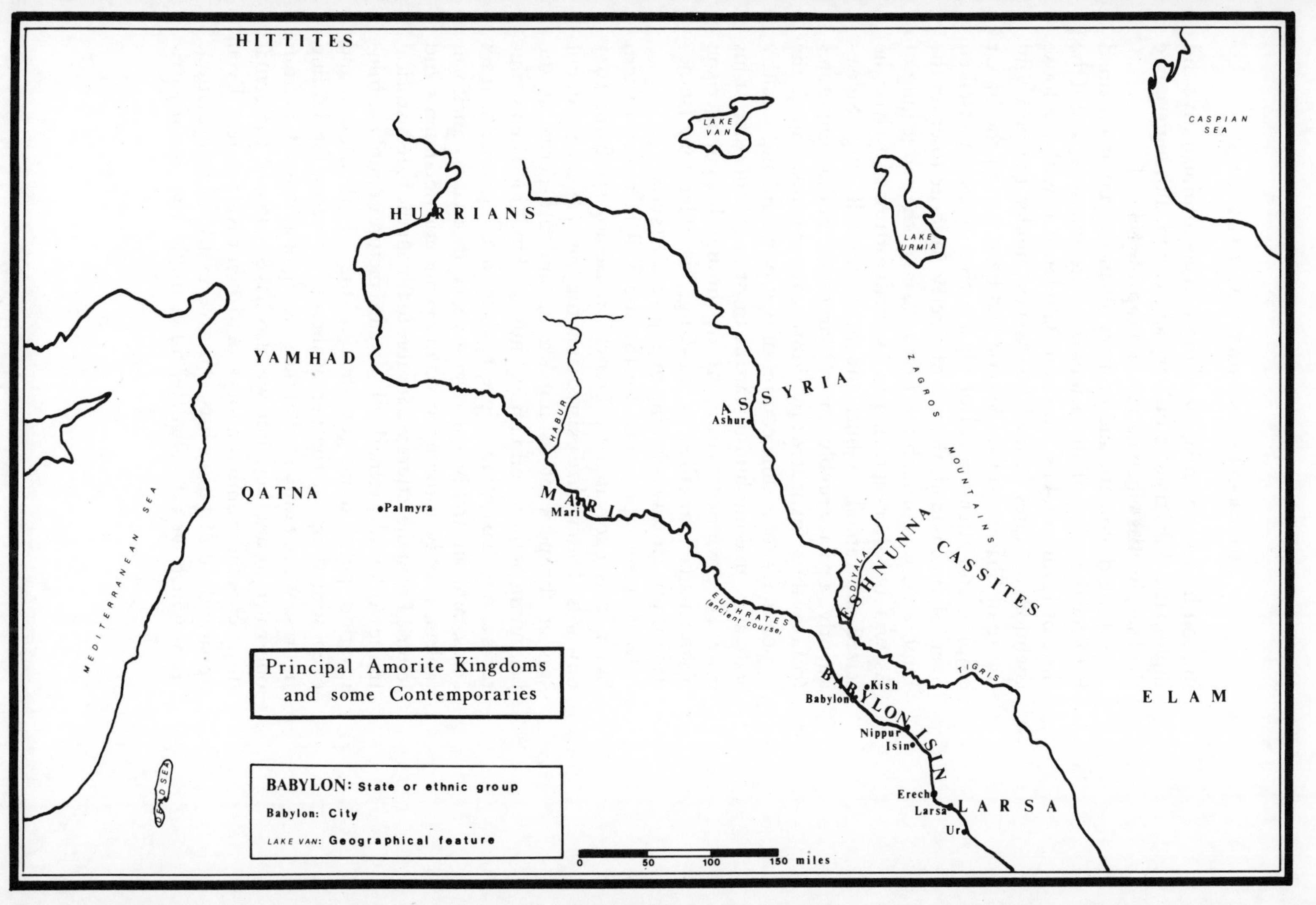

Principal Amorite Kingdoms and some Contemporaries

ing south Mesopotamia, owed more to his administrative and diplomatic skills than to military aggression, although, as we shall see, he was when necessary a capable general.

Shifting diplomatic and military alliances were maintained between the rulers of the various Amorite dynasties, and at the time of Hammurabi's accession Babylon was within a loose coalition of states headed by Assyria, under the powerful figure of Shamshi-adad. Assyria had been part of the III Ur empire, and after the fall of Ur a native dynasty had taken over. Shamshi-adad, the son of a petty Amorite ruler on the Euphrates, was probably at first a vassal of the native king of Assyria, but after capturing an Assyrian fortress as his base, he seized the capital, Ashur, and made himself king. Subsequently, a palace revolution in Mari on the middle Euphrates (conceivably instigated by him) gave Shamshi-adad the opportunity to assume control of that powerful and wealthy state also, making him by far the most powerful ruler of his time. He governed Mari indirectly through his younger son Yasmah-adad, installed as sub-king; his older son, Ishme-dagan, was already sub-king over part of Assyria.

Mari, now represented by the site Tell Hariri in eastern Syria, was excavated by French archaeologists from 1933 onwards. The city had existed since the *Jemdet Nasr* period, but was at the peak of its importance and prosperity at the beginning of the second millennium BC. Finds included sculptures and wall paintings, a great palace covering more than six acres, and an archive of over twenty thousand cuneiform tablets, mainly administrative and economic documents and letters. From the letters we are able to fill out the bare historical framework with a remarkably detailed picture of public administration, political intrigue, the workings of officialdom, and even something of the personality of some of the leading figures. We not only read of the sending of ambassadors from one ruler to another, but we also have many of the actual dispatches those ambassadors sent to their royal masters. Even apparently dull ration lists can give us useful information, from which we can calculate, for example, the size of garrisons: thus we know that four thousand troops were stationed in the capital. The duties of such garrisons were largely concerned with protecting the settled populations against marauding nomads; the sub-king of Mari, Yasmah-adad, writing to his senior brother Ishme-dagan about the disposal of a contingent of a thousand troops, explained that five hundred had been put to guard the town and the remainder to protect the cattle. Economic as well as military and political cooperation was the custom with Amorite rulers. When pasturage was scarce in the territory of Mari, the sub-king asked the permission of the king of Qatna to have his flocks pastured with the Qatna flocks, a request which was granted.

The correspondence concerning Yasmah-adad shows that he was a loyal subordinate to his father and senior brother, but not one of the most able of administrators; there were times when his older brother had to help him out of scrapes. In one letter his father rebuked him vigorously for his discourteous treatment of some persons of royal blood. In another, Yasmah-adad quotes his father's contemptuous words to him: 'You're not a man! You haven't a beard on your chin! How long are you going to remain unable to administer your estate?' Elsewhere Shamshi-adad criticizes Yasmah-adad for always wanting advice about matters entrusted to him, and holds up Ishme-dagan as an example of how a sub-king should behave. On another occasion Yasmah-adad had had the audacity to ask his father to add to his territory a city called Shubat-shamash. The impudence of this had annoyed the older man who, according to Ishme-dagan in the letter he wrote to smooth things over, had commented angrily: 'He hasn't put Mari and Tuttul on a sound basis yet and now he wants Shubat-shamash!'

It is clear that although Yasmah-adad enjoyed the title of king of Mari, all political and strategic decisions there remained in the hands of his able father, Shamshi-adad. Shamshi-adad was certainly the major ruler of his time, and by expanding eastwards from Assyria he ended with an empire 300–400 miles in diameter, stretching from the middle

Euphrates to the foothills of the Zagros, and from north Babylonia to the Taurus.

It was against this background that Hammurabi ruled for his first ten years, until Shamshi-adad died. During this decade he was devoting himself mainly to improving the infrastructure of his own kingdom, Babylon, a situation reflected in some of his date-formulae. The formula for year 2, 'He established justice in the land', refers to economic reforms; that for year 4, 'the wall of the temple-cloister was built', is linked to protection of the rights of a class of female temple personnel who lived there; and the formula for year 9, 'The canal "Hammurabi is abundance" (was built)', clearly recognizes the economic importance of irrigation. Most of his limited military activity during these years was probably in the service of Shamshi-adad's coalition, although in his seventh year he made a significant addition to the territory under his control by taking both Isin and Erech, the latter over a hundred miles to the southeast down the Euphrates. As Erech was less than twenty miles from Larsa, it would seem that he was taking the opportunity, presumably with Shamshi-adad's approval if not his active support, to consolidate his kingdom southwards against Rim-sin of Larsa, the leader of the southern coalition.

When Shamshi-adad died, the leadership of the coalition he had headed passed to Hammurabi. The situation is plainly stated in one of the letters found at Mari:

> There is no king who is strongest by himself alone. Ten or fifteen kings follow Hammurabi of Babylon, the same number follow Rim-sin of Larsa, the same number follow Ibal-pi-El of Eshnunna, the same number follow Amut-pi-El of Qatana, and twenty kings follow Yarim-lim of Yamhad.

Yasmah-adad's kingship of Mari did not long survive his father's death. The king of Eshnunna, east of the Tigris, attacked part of the former territories of Shamshi-adad, and Zimri-lim, heir of the former Mari dynasty, took advantage of this to emerge from his refuge in Syria, and with the backing of Yamhad (the kingdom based on Aleppo) he was able to regain his ancestral throne. Hammurabi did not intervene militarily on behalf of Shamshi-adad's sons. Indeed, the twenty years in the middle of his reign seem, judging by his date-formulae as well as his correspondence, to have been more significant for the digging of canals and building works than for major military operations. For much of this period Hammurabi was on good terms with both Rim-sin of Larsa and Zimri-lim of Mari; we know details from their correspondence. They all had diplomatic representatives at each other's courts, and many of their reports are preserved. These say a great deal about troop movements, and sometimes sieges, but seldom mention pitched battles; and the impression given is that the main use of troops in the field was to bring them to a threatened area as a deterrent against aggression, rather than with the intention of destroying the enemy. Hammurabi and the kings of Mari, Yamhad, Eshnunna and Larsa were accustomed to lend each other troops, in contingents sometimes up to 10,000 strong, but this was usually for defensive rather than offensive purposes. The following, part of a letter sent to Zimri-lim of Mari by one of his ambassadors, illustrates this:

> To my lord say, thus says your servant Yarem-addu:
> . . . Two servants of Hammurabi have arrived at Babylon. I have learnt the report of four ass-riders from Larsa who came with them. [At this time, before the horse became widely used in the Near East, to ride an ass was a mark of status.] Their message is thus: 'In the matter of the troops that you keep writing about, I have heard that the enemy have set their course to another country. That is why I have not sent my troops to you, but my troops are in a state of readiness. If the enemy make for you, my troops will come to your help, but if the enemy makes for me, let your troops come to my help.' This is what Rim-sin has written to Hammurabi.[4]

In Hammurabi's twenty-ninth year he was attacked by a coalition of states east of the Tigris, including Eshnunna, but defeated this, so that two years later he was in a position to call upon Eshnunna for troops. That year saw a change in the old policy of armed coexistence, when Hammurabi made a major attack against Rim-sin of Larsa. The reason for this we do not know, but it was certainly an operation planned in advance and not a mere border clash which happened to escalate, for a letter to Zimri-lim from his ambassador gives the background:

> About the message which Hammurabi king of Babylon has sent to my lord saying 'I am going against Rim-sin king of Larsa and the ruler of Eshnunna is standing by me. Now, send me troops so that I may achieve this.'[5]

Clearly, Hammurabi was organizing a coalition of the three major northern states against Larsa in the south. He succeeded in overthrowing Rim-sin, and thereby made himself sole ruler of all Babylonia (1763 BC). A year later he followed this up by reducing most of the region east of the Tigris, although Eshnunna and Assyria did not finally fall to him until near the end of his reign. In his thirty-third year he attacked and occupied Mari, but left Zimri-lim in possession as a vassal; two years later, after a revolt, he de-fortified the city and removed Zimri-lim.

Hammurabi had thus built up a petty city-state into a major kingdom. Although the final stages involved warfare, this was substantially the achievement of a skilled administrator and diplomatist rather than of a warrior. We learn of his administrative achievements firstly from the famous collection of laws which he promulgated, and secondly from about 150 letters on clay tablets from him to his regional officials.

In his *Laws* (on which see pages 183ff.), he describes how the gods sommissioned him.

> Hammurabi, the reverent god-fearing prince, to make justice appear in the land, to destroy the evil and the wicked so that the strong might not oppress the weak, to rise like the Sun-god over the Black-headed Ones [i.e. humans] to give light to the land,

1 White temple at Warka

2A Cone mosaics from Warka

2B Silver model of a boat, from the 'royal tombs' of Ur

3A The ziggurat of Ur before modern reconstruction

3B Ruins of ziggurat of Borsippa (modern Birs Nimrud), possibly the original 'Tower of Babel'

4A Ruins of ziggurat of Dur-Kurigalzu (modern Aqarquf)

4B Ruins of processional way at Babylon

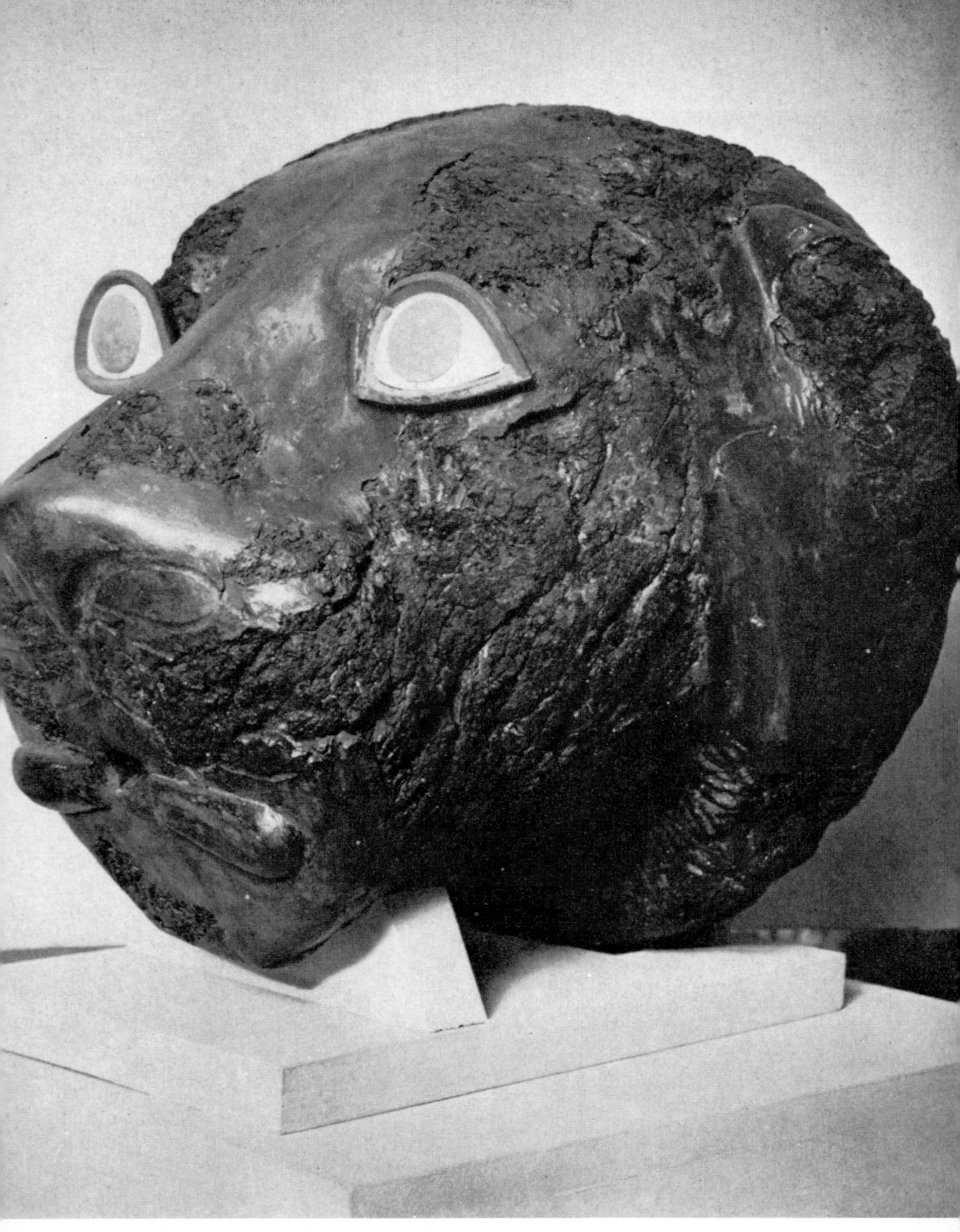

5 Bitumen core of lion head, originally in copper (from Ubaid)

6 The Ishtar Gate (reconstruction)

7 (*opposite*) Harp (restored) from the 'royal tombs' of Ur

8A Alabaster vase from Warka

8B Early Sumerian dress (carving on a stone mace-head)

9A Cattle trough from Jemdet Nasr (early third millennium)

9B Gaming board from Ur (first half of third millennium)

10 The god Imdugud ('Severe Wind') with stags; an early Sumerian monument probably concerned with fertility

11A Cult object, usually described as a lamp cover, in the form of intertwined snakes (late third millennium)

11B Inlaid panel from Ur (first half of third millennium), showing religious representations related to a fertility cult

12 War scene from the 'Standard of Ur' (first half of third millennium)

13A Lavatory, with remains of seat of bitumen (third millennium)

13B Main drain of a palace (third millennium)

14 Bronze mask, perhaps of Sargon of Agade

15A Window grille (third millennium)

15B Bronze 'frying pan'

16A Rock relief of Naram-Sin in Qara-Dagh range, Iraq (*circa*

16B Stele of Naram-Sin (*circa* 2280 BC)

and how, at the command of the god Marduk, he

> set forth truth and justice throughout the lands and prospered the people.

Hammurabi's correspondence shows how well justified this claim was. No detail was too small, and no official too important, for Hammurabi to give clear-cut decisions and orders in the interest of good government. We meet the case of a high official who had been instructed to clear out a canal near Erech but had been tardy in the matter; he was peremptorily ordered to have the work finished in three days and to report. Accusations of land-snatching were investigated and justice served. When a charge of bribery reached the king, he ordered an investigation, with instructions that, if the case were made out, the bribe should be confiscated and the defendants and witnesses dispatched to him. Even the accuracy of the calendar was the business of the king: the calendar in use was lunar, but for agricultural and religious purposes it needed to be kept in line with the equinox, and it was the king who gave orders for the intercalation of a month when necessary. Above all, to ensure the agricultural prosperity upon which the wellbeing of his land ultimately rested, throughout the whole of his reign Hammurabi prosecuted a vigorous policy of canal-building; after he had unified Babylonia, he spent considerable resources upon a great canal in the south, to ensure bountiful harvests on the lands of the old Sumerian centres: appropriately he named it 'Hammurabi is the abundance of his people'.

Letters from ambassadors at Hammurabi's court show him as he appeared to his contemporaries, and supplement his own correspondence to give us a glimpse of the kind of man he was. He was manifestly a hardworking man who spared no trouble to keep in touch with every aspect of the running of his kingdom, and to ensure that everything was done efficiently. It seems that he carried out all duties of state in person, and as far as we know did not delegate responsibility to ministers. He personally received foreign ambassadors, dictated missives to other kings, made the arrangements for court ceremonial, inspected his troops and decided upon their movements, gave orders about canal digging, settled questions of land tenure, investigated maladministration, and administered justice. But accessible though he was, he did not take kindly to criticism. We have a letter in which an ambassador reports the treatment of a complaint at Hammurabi's court. A ceremony was to take place, and robes of honour had been provided for certain envoys. But others were overlooked, and a complaint was made to Hammurabi. His answer was terse: 'I shall clothe whom I wish, and I shall not clothe whom I do not wish.'[6]

Since all Hammurabi's military activities were successful, he was presumably an able general, but on the whole we have to take this on trust. There is, however, just one piece of evidence which shows the clever and original way in which he solved a military problem. This is found in the date-formula for his thirty-eighth year, which reads: 'By the wisdom given to him by Marduk, he destroyed Eshnunna with a great mass of water.'[7] This must mean that, instead of using conventional siege tactics (well known from letters of Shamshi-adad), he breached the city's defences by diverting a river to flood it out.

Hammurabi welded into one kingdom the many former city-states of Sumer and Akkad, and brought them under one legal system. From this time it was recognition at Babylon, not (as formerly) at Nippur, which gave legitimation to a dynasty.

The impress which Hammurabi put upon Babylonia continued to be felt until the end of its history: his military achievements, however, did not long survive Hammurabi himself. His son Samsu-iluna (1749–1712 BC) lost control of substantial parts of his territories: the middle Euphrates region broke away, to form an independent kingdom, Hana; and in south Babylonia a successful revolt ushered in what became known as the Dynasty of the Sealands, which maintained independence for more than the next two centuries. Under Samsu-iluna's three successors, covering nearly a century, the kingdom shrank to little more than it had been when Hammurabi came to the throne.

The end of the First Dynasty of Babylon represents one of the landmarks of ancient history, and introduced a people who played a leading part in the history of the Near East during the succeeding centuries. At the turn of the third to second millennium some peoples speaking Indo-European languages had moved from north of the Caucasus into parts of what is now asiatic Turkey. There the most important group, the Hittites, had formed first a kingdom and then an empire, based on the region of the Halys river. Suddenly, in 1595 BC, Mursilis I, the third major ruler of the Hittite empire, swept out of Asia Minor into Syria (where he took Aleppo), and down the Euphrates, sacking Mari on the way. The conqueror reached Babylon, which he plundered and burnt, and then returned to his capital, as suddenly as he had come, but too late to crush a court conspiracy which led to his assassination. His stay in Babylon had, however, been long enough to bring to an end the reign of the last of Hammurabi's successors, Samsu-ditana (1625–1595 BC), and to disrupt government and administration there. After the Hittites had retreated, Babylon was first taken over briefly by the southern Dynasty of the Sealands, and then by the Cassites.

The Cassites and Hurrians

We know little about the antecedents of the Cassites. They originally came from the Zagros, and their language is not assignable to any known family. They were probably one of the population groups which had inhabited the Zagros foothills from far back in prehistoric times, and they would have gradually come under the influence of Sumero-Babylonian culture as Mesopotamian rulers made repeated forays into the mountains. Individual Cassites are found in Babylonia during the First Dynasty, and the first successor of Hammurabi clashed with Cassite forces east of the Tigris. From this time Cassites began to settle under their own kings in the northeast of Babylonia and on the middle Euphrates: it was one such ruler, Agum II (Agukakrime), who finally took possession of Babylonia after the sack of the capital by Mursilis.

With the Hittite sack of Babylon and the Cassite invasion, the political achievements of Hammurabi had been finally brought to an end. But Babylonian culture continued to exercise a vast influence throughout the Near and Middle East. Not only did the Cassite kings adopt the language and cuneiform script of Babylonia, but also dialects of Akkadian were widely employed for official business far outside Babylonia and Assyria. At the end of the nineteenth century, clay tablets inscribed in cuneiform were discovered at El Amarna in central Egypt, an unexpected find, since ancient Egypt had its own hieroglyphic writing on papyrus. The tablets proved to be some of the diplomatic correspondence which, just after 1400 BC, had passed between the kings of Egypt on the one hand and the rulers of the Hittites, Mittanni, Assyria, Babylonia and various cities in Syria and Palestine on the other. Predominantly the language is Akkadian, but not always good Akkadian, since in some cases it is heavily contaminated by the native tongue of the writer. But the attempt to write Akkadian in such circumstances shows that it was the recognized language of civilized intercourse between nations. This is confirmed by the situation in Ugarit in Syria. There a Semitic language very different from Akkadian was spoken, and a distinct alphabetic system of cuneiform writing had been invented for it and was in use for religious texts. But Mesopotamian cuneiform and the Akkadian language continued to be used for international correspondence and legal texts.

At the same time that Babylonia fell under Cassite control, Assyria and much of the rest of the Near East south of the Hittite area were coming under the growing influence of yet another ethnic group, the Hurrians. These peoples have long been known in the Old Testament as the Horites (Genesis 14:6, Deuteronomy 2:12). The view most commonly taken of their origin is that they migrated into the Near East during the third millennium, coming from the north by a route east of the Black Sea. But there is the alternative possibility that they were one of the original population groups of the Near East, and had been in north Mesopotamia or Armenia (eastern Turkey) since prehistoric times. Their language tells us little about their antecedents, since it has no recognized affinities except the later Urartian, written in Armenia in the first half of the first millennium BC. However, the language does provide one item of evidence. The native name for what we call the 'Hurrian' language was 'the tongue of Su-bir', and third-millennium Sumerian texts mention Su-bir (which we normally anglicize as 'Subarian') as what seems to have been a population element in north Mesopotamia, with no indication that they were thought of as immigrants. Moreover, Hurrians had already formed a small kingdom in the Habur river region of Syria as early as the twenty-fourth century BC, which implies a Hurrian presence in the Near East substantially earlier.

Mursilis I, in his thrust to Babylon, had encountered hostile Hurrian princes on the Upper Euphrates. The dynastic confusion consequent upon the assassination of Mursilis seriously weakened the Hittite state for several generations, allowing an important Hurrian state, known as Mittanni, to develop in the Habur region. Soon after 1550 BC it stood as an equal with Egypt and the Hittite empire, and a century later it was powerful enough to annex Assyria, Babylonia's northern sister kingdom, and hold it for about half a century. At its greatest extent it controlled the whole area from Lake Van to the middle Euphrates and from the Zagros to the Syrian coast. When eventually it declined under Hittite pressure, Assyria was soon to become and remain the main power in north Mesopotamia.

Meanwhile the Cassite dynasty in Babylonia went on to reunify the country, by displacing the Dynasty of the Sealands in the south. To judge by economic documents, and the absence of any hostile tradition, Cassite government was mild and unoppressive. One of the factors which most affected the reaction of ancient cities to a king was his attitude to their traditional rights, which in many cases involved exemption of their citizens from taxes or corvée duties. Charters promulgated by the Cassite kings show them as liberal rulers in this respect. The apparent absence of native risings confirmed the value of such policies. Some of the Cassite kings enhanced their good repute by undertaking building operations and other works of piety in key southern cities, such as Erech and Ur. This benevolent regime made no attempt to interfere with Babylonian institutions, and the Cassite period saw intense literary activity in the scribal schools. It was predominantly a time of peace, when the absence of turmoil put Babylonia in the happy position of freedom from the crises which shape so much of history.

The most important Cassite king was Kurigalzu I, who reigned around 1400 BC. By his time Mittanni had been seriously weakened by a combination of civil war and Hittite expansion, leaving Babylonia in a position to claim the suzerainty over Assyria which Mittanni had formerly exercised; thus, once again, although only until Assyria reasserted itself, Babylon controlled the whole of Mesopotamia. Kurigalzu maintained good relations with Amenophis III of Egypt and expanded his territory by a successful campaign against Elam in southwest Iran. But the work for which he is best known to posterity is the fortified new capital he built to seal the neck where the Euphrates and Tigris come closest: its remains are to be found at Aqarquf not far from Baghdad, the ziggurat (see plate 4A) being a prominent feature of the landscape and (so long as it escapes total restoration) an essential sight for any visitor to Iraq.

4

The Rise of Imperial Assyria

A north Mesopotamian kingdom

FOR the next half-millennium the centre of political interest in Mesopotamia shifts away from Babylonia to its northern neighbour, Assyria. But this occasions no break, since Assyrian history, both cultural and political, was intimately linked with Babylonia.

Although it was in the southern part of the Euphrates–Tigris plain that ancient Mesopotamian civilization began, it quickly spread northwards up the two great rivers. By the middle of the third millennium, a kingdom had developed along the middle Tigris, based on a city called Ashur, and under the subsequent southern expansions it became part first of the Agade empire and then of the empire of the III Ur dynasty. When these outbursts of imperialism receded, Assyria regained its independence, and by early in the second millennium at latest, and probably before the end of the third, merchants from Ashur, setting out northwards by the natural route up the Tigris, had greatly extended the influence of their city by establishing colonies deep in Asia Minor, near modern Kayseri, trading mainly in tin and textiles. This brought a significant spread of Mesopotamian culture, most evident in the subsequent employment of cuneiform writing for the Hittite language used in that area in the second millennium.

Ashur was the native name not only of a city but also of the city's god and of the kingdom centred on that city; 'Assyria', the Greek form of that name, was applied only to the kingdom. The second major city in Assyria was Nineveh, also on the Tigris, but some 120 miles further north, within sight of the foothills of the eastern Taurus. Ashur in the south, Nineveh in the north, and a third city in the plains to the east, Arbail (today Erbil, to the Sumerians Urbillum) marked the basic boundaries of the kingdom of Assyria.

From early in the third millennium, the architecture and institutions of all three of these cities bore unmistakable marks of the influence of Sumerian civilization, and the kingdoms of Assyria and Babylonia always shared a common culture. But there were significant differences, dictated by geography. Much of Assyria, as far south as the city Ashur, enjoys rainfall which is sufficient, although in some place only marginally so, to produce corn crops without artificial watering. This is in marked contrast to Babylonia, where agriculture is impossible without some form of irrigation. There the need for large-scale cooperation in irrigation projects resulted in the growth of a high concentration of urban centres. In Assyria there was no corresponding factor, and although other cities did exist, the three already mentioned were the only ones of ancient foundation comparable in population with the great centres of south Mesopotamia.

There was a second geographical factor which brought differences between the history of Babylonia and that of Assyria. In the latitude of Babylonia, the natural features, taken from west to east, are: desert, the Euphrates, the river plain, the Tigris, another plain, and finally foothills and the main Zagros range. The hills were inhabited by peoples to whom the relative wealth of the plains was a standing temptation to plunder. In Babylonia, most important cities (there were a few exceptions) lay along the main course of the Euphrates or subsidiary channels, and for settlements so sited the Tigris constituted a major safeguard against raids from the mountains. Assyria also had mountains to its east and north, but did not enjoy a corresponding riverine shield: its main cornlands were in the plains to the east of the Tigris, and therefore more vulnerable. Both Babylonians and Assyrians were accustomed to undertake forays into the Zagros in quest of timber and stone, but the Assyrians had an additional reason for campaigning in the mountains – to make deterrent attacks upon mountaineers who were given to raiding the Assyrian plains. Winter, when the mountain peoples could withdraw to impregnable snowbound fastnesses, was not a time for military action in the mountains, and therefore any punitive expeditions by Assyrian kings had to be in summer. In consequence, a pattern gradually evolved: as soon as the harvest was in, Assyrian kings would campaign in the mountains for a month or more, attempting to bring the hill tribes into submission. This became such a matter of course that it was thought of as divinely ordained, and one Assyrian king speaks of the month Dumuzi (roughly July) as 'the month which the Lord of Wisdom, Ninshiku, had prescribed in a tablet of former times for mustering the army'. As there were always other potentially troublesome peoples just beyond those last dealt with, such campaigns brought a gradual extension of Assyrian boundaries, a development which was rationalized in the theological doctrine that the national god demanded wide and secure boundaries. It was this quest for secure boundaries, to conform to the supposed will of the national god, which eventually gave the Assyrians an empire reaching as far as Egypt in the southwest, deep into Asia Minor in the northwest, and to the region of Lake Van, Lake Urmia and Hamadan in the northeast and east.

We speak of 'the Assyrians', but behind this simple term lies a complex ethnic background. Strands in the make-up of the Assyrians as we find them in the fifteenth century BC included the prehistoric population, third-millennium Sumerians who brought their culture up the Tigris, early Semites who arrived in the course of the Agade expansion, Amorite immigrants of whom the dynasty of Shamshi-adad was a part, and Hurrians, both old stock from the third millennium or earlier and those newly settled under the Mittannian expansion. Later, still other elements came in; some, such as Aramaeans, entered by immigration, others arrived under the policy of deportation practised by Assyrian kings from the thirteenth century onwards. By the end of the Assyrian empire, in the seventh century BC, there was probably no ethnic strain throughout the whole Near East which was not represented in the Assyrian homeland. Assyria was a melting-pot of peoples.

In the Mittannian period, Assyria, which had risen to temporary prominence under Shamshi-adad, had sunk to a very low ebb. During this time we find the Hurrian ethnic strand strongly represented in eastern Assyria, in the region around Kirkuk (ancient Arrapkha), now the centre of a great oilfield. The people there spoke Hurrian but wrote their administrative and legal documents in a dialect of Akkadian much coloured by their mother tongue; extensive records of this kind from the fifteenth century BC give us much information about the customs of the area at this time.

Mesopotamia after Mittanni

With the decay of Mittanni, Assyria once again became a force in international politics. It was under Ashur-uballit I (1365–1330 BC) that the long process began by which Assyria ultimately, after repeated setbacks, rose to supremacy in the Near East. His great-grandson said of him that 'his kingship was firmly established as far as the mountains', and we find this rising status of Assyria reflected in the El Amarna tablets. In one of these letters, the Cassite king of Babylonia, Burnaburiash II (1375–1347 BC), indignantly asks his counterpart, the king of Egypt: 'Why have the Assyrians, subjects of mine, . . . come to your country? If you love me, . . . send them away empty-handed.' He was claiming that the Assyrians were still vassals of his, and had no right to send an independent embassy to another power. But the Egyptian king accepted realities, and there are two letters from Ashur-uballit to the pharaoh in which he uses the expression 'my brother' in his greeting, the mark of an equal.

Across the whole Near East in the fourteenth century BC, many rulers were looking outward beyond their own boundaries, seeking to promote international relations. Regular correspondence was maintained between the Egyptian and Babylonian capitals, even though the distance was well over a thousand miles, with hazards from deserts and lawless nomads. Inter-state trade thrived, in the guise of exchange of presents between rulers, and royal families in Egypt, Asia Minor and Babylonia were all inter-linked by marriage alliances; we have the actual correspondence about arrangements for escorting a Babylonian princess with due honour to the Egyptian king. The practical consequences of such alliances are illustrated from the sequel when Ashur-uballit of Assyria gave a daughter in marriage to the Cassite king of Babylonia. When Babylonia had trouble in dealing with the Sutu, troublesome nomads who infested the middle Euphrates region and harassed both states with border raids, Assyria sent military support. At the death of the king of Babylonia, when a revolt broke out against the legitimate Cassite successor, the son of Ashur-uballit's daughter, the dynastic alliance again came into effect. The Assyrian king intervened forcibly, as a text known as the *Synchronistic History* tells us:

> In the time of Ashur-uballit king of Assyria, the Kassite troops rebelled against Karahardash king of Karduniash [Babylonia], son of the lady Muballitat-sherua daughter of Ashur-uballit, and they killed him. Ashur-uballit went to Karduniash to avenge his grandson. . . . He installed Kurigalzu the younger in the kingship.

This was Kurigalzu II (1345–1324 BC).

The good relations between Babylonia and Assyria did not outlive Ashur-uballit, and after the accession of Enlil-narari I (1329–1320 BC), Kurigalzu invaded Assyria, possibly because, as a descendant of Ashur-uballit, he considered he himself had a claim to the Assyrian throne. There was a battle, won by Enlil-narari, who thereupon assumed the title 'slayer of the hosts of the Cassites', and Babylonia was left so weakened that it was unable to offer effective resistance to raids from its eastern neighbour, Elam. Assyria, on the other hand, continued its northward expansion. Particularly notable are the exploits of Adad-narari I (1307–1275 BC), who annexed the rump of the old kingdom of Mittanni, by this time known as Hanigalbat, and so extended Assyrian control up to the elbow of the Euphrates, east and north of Aleppo, beyond which lay the Hittite empire. In the southeast, he was able to push the boundary with Babylonia to the Diyala river. Adad-narari's son Shalmaneser I (1274–1245 BC) continued the northern expansion, defeating a confederation known as Uruatri (the earliest form of the name Urartu or Ararat), towards Lake Van in the Armenian highlands of eastern Turkey. This had an economic dimension, for Shalmaneser developed trade with Anatolia. He also instituted the practice of deportation which quickly developed into resettlement of captives by thousands and even tens of thousands at a time. This too had an economic aspect, since, except for those conscripted into the Assyrian army, the new manpower was mainly put to work in either agriculture or building.

Tukulti-ninurta I (1244–1208 BC) continued his father's policy of expansion, with conquests in the west and north. Again there was an economic dimension: Tukulti-ninurta records bringing back to Assyria a vast booty of herds of horses, asses and cattle; and he also began the systematic exploitation of the eastern Taurus, by imposing upon conquered peoples tribute in the form of timber.

After stabilizing the north, Tukulti-ninurta, provoked by border raids, invaded Babylonia. This brought his most spectacular achievement, the defeat of the Babylonian king Kashtiliash IV (1242–1235 BC), and the sack of Babylon. He narrates:

> My hand took Kashtiliash king of the Cassites. I trod on his royal neck with my feet like a stool. I brought him captive and bound before my lord Ashur.

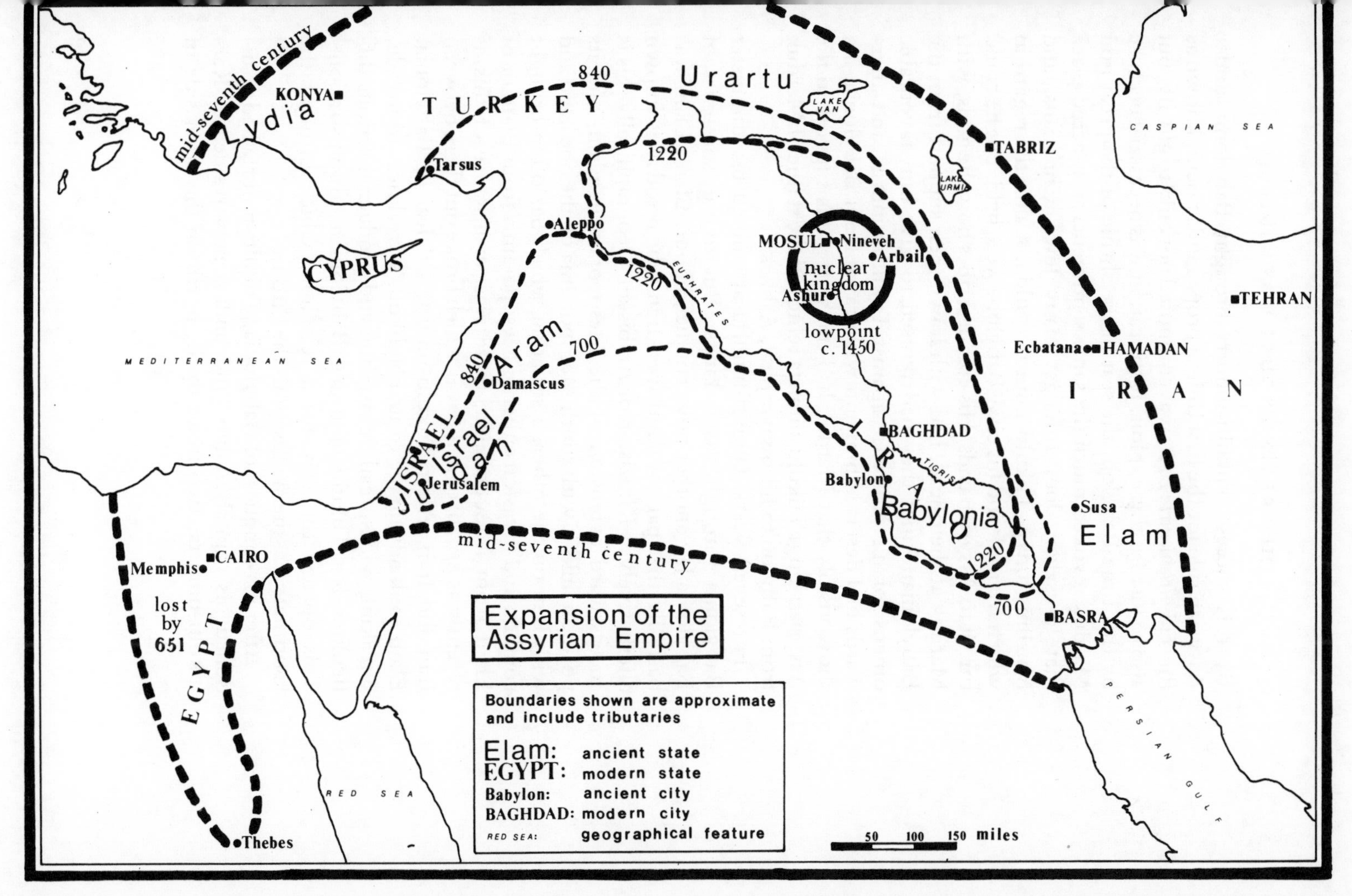
Expansion of the Assyrian Empire
Boundaries shown are approximate and include tributaries
Elam: ancient state
EGYPT: modern state
Babylon: ancient city
BAGHDAD: modern city
RED SEA: geographical feature
50 100 150 miles
CASPIAN SEA
MEDITERRANEAN SEA
RED SEA
PERSIAN GULF
TURKEY
IRAN
IRAQ
EGYPT
CYPRUS
ISRAEL
Urartu
Lydia
Aram
Israel
Judah
Babylonia
Elam
KONYA
Tarsus
Aleppo
Damascus
Jerusalem
MOSUL
Nineveh
Arbail
Ashur
nuclear kingdom
lowpoint c. 1450
TABRIZ
TEHRAN
Ecbatana
HAMADAN
BAGHDAD
Babylon
Susa
BASRA
CAIRO
Memphis
Thebes
lost by 651
LAKE VAN
LAKE URMIA
EUPHRATES
TIGRIS
mid-seventh century
mid-seventh century
840
840
1220
1220
1220
700
700

By this success Tukulti-ninurta brought Babylonia under Assyrian rule for the first time: a propaganda poem, known as the *Tukulti-ninurta Epic*, was composed not only to glorify, but also to justify, this exploit. Justification was necessary because by this time Babylon, the seat of the shrine of the great god Marduk, evoked much the same sentiments as a sacred place that Jerusalem does amongst many Jews, Christians, and Muslims today. Tukulti-ninurta could not alter the regard in which Marduk and his city, Babylon, were held, but he could turn it to Assyrian ends. His epic describes how the gods, with Marduk at their head, had withdrawn their support from the Babylonian king; they had refused to give him favourable omens for his resistance against Tukulti-ninurta, and afterwards had deserted him and withdrawn from Babylonia. To show visibly that Marduk had transferred his support to the Assyrian king, Tukulti-ninurta removed the statue of Marduk from Babylon to his own capital, Ashur.

For seven years Tukulti-ninurta attempted to administer Babylonia through vassal kings. But to the southeast of Babylonia lay another powerful neighbour, Elam. Elam was basically that part of southwest Iran which today is known alternatively as Khuzistan or Arabistan. Geographically this is an eastward extension of the Mesopotamian plain, and its position links it with south Mesopotamia on the one hand and with Iran on the other, a situation which has often brought conflict, and invasion either of Mesopotamia from Elam or of Elam from Mesopotamia; there was an instance of this as recently as AD 1980, in the war which broke out there between Iraq and Iran. After Tukulti-ninurta's defeat of Babylonia, Elam took advantage of its neighbour's weakness to invade, wreaking widespread devastation and producing serious difficulties for Tukulti-ninurta's Babylonian administration.[1] This opened the way for a rebellion, which brought the legitimate Cassite successor to the throne.

After his conquest of Babylonia, Tukulti-ninurta had abandoned his capital, Ashur, and built a new residence, Kar-tukulti-ninurta, two miles to the north on the other side of the Tigris. Such a shift of the centre of government, of which Assyrian history gives several instances, usually reflected political problems, and it may have been so here. The citizens of a capital city gradually acquired privileges, such as exemption from taxes and the corvée, the exercise of which could occasion friction with the king. In addition, Tukulti-ninurta's conquest of Babylon may also have created problems in Ashur; the presence there of the statue of Marduk, which he had brought back with him, must have strengthened Babylonian cultural and religious influences in the Assyrian capital, and produced tensions between those who accepted and those who disapproved of this. Moreover, Tukulti-ninurta's theological justification for his sack of Babylon rebounded on him, since his subsequent loss of the city implied that the gods had now deserted him, because of his sacrilege. This last was one of the factors which led to a palace conspiracy in which Tukulti-ninurta was killed, as a chronicle records:

> Tukulti-ninurta, who had brought his hand for evil upon Babylon, his son . . . and the nobles of Ashur rebelled against him, deposed him, imprisoned him in a building in Kar-tukulti-ninurta, and killed him with a weapon.

Although Babylonia had regained independence from Assyria, it remained subject to the spasmodic ravages of Elam. These reached a climax in 1157 BC, when the Elamites undertook a major campaign which brought the old Cassite dynasty to an end. Once again the statue of Marduk – presumably a new one, unless the one taken by Tukulti-ninurta had since been returned – was taken away by the conqueror.

During the period of Elamite occupation, a new native power centre developed, probably at Isin, to judge by the name, 'the Second Dynasty of Isin', later given to the line of rulers that ensued. This dynasty gradually consolidated itself during the long and mainly peaceful reign of the Assyrian king Ashur-dan I (1179–1134 BC), and by the time of his death seems to have become strong enough to meddle in the

Assyrian succession. By the reign of Nebuchadnezzar I (1124–1103 BC), the fourth and most important king of the dynasty, the central administration was fully in control of events throughout Babylonia, and this ruler was in a position to turn his attention to foreign affairs. He finally rid the country of the Elamite menace by a military defeat of their forces, achieved by a campaign unexpectedly undertaken in the blazing heat of the Babylonian summer, when, as a text describes,

> The axes [carried by the soldiers] burned like fire,
> And the surface of the roads scorched like flame;
> There was no water in the wells, and the drinking supply was cut off,
> The strength of the great horses failed,
> And the legs of the strong warrior turned (weak).[2]

This victory revived the international prestige of Babylonia, and the fame of this event was such that a series of omen texts came into being called 'When Nebuchadnezzar smashed Elam'. Because of his reputation as a restorer of Babylonian fortunes, this king's name was bestowed upon the son of the founder of a much later dynasty, the celebrated Nebuchadnezzar of the Bible. Nebuchadnezzar I went on to extend Babylonian control northeastwards into what was usually Assyrian territory, as far as the Lesser Zab river.

The Aramaeans

A new threat was now becoming apparent, affecting both Assyria and Babylonia. Once again Semitic-speaking nomads were pushing into the settled lands. This new group comprised those usually known as Aramaeans, although the terms Ahlamu and Sutu also occur, and they came from the Syrian highlands between Palmyra and the Euphrates, much as the Amorites had done earlier. We have no specific information as to what set this movement under way, but the likelihood is that over the centuries the Aramaean population in the Syrian highlands had reached the maximum the region would support, and in such circumstances a quite small and temporary climatic change could bring famine and the need to migrate.

The Bible mentions the Aramaeans, and links the Hebrew patriarchs with them, although the Authorized King James Version (AV) obscures this by translating the Hebrew term 'arammi' (= 'Aramaean') as 'Syrian'. Rebekah, Isaac's wife, was 'daughter of Bethuel the Aramaean, and sister of Laban the Aramaean' (Genesis 25:20); Jacob married his cousins, Leah and Rachel, daughters of Laban the Aramaean (Genesis 28:5 and 16–28); and later Israelites had to make a profession of faith beginning 'My father was a wandering Aramaean' (AV wrongly 'a Syrian ready to perish'; Deuteronomy 26:5).

Near the end of the twelfth century BC, a branch of the Aramaeans called Ahlamu were encroaching upon the Habur region, threatening the Assyrian trade routes to the Syrian coast and Anatolia. The vigorous Ashur-resh-ishi (1133–1116 BC) undertook a successful campaign against them, and subsequently described himself as 'crusher of the widespread forces of the Ahlamu'.

Ashur-resh-ishi was succeeded by an equally able son, Tiglath-pileser I (1115–1077 BC), the king who established the main lines of the policy of frightfulness followed by later Assyrian kings. He faced a major problem in preventing Aramaeans from invading Assyrian territory, for he tells us in his inscriptions that he crossed the Euphrates on twenty-eight occasions in pursuit of them. Finally he cleared the way to the Mediterranean coast, where he reopened trading relations with the Phoenicians and the ports of north Syria. His links with the Mediterranean coast extended as far south as Egypt, whose king sent him a live crocodile as a present. The material prosperity which ensued from the trade so established enabled Tiglath-pileser I to engage in munificent works of temple-building, ensuring him a legacy of high respect from his successors.

The already considerable Aramaean pressure intensified after the reign of Tiglath-pileser I, and the kings of both

Assyria and Babylonia faced disaster. This brought them together for mutual support, and Tiglath-pileser's second successor, Ashur-bel-kala (1074–1057 BC), exchanged pledges of goodwill with his Babylonian contemporary, Marduk-shapik-zer-mati (1080–1068 BC), at a time when Babylonia was being overrun by Aramaeans. On the death of Marduk-shapik-zer-mati, a usurper, Adad-apal-iddina (1067–1046 BC), whom a later chronicle describes as an Aramaean, was able to take the throne. His alleged Aramaean origin did not prevent Babylonian cities from being sacked by plundering Aramaeans and other nomads. In Assyria, Aramaean pressure brought economic difficulties and social unrest; and at the death of Ashur-bel-kala the legitimate succession was interrupted.

The situation in Assyria and Babylonia now becomes obscure. In Babylonia, just before and after 1000 BC, there were three insignificant dynasties in less than fifty years; obviously, there was grave political instability. It is recorded of this troubled period that just before 1000 BC distress and famine were so severe that in Sippar the regular temple-offerings were discontinued. Things were even worse in the early tenth century, when there was such disorder around Babylon that for eleven years out of twenty the New Year Festival could not be celebrated – a situation as shocking as the cancellation of Christmas would be in a Christian country. A chronicle gives the details for 971 and 970 BC:

> In the month Nisan [the first month], the Aramaeans were hostile, so that the king could not come up to Babylon and Nabu did not come and Bel did not come out

so that

> the king did not perform the *Akitu* sacrifice.

The *Akitu* was the New Year Festival, in which Nabu of Borsippa visited Babylon's god Marduk (called Bel, 'The

Lord') at his great temple, Esagila, and the king took Marduk's hand to be reinvested with his royal powers (see pages 333ff.). As this was the central event of the Babylonian year, the administration must have been completely disrupted. Assyria likewise suffered, and under Ashur-rabi II (1010–970 BC) Assyrian settlements on the middle Euphrates were lost to the Aramaeans.

Like the Amorites before them, the Aramaeans moved west into Syria and south along the Euphrates. They gradually settled to form kingdoms, the earliest of which were in Syria; one of them, Zobah (Supite of the cuneiform inscriptions), is mentioned in the Bible as clashing with king Saul of Israel just before 1000 BC (1 Samuel 14:47), and it was shortly after this that the Israelite kingdom expanded under David and Solomon to reach as far as the Euphrates. The Bible mentions no encounter with Assyria; clearly it was too weak at this time to intervene.

The temporary Israelite expansion was possible because the consolidation of the Syrian Aramaeans into kingdoms had re-established the security of trade routes through Palestine and Syria, at a time when there was no other major power to compete with Israel for control. In Mesopotamia, Aramaeans continued migrating for two generations more, and it was not until the middle of the tenth century that the situation stabilized there, to bring an upturn into Assyria's fortunes. The first indication of this comes from king Ashur-dan II (934–912 BC), who relates how he rebuilt a certain gate in Ashur; the gate in question was the main entry for traffic with the west, and so clearly trade in that direction was reviving. The situation improved rapidly, so that under Ashur-dan's son, Adad-nerari II (911–891 BC), Assyria entered upon a period of major economic and military expansion. From this point, it is scarcely an exaggeration to say that the political history of Babylonia was little more than a footnote to the imperial career of its northern neighbour.

Adad-nerari took firm control of the Aramaean-populated Habur basin and the regions to the northwest as far as the eastern Taurus. His aim was settled conditions to optimize his use of agricultural resources, and he specifically states:

> I built administrative buildings throughout my land. I harnessed up plough-teams throughout my land. I increased grain stores over those of former times.[3]

Another inscription of his relates to the rebuilding of the quay wall at Ashur: obviously he was promoting riverine transport and trade.

In the southeast Adad-nerari II redrew the frontiers with Babylonia. He went south of the Lesser Zab, the former boundary, to take a wide stretch of territory east of the Tigris, and pushed the Euphrates frontier to south of Hit. To emphasize his dominance over Babylonia he gave himself the title 'conqueror of the entire land of Karduniash [Babylonia]'. His successor Tukulti-ninurta II (890–884) held and extended these advances in Assyrian power. The tribute he received from Aramaean settlements along the trade routes shows the wealth their trading activities brought them: it included myrrh, which must have come from south Arabia, dromedaries from the Arabian desert, ivory-inlaid furniture from Phoenicia (recalling the 'ivory house' of Ahab, 1 Kings 22:39, and ivory beds mentioned in Amos 6:4), textiles, iron, cattle and sheep. From the northern regions Tukulti-ninurta received horses in thousands as tribute, and it was he who introduced the large-scale use of cavalry into the Assyrian army. Like his father, he took steps to increase agricultural production by irrigation and the forced settlement of population in underdeveloped areas of Assyria.

Beginning of the Neo-Assyrian empire

From the ninth century onwards the inscriptions of most Assyrian kings are so detailed that the modern writer is in a position, if he so chooses, to pass off as history an extensive roll-call of places overrun or rulers conquered, chronologically arranged. But a more productive approach, and one which will be attempted here, is to use this extensive material not for its details but as a key to the understanding of Assyrian imperial policy and the part this played in the spread of Mesopotamian civilization.

Ashur-nasir-pal II (883–859 BC) (see plates 28, 29) has generally been castigated by modern writers for the frankness with which he relates the brutalities he inflicted upon the conquered; and in the heat of moral indignation his positive achievements have sometimes been overlooked. He made a major extension of the area of influence of Mesopotamian civilization, and it was he who was the real founder of the Neo-Assyrian empire. He clearly had an imperial strategy. He first dealt with Aramaeans in the Habur and middle Euphrates regions, and then extended Assyrian power eastwards into Kurdistan and northwards beyond the eastern Taurus. That done, he neutralized Babylonia by marching down the Euphrates to capture a border town with the deliberate political objective of impressing his might upon his southern neighbour. This assessment of his objective is not a guess; he specifically tells us what he intended by it:

> The fear of my dominion reached as far as Karduniash; the terror of my weapons overwhelmed Chaldea [south Babylonia].

What he was doing was to prepare a ring of security around Assyria as a prelude to a major expansion. Finally, after dealing with the hostile Aramaean state of Bit-adini (the 'Beth-Eden' or 'House of Eden' of Amos 1:5) in the elbow of the Euphrates east of Aleppo, he went westwards to the Mediterranean, where no Assyrian ruler had penetrated since Tiglath-pileser I, two centuries before. There he established friendly relations with the rulers of a number of states of Syria and the southern part of the old Hittite area, and received tribute from as far south as Tyre; he was in fact using a combination of a military demonstration and diplomacy to secure access for Assyria to the trade routes from the Phoenician ports on the Mediterranean which linked Egypt and Cyprus to Syria and the rest of Asia.

In domestic policy Ashur-nasir-pal's most notable achievement was the founding of a new capital of Kalhu (the biblical Calah of Genesis 10:12, modern Nimrud), which was ceremonially opened in 879 BC. It is clear that Ashur-nasir-pal, like several other Assyrian kings, was keenly interested in the natural environment, for his new city incorporated gardens containing plants and trees that he had collected in the course of his campaigns. There was also a zoological garden where the king bred herds of bulls, lions, ostriches and apes; and his governors presented elephants. Agriculture was not neglected in the new capital, and irrigation projects were set up to increase the fertility of the district around.

It is significant that Ashur-nasir-pal largely settled his new capital not with native Assyrians but with captives from his various campaigns, an indication that he held an ideal of empire free from narrow racialism.

His son, Shalmaneser III (858–824 BC), continued and extended his father's policies. He spent his early years in strengthening the Assyrian position in the west. Bit-adini, which Ashur-nasir-pal had made tributary, was brought under direct rule as an Assyrian province, a move which strengthened Assyria's hold over the important trade routes to Cilicia and Asia Minor. But this threatened the interests of the rich trading states of Syria, and they formed an anti-Assyrian coalition. In 853 BC the coalition – which included a strong contingent from Ahab of Israel, although the Bible does not mention this – faced the Assyrians in a major battle at Qarqar on the Orontes. Shalmaneser claimed to have won, although the fact that he made no immediate further advance puts that in question. But if this was a setback to Assyrian strategy in Syria and Palestine, it was only temporary. Twelve years later king Jehu of Israel, the usurping successor of Ahab's son Joram (2 Kings 9:14ff.), had become an Assyrian vassal; on a monument in the British Museum we see him doing obeisance to Shalmaneser[4] (see plate 35). The same monument witnesses to the friendly attitude of Egypt, which sent Shalmaneser a gift of dromedaries, a hippopotamus and other exotic animals.

Shalmaneser also extended Assyrian control into what is now Turkey, from the western Taurus north of Cyprus to beyond Diyarbekr in the east, and undertook campaigns against the rising kingdom of Urartu (Ararat) towards Lake Van. These activities had an economic component. Iron production was still largely centred in the region of Shalmaneser's operations in Asia Minor, and the region further east was a major source of horses and copper. Assyria was increasingly gaining control of the resources of the Near East, and an aspect of this was Shalmaneser's use of Syrian craftsmen. Just as Solomon in the previous century had brought craftsmen from Tyre and Gebal (Byblus, north of Beirut) to build his palace and temple (1 Kings 5:18; 7:13, 14), so did Shalmaneser deport many Syrian craftsmen to the Assyrian cities; vast quantities of carved ivories of Syrian workmanship have been found at Nimrud (Calah). Shalmaneser also left some famous 'bronze gates' – metal bands on gates, decorated in *repoussé* work with scenes from his principal campaigns (see plates 33A, 33B and 34) – which may owe something to metalworkers of the type of Hiram of Tyre in the previous century, who 'was filled with wisdom and understanding and cunning, to work all works in brass [i.e. bronze]' (1 Kings 7:14).

Shalmaneser made a significant eastward extension of Assyrian influence, by crossing the Zagros from Kurdistan into northwest Iran. There he came into contact for the first time with the Iranian tribes of the Medes and Persians, who had migrated from the north late in the second millennium. The subsequent history of these peoples well demonstrates the part Assyrian imperial expansion played in the spread of Mesopotamian civilization, since it was the Persians who, from their contacts with Assyria, were to be the ultimate heirs of the Assyrian empire and to transmit many features of Babylonian and Assyrian culture to the Greeks, and through them to the world.

It remains to mention Shalmaneser's policy towards Babylonia. There the settlement of the Aramaean tribes had removed the threat of invasion, and common trading interests resulted in predominantly friendly relations with Assyria. The most important Babylonian ruler during this period was Nabu-apla-iddina, contemporary in part with both Ashurnasir-pal and Shalmaneser. He made a treaty with Shalmaneser, who in fulfilment of it later gave military assistance to Nabu-apla-iddina's legitimate successor, Marduk-zakir-shumi I, to put down a rebellion in north Babylonia.

Since the beginning of the first millennium, another Semitic-speaking tribal people had settled in the south of Babylonia. They were the Kaldu, the Chaldeans of the Bible, who came to play an important role in the Persian Gulf trade. While many of them lived in settlements hidden in the extensive southern marshes, by the time of Shalmaneser they also had fortified cities. They took advantage of Marduk-zakir-shumi's troubles to assert their independence, but Shalmaneser followed up his action in north Babylonia by reducing the Chaldean tribes. They marked their submission by the payment of tribute of gold, ebony and ivory, an indication of the considerable wealth they had acquired from trade.

The final years of Shalmaneser's reign were marked by a widespread rebellion headed by one of his sons. The legitimate successor, Shamshi-adad V (823–811 BC), only established himself with help from Babylonia, given at the price of a humiliating treaty which made him virtually a vassal. This must have rankled, and led Shamshi-adad, after consolidating himself in the north, to march down the Tigris and devastate eastern Babylonia. Although the king of Babylonia, successor of the one who had imposed the humiliating treaty, organized a defensive coalition of all possible allies, including Elam and Chaldean and Aramaean tribesmen, he was defeated in a pitched battle. From this time until the final collapse of the empire two centuries later, Babylonia was almost always dominated, sometimes actually ruled, by Assyria.

Although Assyria was now paramount in Mesopotamia and Syria, with a major foothold in Asia Minor, its Near Eastern empire was not unchallenged. In the region later known as Armenia, now eastern Asiatic Turkey, a number of petty states had federated into the kingdom of Urartu (Ararat). This, like other peripheral regions, had come under the influence of Mesopotamian culture and adopted its cuneiform writing system (adapted for the native language) and other institutions. It now came into economic competition with Assyria for the trade routes from Asia Minor and the Mediterranean and for control of resources further north. Assyria used the northern regions from Cilicia to Lake Van as a source of iron, copper and horses, but from the reign of the Assyrian king Adad-nerari III (810–783 BC) these were under threat. A Urartian thrust in the west dispossessed Assyria of almost the whole region north and west of Carchemish, and further east Urartu made substantial encroachments on northern territories previously controlled by Assyria. Across the Zagros also, where Assyria had recently come into contact with the Medes and Persians, Urartu extended its influence south of Lake Urmia to gain control of the trade routes across northern Iran. The loss of economic resources severely damaged Assyrian military efficiency. One facet of this is reflected in the Bible. It is during this period that the reign of Jeroboam II of Israel is to be placed, and 2 Kings 14:25–28 tells us that he extended his borders at the expense of Hamath and Damascus. This was only possible because there was no strong imperial power in Syria to hold the balance between vassals.

Within Assyria itself, the economic problems arising from the cutting of trade led to revolts in a number of cities. In 746 BC this spread to the capital, Calah, itself, and Ashur-nerari V, the last of the three kings following Adad-nerari III, was murdered with the whole of the royal family.

The revolution which overthrew the old royal family brought to the throne the most able Assyrian ruler for over a century. Of the antecedents of this king, Tiglath-pileser III, the Pul of the Old Testament, little is known, except that he had been governor of Calah. In one inscription he claims descent from Adad-nerari III, and there is no good reason to question this. He was known as 'Pul' not only in the biblical milieu but also in Babylonia, and it is possible that this was his personal name. If so, he took Tiglath-pileser as his throne-name to indicate his intention of following in the steps of the all-conquering ruler who had borne it more than three centuries before.

5

Assyrian Supremacy

WHEN Tiglath-pileser III (745–727 BC) came to the throne, Assyria was in a difficult, even desperate, military and economic situation. Much of the western territories had been lost, Babylonia was near anarchy, and the mountain regions to the east and north of Assyria were largely in the control of Urartu. The succeeding forty years saw Assyria recover all its old territories and re-establish itself firmly as the pre-eminent military and economic power of the Near East.

These striking changes did not result from any cardinal improvement in the external situation, but may be laid very largely to the credit of administrative reforms undertaken by Tiglath-pileser. The provinces were in some cases reduced in size, in the interests on the one hand of efficient administration and on the other of preventing the acquisition of a dangerous measure of power by provincial governors. The reorganized provinces in turn were subdivided into smaller areas under the control of lesser officials, who generally speaking were responsible to the governor but had the right to make complaints and representations directly to the king: this was a useful check upon the efficiency and loyalty of the provincial governors. A system of posting stages (for the introduction of which the Persians have generally been given the credit) was organized across the empire, permitting the rapid passage of messengers between the king and his governors; the latter were required to make regular reports on the affairs of their provinces. In the buffer states beyond the Assyrian provinces Tiglath-pileser and his successors appointed representatives to watch Assyrian interests at the court, control being exercised indirectly through the local royal family. Such local dynasts, provided they paid tribute and accepted the direction of the Assyrian Resident in matters of foreign policy and trade, were assured of the backing of the imperial power in the event of internal revolution or enemy attack: an example of this is seen in the Old Testament, when Ahaz of Judah, threatened by a coalition of Syria and Israel, appealed, not in vain, to Tiglath-pileser (2 Kings 16:7–9).

Tiglath-pileser's first military concern was the settlement of the southern border, where Aramaean tribes along the Tigris had been giving trouble for several decades. The tribal lands of Puqudu (biblical Pekod), east and north of what is now Baghdad, were conquered, resettled and incorporated into the province of Arrapkha (now Kirkuk), which became a long sausage-shaped strip of territory right down the eastern side of the Tigris and served as the key to Assyrian control of Babylonia. Tribal areas further to the southeast, towards Elam, were made into a province under Assyrian administration. Such action strengthened the position of the native Babylonian king, Nabu-nasir, with whose authority west of the Tigris Tiglath-pileser did not interfere. Nabu-nasir maintained civil peace and a pro-Assyrian policy until his death in 734 BC.

Tiglath-pileser, for the present relieved of problems in the south, was able to turn his attention to Assyria's main adversary, Urartu. He began in 743 BC in north Syria, with the siege of Arpad, northwest of Aleppo, at that time held by Urartian forces. Although the city was not finally taken until 740 BC, there were early successes which brought the submission of many states of north and south Syria. During the following years extensive administrative changes were made to consolidate the Assyrian position in the west, kingdoms which had proved unreliable as vassals becoming directly-ruled Assyrian provinces. Isolated trouble spots remained, as we know from mention of anti-Assyrian activities in the annals or the royal correspondence. Such activities ranged from open rebellion to local rioting against unpopular economic measures. A letter to Tiglath-pileser from the Assyrian administrator in the commercial seaports of Tyre and Sidon gives an instance of the latter. The Assyrian authorities had imposed a tax upon the timber brought down to the quays from the Lebanon mountains, whereupon the outraged citizens had rioted and seized the Assyrian customs officer. The governor reacted energetically, bringing into the towns concerned a contingent of Itu'a troops, a tough tribal body used for police duties amongst troublesome urban populations: the presence of these troops, so the writer tells the king, 'put the people into a panic'. When the lumber merchants had been brought to heel, the Assyrian official instructed them to continue felling as before, but put an embargo upon export to Egypt or the Philistine cities, a clear indication of the economic dimension of Assyrian imperialism. In 738 BC Tiglath-pileser made a demonstration of force into south Syria to secure the submission of native rulers of doubtful loyalty, amongst them the king of Israel, Menahem, who had to pay tribute of a thousand talents of silver, as 2 Kings 15:19–22 relates. It is possible that the king of Judah, Azariah (Uzziah) (2 Kings 15:2–7 and 2 Chronicles 26:1–23), was also involved in anti-Assyrian activities, if a certain Azriyau of Yaudi, mentioned in Assyrian inscriptions, is to be identified with him.

Tiglath-pileser's activities were not limited to Syria; he acted energetically against Urartu along the northern frontier, as far east as the land of the Medes in northwestern Iran. Letters to the king from military officers on the Urartian front show that the Assyrians had a very efficient system of military intelligence, which kept them well informed of the disposition and movements of Urartian forces.

In 734 BC fresh anti-Assyrian movements broke out in Palestine, perhaps in concert with a rebellion in Babylonia. 2 Chronicles 28:16–21 tells us that Edom and the Philistine cities attacked Judah under Ahaz, and 2 Kings 16:5–9 speaks of an attack upon Judah by the kings of Syria and Israel, whom we know from the Assyrian records to have been engaged in an anti-Assyrian coalition. According to the consistent story of the Old Testament, Ahaz loyally maintained a pro-Assyrian policy throughout and called upon Tiglath-pileser for assistance. This was given, the Assyrian king easily disposing of the opposition from the Philistine cities and Syria, and intervening in Israel to replace king Pekah by Hoshea.

The same year (734 BC) saw fresh trouble in Babylonia, at the death of its pro-Assyrian king. A certain Ukin-zer, head of the Chaldean tribe of Bit-Amukkani, occupied Babylon and seized the throne. Non-Chaldean tribes, such as the Puqudu (biblical Pekod), remained loyal to Assyria, as in the main did the urban population, to whom Assyria represented stability against disruptive Chaldeans. Tiglath-pileser responded by sending military forces, and we have a letter giving an account of a parley at the gates of Babylon between Assyrian officials and the people barricaded within. It is curiously reminiscent of the interview between the Rabshakeh official and the ministers of Hezekiah at the siege of Jerusalem in 701 BC (2 Kings 18:17–36), justifying us in accepting the biblical narrative as an eyewitness account.

The Assyrians did not rely exclusively on military force against Ukin-zer; they also used diplomacy. A letter reveals that another Chaldean leader, Marduk-apil-iddina of the tribe Bit-Yakin, was secretly accepting a subvention from the Assyrians; this was the Merodach-baladan of Isaiah 39:1 and 2 Kings 20:12, and his double-crossing of his fellow-Chaldeans shows how right Isaiah was to mistrust him.

Tiglath-pileser's military action against Ukin-zer showed clever tactical planning. The attack was directed from the province of Arrapkha, so that the Assyrian army could march southwards east of the Tigris and approach Babylon from the east, bypassing the powerful defences placed north of the capital between the Euphrates and Tigris where they come closest. Babylon was taken, and Ukin-zer fled to his stronghold deep in the marsh country on the lower Euphrates, where an Assyrian army besieged him and devastated his territory and that of other hostile Chaldean tribes. The whole affair occupied three years. Babylonia was placed under Assyrian administrators, and in 729 BC Tiglath-pileser himself 'took the hand of the god' in the New Year ceremony at Babylon, whereby he was formally invested by the national god Marduk with kingship over Babylonia; no Assyrian king had formally held the kingship of Babylonia for over four and a half centuries. When Tiglath-pileser died in 727 BC, he left Assyria with an empire extending from the Persian Gulf to the borders of Egypt, and including a substantial part of Anatolia and Asia Minor.

Assyrian military operations had won control of the Palestine coast as far south as Gaza; this, coupled with the Assyrian interference with the trade of the Phoenician ports, was felt as a threat by Egypt. During the brief reign of Tiglath-pileser's successor, Shalmaneser V (727–722 BC), the Egyptians embarked upon a diplomatic counter-offensive, attempting to subvert the petty kingdoms of Palestine and south Syria. Hoshea of Israel was implicated, bringing down upon himself attack by Shalmaneser (2 Kings 17:3–5), which ended with the capture of the Israelite capital, Samaria, in 722 BC after a three-year siege. This was followed by the usual policy of deportation (2 Kings 17:6), in which the 'ten lost tribes of Israel' – the fate of which has given play to much sterile fancy – were transferred to areas of Assyria and northwest Iran. This deportation is reflected in Israelite names, such as Hananeel, Menahem, Uzzah, Elisha, Haggai, written on a piece of pot found at Nimrud (the ancient Calah).

There was nothing unusual about this deportation; it was in accordance with established Assyrian policy. A state newly brought into vassaldom was normally left undisturbed in its internal affairs, subject to the payment of tribute. In the event of subsequent anti-Assyrian activity, the ruler was likely to be replaced by another native more acceptable to Assyria: in the case of Israel this stage had been reached with the accession of

Hoshea (2 Kings 17:1), known from the annals of Tiglath-pileser to have been an Assyrian nominee. If such a ruler subsequently proved unreliable, the usual outcome was deportation of the leading elements of the population and conversion of the state to a directly ruled province. This policy of deportation had an important consequence for the future of the Near East, since it contributed to the breaking down of ethnic barriers and prepared the way for the later spread of first Hellenism and then Christianity.

Sargon II of Assyria

The manner in which Shalmaneser's reign ended illustrates one of the constraints upon ancient rulers. Ashur, the most ancient of Assyrian cult-centres, had enormous prestige, and its citizens enjoyed considerable privileges in the form of exemption from taxation and forced labour. When Shalmaneser attempted to modify this, there was an insurrection, which brought to the throne Sargon II (721–705 BC), possibly his brother. In recognition of the support he had received, Sargon had to confirm the privileges of the people of Ashur and of all the temples of Assyria.

The insurrection in the homeland brought unrest elsewhere, and the beginning of Sargon's reign was marked by fresh trouble in Babylonia. There Merodach-baladan, the chief of the Bit-Yakin tribe, under Tiglath-pileser an Assyrian ally, had worked himself into a very strong position. Now paramount sheikh of the Chaldeans, he had secured widespread tribal support in Babylonia, and had made an alliance with Elam; immediately upon Sargon's accession, he entered Babylon and claimed the kingship by 'taking the hand of Bel' at the New Year Festival of 721 BC. When the Assyrian army attempted to repeat the manoeuvre by which Ukin-zer's defences had been outflanked, they were confronted by the Elamite army; they failed to force a crossing into metropolitan Babylonia and had to withdraw to the homeland. Sargon was compelled to leave Merodach-baladan in possession for ten years, during which time the economy of the great cities of Babylonia suffered severe damage, as the tribesmen interfered with the free flow of trade and practised various extortions. This made the Chaldeans highly unpopular with the major urban centres, so that, down to within a few years of the final extinction of Assyria itself, these cities were constantly appealing to the Assyrian king for assistance against them.

When rebellion broke out in Syria, Sargon had to leave Babylonian problems unresolved. This came so conveniently for Merodach-baladan that one wonders if he was behind the affair, as he certainly was in the later rebellion of Hezekiah of Judah (2 Kings 20:12–17). The current rebellion was headed by Hamath, the sole remaining independent princedom in Syria, whom Sargon attacked and defeated in 721 BC. Amongst Hamath's minor allies were forces from the former Israelite capital, Samaria, and in inscriptions later in his reign Sargon used this circumstance to claim credit for the earlier major operation of 722 BC against Samaria, actually an achievement of Shalmaneser V, as 2 Kings 17:5–6 implies. In the little tributary state of Judah, the statesman and prophet Isaiah pointed out the lesson to be drawn from the fate of the cities of Syria, regarding Assyria as the instrument of God:

> Ah, Assyria, the rod of my anger, the staff of my fury!
> Against a godless nation I send him . . .
> . . . he says:
> 'Are not my commanders all kings? Is not Calno like Carchemish?
> Is not Hamath like Arpad? Is not Samaria like Damascus?'
> (Isaiah 10:5–6,8–9; RSV)

Apart from an abortive attempt in 712 BC by the coastal city of Ashdod to organize with Egyptian encouragement an anti-Assyrian coalition, Sargon had no further trouble with Palestine. Isaiah 20:1–6 refers to the capture of Ashdod, and points out the futility of looking to Egypt for military support against Assyria.

As with Tiglath-pileser, Sargon's main problems were with

Urartu in the north, which itself was under pressure from Iranian tribes who since the beginning of the millennium had been migrating south from the steppes of Russia. The most important group of these was the Medes. The Urartian king Rusas I (733–714 BC) came to terms with some of the Median chieftains, securing their support against Assyria and their cooperation in keeping open the trade routes to Urartu from further east. At this period the main route from Iran went via Lake Urmia to Erzerum (where eighth-century Urartian bronze objects have been found) and on to Trebizond on the Black Sea, which according to tradition was founded in 757 BC. Urartu may also have had trading relations with lands beyond Greece, since allegedly Urartian bronzes are found in Etruscan tombs in Italy. It has even been suggested, on the basis of art motifs, that silk caravans reached Urartu all the way from China. Some of the trade across Urartu had probably earlier passed through Assyria, and the desire to re-divert this into the old channels may have been one element in Sargon's subsequent campaigns in the region. Another factor was that the area was an important source of horses.

South of Lake Urmia were the Mannaeans (the Minni of Jeremiah 51:27), who were Assyrian tributaries. Shortly after Sargon's accession trouble broke out there, fomented by Urartu, and Sargon had to make several interventions to defend the Mannaean ruler. In addition to this Urartian interference in the affairs of a loyal Assyrian vassal, there were frontier clashes. Sargon decided upon a major military response. Plans were laid, and intelligence reports streamed in to him, from Assyrian officials and from foreign spies. One writer suggested that the king should make a direct attack upon Urartu, and seemed confident that the capital, Turushpa, would fall to Assyria. Another letter spoke of an insurrection inside Urartu, and expressed the view that the tribes concerned would prove pro-Assyrian in the event of an invasion. An invasion was evidently expected, for a disaffected informant from Urartu spoke of 'when the forces of the king of Assyria come for the third time'.

The forces of Sargon undertook the planned major action against Urartu in the summer of 714 BC. Details are known from a report on the campaign, drafted in the form of a letter to the national god Ashur. Having crossed the Zagros into northwest Iran, Sargon outflanked the Urartian defences by marching northwards up the east bank of Lake Urmia and then turning west towards Urartu. By the time he made contact with the main body of the enemy, Sargon's forces, exhausted from the long march through mountainous terrain, were near to mutiny. Unable to rely on the discipline of his main army, Sargon in his battle-chariot led his personal corps of mounted guards in a cavalry attack against one wing of the opposing force. The enemy line gave. This put new heart into the main Assyrian army, which fell upon the Urartian coalition, breaking their lines and causing panic. The Urartian general led his own force in a hurried yet disciplined retreat, but the other contingents, now a leaderless and terror-stricken rabble, fled in disorder over the mountains, where great numbers perished from the severe climatic conditions. The defeat and flight of the main Urartian army was a shock to Urartian morale, and Sargon was able to penetrate, with negligible opposition, deep into Urartian territory. Rusas abandoned his capital, Turushpa, and took to the mountains, where, according to Sargon, he eventually died of grief (although in another inscription he said it was suicide):

> He took to bed like a woman in confinement; he refused to let food or water touch his mouth; he brought on himself an incurable illness.

Sargon marched through Urartian territory, looting towns and leaving them ablaze, destroying gardens and setting growing crops on fire, felling and burning trees, and smashing down dams. One district, Musasir, cult-city of the Urartian national god Haldi, deep in forests and mountains, failed to give formal recognition to Sargon as overlord. Sargon decided to make an example of Musasir, holy city though it was and difficult of approach. Allowing his main force to proceed homeward, Sargon led a contingent of a thousand cavalry against the city. He arrived to find a coronation festival in progress at which Haldi was appointing a successor to the kingship of Urartu. The god and his consort were taken captive, the citizens deported, and a vast treasure of precious metals and bronzeware taken back to Assyria.

In 710 BC Sargon returned to deal with Babylonia. Ten years of tribal rule and dislocation of trade had left the inhabitants of the great cities ready for Assyrian intervention. As the Assyrian forces approached, the Chaldean army retreated and the cities of north Babylonia opened their gates and welcomed Sargon, who duly 'took the hand of the god' at the New Year Festival in Babylon. Merodach-baladan's tribal area was overrun, and he had to pay a heavy tribute, but finally Sargon left him in control of his territories, either from policy or from inability to catch him.

Shortly afterwards another problem appeared on the horizon, when a great horde of barbarians, known in cuneiform sources as Gimirraya, in the Bible as Gomer (Ezekiel 38:6, etc.) and in classical sources as Cimmerians, entered Urartu from the north. The Urartian king Argistis failed in an attempt in 707 BC to check them, and they passed westwards towards Asia Minor, where they came into territory controlled by Assyria. This is an appropriate point at which to examine Assyrian interests in Asia Minor during the reign of Sargon.

North of the Taurus in central Asia Minor, astride main trade routes from Europe to Asia, lay the powerful and wealthy state of Mushki (biblical Meshech, classical Phrygia). By Sargon's reign its interests were beginning to clash with those of Assyria, and in 716 BC Sargon undertook military action against Mushki on the pretence that the latter had encroached on territories of the province of Que (Cilicia in southeast Asia Minor). Urartu, struggling for recovery after the invasion of 714 BC, made common cause with Mushki; and they succeeded in subverting several Assyrian vassals in north Syria and Asia Minor. Disturbances ensued.

In 709 BC an attack was made upon Mushki from Que. Whether for this reason, or because of the first rumblings of the Cimmerian invasion, the policy of Mushki suddenly changed in favour of Assyria, its king, Mita (Midas to classical authors), sending a present to Sargon and seeking a treaty of friendship. Sargon was delighted, and in a letter to his emissary in charge of negotiations, almost certainly his son and eventual successor Sennacherib, he asked that Mita should be informed of his pleasure.

This was the situation when the Cimmerians appeared northwest of Assyria. It is not impossible that they actually raided one or more of the great Assyrian cities, since archaeological evidence indicates that the city Calah was the scene of violent destruction at some time in the last decade of the eighth century BC. In 705 BC Sargon marched to Tabal, the province north of Que, and there met the Cimmerian hordes in battle. A chronicle entry for 705 BC, succinctly worded 'the king killed; the camp of the king of Assyria [captured?]', suggests that Sargon fell in battle. There is probably also a reference to his fate in the Bible, in Isaiah 14:4–20, part of which reads:

> All the kings of the nations lie in glory, each in his own tomb;
> but you are cast out, away from your sepulchre, like a loathed
>   untimely birth,
> clothed with the slain, those pierced by the sword. (verse 19; RSV)

Sargon's death was not in vain, for the barbarian hordes moved off from Assyrian territories into the interior of Asia Minor.

Sennacherib

Sargon's successor, his son Sennacherib (704–681 BC), came to the throne with experience as an administrator and soldier on the northern frontier. Profiting by the favourable military situation bequeathed by his father, Sennacherib made his first work the rebuilding of the ancient city of Nineveh, which he adopted as the capital: such it remained until the overthrow of the Assyrian empire, and long after that it continued to be remembered in tradition. So also was Sennacherib remembered: the Talmud makes him an ancestor of the teachers of the liberal Pharisee Hillel, grandfather of the Gamaliel mentioned in Acts 5:34.

Babylonia remained a major problem to the Assyrian rulers. It had to have a king, as the state religion could not function without one to officiate at the annual New Year Festival in Babylon. But since the death of Nabu-nasir in 734 BC, there had been no native dynasty capable of governing the country. Also, the country was split ethnically. Much of south Babylonia was dominated by Chaldean tribes, to the detriment of the urban centres; the trading interests of the latter generally coincided with those of Assyria. To the southeast, Elam was usually ready to meddle in Babylonian affairs in support of the Chaldeans. In the absence of a strong Babylonian king, an Assyrian presence was therefore necessary to protect the interests of the Babylonian cities no less than those of Assyria.

Tiglath-pileser and Sargon had both come finally to direct personal rule of Babylonia, but Sennacherib attempted devolution through native Babylonian puppet kings. But after two years, in 703 BC, Merodach-baladan deposed Sennacherib's nominee and proclaimed himself king. Sennacherib sent an army which overthrew Merodach-baladan's forces, and Babylon received Sennacherib, as it had done his father, with enthusiasm. Sennacherib used his army to subjugate and de-fortify the whole of the Chaldean area in southern Babylonia, and put it under Assyrian officials. Northern Babylonia was placed under a native Babylonian king, Bel-ibni, one of the many foreign princes who had lived as hostages at the Assyrian court and been educated in readiness for such a situation.

Merodach-baladan was a skilful diplomatist, and had made overtures as far afield as Palestine, as we learn from the biblical account of his embassy to Hezekiah of Judah (Isaiah 39:1–2 and

2 Kings 20:12–13). A rebellion, possibly related to this, broke out in Palestine in 701 BC, under Hezekiah of Judah. Hezekiah was the most powerful of the petty kings of Palestine (2 Kings 18:13ff.); according to 2 Kings 18:8, he had established suzerainty over some of the Philistine cities, and Isaiah 30:1–5 indicates that he had made an alliance with Egypt. But he was no match for the Assyrians. A strong Assyrian force overran Palestine, defeated the Egyptian troops, took the rebel cities (with the exception of Jerusalem), and rewarded loyal vassals in the Philistine cities with territories stripped from Judah. Possibly because developments in Babylonia necessitated the early return of his forces to the homeland, but according to the Bible because of divine intervention, Sennacherib did not press the siege of Jerusalem, and Hezekiah's city was spared by his submission and payment of a heavy indemnity.

In Babylonia, Bel-ibni proved a broken reed. He was unable to maintain effective government against Merodach-baladan's intrigues, and in 700 BC Sennacherib removed him, and decided to rule through one of his younger sons, Ashur-nadin-shum.

Ashur-nadin-shum reigned in Babylonia for six years. Merodach-baladan is heard of no more, and presumably died at about this time. But his tribe, Bit-yakin, remained a threat to Assyrian interests, and was not easily dealt with, since when Assyria attempted to act against the tribesmen, Elam allowed them to take refuge in its coastal areas. In 694 BC the Assyrian authorities finally decided to lance this festering sore. They planned a direct attack by sea upon the part of Elam which harboured the rebel tribe. Sennacherib had a fleet of ships built by Syrian craftsmen in Nineveh, sailed down the Tigris by Phoenician sailors, and transferred by canal to the Euphrates to be sailed to the Persian Gulf, where troops were embarked and taken over to the coast of Elam. There they destroyed and looted the Elamite cities in the neighbourhood, and captured the troublesome tribesmen of Bit-yakin.

Sennacherib claimed in his annals that he had 'poured out terror over the broad lands of Elam'. Doubtless he had, but it was not sufficient to cow the Elamites. The Elamite king reacted energetically by a raid into metropolitan Babylonia, where he captured Sennacherib's son, Ashur-nadin-shum, and set up his own nominee as king, whom, however, the Assyrians quickly dispossessed.

Elam was now the decisive factor in Babylonian politics, and in recognition of this Sennacherib in late 693 BC invaded it from the province of Der in eastern Babylonia. Another Chaldean leader, Mushezib-marduk, now proclaimed himself king of Babylon, and raised a rebellion. The king of Elam mustered a powerful army and joined forces with Mushezib-marduk. Marching northwards, they met the Assyrian army at the Diyala river. Sennacherib's annals give a graphic picture of the carnage which ensued. Assyrian chargers wading through blood; the plain littered with mutilated bodies of the slain, hacked to bits for the sake of their rings and bracelets or for mere blood-lust; terrified horses plunging madly across the battlefield dragging chariots of the dead – with such strokes the annals describe the carnage.

Sennacherib claimed a victory, but the Assyrian army was so mauled that it could not campaign during the succeeding year. In 689 BC affairs in Elam kept the ruling house from external adventures, and the Assyrians were able to deal with Mushezib-marduk. The Chaldean forces stood siege in Babylon for nine months, finally succumbing to famine and disease. Sennacherib's well-intended attempts at settling Babylonia had repeatedly failed, and he now applied his final solution. Despite the awe in which Babylon was held internationally as a centre of religion and culture, he set out deliberately to destroy it. He gave his troops general licence to loot; he razed houses and temples; and he had canals dug across the city to destroy it to its very foundations. The statue of the god Marduk was taken captive to Assyria, and Sennacherib himself assumed the kingship of Babylonia, with the title 'King of Sumer and Akkad'. There was no further trouble in Babylonia for the rest of his reign.

Outside Babylonia and Palestine, Sennacherib's reign was

largely peaceful. Early in his reign he annexed certain territories in the Zagros, and in 696–5 BC there were disturbances in Que. Otherwise the situation along the northern and eastern frontiers was stable, with no further trouble from Urartu.

In his domestic policy Sennacherib is notable for his building activities and his interest in technical problems. He it was who rebuilt Nineveh, cutting new streets, enlarging squares, diverting watercourses and building great stone flood-defences to protect his new palace. Around the palace a great park was laid out 'like Mount Amanus, wherein were set all kinds of plants and fruit trees such as grow in the mountains and in Chaldea', and with 'all the plants of the land of Syria, myrrh plants, whose luxuriance was greater than in their native habitat, and all kinds of mountain vines'. Beyond these botanical gardens were orchards, and to irrigate all this greenery canals were cut to bring water from mountain streams thirty miles away. Sennacherib used dams to create a large marsh, which he then stocked with waterfowl, wild pigs and deer in imitation of the natural fauna and flora of south Babylonia. Substantial remains still exist of one of Sennacherib's engineering works – an aqueduct for carrying water over the bed of a wadi, over three hundred yards long, twenty-four yards wide and containing half a million tons of limestone blocks. A project of Sennacherib for supplying the city of Arbail (Erbil) with water is also known.

Sennacherib's interest in technology is shown by his claim to have invented new techniques in bronze casting:

> I, Sennacherib, through the acute intelligence which the noble god Ea had granted me and with my own experimenting, achieved the casting of bronze colossal lions . . . which no king before me had done. . . . Over great posts and palm-trunks I built a clay mould for twelve colossal lions together with twelve enormous colossal bulls . . . and poured bronze therein as in casting half-shekel pieces.

The reference is to the application of the lost-wax process to very large objects; the process itself had been in use from early in the third millennium.

Esarhaddon

In 681 BC Sennacherib suffered a fate not uncommon amongst oriental monarchs, being murdered by his sons, as 2 Kings 19:36–7 narrates. The legitimate successor, nominated by Sennacherib and already formally accepted by the gods and the nobles of Assyria, was Esarhaddon. This prince was already an experienced administrator at the time of his father's murder, since Sennacherib had placed him in charge of Babylonia after the sack of its capital in 689 BC. His experience stood him in good stead. He delayed only to secure the formal approval of the gods, and then, without waiting to go through the usual preliminaries for a campaign, he moved swiftly against the parricides. The main Assyrian army prepared to oppose him, but at his approach dissension broke out, as some of the troops learnt of an oracle of the goddess Ishtar favourable to Esarhaddon, and declared for him. The parricides fled to Urartu, and Esarhaddon, now supported by the whole army, was accepted as king. Once he was securely in the saddle, a purge followed, those implicated in the revolt suffering the usual fate.

The unrest which marked the succession gave the current chief of the tribe of Bit-yakin the opportunity to assert his independence in Babylonia. Esarhaddon ordered an offensive. The rebel chief fled to Bit-yakin's old ally, Elam, only to find that a change of king had brought a reversal of foreign policy: the fugitive was promptly put to death. The brother of the late chief made submission to Esarhaddon and was installed as vassal prince over the whole of the Sealands. There was a second troublesome Chaldean tribe, the Bit-dakkuri, which had encroached on territories belonging to the citizens of Babylon and neighbouring Borsippa; and two years later the chief of this tribe was also replaced by a vassal acceptable to Assyria.

Meanwhile Esarhaddon was faced with problems in the west and northwest. A new tribal group was now overrunning much of the territory of Urartu and Asia Minor. This new element was the Scythians, known in cuneiform sources as Ashguzaya and in the Bible (Jeremiah 51:27 and elsewhere) as Ashkenaz, an ancient 'misprint' or mispronunciation of Ashkuz. There is some evidence that Esarhaddon allied himself with one of the Scythian princes by marriage.

The trouble in the west was centred on Sidon, whose king revolted in alliance with a ruler on the Gulf of Antioch. Esarhaddon captured and executed both kings and sacked Sidon, founding an Assyrian fortress on a new site nearby; as an object lesson to prospective rebels he formally dedicated it in the presence of twenty-two kings of western lands. To secure Assyrian interests on the desert fringes of the western provinces, when the king of the Arabs died, he sent a force to ensure the succession of a nominee friendly to Assyria.

In Babylonia, Esarhaddon's firsthand knowledge and conciliatory policy produced a situation favourable for Assyria. Babylon, devastated by Sennacherib, was probably already being rebuilt before the end of his reign, and considerable work was carried out by Esarhaddon. An inscription describing the restoration amusingly illustrates how a divine decree could be circumvented. When Sennacherib sacked the city, the god Marduk had written, presumably through the priest at some divination procedure, 'seventy years as the measure of the city's desolation'. The inscription claims that the god, having recovered from his pique, 'turned the tablet upside down and ordered the city's restoration in the eleventh year'. The meaning is perfectly clear in the sexagesimal system of Babylonian writing, where cuneiform 𒁹 can represent either 'one' or 'sixty', and 𒌋 denotes 'ten'. Cuneiform 𒁹𒌋 is thus seventy, but turned about, it reads 𒌋𒁹, that is, eleven.

Esarhaddon's efficient administration in Babylonia contributed to the wellbeing of its citizens, and exiles returning after the chaos of the Chaldean troubles were reinstated in their property if they could prove their claims. For the time being, the Assyrian position was secure, so that an Elamite raid on central Babylonia in 675 BC met with no answering revolt.

Beyond the Taurus, Assyrian control in the area of their furthest advance to the northeast, the Mannaean region south of Lake Urmia, was becoming precarious from Scythian pressure. The Assyrians compensated by an increasing involvement with the powerful and friendly Medes just to the south, with whose chieftains Esarhaddon made treaties. We have cuneiform tablets which give the text of a series of such treaties; similar treaties were probably drawn up with all vassal rulers. Esarhaddon's primary objective in these treaties was to regulate the succession after his death; doubtless recollection of the circumstances of his own succession drove him to this precaution.

Esarhaddon had six sons, of whom the first died at an early age. Amongst the survivors two, Shamash-shum-ukin and Ashur-ban-apli (Ashurbanipal), were considered the most fitting for the succession: it is disputable which was the older; they may have been twins. At a great assembly in Nineveh in 672 BC, Esarhaddon, having previously obtained the approval of the gods and the assent of the family council, proclaimed Ashurbanipal as Crown Prince of Assyria and Shamash-shum-ukin as Crown Prince of Babylonia. The provincial governors and vassal rulers were required to take oaths to recognize the settlement, the vassals ratifying the oath in a treaty in which they were reminded:

> When Esarhaddon king of Assyria dies, you will seat Ashurbanipal the Crown Prince upon the royal throne; he will exercise the kingship and lordship of Assyria over you. You will protect him in country and town; you will fight to the death for him. . . . You will not be hostile to him nor enthrone any of his older or younger brothers in his place. . . . Should Esarhaddon, king of Assyria, die whilst his sons are minors, you will help Ashurbanipal the Crown Prince to take the throne of Assyria and you will help to seat Shamash-shum-ukin, his coequal brother, the Crown Prince of Babylon, on the throne of Babylon. . . .

These arrangements were made during a brief period of calm shortly before Esarhaddon embarked on a new and far-reaching development of imperial policy. In 675 BC, Tarqu of the Ethiopian dynasty ruling in Egypt (the 'Tirhakah king of Ethiopia' of 2 Kings 19:9) led the king of Tyre into an anti-Assyrian intrigue, and Esarhaddon decided to strike at the root of the trouble. An initial attack upon Egypt was frustrated by a sandstorm, but in 671 BC an organized invasion was put under way. Tarqu's army was routed, and Memphis was besieged and taken, although Tarqu himself escaped. The princes of all Lower Egypt, including the paramount prince, Necho of Sais, hurried to acknowledge Esarhaddon's suzerainty. Assyrian officials were appointed to oversee Esarhaddon's interests within the territories of the native rulers, and Esarhaddon proclaimed himself king of Upper and Lower Egypt and Ethiopia – a claim in which he exceeded the truth. The lie is repeated pictorially in a sculptured monument which Esarhaddon set up at Zenjirli during his return to Assyria: this shows the Assyrian conqueror holding cords which pass through the lips of two kneeling figures, one being the king of Tyre (see plate 37). In fact, Tarqu was still at liberty. As soon as the main Assyrian army was well clear, he returned, induced some of the princes of Lower Egypt to renounce their new suzerain, and re-took Memphis.

There may have been some in Assyria who did not approve of Esarhaddon's Egyptian policy. This suspicion is raised by a line from a chronicle reading 'The eleventh year [i.e. 670 BC]: in Assyria the king put many of his nobles to the sword.' Obviously Esarhaddon had come upon serious opposition of some kind. The following year (669 BC) the king set out to march to Egypt, but was taken ill and died on the way. As his antecedents would not make him much more than forty-five, one is left wondering if perhaps his opponents managed to poison him once he was away from the palace, with its elaborate precautions against such an act.

Ashurbanipal

Upon the death of Esarhaddon the carefully planned arrangements for the succession went smoothly into effect. There was little outward indication that the end of the reign of Ashurbanipal would see the empire plunging to disaster, for geographically it was almost at its greatest extent and still expanding. None the less, factors can already be seen which contributed to the collapse. First was the situation along the northern frontiers: here the order established by Tiglath-pileser III and Sargon II and largely maintained by Sennacherib was beginning to crumble, as hordes of Cimmerian and Scythian barbarians roamed over Asia Minor and the territories of Urartu. The powerful Median tribes in northwest Iran were now settling and coalescing into powerful units which ultimately became a kingdom able to meet the military might of Assyria on equal terms; and their confederacy must have deprived Assyria of an important source of metals and horses, and cut the routes bringing spices and semi-precious stones from India. Babylonia had the problem of disruptive Chaldean tribes, who controlled much of the south of the country, and who had learned from the Assyrians the science of warfare and from the native Babylonians the arts of peace.

At his accession Ashurbanipal was left to carry out the attack planned upon Tarqu. In 667 BC a powerful Assyrian army, with contingents from Syria, Phoenicia, Palestine and Cyprus, marched against Egypt, took Memphis and defeated Tarqu, who withdrew to the southern capital, Thebes. Subsequently, the Delta princes rebelled, but the Assyrians arrested the ringleaders, and Necho, the paramount prince, was taken away to Nineveh. There, however, instead of the expected punishment, he received clemency and favour, and after taking an oath of fealty and being loaded with gifts, he was returned to his post. Clearly, Ashurbanipal saw that in a country such as Egypt, with an unfamiliar way of life and a venerable bureaucratic system of government hierarchically organized, efficient administration was only possible through native princes.

A subsequent attempt by the southern dynasty to regain Lower Egypt brought an attack by the Assyrian army upon the ancient southern capital, Thebes, which was taken and sacked (663 BC). The vivid and lasting impression which this made internationally is reflected half a century later by the prophet Nahum, who refers to the fate of Thebes, under its Hebrew name of No-amon:

> Are you better than No-amon, that sat by the Nile . . . ?
> Ethiopia was her strength, Egypt too, and that without limit; . . .
> Yet she was carried away, she went into captivity.
>
> (Nahum 3:8–10; RSV)

During the Egyptian campaigns Assyrian influence in Asia Minor reached its furthest limits. The Cimmerians, deflected from Syria by Sargon, had overrun Mushki (Phrygia), and were now pressing upon Lydia. This led the king of Lydia, Gugu (Gyges), to send an embassy to Ashurbanipal seeking military assistance. It appears that this was forthcoming, for Gyges was able to inflict a defeat upon the Cimmerians, and after the campaign sent some of the spoil to Nineveh (*c.* 663 BC).

The year of the sack of Thebes also saw the death of Necho, in whose place, as prince of Sais and paramount price of the Delta, the Assyrians appointed his son Psammetichus. But he soon came to assert his independence, and with the assistance of mercenaries from Greece and Asia Minor he was able to expel the Assyrian garrisons between 658 and 651 BC. One of his allies in this was Gyges, whose country was linked to Egypt by common commercial interests. As a result, Gyges lost Assyrian protection and in or just before 652 BC he fell to a new Cimmerian attack.

The earlier tensions in Babylonia were in the end intensified by the succession arrangements that Esarhaddon had made to minimize them. Although Shamash-shum-ukin held the kingship of Babylonia, the Assyrian garrisons there were under the control of Ashurbanipal, who was also responsible for all major decisions; this left Shamash-shum-ukin in a position in which he was constantly made to feel the emptiness of his title. There are instances in the imperial correspondence of Assyrian officials in Babylonia declining to act upon orders other than those emanating from the king of Assyria, and this would give many opportunities for friction. A letter is extant in which Shamash-shum-ukin mentioned to his brother that he had been obliged to countermand his own orders. However, despite this the diarchy worked for about sixteen years.

Events in Babylonia at this time depended upon interaction between four main groups. Firstly, there was Assyria, which regarded Babylonia as the central part of its empire and an indispensable trading partner. Then there were the citizens of the Babylonian cities, for many of whom Assyria represented stability and a guarantee of favourable conditions for international trade. Thirdly, there were the increasingly powerful Chaldean tribes, mainly in the south of the country, whose activities were often in conflict with the vested interests of the old cities. Lastly, there was the kingdom of Elam in southwest Iran, historically always closely linked with south Babylonia and because of that and common trading interests now usually ready to support the Chaldeans.

Elam was now showing signs of decline. One factor was the arrival from further north of the powerful Persians, who were occupying more and more of Elam's eastern territories. Dynastic instability was another factor; the royal family was extensive, with a large number of claimants to the throne, and consequent severe internal dissension. Several Elamite kings died sudden and unexpected deaths, but whether this was due to a genetic defect in the royal family or to secret poisoning we do not know.

Ashurbanipal's relations with Elam began well. At the beginning of his reign, Elam was suffering from drought, and Ashurbanipal sent corn for famine relief. But despite this, by 665 BC the Elamites were giving the Chaldeans assistance in an attack upon Babylon. Assyria's military response was no more than limited and local, but relations between Assyria and Elam continuously deteriorated over the next decade, with constant anti-Assyrian intrigues between Chaldeans and Elamites. Eventually Shamash-shum-ukin himself was drawn into this.

In 653 BC Ashurbanipal, learning that the Elamite king was mobilizing his army, pre-empted his intentions by a raid on Elam. The following year Shamash-shum-ukin attacked the Assyrian garrisons in Babylonia, and an Elamite army came to his aid. But the Elamite army was defeated, and civil war in Elam prevented any further intervention. The Assyrians seized the initiative, cleared south Babylonia of organized Chaldean forces, and put Borsippa and Babylon, held by Shamash-shum-ukin, under siege. Famine compelled surrender in 648 BC: conditions had become so appalling that the defenders had resorted to cannibalism. Shamash-shum-ukin died, probably by suicide by casting himself into a fire, and his wife with him. However, Ashurbanipal was scrupulously careful that his dead brother and sister-in-law should have proper burial with due rites. But surviving rebel leaders bore the full weight of Ashurbanipal's fury; they were hunted down and destroyed, and their corpses were cut up and 'fed to the dogs, the swine, the wolves, the vultures, the birds of heaven and the fish of the deep'. Ashurbanipal himself occupied the throne of Babylonia for a year, but for the rest of his reign ruled through a shadowy sub-king known as Kandalanu.

Elam continued to support the anti-Assyrian activities of the Chaldeans, headed by Merodach-baladan's grandson, Nabu-bel-shumati, until it drove Ashurbanipal to seek a final solution. Between 642 and 639 BC the Assyrian army marched through the whole of Elam, devastating its cities, capturing and looting the capital, Susa, and carrying off its deities to Assyria. The sanctuaries were desecrated, and the tombs of the Elamite kings violated, in order that punishment might follow them after death, their ghosts being made to suffer the horror of restlessness and thirst from lack of the accustomed food-offerings and libations. Many senior administrators together with the whole royal family in all its branches were taken prisoner to Assyria, whilst specialized fighting units were incorporated into the Assyrian army. Many of the common population were also deported, together with vast herds of cattle and horses. Ashurbanipal summed up what he had done to Elam: 'I left his fields empty of the voice of mankind, the tread of cattle and sheep, the merry shout of harvest-home; I made them a lair for wild asses, gazelles, and all kinds of wild beasts.'

The king of Elam was no longer in a position to protect the Chaldean leader, and when Ashurbanipal demanded his surrender, Nabu-bel-shumati, like king Saul (1 Samuel 31:4–5), ordered his armour-bearer to kill him. The Elamite king sent the body to Ashurbanipal, preserved in salt; unable to inflict punishment on the living man, the vindictive monarch avenged himself on his victim's ghost by refusing the body burial.

Some Arabs had also played a part in the Babylonian revolt. They were not forgotten. Between 641 and 638 BC an Assyrian army defeated the tribes and captured the principal leaders, two of whom were chained to dog kennels at one of the great gates of Nineveh.

The downfall of Assyria

The inscriptions of Ashurbanipal do not extend beyond 639 BC, and we are ill-informed on the remainder of his reign. We know the year of his death from the funerary monument of the mother of a later king, which traces her life in terms of the regnal years of earlier kings and gives the end of Ashurbanipal's reign as his forty-second regnal year, which would be 627 BC. He was succeeded briefly by his son, Ashur-etillu-ili, and then by another son, Sin-shar-ishkun, who reigned until 612 BC. But the major figure in this period was a Chaldean leader, Nabopolassar, who seized the kingship of Babylonia in late 626 BC and later entered into alliance with the Medes – now a single kingdom under Cyaxares – in an alliance against Assyria.

Assyria was not entirely without allies. The Mannaeans

Assyrian scribes recording enemy dead

gave active support to their former suzerain, and even in Babylonian cities there were adherents of Assyria until the final fall of Nineveh; this was particularly marked in Erech, where it seems that a pro-Assyrian revolt broke out as late as 614 BC. Above all, Egypt offered powerful military support. The Egyptians had an interest in stability and would not wish to see Syria and north Mesopotamia under the entirely new dispensation which Median control would have represented. Furthermore, there was the menace of the wandering hordes of the north, the Cimmerians, the Scythians, and various other nomadic tribes of Indo-European origin; and Assyria, with its military prestige won over the centuries, appeared to be the only reliable bulwark against this tide of barbarism. Jeremiah's reference in 626 BC to seeing 'a seething cauldron; and the face thereof is from the north' (Jeremiah 1:13) is generally taken as referring to an expected invasion by those dreaded nomads.

By 617 BC, Nabopolassar had cleared all Assyrian garrisons out of Babylonia. Now – to judge by his subsequent actions – he decided that his control of Babylonia would not be assured without destroying Assyria. But a frontal assault on the powerful Assyrian army in its own bases would have been military madness, and Nabopolassar settled for a series of probing piecemeal attacks. He first marched against Assyrian territories on the middle Euphrates, but after initial successes retreated at the approach of the Assyrian army reinforced by Egyptian troops. The Assyrian forces, instead of pursuing, moved eastwards to invade Babylonia from east of the Tigris, but Nabopolassar anticipated this and met them south of the Lesser Zab and forced them to retire.

Early in 615 BC, an over-bold attack upon Ashur, the ancient capital, almost brought disaster upon Nabopolassar, who was forced to retreat to the citadel of the town known then, as now, as Takrit. But Nabopolassar had been working with diplomacy as well as war, and the Medes were now actively on his side. The Assyrians, instead of pressing their advantage, withdrew, presumably because their intelligence system had given them information of an incipient Median attack, which was actually made in eastern Assyria later in the year, to establish bases for an assault upon Nineveh itself. In 614 BC the Medes closed in to attack metropolitan Assyria, and took both Tarbisu (modern Sherikhan, only nine miles north-west of Nineveh) and Ashur. Nabopolassar arrived in Ashur at the head of his army, and the common action of the Medes and Chaldeans was sealed by a formal treaty between Nabopolassar and Cyaxares, ratified, according to later tradition, by marriage alliances.

With the Medes denying the military route east of the Tigris to the Assyrian strategists, the imperial power in 613 BC counter-attacked down the Euphrates. This brought out the tribal peoples along the middle Euphrates in revolt against Nabopolassar, threatening his bases; and whilst Nabopolassar was undertaking siege operations against the tribesmen, an Assyrian army appeared and forced him to retire. It is curious that the Medes, so spectacularly successful the previous year, were now inactive, leaving Assyria free to deploy an army at a distance from the homeland. Probably the restraint upon the Medes was fear of an attack from the Scythians. The Scythians, although a potential menace to any of the settled peoples of the Near East, had often had friendly relations with Assyria since their first appearance in the north in the time of Esarhaddon; they constituted a potential ally of great strength, and Assyria would not have failed to attempt to secure their assistance now. Traditions in later Greek writers suggest that the Medes were at one time seriously threatened by the Scythians but finally induced the leaders to make common cause with them. In the Babylonian cuneiform sources the northern nomads are referred to not as Scythians but as Ummanmanda, a term which seems to have meant much the same as 'hordes'. The Ummanmanda undoubtedly contained Scythian elements, and it seems probable that until Cyaxares had won over the most influential leaders of the Ummanmanda coalition of tribes, there was doubt as to which side it would take.

In 612 BC Nabopolassar, the Ummanmanda and Cyaxares effected a junction and marched to Nineveh. After a siege of three months the city fell, its last king, Sin-shar-ishkun, dying – according to Greek tradition – in the flames of its destruction, although this detail may simply mirror the fate of Shamash-shum-ukin earlier. Nineveh was sacked and looted and the survivors enslaved. Traditions in Greek authors and the Bible (Nahum 1:8) assert, credibly, that the capture of this powerfully fortified city was made possible by a flood – probably of the tributary Khosr rather than the Tigris – which swept away a section of the defences.

The capital was destroyed, but a nominal kingdom of Assyria still stood. Those of the Assyrian army who escaped from Nineveh fled a hundred miles westwards to Harran, where Ashur-uballit, a junior member of the royal family, was made king, and called upon his Egyptian allies.

6

The Neo-Babylonian Empire

LADEN with the loot of the imperial city, the forces of the Medes and the Ummanmanda retired. Nabopolassar's efforts were now directed to securing as much as possible of the Assyrian empire, to which end he occupied the Nisibin region west of Assyria, central Assyria itself and the provinces along the middle Euphrates. In the areas further north, the entrenched interests of the Scythians prevented Nabopolassar from gaining permanent control anywhere except in Cilicia. The remnant of the Assyrian army was left unattacked at Harran, possibly because Nabopolassar's most urgent concern was to establish a claim to as much of Assyria as possible before the return of the Ummanmanda. Their return in 610 BC brought an attack upon Harran, in which Nabopolassar joined. Ashur-uballit withdrew southwestwards to await Egyptian reinforcements, and on their arrival returned to mount a counter-attack upon Harran. This had some initial success, but the approach of an army under Nabopolassar compelled the Assyrian and Egyptian forces to withdraw to Carchemish.

At this point there was a change of king in Egypt. The new king, Necho II (610–595 BC), decided upon more vigorous measures in support of Ashur-uballit, and led the main Egyptian army into Syria (2 Chronicles 35:21). The outcome shows the success of Chaldean diplomacy in Palestine: Necho had to put down a rising in Gaza (Jeremiah 47:1), and Josiah of Judah, the principal remaining native ruler in Palestine, attempted to harry the Egyptian forces on their way northwards. Josiah was defeated and killed at Megiddo (608 BC; 2 Kings 23:29), his kingdom temporarily becoming a vassal of Egypt. Despite this hindrance, Necho had no difficulty in subduing Syria, and making a junction with Ashur-uballit's forces at Carchemish. But now came disaster. Under Nabopolassar's son, Nebuchadnezzar, the Babylonians made a direct attack upon the powerful Egyptian army (605 BC). There was heavy slaughter on both sides – 'the mighty man hath stumbled against the mighty, they are fallen both of them together' (Jeremiah 46:12) – but the Egyptian army had the worst of the engagement and according to Jeremiah 46:5 bolted in panic for Egypt. The propaganda effect of the Egyptian defeat was felt far and wide, and the subject peoples recognized that it was too late to resist the Chaldeans: 'Pharaoh king of Egypt is but a noise,' they said; 'he hath let the appointed time pass by' (Jeremiah 46:17). Nebuchadnezzar pursued the retreating Egyptians to their own borders, and might well have continued into Egypt but for the death at this moment of his father Nabopolassar, which demanded his presence in Babylon.

Nebuchadnezzar

Nebuchadnezzar's ability as a statesman and military commander have made him one of the most notable figures of the ancient world. His contemporary, Jeremiah, quickly recognized that he was the new power in international politics, and with fair accuracy estimated the duration of his empire as three generations (Jeremiah 27:7). Jehoiakim, the king of Judah appointed by Necho of Egypt, made submission to Nebuchadnezzar at his defeat of the Egyptian army, but returned to allegiance to Egypt when the time appeared opportune. Events proved, however, that Jeremiah had appraised the situation more wisely than the politicians, for in 597 BC Nebuchadnezzar sent forces to besiege Jerusalem. Jehoiakim had the good fortune to die during the siege, and it was his son, Jehoiachin, who was taken captive to Babylon, together with the nobility, craftsmen and troops (2 Kings 24:10–16).

With the whole of Palestine and Syria once more in the hands of a hostile power, Egypt's trade, which depended largely upon the Phoenician ports, was bound to suffer. This may explain the decision of Hophra (Apries) of Egypt (589–570 BC), mentioned in Jeremiah 44:30, to invade Palestine. The Egyptian forces had some preliminary success. They took Sidon, and in Jerusalem and elsewhere Babylonian garrisons had to withdraw, leaving anti-Babylonian statesmen in control. As Jeremiah foresaw, Nebuchadnezzar reacted strongly, dispatching a powerful army to the west. The Egyptians made a hurried withdrawal, leaving their erstwhile vassals to be dealt with piecemeal by the Babylonian forces. Jerusalem was blockaded for eighteen months, and finally starved out (586 BC). Zedekiah, the last king of Judah, was blinded and taken captive by Babylon (2 Kings 25:7); Jerusalem was looted, sacked and de-fortified; the leaders of the anti-Babylonian party were put to death; a pro-Babylonian nobleman was appointed governor; and a section of the remaining population was deported to Babylonia (2 Kings 25:9–11). Other rebel cities were successively subdued, and the great port of Tyre was put under siege. According to Menander (342–292 BC), the siege of Tyre lasted thirteen years. Ezekiel, a contemporary of the event, also refers to it (Ezekiel 26–29). He first pictures Tyre as gloating over the fall of Jerusalem: 'I shall be replenished, now that she is laid waste' (26:22), a reference to the fact that trade between Egypt and regions to the north could go either by caravan through Palestine or by sea into the Phoenician ports. The trading ventures and the commercial wealth of Tyre are then graphically described:

> Tarshish [Tarsus in Asia Minor] was thy merchant by reason of the multitude of all kinds of riches. . . . Javan [Greece], Tubal and Meshech [Tabalu and Mushki of the Assyrian sources, in Asia Minor], they were thy traffickers. . . . They of the house of

> Togormah [Til-garimmu of the Assyrian sources, in Asia Minor] traded for thy wares with horses and war-horses and mules. The men of Dedan were thy traffickers: . . . they brought thee in exchange horns of ivory and ebony. Syria was thy merchant by reason of the multitude of thy handyworks. . . . The traffickers of Sheba [in Arabia], Asshur and Chilmad . . . were thy traffickers in choice wares. (Ezekiel 27:12–16, 23–24)

The city of Tyre was finally taken in 571 BC and a Babylonian administration set up there.

Meanwhile Cyaxares had completely overrun Urartu (Armenia) and pushed into Asia Minor, where he came into contact with the kingdom of Lydia. Initial conflict of interest was settled in 585 BC by a treaty mediated by Nabu-na'id (Nabonidus), an officer and later a successor of Nebuchadnezzar.

Nebuchadnezzar maintained friendly relations with the Medes, and his main problem in foreign politics was Egypt. There were economic as well as military reasons for his concern in the west. Babylonian trade eastwards was adversely affected by the Medes' control of Iran, and this led the Neo-Babylonian kings to turn increasingly to try to capture the routes coming northwards from Arabia. Egypt, however, consistently opposed attempts at Babylonian expansion in the west. 2 Kings 25:22–26 tells of the murder of the native governor of Jerusalem appointed by Nebuchadnezzar, and since the assassins fled to Egypt, this was evidently with the approval, if not at the actual instigation, of the Egyptians. Eventually this drove Nebuchadnezzar to undertake an invasion of Egypt, as a fragment of cuneiform tablet shows; Ezekiel 29:19–21 also refers to this, but no further details are known. Traditions in Jeremiah 49:28 and Herodotus refer to a successful attack on the Arab tribes of the desert.

Nebuchadnezzar's reign was a time of great building activity in Babylonia, and the extant remains of Babylon (see plates 4B and 6) are substantially from his period. He strengthened the fortifications of the city by rebuilding massive inner and outer walls, which, with the river and a chain of fortresses north and south of Babylon, constituted a powerful defence system round the capital.

Successors of Nebuchadnezzar

At Nebuchadnezzar's death in 562 BC he was succeeded by his son Amel-marduk (Evil-Merodach of 2 Kings 25:27 and Jeremiah 52:31), who reigned only two years before he was killed in a revolution. Little is known of him beyond the statement in 2 Kings 25:27–30 that he showed special favour to Jehoiachin, one of the two ex-kings of Judah held at Babylon: curiously enough, there is a direct reference to Jehoiachin in some cuneiform tablets found at Babylon. These tablets are lists of ration issues, and the relevant part of one of them reads:

> For Ya'u-kina king of the land Yahuda, for the five sons of the king of the land of Yahuda, and for eight Yahudaeans, each ½ sila (of corn).

Ya'u-kina of Yahuda is unmistakably the name which our Bible translators render Jehoiachin of Judah.

The man who benefited by the death of Amel-marduk was Nergal-shar-usur (Neriglissar of Greek sources, Nergal-sharezer of Jeremiah 39:3), a son-in-law of Nebuchadnezzar. He undertook a major campaign beyond the Taurus, probably in anticipation of a thrust by the Medes across the Halys. This ended in defeat, and he returned to Babylon in 556 BC, dying so soon afterwards that one is tempted to wonder if his rivals at home took advantage of his loss of prestige to hasten his end. Certainly his son, Labashi-marduk, who attempted to assume the throne in succession, was very shortly removed by a rebellion of the chief officers of state, who put on the throne Nabu-na'id (Nabonidus), the diplomatist who had assisted negotiations between the Medes and Lydians in 585 BC.

Nabu-na'id was not of the royal house of Nabopolassar but was the son of a nobleman and of the high-priestess of the god

Sin at Harran: his mother may, however, have been of the Assyrian royal family, for she was born in the middle of the reign of Ashurbanipal, and before and after this time high-priestesses of the great shrines were commonly princesses of royal blood.

It was once customary to dismiss Nabu-na'id as a learned antiquary, 'never happier than when he could excavate some ancient foundation-stone', but it is now clear that he was a statesman of high ability. He recognized that there were two main problems to be faced: one was the economic difficulties of the empire; the other concerned religion. The Babylonians were now in close contact with the Medes and the Jews, and amongst both these peoples new religious ideas and ethical conceptions were afoot, implying derision of the ancient polytheistic idolatry. It is likely that it was in response to this situation, and the inadequacy he recognized in the old polytheism, that Nabu-na'id now attempted to make the Moon-god, Sin or Nanna, who was the deity both of Ur and of his mother's city of Harran, into the supreme god of the empire. This is not to be thought of as a movement towards monotheism; rather, it was an attempt to provide a reformed type of Babylonian religion which would be acceptable to all the subject peoples. The supreme Babylonian deity, Marduk, an old Sumerian Sun-god specifically associated with the city of Babylon, had no place in the pantheon of the Arabians and Aramaeans; it was otherwise with the Moon-god, who, under various names, was highly honoured by these peoples.

A point at which the economic and religious problems met was the city of Harran. The very name means 'road', and was applied to the place because it was the great meeting-point of the routes northwestwards from Babylonia on the one side and from Egypt, Arabia, Palestine, Anatolia and Asia Minor on the other. It also housed one of the great shrines of the god Sin, which the Ummanmanda had destroyed when they captured the city in 610 BC. Nabu-na'id's inscriptions relate that in his first year of reign the great god Sin (in another version promulgated in Babylonia he tactfully adds the name of Babylon's god, Marduk) appeared to him in a dream saying: 'Make haste and rebuild Ehulhul ["House of great joy"], Sin's temple in Harran, since all lands are committed to your hands.' In the version from Babylon Nabu-na'id then points out to Marduk: 'The Ummanmanda surround (that temple), and their strength is formidable.' Marduk makes the surprising reply: 'The Ummanmanda that you mention, they, their land and the kings their allies no longer exist. In the third year coming I shall make Cyrus king of Anshan [i.e. Persia], his petty servant, expel them.'

The Persians were one of the migratory Indo-Aryan tribes, who had ultimately settled in Elam. Their royal family was founded in the middle of the seventh century, after Ashurbanipal had knocked out the old Elamite dynasty, by Achaemenes (Hahmanish), whose son took the title 'King of Anshan', Anshan being originally one of the princedoms of the kingdom of Elam. The rising power of the Persians led the Median king Astyages to give a daughter in marriage to Cambyses I, the third king of Anshan, and from this marriage Cyrus was born.

In the account of Nabu-na'id's dream, the Ummanmanda referred to were a garrison controlled by the Medes. The dream shows (if we may take it as reflecting political developments on the human plane) that the old tradition of diplomatic relations between the ruling houses of Babylonia and Elam still continued, since evidently Nabu-na'id and Cyrus were intriguing together for united action against the Medes in Nabu-na'id's third year, 553 BC.

Nabu-na'id ordered a general levy of troops from the western provinces. The Medes, occupied with the insurrection of Cyrus, withdrew from Harran, and Nabu-na'id was able to commence the projected work of restoration. But this brought insurrection in the great cities of Babylonia: 'The sons of Babylon, Borsippa, Nippur, Ur, Erech, Larsa and the people of the cities of Akkad [north Babylonia] . . . forgot their duty and talked treason.' There is evidence that Nabu-na'id had been preparing for something of this kind. He owned large estates in south Babylonia, and contracts from temple archives prove that at the very beginning of his reign he was leasing these to the administrative authorities of Eanna, the great and wealthy temple corporation of Erech. Administrative reforms were made in the temples at this time, and at Erech there were new appointments to all the senior posts in the early years of Nabu-na'id's reign.

Famine now appeared in Babylonia, attributed by Nabu-na'id to the impiety of the people, although more soberly traceable to general economic conditions. The withdrawal of manpower for years at a time from productive labour on canals to unproductive temple-building or war, as happened under Nebuchadnezzar and Neriglissar, had brought a severe decline in agricultural production and also inflation. Although the rate of inflation averaged only about 5 per cent per annum, which is considered moderate in the modern world, this was disastrous in an ancient economy when it continued over decades, since a family which originally could just afford a subsistence diet would face starvation by the time food prices had doubled. The results are seen in the commercial documents. One such, dated in the first year of Nabu-na'id, relates to a loan of corn made to a herdsman whose cattle were starving. Other texts concern the handing over of children to the temples as slaves, an evident result of extreme hardship. The economic situation was further aggravated by the loss to the Medes of the trade routes to east and north.

In his inscriptions Nabu-na'id scarcely mentions the economic aspects of his undertakings, but this is simply explained: royal inscriptions were in the main intended to be read by the gods, not humans, and it was therefore reasonable for the king to claim piety rather than economic benefit as the mainspring for what he did. But commercial and administrative documents prove beyond doubt that he was aware of economic problems.

Nabu-na'id's response to the situation in Babylonia was an attempt to move the centre of gravity of the empire westwards and secure the trade routes from south Arabia. Investing his son Bel-shar-usur (Belshazzar of Daniel 5:22; 7:1; 8:1) as regent of Babylonia, he led an army through Syria to the oasis of Teima in northwest Arabia, which he made his base for the next ten years. During this period he pushed 250 miles further southwards until he finally reached Yathrib, deep in Arabia, the Muslim Medina, the city of Muhammad. He states that he established garrisons as colonies around six oases on the way there, and described his forces as 'the people of Akkad and of Hatti-land', that is, both Babylonians and people from the western provinces. It is a fascinating side-issue that a thousand years later, at the time of Muhammad, five of these six oases were occupied by Jews. The conclusion can hardly be avoided that amongst the troops and colonists accompanying Nabu-na'id was a strong contingent of Jews.

This ten-year withdrawal of Nabu-na'id from his capital may well be the basis of the tale of the seven years of madness ascribed to Nebuchadnezzar in Daniel 4:28–33: it often happens that traditions properly relating to one man are transferred to a more famous person with whom he was historically associated. Another form of the same Jewish tradition of divine wrath upon a Neo-Babylonian king – though in this case linked specifically with Nabu-na'id rather than Nebuchadnezzar – has appeared amongst the documents from Qumran, the so-called 'Dead Sea Scrolls'.

The document concerned dates from the second half of the first century BC, and is a fragment of a manuscript written in Aramaic (a language akin to Hebrew and employed for parts of Daniel and Ezra). It reads:

> The words of the prayer which Nabu-na'i(d), king of Assyria and Babylon, the great king, prayed when he was infected with a nasty skin disease by the ordinance of God Most High in the city of Teima: 'I was infected with a nasty skin disease for seven years. . . . But when I confessed my sins and my faults, He granted me a (favourable) verdict. And there was a Jew . . . , and he wrote and told (me) to give honour . . . to the name of God Most High.'

At the end of the ten years at Teima, conditions had so changed that Nabu-na'id, now at least sixty-five and probably more than seventy years old, was able to return to Babylonia. The temporary improvement in the position of Nabu-na'id may have been linked with the fortunes of his rising erstwhile ally Cyrus, king of the Medes and Persians; he had become involved in war with Croesus of Lydia in Asia Minor, and this had temporarily removed any risk of Cyrus expanding into Babylonia. But in 547 BC Cyrus defeated Croesus, and made Lydia into a Persian province. This left him free to embark upon operations against the Babylonian empire, which he began in the same year, when he gained control of part of eastern Assyria. It is reasonable to assume that it was the military threat from the east which produced a temporary unity in Babylonia and a call for the return and active leadership of the king.

The end of independent Babylonia

Southern Babylonia has always been subject to raids from Elam, and it suffered another in 546 BC. But the situation was by no means desperate: Erech, the main city of the south, remained securely in Nabu-na'id's hands, Syria and the west gave no evidence of disaffection, and one may infer from Herodotus that Egypt was a potential ally. However, whilst the aged king was continuing his restoration of the temple Ehulhul in Harran, Cyrus was engaged in propaganda throughout the Babylonian empire. His action towards the defeated Croesus, whom he treated with kindness and respect, and towards the Greek oracles of Asia Minor, which he forbore to plunder, gained him a reputation for clemency and religious tolerance, which is reflected in the Book of Isaiah. The anonymous prophet commonly known as Deutero-Isaiah (Isaiah 40–55) claims to speak for the Lord 'to his anointed, to Cyrus, whose right hand I have holden, to subdue nations before him . . .', saying 'For Jacob my servant's sake, and Israel my chosen, I have called thee by thy name: I have surnamed thee, though thou hast not known me' (Isaiah 45:1, 4). Similar propaganda must have been fermenting in Babylon, and is reflected in the venomous compositions written upon Nabu-na'id at his fall. The following is a translation of such a text, unfortunately very damaged, referring to Nabu-na'id:

. . . he did not cause justice to come forth from him.
. . . he killed the weak with a weapon;
. . . he obstructed the road for the merchant,

and in his religious reforms

. . . he formed a phantom;
He formed the image of a god that no one had ever seen in the land;
He set it on a dais within the temple;
. . . he called its name 'Moon-God'.
. . .
He used to interfere with the rites, and upset the order of things;
He would make utterance against the divinely-decreed order.

Cyrus gradually thrust forward over the Zagros mountains into the regions east of the Tigris. He forced a crossing of the Tigris at Opis, north of where Baghdad now stands, and marched upon Sippar, which surrendered. Babylon itself was then attacked, and submitted with scarcely a struggle. Herodotus attributes this to the Persian stratagem of breaching the Euphrates, which constituted one side of the defences of the city, to render it temporarily fordable. But the real reason for the collapse of the city's defences was the presence within it of a 'fifth column'. Nabu-na'id's attempt to question the supremacy of Marduk had bequeathed him a legacy of discontent. The propaganda of Cyrus had found fertile ground amongst the citizens of Babylon, and they gladly transferred allegiance to the liberal-minded Persian king. He allowed the city to be neither sacked nor looted, and without disturbing either the religious institutions or the civil administration he appointed a Persian representative as governor. Cyrus' own son, Cambyses, officiated on his behalf at the New Year Festival in Babylon. According to one interpretation of a damaged text, there was a hitch in the ceremony: it could not proceed because Cambyses was not wearing the prescribed vestments. But the problem was resolved and Cambyses duly performed the royal ritual: henceforth the dynasty of Cyrus held kingship over Babylonia not only by right of conquest but also by divine vocation.

So came to an end the last of the ancient native dynasties in Babylonia and Assyria. Achaemenid (Persian) rule continued until 331 BC, after which for the remainder of the pre-Christian period Mesopotamia was successively in the hands of Seleucids (Greeks) and Arsacids (Parthians). Many parts of Mesopotamia had been under temporary foreign domination before, but the Achaemenid conquest came when new forces were being increasingly felt in the Near East and the two-millennia-old civilization of Babylonia was, irrespective of political considerations, dying. We have already noticed the growing sense of the inadequacy of the old Babylonian polytheism, and apart from Nabu-na'id's attempts at reform there is evidence from as early as the New Assyrian period of a conscious questioning of some ancient religious concepts, and a rejection of old religious values.

Moreover, since the turn of the millennium Aramaean influence had been penetrating Babylonia ever more strongly, both in social institutions and in language. In the former, by emphasizing tribal organization, it had tended to weaken the dominance of the city; in the latter, Aramaic had the advantage of being the native tongue of a much more widely-spread ethnic group than was Akkadian, whilst for writing purposes the script of the West Semitic alphabet, with its twenty-two letters, was a far easier vehicle of communication than cuneiform Akkadian, with hundreds of signs. Even when Akkadian cuneiform on clay tablets was still the usual vehicle for legal documents, Aramaic writing was sometimes used as a more convenient way of endorsing such tablets for filing purposes. Only the learned could, after many years' study, ever master the use of Akkadian cuneiform; and it was amongst the learned that cuneiform writing remained in use for scholarly and esoteric purposes for some centuries more. By 140 BC it had completely disappeared except amongst a few priests who employed it for religious purposes for another half-century, and amongst astronomers. For astronomical texts cuneiform continued in use right down to the time of Christ, and if there were indeed Three Wise Men from the east, they could well have been consulting cuneiform texts.

7

The Foundations of the Babylonian Way of Life

TWO basic problems face us in examining any human society. Firstly, what provides the cohesion which makes its members live together and cooperate in groups wider than the family? Secondly, what factors enable a minority to enjoy a disproportionate share of wealth and power, and lead the majority to accept this situation? Because ancient Mesopotamia is the ultimate point of origin of our own civilization, the answers to these questions about life in south Iraq five thousands years ago are not without relevance for us now.

There is no single source to give us answers. There are texts from about 2500 BC to tell us of the situation as it had developed, but there are none to tell us directly how that stage had been reached. We have to build up the picture from a combination of evidence. Mesopotamian civilization was essentially irrigation-based, and irrigation works bring changes in the landscape, in the ecology and eventually in the structure of society. Details of the effects of irrigation elsewhere can give us hints as to what is likely to have happened in early south Iraq. Myths are another source of information. They often reflect circumstances of life between prehistory and history, and, used with due caution, can tell us something of early conditions in Mesopotamia. Trends that we see under way in historical times can provide pointers for what is likely to have happened earlier. And archaeology may offer valuable data, particularly about settlement patterns, the development of cities, and centres of wealth and power.

Family landholdings

Let us begin by imagining south Iraq as it was before human interference (see page 4). For thousands of years the Euphrates and Tigris had been depositing silt, flooding, changing course to leave numerous subsidiary channels, and leaking out in seepages. In consequence, much of the country was a swampy jungle, with vegetation ranging from reed-beds to extensive stands of willow and poplar, and full of birds, snakes and wild pigs; conditions much like these still hold in the undrained southern marshes today.

Amongst terrains ranging from swamp to desert, the earliest settlers would find some areas, particularly banks of former or current river channels, which were naturally irrigated and adequately drained, so that cereals could be grown on them. In such places villages would develop, with each family having a share of land and all on a parity. If they flourished, eventually the population would grow to the maximum that the naturally irrigated land could support. This would be a stimulus for digging ditches to drain areas that had hitherto been too wet or to bring water to those that had been too dry. But large-scale cutting of ditches would eventually produce major changes in the water flow at a distance from the main channels of the rivers. The result would be vastly to increase the original difference in productivity between different patches of land; at one extreme there would be large stretches that were well irrigated and fertile, and at the other extreme, areas that had been rendered arid by draining off the natural seepages that had formerly watered them. So long as the arable land newly created by irrigation kept pace with the increasing population, this might occasion no problem, but in a successful settlement the balance would not be maintained indefinitely. Apart from natural population increase, a flourishing centre would attract into it the populations of surrounding villages, and so would grow rapidly, whilst the villages around became deserted. This is not a guess; the archaeological evidence for the pattern of settlement around Erech shows this in progress.

A time would inevitably arrive in a successful and growing settlement when all available arable land had been taken up. Our knowledge of human nature makes it reasonable to suppose that the earliest families there would have taken all the best land, leaving the later comers to make do with poorer land or none. Theoretically this inequality could have been overcome by periodic redistribution of land, but there is no evidence for such a measure. The result would be that the families on the best land would prosper, those on inferior land would be relatively poor, and those with none would form a depressed group. Thus began the stratification of wealth.

Temple estates

There was another very early factor in the inequality of wealth in ancient Mesopotamia: religion. Any settlement needed a religious functionary for the rituals to mark events of particular significance to the community, such as births and deaths, or sowing and harvest, and to avert threatening omens. Thus every early Mesopotamian settlement would have a priest, who would receive a share of the best land and be in charge of the community's cultic building. In view of the calls on the priest's time for specialized functions in the cult, it is likely that the community would volunteer assistance in the cultivation of his land. Such assistance, originally voluntary, would quickly become prescriptive, and it would become accepted that the priest and temple were entitled to a staff of workers and further land to support them. Moreover, priests had a ready way of securing additional privileges from the community: any disaster – flood, crop failure, epidemic disease, attacks by wild animals, infertility – could be attributed to the anger of the god, only to be appeased by a donation to the temple. This opened the way for a rapid increase in the temple's wealth and power; we see this reflected archaeologically in the growth of the temple at Eridu from a chapel no more than ten feet square at the beginning of the *Ubaid* period to a splendid building on a platform with a columned portico at the dawn of history. By historical times we find that the temples are powerful and rich corporations, with huge estates and thousands of personnel.

There could be a substantial number of temple estates within a single city-state, which often comprised several major urban centres and was sometimes as large as a small English county. This multiplicity of temple estates derived from the various cult buildings of the prehistoric communities from which the city-state had evolved. The Sumerians had a great sense of order, and this led them to bring the different temple estates into a system. They customarily explained the relationship between them on a familial basis, the deity of the most powerful temple estate being the chief city god (or goddess), and deities of other temples being linked to the chief deity as his or her spouse or children.

The city-state administration and the city ruler

Sumerian myths suggest (see page 34) that the earliest form of political organization in Mesopotamia was what Th. Jacobsen called 'primitive democracy',[1] meaning a form of society in which power rested with an assembly of all adult citizens. The myths show a characteristic procedure for decision-making. All the deities, female as well as male, would assemble and drink together until the business was broached by a senior god. In the succeeding discussion, any deity might state a view, although there was a group of senior gods whose word carried particular weight. When a consensus emerged, two senior gods framed a decision and put it to the assembly; if they had correctly crystallized the general opinion, the members responded with a unanimous 'So-be-it'. Jacobsen saw this as a counterpart in myth of a Sumerian national assembly which, he argued, was held periodically at the central city of Nippur at the beginning of the third millennium. We would be less specific and take it as reflecting merely an early method of decision-making, with no particular localization. The senior gods who carried greater authority presumably reflected heads of families.

The assembly would need to make decisions on such matters as irrigation projects, land surveying and trade missions abroad, appointing individuals in charge. This would provide the nucleus of a city-state administration, at first under the control of the assembly, but, in the way bureaucrats have, gradually acquiring autonomy.

In the picture of society given by the epics, a significant development is the appearance of powerful city rulers. The epics reflect a period a century or two later than the myths, probably about 2800–2700 BC, when city fortifications were being built. Fortifications imply warfare, probably triggered by inter-city disputes over irrigated land and the control of trade routes. War creates a situation in which leadership has to be vested in a single person, and he, like other officials, would be chosen by the assembly. This again is not hypothetical: there is a reference to the assembly of the city of Kish choosing a king as late as 2300 BC; he took the throne-name Iphur-kish ('Kish assembled') to emphasize the popular basis of his rule.[2]

The epics depict the city ruler as still consulting the citizen body for advice, and it is probable that originally his authority was understood as subject to the consent of the assembly. But a person suitable for appointment as war-leader would be an able and forceful personality, unlikely willingly to relinquish power once given, and such persons would tend to become permanent kings set apart from their subjects.

This tendency was, at least in some city-states, enhanced by a religious consideration. With the Neolithic Revolution, man had in effect taken over from Nature responsibility for food supply; it was therefore essential that he should unfailingly ensure the fertility of the flocks and herds and fields. To achieve this he called on the help of the divine world, and did so in the most intimate way possible, by a festival in which fecundity was magically generated by supposed sexual union between the deity and a human. The human participant, male or female according to whether the chief city deity was a goddess or a god, was called the *En* and lived in a sacred building called the *giparu*, where the so-called Sacred Marriage took place. Well before the end of the third millennium the king, for reasons which will become clear, had taken over the Sacred Marriage role from the male *En*, leaving him simply as a high priest, but the female *En*, who was usually of royal birth, remained thought of as the wife of the god down to the first millennium.

This digression was necessary to explain how the role of the city ruler developed in early Sumer. Judging by later practice, the *En* was selected by omens: this made him, according to ancient thought, the choice not of the community but (in the case of a city-state like Erech whose supreme deity was a goddess) of the city goddess herself. In the nature of the situation he would be young and vigorous, and when the assembly needed to appoint a war-leader, they might well decide to appoint the *En*. We do in fact find that in several cases ancient epics derived from Erech mention the same man as both *En* and city ruler. Such a man, thought of as the human representative of the city deity, would have enormous authority in the city-state, and every opportunity of becoming a permanent king. Once kingship was firmly established, the Sacred Marriage role became associated with the king to the exclusion of the male *En*; where the city deity was male, this of course needed some adjustment of the concept. This was achieved by thinking of the king's role in the Sacred Marriage as representing the god in a sexual union with a priestess.

The interests of the three economic groupings in the third-millennium city-state – the city-state administration under the city ruler, the temple estates, and private landowning families – were not mutually exclusive nor necessarily opposed to each other. Conflicts of interest could and did occur, but they were limited. The most vulnerable group were the private landowners, subject to taxes by the state and various impositions by the temples. But such persons might, alongside their rights over family land, have interests in either or both of the other sectors; by the long-established position of such families in the community, they were likely to be of high status, and we know that consequently, in addition to their own land, they often held plots from the ruler of a temple estate, and served as officials within one of those power structures. The city ruler might sometimes seek to curb abuses of power by major temple estates, but he would be aware that the priesthood exercised religious sanctions – particularly the interpretation of omens – which could be used to undermine his own position. The temple authorities in turn well knew that economic stability, trade and freedom from invasion depended upon a powerful ruler backed by a sound administration. The mutual interdependence of the three structures was a force against violent change.

Landless citizens

In time there came to be a fourth group: citizens without land. Presumably originally all citizens belonged to landowning families, but one can envisage many paths by which a class of landless citizens might grow up. It might be by immigration of new population, by the gradual exclusion of younger sons of younger sons from a share in the family's land, by the voluntary choice of some citizens who preferred to use their professional skills full-time in the service of the king or a temple, or by pressures which compelled a family to sell its land. Such landless people necessarily became dependants of one of the other groups. We know most about this class in relation to those who became dependants of a temple.

Basically such people might either serve in various crafts or professional activities in return for maintenance, or cultivate plots on the temple lands as sharecroppers. There was a substantial degree of specialization and division of labour, and many different types of craftsmen and manual and professional workers are mentioned in the texts. Without attempting an exhaustive list, we may note such workers as bricklayers, carpenters, ropemakers, smiths and masons, spinners and weavers, butchers and cooks, brewers and bakers, potters, jewellers and hairdressers, in addition to those engaged on purely agricultural operations. The latter in turn were divided into specialized groups, and besides common labourers we meet ploughmen, shepherds, oxherds and swineherds, and gardeners who looked after date plantations and vegetable gardens. In some areas there were marshes abounding in waterfowl, and so we meet professional bird-catchers. Because fish was an important item of diet in the early period, there was need for fishermen in large numbers, and they are duly listed amongst temple personnel, the temple of the goddess Bau of Lagash alone having more than a hundred. They were divided into 'fresh water fishers', 'sea fishers', and 'fishers in salt waters', the last being those operating in the tidal lagoons of the delta of the Tigris and Euphrates. The same texts show that at the middle of the third millennium the whole working force of the estate of the goddess Bau amounted to about twelve hundred, not counting wives and children.

There is nowhere any indication that the landless dependants ever made any protest at their lot.[3] There are two factors which help to explain this. Firstly, whilst there may have been individual abuses, as a class they were not oppressed. They received adequate rations and maintenance, and, to judge by occasional references to industrial strikes (see page 357), there were mechanisms for ensuring that they were not grossly overworked and exploited. The other factor was the force of religion. During the early third millennium the whole city-state, not simply those parts actually owned by temple states, became thought of as the estate of the city-god, with all the inhabitants his servants and the ruler or priest-king his steward. Myths developed to reflect and reinforce this view of life. It was held that the very purpose for which man was created was to work for the gods, and several myths develop this theme. The ancient Mesopotamians recognized that the primeval earth was no Garden of Eden producing its crops without labour, and they concluded that before the creation of man the gods themselves had had to bear the toil:

> At that time the pure water coming out of the earth did not irrigate the fields,
> . . . .
> And because of this the gods of the land were in servitude,
> Bearing the mattock and the dirt-basket.[4]

The gods did not like this situation. One Akkadian myth, *Atrahasis*, relates how objectionable the junior gods found the work of making the earth fertile:

> When the gods like men
> Bore the labour, suffered the toil,
> The toil of the gods was great indeed,
> The labour was heavy, the distress was severe.
> . . . .
> They kept complaining and laying blame,
> They grumbled about the work of excavation.

So troublesome did it become to the gods who bore the brunt of the toil, that they went on strike and burnt their tools:

> They set their tools on fire.
> They set fire to their mattocks
> And put their baskets aflame.[5]

They then marched on the residence of the divine chief executive, Enlil, and compelled him to call the two other senior gods for negotiations. To allay the trouble, the senior gods decided to create man to take over the labour which had formerly been the lot of the junior gods. They summoned a goddess named Mami, and instructed her:

Create Prototype Man (*lullu*),[6] that he may bear the yoke;
. . . .
Let Man (*awilum*) bear the toil of the gods.

Another myth, this one Sumerian, illustrates the same idea. The god Enlil separated Heaven from Earth, and bound up Earth's wound at the former point of juncture, the city of Nippur, whose main temple was called Duranki, 'Bond of Heaven and Earth'. This done, Enlil

. . . drove his pick into the 'flesh-producer' [the ground];
In the hole was the vanguard of mankind;
As (the people of) his land broke through the ground towards Enlil,
He eyed his Black-headed Ones [humans] in steadfast fashion
The Anunnaki [one of the two main groups in the pantheon] stepped up to him, . . .
Black-headed Ones they requested of him.

Slaves

Below the landless citizens in the social scale there were slaves. During the *Early Dynastic* period slaves were not a very significant social element; they never became a majority in the population and the work of the community was never dependent upon them. In the earliest times slaves were obtained by raids into the hill country, for which reason the ideogram for 'slave girl' is a compound of the signs for 'woman' and 'mountain'. Prisoners of war also were made slaves.

We do not know precisely at what period it became possible for native citizens to lose their freedom, but from the III Ur period (*c.* 2100 BC) cases are known of free citizens being reduced to slavery either by selling themselves because of debt or hunger, by being seized by creditors, or by being sold as children by poverty-stricken parents. Such procedures had become very common two hundred years later; a factor contributing to this may have been economic hardships resulting from Amorite invasion. By the period of the First Dynasty of Babylon, the laws of Hammurabi imply that the main source of slaves was importation from abroad in the way of commerce, rather than as prisoners of war.

In the third millennium female slaves seem to have been more numerous than male, and apart from the obvious use for the young and fair their main occupation was in the temple mills and in the workshops where spinning and weaving were carried out. In the *Early Dynastic* period almost all slaves were owned by the temples or the palace, being housed in barracks in labour gangs; but private ownership of slaves gradually developed, so that by the first millennium BC the average household in Babylonia owned two or three. Although female slaves might normally be used as concubines, sometimes a girl sold into slavery was safeguarded by a provision in the sale contract that she should be married to a husband, normally another slave, although the husband could be a free man. Such a provision could even be extended to cover remarriage several times if the first and subsequent husbands died.

Because free men could fall into slavery, slavery in Babylonia was never a caste system, and marriage between a free woman and a slave was by no means uncommon. A slave could acquire property, with which (if his master were agreeable) he could buy his own freedom: at the death of a slave, however, his property passed to his master.

There seems to be no proof that slaves carried any distinctive mark in the third millennium, but from Old Babylonian times and perhaps earlier they were identified by a distinctive tonsure. There was also often some kind of mark, either tattooed or branded on the face or the back of the hand. Such markings would be more likely on a slave with known runaway tendencies, and such a one could be fettered and have the words 'A fugitive, arrest him!' incised on his face. We also find mention of a slave with the name of his owner written in two languages on the back of his hand. Marking was most commonly met with amongst a class of temple personnel prominent in the first millennium. These were persons dedicated to the temples, who included not only state prisoners of war and donated slaves, but also people of free birth, such as rescued waifs and children of poor parents who had been handed over in times of famine to save them from starvation.

The pattern of Sumerian society

The circumstances of the first half of the third millennium BC, the *Early Dynastic* period, when Sumerian civilization was taking its characteristic shape, laid their imprint upon the next two thousand years. Despite development, decay, and changes in many details, Sumerian institutions were so well established that in many aspects of life they remained as long as Babylonian civilization endured. To the very end, Babylonian civilization retained a Sumerian framework and many details characteristic of the earliest times.

As we have seen, Sumero-Babylonian life was founded upon irrigation. The city-state arose from the joint effort of large numbers of people of diverse origin in a form of cooperation transcending the family, clan or language group; and as a corollary it was upon the city-state and not upon the family, clan or language group that the social structure was based. When, in several subsequent periods, tribal peoples entered Mesopotamia, they did not fit into the existing structure unless or until they made a radical change in their way of life.

The rise of the irrigation-based state led to developments in many other directions. Those with access to the irrigation system had to accept control in its use, since one man's reckless opening of a watercourse might well wreak havoc on the land of his neighbours. This made it necessary to lay down rules for the use of irrigation channels and to ensure that they were observed. This was one of the factors which gave rise to written legislation, an administrative system, and the creation of an embryonic police system in the form of the canal inspector (Akkadian *gugallu*). The bursting of the banks of the rivers at the time of the spring floods – a constant threat right up to the middle of the twentieth century AD – might obliterate old boundary marks of fields; this was an obvious stimulus to the development of mensuration and, through it, of geometry. The constant need to struggle against the waters had its influence in mythology, where the primeval being, finally overcome by the great gods her children, was Tiamat, the Sea. The behaviour of the rivers, sometimes beneficent, sometimes harmful, seemed arbitrary. Their rise, which depends on the melting of the snows in the mountains of Armenia and in the case of the Tigris on the spring rainfall in the drainage basins of the two Zab rivers, was to the Sumerians unpredictable; and when floods occurred, it was just before harvest at a time potentially disastrous for the crops: this element of perennial anxiety is reflected in Sumerian religion, and the whole later Babylonian way of looking at life.

Sumerian cities as they first developed were enclaves within marsh, jungle or desert, but the rivers ensured good communications between them, so that from the very beginning there was a marked cultural unity throughout the land. This is shown, for example, by a uniform architecture; the ziggurat, or great stepped tower, became, and in some cases remains (see plates 3A, 3B and 4A), the most striking landmark of the Sumerian or later Babylonian city. Uniformity was also shown in common political and religious institutions, and by the fact that writing, once invented, was rapidly diffused through all Sumer, not only as a general principle but in its details; lists of signs in the different cities are substantially the same, with only minor variations.

Irrigated land in south Iraq is highly productive and from the early third millennium onwards the temple estates usually produced considerably more grain than was needed for their personnel and seedcorn. Much of the surplus would normally be exported, but the temple granaries formed a valuable reserve for the community against shortages in the months before the new harvest or against crop failure at any time; this parallels the Pharaoh's storing of grain against an expected famine in the story of Joseph (Genesis 41:33–36). Loans of grain by Sumero-Babylonian temples in times of shortage were not necessarily wholly philanthropic: such loans to small private landowners brought the likelihood that eventually heavy indebtedness would force such citizens to surrender their land to the temple and become clients.

The temple magazines, which can still be recognized in the ruins of a number of excavated sites, contained a wide range of supplies, and the temple precincts must be thought of as a hive of commercial activity. Here were brought all the products of the temple lands – corn, vegetables and dried fish, cheese, dates, onions, linseed[7] for the production of oil, wool, skins for tanners, and reeds for building purposes. Some of these (notably corn, oil and wool) were issued as rations to the people of the god's estates, whilst others were either used in the service of the temple as they were or worked up into manufactured products. Some were destined for export. Sumer lacked three important raw materials: timber (except the date-palm, Euphrates poplar and willow, none of them of use for building), stone and metals; and from earliest days these had to be obtained from abroad, the principal trade routes being opened up in *Early Dynastic* times. As early as *c.* 2800–2700 BC, the period with which the *Enmerkar* epic deals, trading caravans passed between Sumer and the mountains of Iran laden with barley from the surplus of the fertile plains and returning with lapis lazuli, carnelian and other semi-precious stones for the beautification of the temples. Exports other than grain included woollen textiles and Sumerian manufactures such as tools and weapons. The merchant or caravan leader was a respected member of society, with an allotment of land on either the royal or the temple estates.

The network of canals set up during the first half of the third millennium and subsequently extended made possible the transport of large quantities of goods from city-state to city-state, and thus gave shape to the whole pattern of internal Babylonian commerce. Communication between the various parts of a city-state or different states was at all times easy by river, and before the end of the third millennium presented little difficulty by land. The ruler Shulgi of the III Ur Dynasty boasts in a hymn of the attention he had given to the communications in his land:

I went along the roads of the land,
I worked out the mileages, built official posts there,
Put gardens alongside, established rest-houses,
Installed experienced men there.

Shulgi's reference to the establishment of official posts along the roads brings out another consequence of inter-city trade. No city-state was by itself in a position to safeguard the trade routes upon which the prosperity of all depended, and this provided an incentive to political expansion by the wealthier and more powerful states. Thus trade served as a factor in the creation of a unified administrative and political system, and ultimately fostered what is nowadays stigmatized as imperialism, which in the third millennium found its fullest expression in the III Ur Dynasty. From the earliest period, trade assisted the diffusion of Sumerian culture far beyond the bounds of Sumer itself. Thus at Tell Brak in northeastern Syria there was, at about 3000 BC, a temple built on the same plan as those in Sumer and similarly equipped and decorated. Even further away, the major city of Ebla in northwest Syria, which flourished in the twenty-fourth century, although politically independent until conquered by the Agade dynasty, enjoyed a culture of a markedly Sumerian type.

Marriage and sexual relations

Much can be learnt about a society from the relations between its men and women. Throughout the whole of Sumerian and Babylonian history marriage was monogamous, in the sense that a man might normally have only one woman who ranked as a wife and enjoyed a social status corresponding to his. One of the few exceptions to strict monogamy, provided for in the laws of Hammurabi, was that if a man's wife had a disabling illness he might marry a second woman; but the law gave protection to the disabled wife by providing that the husband might not divorce her but must maintain her as long as she lived. Monogamy was based on social and not moral considerations, for no stigma attached to resort to temple prostitutes or to the keeping of concubines (sometimes thought of as secondary wives), although individual women might object to the latter; instances are known in which a marriage contract prohibits a man from taking a concubine. It was quite usual for a slave-girl to be used as a concubine, but this did not automatically alter her slave status, and any children born to her also had the status of slaves unless her master formally accepted them as his own legitimate children. It was possible for a free man – presumably a bachelor or a widower, or perhaps even a married man with a complaisant wife – to make a slave-girl head of his household, but such a course of action is forcefully criticized in a proverb. Where there were concubines, the principal and subsidiary ladies of the household did not always agree, and they might make it an uncomfortable home for the husband: we learn this from an omen:

> If . . . wife and wife agree, that household will get along all right,

which suggests that the opposite state of affairs was not unknown. A biblical instance of discord in such circumstances is that of Sarai and Hagar (Genesis 16:4–6).

Some texts, mainly proverbs and omens, provide details about love-making: they indicate that both the normal behaviour from love play to consummation, and the typical perversions (such as sodomy, transvestism, cunnilinctus, masturbation), were much the same in ancient Babylonia as in modern Europe. We find mention of the shrieks and whimpers which some women make during sexual intercourse; some lines of a Sumerian epic, dealing with the Sacred Marriage when the city ruler made love to a priestess representing the fertility goddess, read:

> The sacred hierodule screeched like a young crow;
> She was no duckling, but she quacked like one.[8]

Maladjustments familiar in modern society, such as impotence and premature ejaculation, were also well known in Babylonia. However, despite all this, married bliss was no rarity. Relations between husband and wife could indeed be as varied as in our own society. At one extreme we meet references to love continuing into old age, and a Sumerian proverb mentions a proud husband boasting that his wife had borne him eight sons and was still ready to lie down to accept his nuptial embrace. At the other extreme there were husbands who ran away from their wives, leading the wives to use incantations in an attempt to bring them back. We even find mention of a wife under such stress that she deliberately set the house on fire.[9] One of the earliest of known letters, written in Sumerian at about 2000 BC, seems to reveal tension in a marriage. It is written to a man by a woman, presumably his wife, who was defending herself against an accusation of squandering her husband's household goods.[10] He seems to have been a very tightfisted man, for the unfortunate woman ended her letter by pleading for him to send grain urgently, as there was no more in the house.

Whilst some husbands might resort to prostitutes or concubines, wives did not always lack opportunity for variety. There were wives who left their husbands for other men; one text mentions a wife urging her lover to kill her husband, and another refers to a woman who had taken a fancy to her brother-in-law. There is also a text which speaks of a wife, pregnant by a lover, who hoped to conceal her secret by gazing at her husband to make the expected baby look like him. At some periods and places women could be tried for adultery. One Sumerian text recording a decision against a wife found guilty of adultery speaks of the lovers being tied to the bed and taken to court.[11] Nymphomaniacs were known: the goddess Ishtar is said to have coped with 120 men and not been tired.[12]

The commonest position for intercourse seems to have been face to face with the woman on her back, but other positions are also attested (see plate 51C, one of many such plaques, mostly unpublished, which depict intercourse taking place as a cult act). There are texts which refer to a high priestess permitting intercourse *per anum*, specifically explained as a means of preventing conception.

Law codes show that in some circumstances a man might divorce his wife, but there are very few documents dealing with actual cases. Such as there are show that the ceremony involved cutting off the hem of the lady's garment before witnesses.

As in most societies, weddings were occasions of rejoicing, marked by feasting. Although marriages were normally arranged by the parents, unmarried young men and women must have had more opportunity of meeting than their counterparts today in the Islamic society of the same region, for we find incantations to assist those in love, pining for a particular person. One third-millennium example puts the beloved maiden under a spell in the name of two goddesses, with the words:

Whilst his neck and your neck
Do not lie side by side,
May you have no rest.[13]

Women as well as men could resort to witchcraft, using magic charms to win back a renegade lover.

There is also mention of young people sleepless for unrequited love. Another text refers to a man and a woman sitting looking at each other, with the woman becoming so excited that she kept touching her vulva.

The status of women

There are hints that at the very beginning of Sumerian society women enjoyed a much higher status than later: in early Sumerian religion a prominent position is occupied by goddesses who – with the one exception of Ishtar – afterwards virtually lose their independent functions and appear only as consorts of male deities. Extant Creation myths reflect several different conceptual stages, and in their oldest stratum Creation is attributed to a mother-goddess; it is only later that the creator-deity is specifically male. The Underworld itself was originally under the sole rule of a goddess, for there is a myth giving an elaborate explanation of how she came to take a male consort (see page 290). Furthermore, myths show goddesses playing an equal part with gods in the divine decision-making assembly. It is difficult to explain these aspects of the early status of goddesses unless they reflected the status of women at the time the myths arose.

In the Sumerian city-state we also find women amongst the owners of family land, and this must reflect the original prehistoric situation, since the trends in historical times were certainly not such as to add rights of this kind to women, which they had not traditionally enjoyed. There are even grounds for thinking that polyandry may at one time have been practised, for the reforms of the ruler Uru-inim-gina, at about 2400 BC, refer to women who had taken more than one husband: some scholars shy away from this conclusion, and want to see this as a reference to the remarriage of widows, but this is not the natural meaning of the Sumerian text. The wives of some third-millennium rulers attained positions of great importance, and the daughter of Sargon of Akkad, the high-priestess of Ur, was a major poet and a woman of considerable prominence.

By the end of the third millennium society had become definitely male-orientated in Babylonia. An unmarried woman was under the authority of her father or, if the father was dead, her brothers. Nevertheless, in Sumer and Babylonia women were not explicitly considered to be inferior to men: they could own property, engage in business, and be parties to contracts. Women never suffered the disadvantages in Babylonia to which they were subject in some later Near Eastern societies, including that of Assyria in the late second millennium, from whence comes a group of laws markedly oppressive towards women (see page 190 and my *The Might that was Assyria*, pages 142f.).

Children

In general children were desired and loved in the ancient Near East. On the other hand, they were required to show respect for their parents, and gross offence in this matter could give valid grounds for disinheritance or even reduction to slavery. Corresponding respect, although with less powerful sanctions, was due to an older brother or older sister.

One of the most touching stories in the Old Testament is the account of the grief of a barren woman (1 Samuel 1:5–10), and in Babylonia one of the greatest possible afflictions of a married couple was childlessness. The laws of Hammurabi presuppose that barrenness in a wife was a ground for divorce; alternatively the husband might take a secondary wife.

When a woman was fortunate enough to have a child she would, if able, suckle it to the age of two or three; the effect of this on her hormones would reduce her liability to conceive during that period, so that typically a woman gave birth to no more than about six children. If the mother did not lactate adequately, the child of a family which could afford it would be entrusted to a wet-nurse; in a poor family, if the mother's milk failed the baby would inevitably die. One of the tragedies of ancient Mesopotamia was its appalling infant mortality (see page 260).

But not all child death was unavoidable. Exposure of unwanted newborn infants was apparently accepted by many people in the ancient Near East with the same indifference with which many non-Catholics today accept abortion. It was so familiar to the biblical writers that Ezekiel 16:4–6 uses it to make a theological point:

> In the day thou wast born, . . . none eye pitied thee, . . . but thou wast cast out in the open field; . . . and when I passed by thee, . . . I said unto thee, . . . Live.

God is represented here as taking pity on an exposed infant and rescuing it for adoption. This is precisely what happened to some children in Babylonia. To have an heir was so important that adoption was widely practised, sometimes of babies rescued from the streets (the standard expression for such cases was 'snatched from the dog's mouth') and, in other cases, of orphans or children of the destitute. Legislation about adoption occurs in the law codes, and numerous documents concerned with the rights and duties of adopted children have been found. One such reads:

> Yahatti-il is the son of Hillalum and of the lady Alitum. He shall benefit by their benefits and suffer ill by their ills. If Hillalum his father or the lady Alitum his mother say to their son Yahatti-il 'You are not our son', they shall forfeit house and furniture. If Yahatti-il says to Hillalum his father or the lady Alitum his mother 'You are not my father' or 'You are not my mother', they may shave his head and sell him for silver.
>
> (As to) Hillalum and the lady Alitum, however many sons they get, Yahatti-il is the heir. From the house of Hillalum his father he shall receive a double (inheritance) share and (any) younger brothers of his shall share (the rest) equally.

One does not look in the ancient world for social insurance as we know it, but there are indications (apart from what has just been mentioned) that the poor and weak might find assistance and protection. As early as the time of Uru-inimgina (*c.* 2400 BC), that ruler set out, according to his own statement, to protect the poor and weak against the rich and strong (see page 43), and the laws of succeeding periods reflect the same noble intention. We find instances of the principle not only in legal codes but also in benevolence towards particular persons. A letter from Mari (*c.* 1800 BC) shows the young orphan of an old palace servant being recommended to the protection of the sub-king Yasmah-adad:

> To my lord Yasmah-adad say, 'Thus says Hasidanum your servant: "The son of the palace postal official was transferred from Mari and now that man has died. He has left a son, who is still an infant. Let my lord see the child, and (having confirmed that) he is an infant and has no guardian, let my lord ease the situation for him."'

Clothing

Fashions changed considerably over the two and a half millennia from 3000 BC to 500 BC. There is some evidence suggesting that in the period before 3000 BC the people of south Iraq still went naked in their daily work in the fields. Consonant with this is that from the *Early Dynastic* period onwards the *Ensi* (city governor) is sometimes depicted kneeling before the god naked; this cultic nudity may possibly have reflected the everyday practice of Sumer several centuries earlier.

Monuments often depict Sumerians wearing garments which appear to be made of sheepskins or goatskins, and these reflect the form of dress in the earlier part of the third millennium. Once the people of Sumer and Akkad had advanced beyond skins and fleeces, most garments were made of woollen cloth, although linen was an alternative. Cotton was not introduced into Mesopotamia until the first millennium BC. The production of garments in wool and linen called for weavers (it was mainly women who were engaged in this) and fullers; workers of these classes are referred to in economic documents. There were also garments of leather, with corresponding mention of leather-workers.

Where textiles are represented, it is clear that amongst Sumerians the common garment was a kind of kilt, as shown in plate 8B. An inlaid panel from Ur (see plate 12) shows soldiers wearing such kilts, together with long cloaks draped over the shoulders and fastened together in the manner of a duffel coat with a peg. Some Sumerian rulers are depicted wearing a kind of loose-fitting ankle-length shawl draped over the left shoulder. During the second millennium the typical dress consisted of an undergarment with lengths of cloth draped around, often belted at the waist. Stitched clothing was introduced into Mesopotamia in this period, and in the first millennium BC the typical dress was a tunic, fitted rather than draped.

Textiles ranged in quality from cheap materials suitable for servants to those fit for royalty. Assyrian bas-reliefs show that the robes of kings and noblemen were heavily decorated with embroidery.

The wool for most textiles was, of course, obtained from sheep, but not necessarily by shearing as practised by us. This was certainly used – the animal being given a bath before shearing – but an alternative technique was to pluck it. Goat's hair was probably also used for some purposes, as it still is in Iraq. From extensive Sumerian records on tablets found at Nippur, technical experts have succeeded in deriving considerable information about the bleaching, dyeing, spinning and weaving of wool in the third millennium.

Hair styles

Evidence on hair styles comes almost entirely from representations in art, in the third millennium most commonly cylinder seals.

In the *Jemdet Nasr* period (*c.* 2900 BC), both sexes wore long hair, tied back in a bunch. In the succeeding period (down to *c.* 2400 BC), the most common style, with various modifications, was long hair coiled round the head turban-wise.

In the Agade period (*c.* 2370–2230 BC), the hair fashion for women was waves or curls. The lady would have a parting in the middle, with sometimes a fringe at the front and over the temples. The mass of the lady's hair was generally done up at the back in a chignon or bun. Subsequent fashion dictated a very large chignon, held with a snood and headband. Other accessories used for the coiffures of ladies of those ancient times included hairpins of bone, copper, silver or gold.

The Sumerian male of the latter half of the third millennium might either be completely shorn, or wear his hair and beard carefully waved. From the beginning of the second millennium, kings and warriors are usually shown with luxurious wavy beards, and often with long wavy hair, clear of the ears, falling loosely over the shoulders. Alongside these bearded men there are often others, also with long hair but beardless and with rather fleshy faces; these are usually taken to be eunuchs.

Slaves had their own characteristic tonsure, probably a topknot, as did also priests. So apparently did doctors, to judge from the Babylonian story called *The Poor Man of Nippur* (see page 415), in which, when the hero wishes to impersonate a doctor, he first went to have his head shaved.

Food and drink

The diet of the people of Babylonia, slave and free alike, was largely based on barley, which provided the staple drink, beer, as well as the staple cereal food. It was eaten in the form of unleavened bread, probably as thin discs cooked by spreading the dough on a hot surface, giving a very palatable food (now known as *khubuz*), still eaten by peasants in Iraq although despised for its primitiveness by the more sophisticated. Other cereals used for human food were millet, wheat, rye and (in the first millennium BC) rice; these were eaten in the form of bread or a kind of porridge. Another way of eating cereals was to mix them with honey, ghee, vegetable oil, milk or various fruits, and cook the mixture to make pastry, cakes or biscuits.

The commonest vegetable was probably the onion; others widely used included lentils, beans and peas (valuable sources of protein), often in soup. The cucumber and other plants of that family were eaten, as was the cabbage. The lettuce was grown then as now, and was probably responsible, as it still is, for the transmission of a great deal of waterborne disease. Dates, a valuable source of sugar, were an important part of the common diet, whilst the date-palm also provided date-wine, as well as a celery-like delicacy cut from the growing heart of the male palm. Other fruits were the apple, pomegranate, fig, quince, medlar and apricot. Amongst beverages, the commonest were beer and date-wine, although wine from the grape was known as early as the *Jemdet Nasr* period (*c.* 2900 BC), probably as an import from the highlands. Such

Drinking tube

beverages, which probably contained a good deal of lees, were in the third millennium imbibed through drinking tubes, with an end perforated with small holes to form a kind of filter.

Beer was known in many varieties, and one Babylonian lexical work contains an extensive list of technical terms for the processes and materials employed in making the different kinds. Down to the time of Hammurabi, brewing seems to have been in the hands of women, for this craft was under the protection of female divinities, and the alewife is specifically mentioned in the laws of Hammurabi. Occasionally brewing is depicted in art.

Brewing

Milk was used from sheep, goats and cows, but because of the rapidity with which it turns in the climate of south Iraq it was chiefly consumed in the form of yoghurt, butter, ghee or cheese. An inlaid frieze from the middle of the third millennium illustrates the production of milk and milk foods. We see a calf placed at its dam's head, a practice well known to have

Milking scene

the effect of making the cow let down its milk more readily. By exploiting this aspect of animal behaviour, the Sumerians showed themselves more acute observers than the Scythians two millennia later, whose blinded slaves were known, according to Herodotus, to 'use tubes of bones . . . which they thrust up the vulva of the mare; some engage in milking the mares, whilst others are busy blowing. They assert that this practice has the object of inflating the mare's veins with air, so forcing the udder down.' In the Sumerian frieze the milker sits on a stool behind the cow, in a position which I have seen used in England. A little way off, another man sits on a stool rocking the milk in a large stoppered vessel to make the butter-fat coagulate. On the extreme left are shown another pair of men, apparently straining the butter-milk from the butter.

Even slaves ate meat from time to time, but, apart from milk, the only animal protein always widely available on a regular basis was fish. Many kinds are mentioned in documents of the third and early second millennia. A Sumerian text of about 2000 BC describes the habits and appearance of many species of fish in the guise of a deity's invitation to enter the house he had prepared for them.[14] This was probably a piece of scribal erudition which had its basis in more primitive magical spells used by fishermen to charm fish into their nets.

Mutton, and less commonly beef, were always part of the food available at festivals. Goat meat was also eaten. Some of the cattle destined for food must have been fattened to a huge size, for in one letter of the early second millennium BC there is mention of an ox, intended for a palace offering, so fat that it could not stand.

There was no taboo on the pig, which is still found in large numbers in the marshes of southern Iraq and elsewhere in the country. In Sumerian times pigs were tended in large herds, living by scavenging, with a supplement of barley feed. Many early or primitive communities had a shortage of fat in the diet, and in such circumstances fat meat is a greater delicacy than with us. Accordingly, a Sumerian proverb makes the point that fat pork was too good for slave girls, and that they should make do with lean meat.

There was no objection to eating horse-flesh, at least in the Nuzi area east of Assyria in the fourteenth century BC, from where there is a record of a lawsuit in which the defendants had stolen and eaten a horse. Dead asses were used only as dog meat. Geese and ducks were kept from early times; the hen did not reach Mesopotamia until the first millennium BC.

Many of the foods mentioned were preserved for times of scarcity. Cereals would present no problem, whilst legumes could easily be dried. Various fruits were kept in edible condition by pressing into cakes. Fish was preserved by salting, and this process was also used, combined with desiccation, for meat.

Housing

The average citizen's house of the third millennium was in effect a thick-walled, almost windowless, mud hut, often with a common wall with its neighbour. Rooms were fitted together to suit the site available, and the doors were so low that one would need to stoop to pass from room to room. But besides the mud-brick house, there was a superior type made of baked brick, often of more than one storey. Houses of that better kind would be built round a central courtyard, like an older type of good-quality house still found in Baghdad up to the 1960s.

Although Sumerian and Babylonian housing may not be impressive by modern western standards, comparison of Sumero-Babylonian structures with the buildings of western Europe is largely beside the point. The basic purpose of a house in a temperate climate is to exclude the wet and cold draughts: the primary requirement from a house in southern Iraq is that it should keep out the blasting heat which beats down twelve hours a day from May to September from the blazing, pitiless sun. Windows in that climate are not a blessing, and, accordingly, houses in ancient Mesopotamia contained, in the way of windows, at the most a clay or wooden grille set in the wall: examples from the third millennium BC have been found (see plate 15A), almost identical with a type still seen in Iraq up to the 1960s.

The equipment of houses naturally varied a great deal from period to period, area to area, and class to class. The furnishings of palaces are obviously not typical, and no private house complete with a full range of contents has yet been excavated. The following account must therefore necessarily be composite.

At the end of the third millennium, the common people seem still to have slept on reed mats, although by the first millennium wooden bedsteads were in common use and are depicted on Assyrian bas-reliefs. Models of beds in terracotta have been found, and medical texts frequently assume that the patient will be lying on a bed. The gods had tables for their meals, and, in view of religious conservatism, this presumably means that humans already used tables in the earliest times; later examples are depicted on Assyrian monuments. Chairs with legs, a back, and even arms, were common in palaces, and stools were in use as early as the beginning of the third millennium (see illustration on page 165). Built-in mud benches have also been found. The other major pieces of furniture in a house would be wooden storage chests.

Amongst feeding utensils, single-pronged bone forks have been found in large numbers, and knives were common. Spoons of bitumen or bone have been excavated, and terracotta ladles were in use. Typical eating and drinking vessels, in a wide variety of styles, included platters, bowls and cups, made of pottery, wood, stone or metal.

Food would be prepared on an oven, often situated in the courtyard of the house, although indoor hearths are also found. Portable copper braziers (of the type in plate 59) could also be used indoors, where they would be a comfort in the cold season, although the particular specimen illustrated may actually have come from a temple. Amongst cooking utensils, a copper vessel almost indistinguishable from a modern frying pan was found in a stratum of the early third millennium (see plate 15B).

Some cereal foods and legumes were prepared by pounding, and a pestle and mortar must have been a necessity for any industrious Babylonian housewife. Above the residential areas of some ancient Babylonian cities the interested visitor can (if allowed to) pick up quite a number of broken pestles and mortars of baked clay or stone. From the beginning of the third millennium onwards some houses contained handmills of imported volcanic stone for grinding corn.

A Babylonian house might also contain items of jewellery, such as earrings, beads, pendants, bracelets and anklets. Toilet accessories might include pots of unguents with which to anoint the body or the hair, and mirrors and tweezers of copper or even silver or gold. One archaeologist excavating a palace of about 2300 BC found himself in a lady's apartment, identified by the presence of beads, and mussel shells containing kohl (eye-shadow) and rouge. Bathrooms have been found in palaces, but none are known from private houses, whose occupants presumably used the rivers when they wanted a full body bath, although some form of washing certainly took place in the home, since ablutions were a ritual requirement after sexual intercourse. Lavatories, consisting of a platform above a pit or drain, have been found from as early as the third millennium, one having a seat of bitumen for added comfort (see plate 13A).

There was no municipal sewage disposal for private houses, but government buildings as early as the third millennium had an elaborate system of drainage. A palace of about 2300 BC, at Eshnunna (modern Tell Asmar) on the Diyala river, contained six lavatories with raised seats made of baked brick, and five bathrooms. Most of these lavatories and bathrooms were connected with bitumen-lined drains which led into a vaulted baked-brick main sewer three feet deep (see plate 13B), but in one wing of the building there had to be a separate cesspool, because the level was too low for it to join the main system. Each lavatory was equipped with a large water vessel, and at the time of excavation some of these still contained the pottery dipper which must have been employed to flush the lavatory after use. Assyrian palaces of the first millennium BC also had an elaborate system of drainage, the main drain being five feet wide and having its end covered with a grating to prevent the ingress of burglars. Such drains discharged their contents into the river.

Artificial light was provided either by torches, consisting of a bundle of reeds dipped in oil or bitumen, or by lamps. Such a lamp would consist of a small shoe-shaped pot of oil, with a wick made from a reed protruding through a hole on top. The oil employed for this purpose would be either vegetable oil from linseed, or possibly mineral oil from the deposits upon which much of Europe now relies.

Various hazards were associated with ancient housing. The actual collapse of a house, particularly of the type made of sun-dried brick, was by no means uncommon. The laws of Hammurabi devote five sections to the problem, laying down, amongst other things, that if a builder builds a house which collapses and kills the householder, the builder himself is to be put to death; if it kills the householder's son, the builder's son must die. Sin-iddinam, king of Larsa, met his death through the collapse of part of the structure of a temple, as we learn from an allusion in an omen text. There were rituals which purported to prevent walls from collapsing, and even omens foretelling death through accidents of this kind:

> (In a dream)
> If (a man) descends into the underworld and a dead person blesses him,
> he will die through the collapse of a wall;
> If he descends into the underworld and eats a dead person,
> he will die through a falling roof-beam.

Another inconvenience in ancient houses was creeping things. Scorpions still find their way into modern houses in the centre of Baghdad from time to time; in the ancient world they

17 Head from Warka (third millennium)

18A (*left*) Bronze foundation depos representing a Sumerian rul bearing the head-pad at the buil ing of a temple

18B (*above*) Head of a Sumerian i diorite (end of third millennium)

19 A goddess holding vase, for use as fountain (from Mari)

20 A Sumerian official

21A (*left*) Babylonian boundary stone (late second millennium BC)

21B (*right*) Cast of the stele of Hammurabi (early second millennium BC)

22 (*opposite*) Part of a cuneiform tablet (from Nineveh, first millennium BC), bearing the end of the Flood story from the *Epic of Gilgamesh*

23 (*above*) Obverse of a cuneiform tablet inscribed with geometrical exercises (early second millennium BC)

24 Reverse of a cuneiform tablet inscribed with geometrical exercises (early second millennium BC)

25 Inscribed cone of Ur-Bau (*circa* 2200 BC)

26A Old Babylonian cuneiform tablet and envelope; a contract for the sale of land

26B (*left*) Cuneiform tablet (*circa* 600 BC) bearing a map of the world. [The ring represents the ocean supposedly enclosing the earth]

26C (*below*) Cuneiform tablet with Egyptian endorsement

27A Impression of cylinder seal, showing Maltese crosses

27B Inscribed clay model of an internal organ, for use in divination

28 King Ashur-nasir-pal II

29 King Ashur-nasir-pal II

30 An Assyrian god

31 Assyrian religious ceremony of the first millennium BC involving the king [the figure on the left]

32 The Assyrian king in a cult scene before stylized sacred tree

must have been uncomfortably common in the mud-roofed mud-brick house of the ordinary man, and a whole group of omens refer to scorpions falling from the ceiling on to a man or his bed. Snakes also sometimes crawl about in search of rodents amongst the branches and mud forming the roof of mud-brick houses, and Babylonian omen texts contain many references to snakes falling into the room: in some circumstances this was considered lucky.

Town planning; water supply

In the beginning towns grew up gradually around the temple area, but town planning was not unknown in ancient Mesopotamia, and in the first millennium several Assyrian kings created new towns on a planned basis. A notable example is Calah (represented by the modern mound Nimrud), rebuilt by Ashur-nasir-pal in 879 BC and populated with about 70,000 people. It was, of course, planned with military needs in mind; another instance in which this factor applied is Dur-sharrukin (Khorsabad), northeast of Nineveh, planned and founded by Sargon II as a new capital on the site of a small village. Sargon's son, Sennacherib, undertook a major re-planning of his capital, Nineveh. Such royal cities were provided with main exit roads, well surfaced with cobblestones for the benefit of the royal armies proceeding on campaign. A stretch of a road of this kind was excavated at Nimrud, whilst Sennacherib mentions another when he threatens, in connections with his re-planning of Nineveh, that anyone attempting to build on the royal road will be impaled.

Good rulers were always concerned about the water supply of ancient cities, and the Bible in 2 Kings 20:20 regards the improvement of Jerusalem's water supply as one of the notable achievements of Hezekiah of Judah. Babylonian cities had few problems in this respect, since most of them lay on branches of the Euphrates. But the situation was different in some of the cities of Assyria. The main river there, the Tigris, is more variable in level than the Euphrates and lower in its bed, so that its use for irrigation can present problems. Sennacherib made strenuous efforts to bring water to Nineveh to irrigate the orchards and parks he had laid out, cutting canals from the mountains up to thirty miles away (see page 115).

Calah also had a canal system, but in addition there were several wells cut down to a depth of ninety feet to ensure the acropolis a constant water supply, which would also have been very useful in case of siege: one of the wells (cleared out in 1952) proved still to yield five thousand gallons a day. In the same well there was found a wooden pulley wheel on which were clearly visible the marks of wear caused by a rope. There were also several score of pots, some with pieces of rope still round their necks, which must once have constituted an endless chain of vessels worked by a windlass to draw water. Sennacherib proudly refers to some device of this kind when he says, with reference to his works in Nineveh:

> In order to draw water daily, I had ropes, bronze cables and bronze chains made, and I had beams and crossbars fitted over the wells instead of poles.

Health

The evidence of Babylonian texts destroys any fantasy one might have had about the ancient world as a golden age peopled by a happy, healthy race of mankind, free from anxieties, inhibitions, worries and want. Mental illness was not uncommon, and attempted suicide is attested, as in the case of a slave-girl who had three times been caught with a headband round her neck, trying to strangle herself. Drunkenness was well known. Various psychoses are alluded to, for instance the mental condition of the Babylonian king Nebuchadnezzar, who according to the Bible suffered from lycanthropy (Daniel 4:28–33): whether the tradition was based on fact or on theological fancy, this reflects acquaintance in the ancient world with a particular type of mental disease. The royal family of Elam seems to have been subject to mental illness and in several cases it is said of rulers of this line that 'his mind changed', meaning, apparently, not that the king concerned altered his foreign policy but that he went off his head. Insomnia was a recognized problem, sometimes put down to witchcraft, but in other cases more rationally attributed to worry, or love-sickness. Sexual impotence was one form of maladjustment from which some suffered in the ancient world as in the modern, and there were incantations and rituals to treat this. Involuntary seminal emissions at night were well known to the ancients, as omens of the following kind prove:

> If a man becomes sexually excited during the night and pollutes himself in his dream, that man will suffer a loss.

But if he awoke as it happened, it was lucky:

> If a man becomes sexually excited during the night and wakes up and has a pollution . . . he will acquire wealth.

Amongst other health problems, headaches and fever were extremely common, and sinusitis, tonsillitis, catarrh, rheumatism, various forms of paralysis, and probably tuberculosis, are mentioned. We find mention of blood in the urine, which is one of the symptoms of bilharzia, today endemic along the lower Euphrates. Eye and ear infections were of very frequent occurrence. We find references to symptoms which must relate to various internal complaints, and jaundice and dysentery were very common, as they still are in Iraq. In women, breast disorders and miscarriages were no rarity, and there are references to varicose veins. Venereal diseases are often mentioned. Some men suffered from incontinence of urine. Baldness was a source of worry to some men, and various quack treatments were available for it. The Babylonians were well acquainted with monstrous births, including such abnormalities as Siamese twins and a child with two facing heads, which happened to be recorded because of their significance as omens.

Dreams and nightmares

Records of omens also provide us with information on the kind of thing about which the people of ancient Mesopotamia might dream. The evidence is to be found in A. L. Oppenheim's *The Interpretation of Dreams in the Ancient Near East* (1956), in which omens from dreams are edited. They have the form:

> If a man flies repeatedly, whatever he owns will be lost.

Obviously the ancients, like ourselves, had flying dreams: Freud's quite different interpretation of such dreams will be familiar to many readers. They also had nightmares: an Old Babylonian omen mentions the man who in his dream had the town – doubtless set on a hill – falling on him repeatedly, with no one to answer his cries for help. A sufferer from nightmares might take various magical means for their alleviation, such as burying under his bedroom floor figurines bearing such inscriptions as 'Get out, evil caused by dreams! Come in, pleasantness caused by dreams!'

Embarrassing dreams of walking around naked were as well known to the Babylonians as (according to Freud) to modern Europeans. In the ancient world they were considered lucky:

> If in his dream a man walks about naked . . . troubles will not touch this man.

Many other dreams mentioned in omens shed an interesting sidelight on the mind of ancient man. Thus:

> If a man (in his dream) goes in (sexually) to a wild animal, his household will become prosperous.
>
> If a man (in his dream) goes in (sexually) to his daughter (or) . . . his mother-in-law, [consequences foretold are lost].
>
> If (in a dream) a man's penis is long, he will have no rival.

If (in a man's dream) his urine comes out of his penis and fills the streets, his property will be confiscated and given to the town.

We also find mention of dreams which refer to cannibalism (see example on page 170) and to eating parts of the dreamer's own body.

The basis on which the Babylonians interpreted dreams can in many cases only be guessed, but sometimes the symbolism is transparent enough. Thus:

If (in a dream) someone gives (the dreamer) a wheel, he will have twins. [There is the obvious connection that wheels come in pairs.]

If (in a man's dream) someone gives him an empty cup, the poor man will become poorer.

If (in a man's dream) someone gives him a full cup, he will have fame and prosperity.

Some interpretations depended upon a pun. Thus:

If (in a man's dream) someone gives the man *mihru*-wood, he will have no rival [Akkadian *mahiru*].

8

Law and Statecraft

ONE of the most marked features of ancient Mesopotamian civilization was its respect for the rule of law. Over 90 per cent of the cuneiform documents so far recovered consist of receipts, accounts and records of transactions concerning property. It was generally recognized that a property transaction without written record was not valid, and to alter such a document was a heinous offence.

The people of ancient Mesopotamia attributed the origin of law to the gods, in particular to the Sun-god, who dispersed all darkness and in his course across the heavens looked down upon all the deeds of man. Many third-millennium rulers claimed to have promoted the cause of law and justice, but whether or not such activities always involved the promulgation of written laws is uncertain.

For long the oldest collection of laws known was that of Hammurabi in the early second millennium, inscribed on a diorite stele discovered in 1901–2 at Susa in southwest Iran, the capital of ancient Elam. When first found, the obvious parallels between these laws and those attributed to Moses in the Bible, which even on the traditional view were indisputably later by several centuries, led some rationalists to lay down as dogma that 'the Hammurabi Code must have been the immediate or remote progenitor of the Hebrew legal system'. Later discoveries have put the matter in better perspective. We now have at least three collections of laws antedating those of Hammurabi by a century or more, and others of a later date from the Hittite area and Assyria. Further small groups of laws are also known. All these collections have both points in common and their own peculiarities, and it has become clear that the ancient Near East possessed a large body of generally recognized law. Some of this was incorporated in various local collections, modified to suit local circumstances, and this is adequate to explain the parallels between Hebrew and Babylonian law.

Evidence now available shows that written collections of laws were by no means uncommon at the turn of the third millennium BC; some scholars suggest that every city-state had such a collection, written in either Akkadian or Sumerian according to local conditions.

The concept of justice

Justice – for which the word used meant literally 'the straight thing' – was an accepted responsibility of the king. Hammurabi, for example, made the establishment of justice one of his first concerns at his accession; and the formula by which his second regnal year was known was 'the year in which he set forth justice in the land'; some other rulers used the same formula. This does not refer to the promulgation of the famous Code, which took place much later in Hammurabi's reign, but rather to measures intended to improve the lot of the citizens. The 'justice' referred to was primarily economic justice; for the king to 'set forth justice in the land' involved some kind of moratorium or general remission of debts. Before the end of the third millennium, inequalities of economic power which had gradually developed between temple estates and owners of family land, and between large landowners and small landowners, had brought a situation in which it was small landowning or land-renting peasants who took the first shock of catastrophes such as flood, famine or blight. To survive such difficulties, small independent peasants had to borrow at interest from the temple or from wealthy merchants. Over the years this would result in much of the peasantry becoming the victim to a crippling load of debt, a situation which could only be cleared by a general remission and a fresh start – which is what 'setting forth justice in the land' meant. There are traces of a corresponding situation in the Old Testament, where Leviticus 25, which deals with the Year of Jubilee, lays down that in the fiftieth year the poor man who had had to pledge property or mortgage land or sell himself into bondage should have his former rights restored.

Although Hammurabi's year-formula 'he set forth justice in the land' does not refer specifically to his laws, economic measures of the kind referred to may well have been a factor in the origin of collections of laws. Economic distress could bring political instability, and it was therefore a matter of concern for a wise king to prevent exploitation of the population by the temples and owners of large estates. This involved the issue of decrees to fix prices and wages. It seems likely that behind the stele of Hammurabi, set up to give the text of the royal laws, lie simpler monuments bearing lists of authorized prices. There are vestiges of this in Hammurabi's laws themselves, where we find sections dealing with rates of hire and wages. The origin of written laws from documents to fix prices is quite clear in the earlier laws of Eshnunna, which actually begin with a list of controlled prices of commodities such as barley, oil, lard, wool, salt, spices and copper, basic to the economy, and continue with clauses fixing the rate of hire of wagons and boats and the wages of agricultural workers.

Laws of Ur-nammu

The earliest collection of laws at present known are those of Ur-nammu, founder and first king of the III Ur dynasty, known from two damaged copies, first published in 1952 and 1965. The text (in Sumerian) begins with a brief review of the history of the world and the rise to supremacy of Ur, whose king Ur-nammu was representative of the city's god, Nanna.

Ur-nammu tells us that after attention to the political and military security of his city, he turned to rectify a number of economic abuses: he 'established justice in the land', and ensured that

> the orphan was not given over to the rich man, the widow was not given over to the powerful man, the man of one shekel was not given over to the man of one mina.

The remainder of the introduction is broken away, and when the text becomes legible again the laws proper have begun. The text of seventeen laws is substantially complete, and sufficient remains of a few others to give their sense. The matters with which the extent laws deal are: adultery, betrothal, marriage and divorce; false accusation and perjury; runaway slaves and insolence by slave-girls; personal injury; and rights over land. One of the laws on personal injury reads:

> If a man . . . has broken another man's limb with a weapon, he shall pay one mina of silver,

and four other sections, less well preserved, demonstrate the same principle of a financial penalty for personal injury. Thus in third-millennium Sumer the *lex talionis*, or principle of 'an eye for an eye', had – if it ever existed there – already been superseded. The more barbaric principle of direct revenge, found in the laws of Hammurabi, of Assyria and of the Hebrews, reflects the unmodified practice of less civilized Amorites and other West Semites, who came relatively late to life in cities.

Laws of Lipit-ishtar

We know of other laws written in Sumerian. Foremost amongst these are the laws of Lipit-ishtar, king of Isin, a ruler midway between Ur-nammu and Hammurabi. They are preserved on fragments of several clay tablets. Thirty-eight laws are preserved wholly or in part, set between a prologue and an epilogue. The subject-matter of the more intelligible laws may be analysed as follows:

7–11 Rights over gardens and orchards.
12–16 Slaves and dependent free men.
18 Land tax.
21–33 Marriage and inheritance.
34–37 Fines for damage to a hired ox.

The following are examples of some of the better preserved of the Lipit-ishtar laws:

11 If someone's uncultivated land next to a man's house has been left waste, and if the owner of the house has said to the owner of the uncultivated land: 'Someone may break into my house because of your land being left waste . . .', and if an agreement on this matter has been ratified by him [i.e. the owner of the uncultivated land], the owner of the uncultivated land shall make good to the owner of the house any property of his that may be lost.

24 If a second wife whom (a man) married has borne him children, the marriage-settlement which she brought from her father's house belongs to her children; the children of the first wife and the children of the second wife shall divide the property of their father equally.

25 If a man has taken a wife and she has borne him children and those children have survived, and a slave-girl has also borne children to her master and the father has granted freedom to that slave-girl and her children, the children of the slave-girl shall not share the estate with the children of their (former) master.

27 If a man's wife has borne him no children but a prostitute from the street has borne him children, he shall provide corn, oil and clothing for that prostitute, and the children which the prostitute has borne him shall be his heirs; but as long as his wife lives the prostitute shall not reside in the house with the wife.

29 If a son-in-law has entered the house of his (prospective)

father-in-law and has gone through the betrothal procedure, but subsequently they reject him and (propose to) give his wife to his comrade; they shall deliver to him the betrothal gift which he brought and that wife shall not be given in marriage to his comrade.

35 If a man has hired an ox and damaged its eye, he shall pay half its price.

Not all documents in Babylonia containing laws came direct from legislators. An example of one which did not is a text which the ancient scribes named, from its initial words, *ana ittishu* (meaning 'upon notice given'). Internal evidence shows that this originated at about 1950 BC, the period of the Lipit-ishtar laws. It contains a listing of Sumerian words and clauses excerpted from contracts, with Akkadian translations along-side. Its final tablet incorporates the text of twelve laws dealing with family relationships, of which the following extracts are typical:

If a son says to his father, 'You are not my father', (the father) may give him a tonsure, put a slave-mark on him and sell him.

If a wife hates her husband and says, 'You are not my husband', they shall throw her into the river. [This does not necessarily imply deliberate drowning; it could refer to trial by ordeal, if the woman's denial of her husband raised a presumption of adultery.]

If a husband says to his wife 'You are not my wife', he shall pay half a mina of silver.

Laws of Eshnunna

The earliest laws yet known in the Akkadian language are those on two clay tablets found in 1947 at Tell Harmal, then a village outside Baghdad, now a part of the expanding city. Tell Harmal represents ancient Shaduppum, a city of the kingdom whose capital was at Eshnunna, modern Tell Asmar on the Diyala; these laws are therefore referred to as the laws of Eshnunna. Linguistic and other features of the tablets show that they probably derive from between one and two centuries before Hammurabi.

The prologue takes the form of a list of commodity prices, followed by sections dealing with rates of hire and wages and possible penalties arising; on the significance of this, see page 178. The main concerns of the remaining forty-eight sections are:

12–13 Penalties for trespass and unlawful entry – a fine if by day; death if by night.
14–21 Regulations on making loans, and loan interest.
22–24 Unlawful distraint upon a slave-girl or wife of a dependent free man.
25–28 Betrothal, marriage, rape, adultery.
29–30 Husband loses rights over his wife by voluntary desertion but not by unavoidable absence.
31 A fine is imposed for deflowering another man's slave-girl.
32 Regulations governing a foster-mother.
33–35 Ownership of children of slave-girls.
36–37 Liability for loss of property deposited for safekeeping.
42–48 Assaults and personal injuries.
49–52 Theft, flight and ownership of slaves.
53–58 Responsibility for damage caused by an ox, dog or collapsing wall.
59 Penalty upon husband who illegally divorces his wife.
60 [Too damaged for certain interpretation].

To give some idea of the style and contents of these laws, a few are translated in full:

25 If a man offers service in the house of a(n intended) father-in-law and his father-in-law takes him into service but then gives his daughter to another man, the father of the girl shall refund twofold the bride-price which he has received (in the form of service). [This situation may be compared with the case of Jacob serving Laban seven years for each of his two daughters (Genesis 29:18–28).]

27 If a man takes a man's daughter without asking her father and mother and has not made a formal contract with her father and

mother, she (has) not (the legal status of) wife, even though she lives a full year in his house.

30 If a man hates his town and his lord and runs away, and another man takes his wife, if he [the first man] returns, he shall have no claim to his wife.

39 If a man becomes insolvent so that he sells his house, when the buyer resells it the original owner shall be entitled to redeem it. [This recalls the provision of Leviticus 25:29: 'If a man sell a dwelling house in a walled city, then he may redeem it within a whole year after it is sold'. In the biblical passage, there is no time limit if the house is outside the city.]

42 If a man bites the nose of another man and severs it, he shall pay one mina of silver; for an eye, one mina; for a tooth, half a mina; for an ear, half a mina; for a blow on the face, ten shekels of silver.

54 If an ox is one that gores and the authorities have notified its owner, but his ox is not kept under control(?) and it gores a man and causes his death, then the owner of the ox shall pay two-thirds of a mina of silver. [This is closely parallel to §251 of the laws of Hammurabi, where a fine is likewise imposed, and to Exodus 21:29, where both ox and owner are put to death.]

58 If a wall bulges and the authorities have notified the owner of the wall, but he does not strengthen his wall and the wall falls and causes the death of a freeman, it is a capital case, in the jurisdiction of the king.

59 If a man divorces his wife after having made her bear sons and takes a second woman, he shall be expelled from house and property, and shall go off after anyone who will take him.

Laws of Hammurabi

The Eshnunna laws find many echoes in the more extensive laws of Hammurabi. Hammurabi's laws show a significant difference from the others so far discussed in their much more ordered arrangement. It is by virtue of this that the term 'code' is often applied to them.

The considerable amount of material common to the Eshnunna laws and the Hammurabi Code raises the question of their interrelationship. Detailed comparison produces no clear proof of direct borrowing, and the explanation of the undoubted overlap is probably that both incorporated traditional material.

The laws of Hammurabi are sandwiched between a prologue and an epilogue. The prologue gives the titles of Hammurabi and a review of his previous achievements, whilst the epilogue proclaims the purpose and authority of his laws, and calls upon succeeding rulers, upon pain of his curses,

> to pay attention to the words which I have inscribed on my stele, . . . so that he may make straight the way for his people [literally, 'Black-headed Beings'], that he may judge their causes and make decisions on their cases, that he may pluck out the evil and the wicked from his land, and make the flesh of his people glad.

In the epilogue, Hammurabi also lays down the procedure an oppressed man should follow:

> Let the wronged man who has a cause go before my monument (named) 'King of Justice', and let him have my inscribed stele read out and let him hear my precious words; let my stele show him his cause, let him see his judgement, let his heart be at ease.

The laws themselves, in which few substantial gaps now remain, amount to more than 260 sections. In modern editions paragraphs of the original stele are denoted by numbers, whilst paragraphs restored subsequently from clay tablets are indicated by letters. The following briefly outlines the subject matter of the laws:

Administration of justice

1–5 False witnesses; corrupt judges.

Offences against property

6–14 Theft; kidnapping.
15–20 Runaway and stolen slaves.
21–25 Housebreaking, robbery, looting.

Land and houses

26–41	Tenure of land held as a fief from the king.
42–48	Cultivation of arable land by tenants.
49–52	Financing of tenant-farmers.
53–56	Negligent irrigation.
57–58	Trespass of cattle on corn-land.
59	Unauthorized cutting of trees.
60–65, A	Cultivation of palm-plantations.
B–E, G, H	Renting, building and repairing of houses.
F, J, K	[Fragmentary.]

Merchants and agents

L–R	Loans from merchants; interest rates.
S, T	[Fragmentary.]
V	Division of profit and loss between business partners.
100–107	Transactions of merchants' agents.
108–111	Regulations concerning ale-wives (who apparently also served as small brokers).
112	Fraud by a carrier.
113–117	Distraint for debt.
118–119	Delivery of dependants into bondage for debt.
120–126	Deposit of goods.

Women, marriage, family property and inheritance

127	Slander of a high-priestess or married woman.
128	Cohabitation without contract does not give a woman the status of 'wife'.
129–132	Adultery.
133–136	Remarriage of a wife: permitted until husband's return if he is taken captive leaving insufficient to maintain her; permitted unconditionally if husband runs away.
137–143	Divorce.
144–149	Concubinage: bigamy permitted if wife is disabled.
150	Inheritance of property settled by husband on wife.
151–152	Liability of spouses for debt.
153	Impalement as penalty for wife who murders husband.
154–158	Incest.
159–161	Breach of contract after betrothal.
162–164	Inheritance of dowry after death of wife.
165–167	Division of inheritance amongst sons.

168–169 Disherison.
170 Legitimation of sons of concubine.
171–174 Rights of concubine and non-legitimated sons; widow's property.
175–176 Rights of a free woman married to a slave.
177 Property disposal at remarriage of a widow.
178–184 Rights of cult women [the ancient equivalent of nuns] to dowry or paternal inheritance.
185–193 Adoption.
194 Substitution of changeling by wet-nurse.

Assault and personal injury

195 Assault by a son on his father.
196–205 Penalties for inflicting bodily harm: talion when the victim is a freeman; a fine when he is a villein or a slave.
206–208 Penalty for accidentally causing injury: a fine or costs, not talion.
209–214 Assault upon a woman resulting in miscarriage.

Professional fees and responsibilities

215–225 Fees payable to surgeons and veterinary surgeons; penalties in event of failure.
226–227 Penalties for removing a slave-mark.
228–239 Fees payable to housebuilders and builders and operators of boats; penalties for negligence.
240 Collision between boats.

Agriculture

241–249 Distraint, hire, death and injury of oxen.
250–252 Responsibility for damage by a goring ox.
253–256 Embezzlement by a bailiff.
257–258 Hire of ploughman and ox-herd.
259–260 Theft of agricultural implements.
261 Hire of stockman or shepherd.

Rates of hire

268–277 Rates of hire of animals, wagons, labourers, craftsmen, boats.

Ownership and sale of slaves

278–279 Liability for a slave sold when diseased or subject to a legal claim.

280–282 Ownership of slaves bought abroad or in disputed ownership.

Translations of a few of the laws are given as specimens:

1 If a man has accused someone and has cast an accusation of murder against him and has not proved it, the accuser shall be put to death.

22–23 If a man has committed robbery and is arrested, that man shall be put to death. If the robber is not arrested, the robbed man shall certify before the god whatever of his is lost, and the city and the mayor within whose territory or bounds the robbery was committed shall replace the lost thing for him.

55 If a man has opened his ditch for irrigation and has been slack and consequently has caused the water to carry away his neighbour's field, he shall pay corn corresponding to (the crop of the field) adjoining it.

117 If a man is in the grip of a bond (for debt) and has handed over his wife, son or daughter for silver, or has given (them) into bondservice, for three years they shall serve in the house of their buyer or the one who took them into bondservice; in the fourth year their release shall be granted.

128 If a man has taken a wife and has not set down a contract for her, that woman does not have the status of wife.

153 If a woman has caused the death of her husband on account of another man, they shall impale that woman.

170 If a man's bride has borne him sons and his slave-girl has borne him sons, and the father in his lifetime says to the sons whom the slave-girl has borne him, 'You are my sons', he shall count them with the sons of the bride. After the father goes to his fate, the sons of the bride and the sons of the slave-girl shall share equally in the property of the father's estate. The heir, a son of the bride, shall take (first) choice at the division.

209–210 If a man strikes the daughter of a freeman and causes her to cast that which is within her womb, he shall pay ten shekels of silver for that which is within her womb. If that woman dies as a result, they shall put his daughter to death. [Where the woman struck was of the villein or slave class, her death involved only a further fine.]

215, 218 If a surgeon has made a deep incision in a freeman with a bronze instrument and saved the man's life, or opened a cataract(?)[1] with a bronze instrument and so saved the man's eye, he shall take ten shekels of silver. If a surgeon has made a deep incision in a freeman with a bronze instrument and caused the man to die, or opened a cataract(?) with a bronze instrument and thereby destroyed the man's eye, they shall cut off his hand.

229–230 If a builder has built a house for a man and has not made his work sound, so that the house he has made falls down and causes the death of the owner of the house, that builder shall be put to death. If it causes the death of the son of the owner of the house, they shall kill the son of that builder.

It will be clear that the Code of Hammurabi does not constitute a complete system of law. Hammurabi in his prologue and epilogue makes no claim to having codified the whole of the existing law, and one can envisage matters which must at times have needed legal decisions, for which no laws are given. For instance, there is a law about kidnapping a freeman's son, but nothing about kidnapping a freeman's daughter or wife.

If Hammurabi was not codifying existing law, he must have had some other purpose. Part of this must have been related to his political and military achievements. The kingdom he had created, extending from southwest Iran to east Syria, contained a large number of former city-states and petty kingdoms, and although these shared a single culture, there were local variations in customs. In addition, the area contained citizens of two different strata, on the one hand those descended from the populations of the old city-states, and on the other those whose ethnic background was immigrant Amorites from the previous two or three centuries, and in some respects, such as penalties for causing personal injury, these two groups would have widely conflicting customs. Anyone involved in a legal case would expect to have it settled in accordance with the practice of his own background. But inevitably disputes would arise between two parties from different city-states or with different antecedents, and then a decision would have to be made about which of two different legal practices should prevail. It fell to Hammurabi to make the decisions in such cases, and this is what the laws are and what he called them. They were decisions in particular cases, incorporating principles which Hammurabi had applied in certain actual cases, and which he caused to be recorded as specimen decisions for future comparable cases.

There are cuneiform tablets which show that Hammurabi and his successors issued 'royal ordinances' to their officials as guidance for procedures in lawsuits. A letter from the king to an official directs him to try a case 'according to the ordinances which are in your presence'. Such royal ordinances, which might modify customary law, decide between variant practices in two cities, or recapitulate laws falling into disuse, may lie behind such an imposing document as the Code of Hammurabi; indeed, the core of the Code seems to be based not on abstract decrees but on collections of decisions in particular cases.

That the principles incorporated in Hammurabi's laws were observed in Babylonia, even more than a millennium after his time, is clear from records of several court cases. One such dates from as late as 527 BC. Four workmen were arraigned before the Assembly of Erech on a charge of having stolen two ducks belonging to the temple, and the case was heard in the presence of not only the two principal temple administrators but also representatives from the capital. This seems to be making very heavy weather of the theft of two ducks. Reference to the laws of Hammurabi explains why. §6 of the laws decrees that 'if a man has stolen property of a god or the palace, that man shall be put to death', whilst §8 says 'if a man has stolen either ox, sheep, ass, pig or a boat, if it belongs to a god or the palace, he shall pay thirty-fold'. Theft from actually within the temple or palace precincts was the more serious case because it was sacrilegious. Clearly the question at issue in the case of 527 BC was whether or not the offence was a capital one. This is borne out by the nature of the evidence given by the accused, who testified: 'We were digging behind the wall by the river; the two ducks . . . that we killed we buried in the mud.' That is, they were claiming that when they committed the offence they were on the river side of the boundary wall of the temple and so technically outside its precincts. Their evidence was accepted and the penalty was the lighter one – thirty-fold restitution.

There were other collections of laws from ancient Mesopotamia, amongst the most important of them being two groups of Assyrian laws from the late second millennium, one of which dealt mainly with land tenure and the other with matters concerning women. The latter are discussed in my *The Might that was Assyria* (1984), pp. 140–143.

Administration of justice

Details of the administration of justice varied widely over the two millennia with which we are concerned, but certain permanent principles are discernible. In ancient theory it was a divinely ordained duty to the king, the god's representative, to see that his people received justice; therefore justice was always a concern of a good ruler. Alongside this, in the earliest form of Mesopotamian society private disputes could go to the citizens' Assembly for decision, and relics of this remained in Babylonia down to the middle of the first millennium, with the Assembly frequently playing a part in cases involving private individuals, long after the last shadow of its political authority had passed away.

In the Old Babylonian period, attendance at the judicial Assembly seems to have been open to all male free citizens, to judge by a proverb which, with a notable lack of public spirit, counsels:

Do not go to stand in the Assembly; do not wander to the place of strife. It is in strife that fate may overtake you, and you may be made a witness for them, to testify in a lawsuit not your own.

A murder trial

An account of a murder trial in the kingdom of Isin, just before the time of Hammurabi, clearly shows the part played by the king on the one hand, and the Assembly on the other, in the administration of justice. When the charge was made, the case was first brought to the king, as the fountain of justice; he then referred it to the Assembly of Nippur, which heard the evidence and pronounced the verdict. Slightly abbreviated, and with Babylonian personal names replaced by letters, the text reads:

A . . . , B . . . , and the slave C . . . killed D. . . . After D had been killed, they told D's wife E, that her husband has been killed. E did not open her mouth, she concealed (the matter).

Their case was brought to Isin before the king, and . . . he ordered their case to be taken up in the Nippur Assembly.

There [nine named men] addressed (the Assembly) and said: 'They who have killed a man are not fit to live. Those three men and that woman should be killed in front of D's chair . . .'

[Two named persons] addressed the Assembly and said: 'Did E . . . kill her husband, that that woman should be put to death?'

Then the Nippur Assembly addressed (them) and said: '(Granted that) a woman who was not loyal to her husband knew his enemies (and that the latter) killed her husband. . . . (But) did she herself kill her husband . . . ? (It was) they (who) killed the man.'

In accordance with the decision of the Nippur Assembly, A, B, and C were handed over to be killed.

Judges

There is no mention of judges in the document, although the existence of men called 'judges' is attested from at least the twenty-fourth century. One school of thought on the history of ancient law speaks of judges sitting 'as a college or bench', but whilst judges are often mentioned as a group, they are probably to be regarded as assessors sitting with the Assembly. This is clearly indicated by a section of Hammurabi's laws, which reads:

> If a judge has judged a case, decided details of the decision, caused a sealed document to be deposited, and afterwards he changes his judgement, they shall establish that that judge has made alteration in the judgement he judged, and he shall pay twelve-fold the penalty appropriate in the case concerned; furthermore, they shall expel him from the seat of his judgeship in the assembly, and he shall not return to sit with the judges in a case.

Judges are sometimes mentioned in Old Babylonian times with no indication that there was an Assembly alongside them. In some such instances, judges may have been regarded as presidents of the Assembly, which sat passively by; there is also the possibility that sometimes the apathy of free citizens, following literally the advice of the proverb quoted on page 191, had the result that there were no citizens present other than those involved in the case, to constitute an Assembly.

In the course of the court proceedings, there might be a clash of evidence. The Assembly or the judges might then order those concerned to take an oath at a temple. Here is an example:

> Tablet in connection with the house of A, daughter of X.
>
> B, daughter of Y, made a claim against A.
>
> The judges in the Shamash temple gave judgement that A should take an oath by the life of the deity. A took the oath by the life of the goddess Aya her Lady and rebutted her [B's] claim.
>
> Since she [A] did not turn back (from the oath), B shall make no claim to A's house, paternal inheritance, property, or inheritance from her husband, as much as there may be, from straw to gold.
>
> She [B] has sworn (to accept this) by (the gods) Shamash, Aya and Marduk and by (king) Sumu-la-ilum.

Judgement of the Shamash temples. [Names of the judges are given.]

Before [two named persons, who were witnesses constituting or representing the Assembly].

Before [a named woman], the female scribe.

Perjury before a deity could, in the ancient view, bring terrible retribution, and cases are known in which one party recoiled from the oath, as the following shows:

> The witnesses of A testified before the judges, 'B beat A and took oxen away from him.' So the judges said to B, 'Take the oath of the gods against the witnesses.' And this is the declaration of B; before the judges he admitted, 'I did strike A.' B was afraid of the gods, A won the case and the judges made B pay 30 shekels of silver to A.

When there was a clash of evidence, and neither side admitted guilt by refusing the oath by the life of the gods, the decision would be handed over to the gods themselves. This was given, as in many other cultures, by the ordeal. In Babylonia the ordeal was by the river, and the rule – opposite to that found in mediaeval England and more humane – was that the guilty person sank and the innocent was saved. The laws of Hammurabi decree that charges of witchcraft were to be judged by this means:

> If a man has cast a charge of (using) black magic against a man and has not proved it, the one charged with black magic shall go to the Holy River and jump into the Holy River. If the Holy River clutches him, his accuser shall take his estate. If the Holy River clears that man and he comes safely back, he who cast the charge of black magic against him shall be put to death. He who jumped into the Holy River shall take his accuser's estate.

Normally the ordeal was reserved as a last resort after the parties concerned had been put to the oath. A letter between two kings, approximately contemporary with Hammurabi, sheds light on this practice. It reads:

Now as to these two men whom I have sent with A, . . . they have been accused in these terms: 'They have been talking with X; they know something about the affair.' [This must be a reference to some crime in their home town in which they were alleged to be implicated.] So now I am duly causing them to be brought to the Holy River. Their accuser is being guarded here under detention. Let one of your servants, a security officer, lead these men, in the company of A, to the Holy River. If these men come safely back, I shall burn their accuser in a fire. If these men die, I shall hand over their estates and people to their accuser. Please let me know the result.

The aim of Babylonian legal procedure was to secure a decision accepted by all parties as just and binding. Thus, in the case quoted earlier concerning the dispute between two ladies over the ownership of a house, the loser took an oath to accept the decision. The record of a case often specifically stipulates that it shall not be reopened. The following illustrates this, and also sheds further light on the relationship between the judges and the local Assembly.

In the matter of the orchard of Sin-magir which Mar-amurrim bought for silver.

Anum-bani made a claim in accordance with a royal ordinance and they went to the judges and the judges sent them to the Bab-ninmar shrine. Anum-bani took the oath at the Bab-ninmar shrine before the judges of the Bab-ninmar shrine. Thus he said: 'I am the son of Sin-magir. He took me for sonship and my official (adoption) document was never cancelled.' Thus he took the oath, and they [the judges] in pursuance of (the ordinance of king) Rim-sin established the orchard and house as belonging to Anum-bani.

Sin-muballit [presumably heir of Mar-amurrim] returned [i.e. reopened the case]. He claimed the orchard of Anum-bani, and they went to the judges. The judges sent them to the City (Assembly) and the witnesses [i.e. of the original sale]. They stood in the gate of Marduk (near) the divine *shurinnu*-emblem of Nanna, the divine Bird of Ninmar, the divine Spade of Marduk, and the Stone Weapon. When the former witnesses of Mar-amurrim said, 'At the Bab-ninmar shrine they administered to Anum-bani the oath, "I am indeed the son" ', they established the orchard and house as (belonging) to Anum-bani.

Sin-muballit has (now) sworn by Nanna, Shamash, Marduk and king Hammurabi that he will not return and make a(nother) claim.

Before A the mayor [and eleven other named persons].

The seals of the witnesses.

The substance ot the case seems to have been that if Anum-bani could prove that he had been adopted as son, he could reclaim land that had belonged to his father, regardless of his father having sold it. The context suggests that the 'royal ordinance' which 'Rim-sin established' gave a son the right to reclaim family land sold by his father. In some parts of the ancient Near East family land was regarded as inalienable, and the ordinance of Rim-sin may have been an attempt to reinforce a tradition about land ownership that was falling into desuetude. Alternatively, the orchard and house in question may have been held by Anum-bani's father as a royal fief which could not be sold.

In first-millennium Assyria, where administration was highly centralized and an efficient civil service functioned, the administration of law was largely in the hands of royal officials, and many records of legal decisions of the period are introduced by the formula, 'The judgement which (such-and-such an official) imposed'. However, it still remained a general principle that legal decisions should be acquiesced in by all parties. A typical record of a case includes the clause:

The case which A argued with B over the damage to his house. The damage which B did to the house has been paid in full to A. There is peace between them. One shall not dispute with the other over any further payment due from the other. Whoever transgresses against the other shall pay ten minas of silver: the gods Ashur, Shamash, Bel and Nabu are the lords of his case.

Assyrian documents of sale often stipulate heavy penalties, should one of the parties bring a lawsuit to upset the agreement.

International law

Not only was justice between individual men one of the gifts of civilized society provided by the bounty of the gods, but also relationships between states, of the kind we know as international law, were thought of as a system of divinely decreed behaviour. Kings and states were subject to the will of the gods: the making of treaties and alliances, the treatment of defeated nations, the relationship between vassals and overlords, were not conducted arbitrarily but according to a recognized code, supposed to reflect the divine will. Treaties and alliances involved a written contract in which the parties were bound by oath before the gods.

We have a great deal of cuneiform material dealing with inter-state relations in the second millennium BC, from two principal periods. The earlier source is the diplomatic archive of the early second millennium excavated by French scholars at Mari on the middle Euphrates in eastern Syria. The other main group comes from just after 1400 BC, and was found in central Egypt at El Amarna, being in fact part of the diplomatic archives of a pharaoh named Akhenaten. These latter documents show that Babylonian influence in the development of international law was so pre-eminent that Akkadian became the principal language of diplomacy between rulers even where, as between Egypt and the Hittites, it was the mother tongue of neither party. Smaller collections of cuneiform material bearing on inter-state diplomacy in the second millennium come from other sites, such as Boghazkoi in eastern Turkey and Ras Shamra (ancient Ugarit) on the coast of north Syria. In the latter case again, although the local language, written in an alphabetic script, was used for most purposes, including religion, it was Akkadian, written in syllabic cuneiform, which was largely employed for law and international affairs.

As early as the *Early Dynastic* period, inter-state relations were governed by certain conventions and standards of decency. We know this from epics. One of these deals with a dispute which developed between Enmerkar, lord of Erech, and the lord of Aratta (a state in Iran). It mentions extensive and detailed negotiations between the two parties, conducted through an ambassador. The epic dealing with the siege of Erech by the king of Kish shows that Gilgamesh, the ruler of Erech, having defeated his rival, neither put him to death nor humiliated him, but showed clemency and returned him to his own kingdom.

It is the Mari letters, from early in the second millennium, just before Hammurabi finally united Babylonia, which give us our clearest glimpse of inter-state diplomacy in the ancient world. This was a time of many small kingdoms, continually entering into relationship with each other, either as vassals or allies, a situation explicitly referred to in a letter (see page 72), in which the writer identifies four different coalitions.

The king of a small state not within such a coalition would find himself at the mercy of more powerful neighbours, as the following letter, from a lesser ruler to a greater, illustrates:

> To Yahdu-lim say, thus says Abi-samar: 'Make an alliance! . . . My towns which have not (yet) been captured will be captured now. These towns have not been lost to the hostile action of . . . the lord of Carchemish (or) Yamhad, (but) they are (now virtually) lost to the hostile action of Shamshi-adad [king of Assyria].'

In a subsequent letter Abi-samar tells Yahdu-lim:

> If you abandon Abi-samar, then you abandon your own cities. . . . Perhaps you are saying 'Abi-samar is not my son and my estate is not (involved with) his estate.' (Yet) indeed my estate is your estate and Abi-samar is your son.

That is to say, Abi-samar was offering to accept the status of vassal to Yahdu-lim in return for protection; obviously this kind of situation strengthened the movement towards larger and larger coalitions.

The treaties by which rulers of states entered into coalitions were ratified by the taking of an oath, with various ritual or symbolic acts. One such act was described as 'the touching of the throat', perhaps an ancient example of a symbolic action still sometimes employed by children in making a solemn statement. Another ritual, for sealing a treaty of peace between former enemies, involved the killing of a donkey foal, as illustrated by the following extract from a letter from an official to his king:

> The tablet of Ibal-adad reached me from (the town) Ashlakku and I went to Ashlakku for 'killing the donkey foal' between the men of Hana and the men of Ida-maraz. They brought (in addition) a puppy and a leafy bough, but I respected (the instructions of) my lord and did not deliver up the puppy and leafy bough; I (only) had the donkey foal killed, (and thereby) established friendship between the men of Hana and the men of Ida-maraz.

The puppy and leafy bough (or, as some think the word means, lettuce) must have been for a further ritual sometimes used in this connection. Another symbolic action which we sometimes meet at the ratification of a treaty was for the junior member of the alliance to 'seize the hem of the garment' of the senior.

Each coalition of states would be headed by the most powerful as suzerain, who would require the others, as his vassals, to accommodate their foreign policy to his, to refrain from having diplomatic relations with his enemies, and to give him military contingents in the event of war. It was understood that troops provided by a vassal, ally or suzerain were made available only for the duration of the emergency for which they were needed. Sometimes there was a difference of opinion between two partners as to when the emergency had ended. Thus we find a certain ambassador, Ibal-pi-El, writing to his king, Zimri-lim of Mari, about personnel of Mari on loan to Hammurabi:

> To my lord say, thus says your servant Ibal-pi-El: 'In accordance with the instructions which my lord keeps sending me, . . . I have now spoken on friendly terms [literally, 'good words'] with Hammurabi. . . . I spoke in these terms: "Inasmuch as the gods have destroyed the enemy and the days of cold weather have arrived, why do you detain the servants of your brother [i.e. 'your ally of equal rank']? Authorize me that I may go back and that the Commanding Officer may reach his estate before the cold weather." This and many (similar points) I have argued with him . . .'

There are very frequent references to ambassadors being sent from one court to another, and great importance was attached to their arrival. On one occasion Yasmah-adad of Mari, always inefficient, received a sharp and sarcastic rebuke from his father, Shamshi-adad, for delaying the members of an embassy on their way to him from Syria. Yasmah-adad was in trouble with his father yet again when he reported that another ambassador could not continue his journey beyond Mari because of some mishap, which may have been (if we may slightly emend the French editor's copy of the cuneiform text) the breaking of the axle of his chariot. 'Can't he ride a donkey?' enquired the indignant Shamshi-adad. Other letters show that omens were taken to obtain divine guidance as to how envoys were to be received. Then as today, diplomatic personnel sometimes engaged in activities which made them unwelcome. We find one sub-king writing to another to declare a certain *persona non grata*; the man was a liar, the writer said, and he did not wish to see him again.

Hostages were sometimes taken before negotiations between powers, and, if negotiations broke down, might be put to death. The following letter illustrates this; Shamshi-adad is writing to his son Yasmah-adad:

> In the matter of the people of Wilanum who are in your charge, I ordered (you) to detain them in case an alliance came about. Now there is no question of an alliance with Wilanum. ... Give instructions that the people of Wilanum, every single one that is in your charge, be put to death tonight.

It is, of course, possible that in this case the victims were prisoners of war whose lives had originally been spared because of the possibility of an alliance. But this is unlikely, as prisoners of war would generally be made slaves. There is no suggestion in the letter that the people of Wilanum were diplomatic personnel.

Often, an alliance concluded between rulers would be sealed by marriage between members of the two families. The following extract from a letter offers an example of this:

> Ishme-dagan [senior son of Shamshi-adad] has made peace with the Turukkians. He is taking the daughter of Zaziya [king of the Turukkians] for his son Mut-asqur. Ishme-dagan has had gold and silver taken to Zaziya as a bridal-gift.

Treaties enabled rulers to follow up troublesome citizens even when they had escaped from their territories, and we find applications for extradition from the Mari period onwards. The following is an example from a letter:

> To Yasmah-adad say, thus says Shamshi-adad your father: 'Ushtan-sharri the Turukkian, who had been deported to Babylon, is . . . in (the city of) Saggaratum. Now examine the antecedents of this man and the place where he is, and let the constables arrest him and let them escort him to me in (the city of) Shubat-enlil. The Babylonian Man [i.e. the king of Babylon, Hammurabi] has requested him from me.'

Inter-state treaties later in the second millennium often included clauses explicitly providing for the extradition of criminals or political refugees. Thus in a treaty (written in

Akkadian) between the Hittite king Hattusilis III (1275–1250 BC) and Ramesses II of Egypt, we read:

> If a man or two men or three men flee from the land of Hatti [the Hittite land] and go to Ramesses, the beloved of the god Amon, the Great King, the king of Egypt, my brother, (then) Ramesses . . . shall arrest them and send them to Hattusilis his brother. . . . And if a man or two men or three men flee from the land of Egypt and go to Hattusilis the Great King, the king of the land of Hatti, (then) Hattusilis . . . shall arrest them and send them to Ramesses.

Correspondingly, international arrangements were made to determine liability if a subject of one ruler were robbed or murdered in the territory of another. The following fourteenth-century document provides an instance:

> Inu-teshub king of Carchemish has made a treaty with the men of Ugarit. If a man of Carchemish is killed in Ugarit, if his murderers are arrested, they [the murderers] shall pay compensation for the man three-fold and they shall make good three-fold the things of which they robbed him. But if his murderers are not identified, they [the Ugaritians] shall pay compensation for the life three-fold; they shall repay the things, as much as he was robbed of, (only) at their capital value. And if a man of Ugarit is killed in Carchemish, the compensation is the same.

Another aspect of inter-state treaty relationships was international transport, and kings had obligations with regard to caravans and personnel crossing their territory. We have a letter in which Yasmah-adad of Mari writes to Hammurabi of Babylon about a caravan from Mari which had passed through Hammurabi's territory to Tilmun (the region of modern Bahrein) in the Persian Gulf. On the return journey it had been held up inside Hammurabi's territory over some question of the use of wells. Yasmah-adad was sending a representative to escort the caravan to Babylon, so that Hammurabi himself might sort the problem out. In another case Shamshi-adad of Assyria writes to his son Yasmah-adad complaining that some people from Yamhad (Aleppo in north Syria) had not been able to cross the Euphrates in his territory because there were no boats available. Boats must be provided, said Shamshi-adad, so that

> as previously, whoever comes along may cross and not be detained.

Rulers were responsible for the conduct of their subjects outside their own territory, and cases are known of one king lodging a complaint with another about criminal offences. Yasmah-adad of Mari complained to Aplahanda of Carchemish that subjects of the latter had kidnapped a young lady in a raid across the border. Aplahanda replied asking for details of the affair; he wanted the names of the lady herself, her abductor, and the person who was alleged to be holding her at present. But his enquiries seem to have drawn a blank, for in a further letter Aplahanda suggested that the young lady's husband should go to Carchemish himself to see if he could trace her.

The suzerain would defend and avenge any vassal of his who became subject to attack, and would act as arbitrator in the event of disagreement amongst his vassals. Cases of the latter occur already in Sumer in the mid-third millennium, and in the fourteenth century we find the powerful Hittite king Mursilis II (1334–1306 BC) settling a border dispute between neighbouring states:

> Thus says Mursilis the Great King, the king of Hatti, son of Shuppiluliuma, the Great King, the hero: 'Of old, the king of Ugarit and the king of Siannu were in a state of unity. Now years have passed by and Abdi-anati king of Siannu has become distant from Niqmepa king of Ugarit and has set his face towards the king of Carchemish. Now Abdi-anati king of Siannu in the matter of these towns [i.e. towns listed later in the document] has cited Niqmepa king of Ugarit for judgement before the Great King, the king of Hatti. . . .'

The Great King then went on to pronounce which towns belonged to which vassal. A parallel document connected with the same piece of arbitration mentions that boundary stones were set up to establish the border, and concludes with the provision:

> In future the king of Siannu or his sons or his grandsons shall not reopen the case with the king of Ugarit or his sons or his grandsons in the matter of these boundaries.

Much of what has been said about international relations in the second millennium could be paralleled from the first, when Assyria was the most prominent power. A letter datable to about 710 BC shows diplomacy in action between kings more or less equal in status. In it, king Sargon of Assyria, writing to an Assyrian dignitary of high rank, possibly his own son and successor Sennacherib, refers to overtures from Mita of Mushki in Asia Minor (that is, Midas of Meshech, the country mentioned in Genesis 10:2 and elsewhere in the Bible). The dignitary had reported that Mita, previously hostile to Assyria or at the best on the unfriendly side of neutral, had now taken the first steps to a *rapprochement*. The Assyrian king warmly welcomed the new situation and gave instructions to further the development of friendly relations. An Assyrian ambassador was to be credited to Mita, whilst consent was given for an ambassador from Mushki to come to the Assyrian court. In addition, the Assyrian king wished Mita to be informed that he was 'very pleased' about developments; furthermore, the Assyrian dignitary's proposal to make reciprocal extradition arrangements was approved. This letter reinforces the view that Assyrian imperialism owed its undoubted success at least as much to careful administration and diplomacy as to military might.

9

Administration and Government

IN any human community the possibility of government and administration depends upon the majority accepting direction by a minority or by a single individual. Differentiation between those who govern and those who are governed inevitably becomes paralleled by an inequality of division of the surpluses produced by the society. The social problems arising from this have produced a multitude of attempts at a form of society embracing social and economic equality, from the primitive Christians (Acts 4:32–35) to twentieth-century revolutions, and shortlived modern communes.

However, throughout the whole two thousand years of ancient Mesopotamian history, the state was so stable that there is no trace of any attempt to challenge it as a system, even though at times individuals or groups felt their own place in society so untenable that they reacted, by flight in the case of slaves, or by rebellion if free men.

Once a situation has arisen in which there is a majority willing to accept direction by a minority, habit becomes a powerful force to ensure continuance, only to be broken by a major catastrophe such as war or famine. But the origin of the situation remains to be explained.

For one human to accept the direction of another, either he must perceive this as in his own interests, or he must be forced to it by some sanction. In the context of ancient Mesopotamia, both self-interest and sanctions played a part in the origin of the state.

The most primitive sanction in any society is the sense of dependence of infants upon parents. Where there is an appropriate social structure the habit of deference becomes extended beyond the parents to the leaders of the clan and tribe. This factor operated amongst some of the later immigrant populations, such as Amorites from the end of the third millennium, and Aramaeans and Chaldeans from the end of the second. But when we first meet the Sumerian city-state, it was not organized on the clan or the tribe, and so this factor can have had little importance in the origin of its social structure.

Another potential sanction is the readiness of some individuals to use physical aggression. In ancient Mesopotamia, physical force was certainly employed in some circumstances in maintaining the state system once established, but there is no indication that the use of force lay at its origin.

A factor which must have played some part as Mesopotamian civilization began was recognition that vesting the direction of certain community operations in a single leader benefited every individual in the community. Such operations might range from major irrigation projects to defence against external attack. But once appointed, the leader would enjoy greater authority than other members of the group, and this would provide a nucleus from which a power structure could grow.

Religion provided another major area for such a development. Fertility was vital to the community and was controlled by the gods. Disposal of the dead required special rituals to avert the dangers from ghosts. When illness struck, it lay with the divine powers to give either recovery or death. All such matters required an approach to the divine powers, but without the proper rituals intrusion into the supernatural world was dangerous. And so in each primitive village community there was a priest or group of priests, whose professional duty it was to approach the gods on behalf of the community, to appease them when they were angry, and to announce their will. This gave them powerful sanctions. If a village prospered and grew to become an urban centre, such sanctions could be used to claim for the gods grants of land and service, providing the beginning of a temple estate. Some of the earliest tablets of which the sense can be made out, from Jemdet Nasr (*c.* 2900 BC), show very large land grants being made to various priests.

Thus we see the beginnings of two structures of social and economic power, the city-state and the temple estates. These are sometimes presented as respectively secular and religious organizations, but that is misleading. The city-state no less than the temple estates had a religious aspect, since the city-ruler became thought of as the city-god's representative. On the other side, much of the activities of the temple estates was economic and administrative.

The two power structures necessarily cooperated to maintain the system, but there was also competition between them for control of economic resources. A strong ruler in favourable circumstances might be able to curb the power of the temple estates; at other times, there might be a considerable shift to the advantage of the temples. Much of the internal history of ancient south Mesopotamia was linked to the relationship of the temple estates to the city-state or the later national ruler. Some examples of this are seen in the characteristic features of the main periods, set out below.

End of the Early Dynastic period (c. *2400* BC)

Although certain kings had claimed kingship over Sumer, the political system had not yet developed beyond loose confederations of city-states under an overlord, and the basic unit remained the city-state. At the head of a city-state was the ruler usually known as the *Ensi*, although if his dominion extended beyond his own city's territory he might bear the more imposing title *Lugal*, king, with governors subject to him in dependent city-states. Within the city-state there might be several temple estates. The economy of both structures depended upon land, with subsidiary production mainly in the form of weaving of textiles. They thus had a considerable need for labour, which was largely supplied by landless free men and women, although there were some slaves. Such workers were provided either with an allotment of land or with rations. A further element in the economic basis of the power of the *Ensi* was his right to levy taxes upon free landowners. Taxes were imposed upon such commodities and activities as cattle, boats, fisheries, the wool-clip, brewing, burial and divorce, and were collected by inspectors who constituted a rudimentary government service.

Each temple estate would have its own administration, subject in the first place to the *Ensi* or king and ultimately to the god whose steward he was. Responsibilities of the temple administrators included organizing the temple personnel, arranging the issue of rations and tools, and overseeing the temple's considerable lands, herds and fisheries.

Conflicts between royal and temple interests are reflected in Uru-inim-gina mentioning, at the end of this period, that the *Ensi* formerly illegally used the temples' oxen and fields.

The dynasty of Agade (2371–2230 BC)

As the first empire, this saw experimentation with centralized control of an area much larger than the city-state. But the absence of an adequate infrastructure brought frequent local revolts of the old city-states (see pages 50, 52). The wider horizons resulted in an increase of foreign state-controlled trade, but in the internal economy the period saw an adverse change. Workers on royal and temple estates had formerly received allotments of land, but now the practice developed of making them totally dependent upon the issue of subsistence rations; in consequence, such workers began to be reduced, in effect although not in name, to the status of slaves. This had become very marked by the succeeding period. However, there still remained large sectors of land owned and worked by private families outside the royal and temple economic systems, but even here royal taxes and the political power of the king put private owners under great pressure to sell; we see a transparent instance of this when we find one of the kings of Agade acquiring very large amounts of land from communities at the absurdly low price of less than one year's crop.[1]

The Third Dynasty of Ur (c. 2100 BC)

Government under the III Ur Dynasty was far more strongly centralized than in the Agade period; and the empire controlled from Ur, which went far beyond the confines of Sumer, was politically the most efficiently organized structure of its kind before Assyrian times.

Provincial administration was in the hands of civil governors dependent upon the king. They were liable to transfer from city to city, a system which restricted their independent power by limiting the development of local ties without which they could not become powerful enough to challenge the central authority. Also, the military administration was made separate from the civil. Such measures served to check the perennial internal rebellions which had been such a problem under the Agade dynasty. Regular reports from all quarters reached the king through royal messengers, enabling him to keep abreast of developments throughout the empire.

The temple estates still existed as separate entities, but, like everything else in Sumerian life in this period, were essentially under royal control. An enormous bureaucracy existed for the administration of the temple and royal estates and trade.

The Old Babylonian period; Mari

The administrative system of the III Ur empire had already broken down before the capital itself was destroyed. Administration in the small splinter kingdoms which took the place of the old empire was therefore a local matter. Gradually these small kingdoms consolidated into larger units, culminating in south Mesopotamia in the kingdom of Babylonia, but the old city-states were no longer of importance as administrative units.

Provincial administration at this time is illustrated by the city of Terqa, part of the territories of king Zimri-lim of Mari. What follows is based on an important study by the Belgian scholar J. R. Kupper.

Terqa was under the jurisdiction of a governor, Kibri-dagan. Its territory comprised a sixty-mile stretch of villages and small towns along the right bank of the middle Euphrates, probably, because of considerations of irrigation, extending not further than five miles away from the river. Within this area there were both settled peoples and nomads from various tribes. The nomads were represented before the governor by their sheikhs (*suqaqu*), and the situation was probably similar for villagers. In the small towns there was a local official called the *hazannu* (overseer or mayor), whilst the *shibutum* or elders constituted a kind of local Assembly. The governor himself was concerned with the maintenance of order, the execution of justice, and, above all, with public works, in particular the canals and irrigation, for, as Kibri-dagan says in a letter to the king, 'if the waters are cut off, the lands of my lord will die of hunger'.

In all these matters the final responsibility rested with the king. This made it imperative for governors to send frequent reports not only on political and military matters, but also on everything which concerned the wellbeing of the territory entrusted to them. And so we find such disasters as epidemics, floods, and invasion by locust swarms being duly reported to the king. A governor could communicate with the king and the governors of other cities by a variety of messengers, ranging from simple carriers of tablets to confidential agents. The king kept a close eye on his officials, and we have letters in which officials had had to defend themselves against charges of negligence.

If a major military emergency occurred, a chain of fire beacons was available to transmit a warning of danger rapidly over the whole land. The only problem was to ensure that the system was not set off irresponsibly. There is a letter which reveals an occasion when the unfortunate Yasmah-adad, sub-king of Mari, always a muddler, had panicked and raised a national alarm for nothing more than a local raid. His helpful and efficient elder brother, Ishme-dagan, writes to advise him how to extricate himself from his predicament:

> To Yasmah-adad say, thus says your brother Ishme-dagan: 'Because you lit two fires during the night, possibly the whole land will be coming to (your) assistance. Have tablets written to all the land, . . . and have your fleetfooted young couriers sent out. You should say, "A considerable body of enemy came on a raid into the land, and (it was) because of this (that) two fires were lit. There is no need to come to (my) assistance."'

Babylon

Hammurabi's laws provide us with a framework for the administrative system in the kingdom he created, which ultimately included Mari; and this is filled out from the evidence of business documents, and correspondence between the king and his local officials. The letters show that administration under Hammurabi was highly centralized, and that no matter was too small to merit his personal attention.

As Hammurabi's ancestors and other Amorite princes gradually gathered the fragments of the III Ur empire into their hands, they were able to bring into their own ownership much land which had earlier belonged to the temples. They had to devise a method of working all this land, and the distribution of royal land became an important part of the administrative system. Plots of such land were allotted to men who performed certain duties for the king; it remained with the grantee, and usually with his son, so long as they rendered the appropriate services; but it was not given as a freehold, and Hammurabi's laws specifically proscribed the sale of such land. There were four classes of military personnel referred to in the laws as holding land in this way, sometimes loosely rendered as sergeant, recruiting officer [literally 'fisherman'], colonel and lieutenant, although there is such a wide difference between Babylonian and modern military structure that such translations do not give an accurate picture. Letters show that it was not only military men who held land in this way; a considerable number of others, such as merchants, scribes, shepherds, jewellers, smiths and soothsayers, to specify only a few, received similar land grants. This is obvious from letters such as this:

> To Shamash-hasir say, thus says Hammurabi: 'When you see this tablet, deliver one *bur* of land [about nineteen acres] to Sin-mushtal, one *bur* to Ili-idinnam, one *bur* to Ili-ihmeani, the three comptrollers of the merchants of Ur, together with their old-standing fields of maintenance.'

'Field of maintenance' was a term denoting fief. Registers recording such grants and rights were kept and referred to in case of dispute. §28 of Hammurabi's laws indicates that grants were given in succession from father to son, and the following shows an instance of this:

> To Shamash-hasir say, thus says Hammurabi: 'Give to Munawwirum the dispatch rider, as his field of maintenance, three *bur* of land [about fifty-seven acres] from his father's estate at Dimti-ili.'

The immediate administration of such matters was in the hands of the governor, who had a threefold responsibility; he was concerned with security, public works (including canals and royal land) and communications, although in all such matters he was closely tied by royal instructions. If a governor did venture to neglect the king's orders, such a dereliction of duty would bring a sharp rebuke. Thus, in one letter, the governor Shamash-hasir is told by Hammurabi:

> Last year I sent some dispatch riders to you for settlement on the

> land. Although they were in your presence for eight months, you did not satisfy a single man.

After giving detailed instructions for rectifying this, the king concludes:

> If these dispatch riders are not quickly satisfied, . . . you will not be pardoned.

Babylonia in the second half of the second millennium

In the Old Babylonian period, although the old city-state system retained little practical importance, kings still called themselves king of a particular city (e.g. Mari or Babylon), and theoretically wielded dominion over the land as a group of subordinate cities; Hammurabi, for example, in the prologue to his laws, enumerates nearly twenty such major cities making up his realm.

The Cassite rulers in the second half of the second millennium began the practice of calling the ruler 'king of Karduniash [i.e. Babylonia]'; thus, the land was now conceived of as a political unit in itself, not a collection of city-states. Subsequently, in the twelfth century, Babylonia was divided for administrative purposes into twenty or more provinces under governors, unrelated to the old city-state structure. Temples still owned some land, but on a much more limited scale than in the third millennium; and economic power and administrative responsibility lay predominantly with the king. Controlling vast tracts of land, the king was able to maintain and extend his influence by judicious grants of estates to private individuals or temples.

From shortly before the end of the second millennium, a new administrative factor began to develop with the arrival of nomadic peoples with a clan structure, Aramaeans who settled in rural areas away from the cities and Chaldeans who took over the southern marshes.

First millennium; New Assyrian period

Politically Assyria was distinct from Babylonia, but the justification for considering Assyria here is that it was the expanding Assyrian empire which in the first millennium spread Sumerian and Babylonian institutions throughout the Near East, far beyond their place of origin in south Mesopotamia.

Byron's celebrated couplet –

> The Assyrian came down like the wolf on the fold,
> And his cohorts were gleaming in purple and gold –

does little justice to the Assyrian system of imperial government. The Assyrians were not simply out for loot. The lands which came under their control they not only attempted to administer, but succeeded in administering with admirable efficiency: indeed, Assyrian administration compares very favourably with the situation which prevailed in much of the area a century ago and in some of it at the present day. Byron's picture of Assyrian hordes sweeping down on defenceless valley populations and withdrawing to leave death and desolation in their wake is a distorted one, as even the Old Testament, written from the point of view of one of the more vocal and nationally conscious subject races, shows. One finds from reading the Old Testament prophets, that where Assyria is condemned, the condemnation is in no case for barbarity nor even for administrative harshness. This is true even of Nahum's gloating prophecy over Assyria's fall. To Nahum, Assyria's offence was its participation in witchcraft coupled with its commercial success: he proclaims that Assyria is doomed

> because of the multitude of the whoredoms of the wellfavoured harlot, the mistress of witchcrafts, that selleth nations through her whoredoms, and families through her witchcrafts (3:4),

and casts against Assyria the taunt

> Thou hast multiplied thy merchants above the stars of heaven (3:16).

Throughout the other prophets, any condemnation of Assyria is not for any specific aspect of its treatment of conquered races but for what one might best call arrogance, that is, for claiming to exercise as of right power merely delegated by God. By Hosea, indeed, Assyria itself is not condemned at all: it is upon Israel that the condemnation falls, for reliance upon the might of Assyria rather than upon God (12:1). Isaiah recognized Assyria – which he described as 'the rod of [God's] anger' (10:5) – as the instrument of Yahweh (Jehovah, the Lord), and for him Assyria was doomed not for any specific misuse of power but for failing to acknowledge the source of the power it wielded by God's will (Isaiah 10:6–16). Zephaniah, in similar strain, foretold the destruction of Assyria not for inhumanity but for pride:

> He will stretch out his hand against the north, and destroy Assyria; and will make Nineveh a desolation, and dry like a wilderness. . . . This is the rejoicing city that dwelt carelessly, that said in her heart, I am, and there is none beside me. (Zephaniah 2:13, 15)

Biblical reflections on the punishment of Assyria subsequent to its fall likewise look back not to any particular form of injustice, but to its arrogance in usurping power belonging properly to God, and impiety in swallowing up the Chosen People. Ezekiel paints a most attractive picture of the Assyrian Empire:[2]

> The Assyrian was a cedar in Lebanon with fair branches, and with a shadowing shroud, and of an high stature. . . . All the fowls of heaven made their nests in his boughs, and under his branches did all the beasts of the field bring forth their young, and under his shadow dwelt all great nations. . . . The cedars in the garden of God could not hide him . . . nor any tree in the garden of God was like unto him in his beauty. (Ezekiel 31:3, 6, 8)

The sin for which the great tree Assyria was felled was Pride (Ezekiel 31:10), but Ezekiel felt no vindictiveness in his reflections upon Assyria's fall. He adds significantly:

> Thus saith the Lord God; In the day when he went down to the grave I caused a mourning. (Ezekiel 31:15)

This is not to deny that by modern standards Assyrian administrative methods were harsh; but the other side of the system must not be overlooked. Far from being simply a despotic militarism holding down conquered races by mere brutal harshness, Assyrian imperialism owed much of its success to an efficient administrative system, and to the attention of an energetic bureaucracy to the day-to-day trifles of government. Even as early as the reign of Ashur-nasir-pal II (883–859 BC), administrative action in conquered territories was not arbitrary but according to recognizable principles; and from the time of Tiglath-pileser III, some 140 years later, in whose reign the Hebrew kingdoms came irrevocably into the Assyrian orbit, a definite pattern in imperial administration may be seen.

Assyria and subject states

Broadly speaking, Assyrian-controlled territory included units of population related to the central government in one of three main ways. Firstly, and most loosely bound, were those states whose rulers had, from motives of prudence, brought tribute to the Assyrian king as the token of a friendly attitude which, according to circumstances, would lie somewhere between alliance and vassaldom. In return for their tribute, the rulers of such states would receive a guarantee to their states and dynasties against aggression: the Assyrian guarantee, unlike that of Egypt – a power derisively described by an Assyrian commander-in-chief as a 'bruised reed, . . . whereon if a man lean, it will go into his hand, and pierce it' (Isaiah 36:6) – was usually implemented, and was so highly regarded that in some cases, of which the best-known instance is that of Ahaz of Judah (2 Kings 16:7–9), a small state would take the initiative in seeking to become an Assyrian tributary. In practice the political status of states in relationship with Assyria would vary within very wide limits, according to such factors as geographical position, matrimonial alliances with other states, and where the nearest Assyrian military forces or officials were. In some cases the interests of Assyria might be secured by an Assyrian adviser or observer permanently attached to a native court.

States which had once accepted – whether of their own seeking or under Assyrian pressure – this kind of relationship with Assyria tended almost inevitably to come in course of time under a closer form of control; for if such a tributary, once having made formal submission, subsequently withheld its annual tribute, this was regarded as a hostile act, and was liable to call down military action. In some cases, by the good fortune or foresight of the delinquent state, Assyria was fully occupied elsewhere and the tributary escaped immediate retribution, but in many instances Assyria's response was to make an attack on the recalcitrant territory with a small force, pruning it back by annexing the outlying parts to a more reliable subject state or province. The Assyrians would then intervene in the internal affairs of the state to replace the unreliable ruler by another prince acceptable to Assyria, or, where a loyal pro-Assyrian ruler had been removed by internal faction, to reinstate the Assyrian protégé or a member of his family. The ruler recognized by Assyria would now be bound by oath before the great gods, whilst an Assyrian official, probably backed by a small military force, would be left in the territory to watch local events, to control the foreign relations of the state, and to ensure due payment of tribute. This marked the second stage of relationship with Assyria.

Subsequent rebellion was an offence, not only against the king of Assyria, but also against the gods by whom the oath of allegiance had been sworn, and as such was punishable by death. The punishment was not so much revenge against the offender or a warning to others as the expiation of an offence against the gods. Such an offence, if not suitably expunged, might bring divine retribution – plague, flood, famine, earthquake or other phenomena manifesting the gods' displeasure – upon the whole territory. It is not hard to find in the Old Testament parallels to this conception of the national ill-fortune likely to result from breaking an oath or otherwise slighting a god. Achan stole from the booty consecrated to the tribal god: defeat at once befell the Israelites and only gave way to success after the sin had been discovered and the sinner executed (Joshua 7). Jonathan broke an oath of fasting to which his father Saul had committed all the Israelites, and although he had done so unwittingly, he faced execution, and only escaped death by the popular feeling that the victory Jonathan had just won demonstrated that God approved his action, Saul's oath notwithstanding (1 Samuel 14:24–25).

Because of its expiatory nature, Assyrian execution in such circumstances might involve tortures such as flaying, immuring, pulling out the lying tongue, burning or impaling. It is atrocities of this type, usually considered without reference to the context of events, which have largely been responsible for the indignation expressed against Assyria by modern commentators. Other sources of offence to modern historians are the heaping up of heads or bodies of the dead, and the holocaust of prisoners, frequently referred to in Assyrian royal annals in phrases like 'Their corpses I formed into pillars; their young men and maidens I burned in the fire'. The former, although offensive to religious susceptibilities, was not in itself an atrocity to living men, and moreover it can be directly paralleled from the twentieth century AD: Sir Philip Gibbs (*The Pageant of the Years*, page 300) mentions a photograph of 'a Turkish officer sitting on a pile of skulls and smoking a cigarette'. As to the phrase about burning in the fire, it is open to question whether or not this meant that children were burnt alive.

Actual tortures on living men (see plate 46A), far from being typical of treatment meted out to conquered peoples as a whole, generally affected only a small number – usually less than a dozen – of the ruling class: the mass of the population was either fined and left to go about its business, or, with increasing frequency as time went on, dealt with by deportation (see plates 33A and 34), the conquered territory being repopulated from elsewhere and reorganized into a province under direct Assyrian administration. If one wishes to pass judgement on the Assyrians in such matters, it should be by comparison with contemporary standards, as revealed in the Bible. A few examples from the Books of Kings will make this clear. King Baasha of Israel, on taking the throne from Jeroboam's successor, wiped out, with the approval of the prophets of Yahweh, the whole family of Jeroboam (1 Kings 15:25–30); Zimri, also with prophetic approval, did the same to Baasha's family on usurping the throne in his turn (1 Kings 16:8–13), and in this case, as Zimri had a reign of only seven days, the royal assassin can have wasted no time in attempting to contrive a pretext to satisfy public opinion. When one king, Ahab, did show magnanimity to a defeated enemy, he was bitterly denounced by one of the prophets (1 Kings 20:30–42). A tradition records, with obvious satisfaction, the fate of forty-two cheeky urchins, cursed by Elisha for calling him 'Baldy' and in consequence eaten by bears (2 Kings 2:23, 24): whether or not the events happened as narrated, prophetic circles and later editors obviously felt it was the kind of thing that ought to happen. Another Israelite monarch, Jehu, having exterminated seventy sons of Ahab and all his surviving relatives, together with most of the Judaean royal family and a multitude of inoffensive if misguided followers of Baal, received the enthusiastic approval of influential sections of the worshippers of Yahweh (2 Kings 10:1–30). As a final example, king Menahem of Israel, on capturing a certain district, disembowelled all the pregnant women (2 Kings 15:16) without bringing down upon himself any obvious condemnation for this particular atrocity, although the biblical editors were ready enough to blame him for his shortcomings in matters relating to the cult. Judged by the moral standards which accepted such events in Israel, Assyria can no longer be indicted for exceptional barbarity. As to comparison with more recent warfare, there is not a single incident in the more gruesome sections of the Assyrian royal annals that cannot be matched from the records of the French Revolution, the Indian Mutiny, or events in Europe, Asia and Africa since AD 1939.

Although the royal annals, our main quarry for Assyrian history in the first millennium, give but scanty hints of the administrative machinery operating within the imperial provinces, it is possible to glean a great deal of information on this from the correspondence between the king and his provincial officials. Nearly two thousand letters of this genre have been found in excavations, most of them at the old royal capitals of Nineveh and Calah (Genesis 10:11, 12), and a few at the provincial city of Guzana on the Habur, the biblical Gozan (2 Kings 17:6).

These letters, covering a wide range of subjects, make it plain that most of the officials we meet in them were actively administering their territories and not merely grinding wealth from the king's subjects by a system of tax-farming. Unexpected consideration is sometimes shown to the people governed, and although this was certainly in the first instance in the interests of efficiency rather than of humanity, can any better claim be made for modern philanthropy in industry? In one instance an official named Ashur-matka-gur had received a royal enquiry about some Aramaeans whom he was responsible for resettling. In his reply he reported: 'They will shortly take the road. I have given them their provisions, clothes, shoes and oil.' But food and equipment did not exhaust the king's arrangements for the settlers: apparently he had also planned to provide wives for them. But here, as we learn from another letter from Ashur-matka-gur, a difficulty had arisen. He reported:

> About the Aramaeans of whom the king said, 'They are to be married off', the women say, 'We find that the Aramaean men are unwilling to give us money', and 'Not until they give us money!'

The ladies seem to have been insisting upon receiving a bridal settlement before marriage; they were justified in this, according to Assyrian law. Ashur-matka-gur's proposed solution was that the Aramaeans should be given the money necessary to meet the ladies' demands. This kind of planning was doubtless not for abstract humanitarian considerations but to ensure the stability of the resettled populations: none the less, attention to such details must have alleviated many hardships.

In another letter an official, probably a provincial governor in the east of Assyria, had been accused of settling farmers on land subject to flooding, and hastened to defend his record. 'The harvest,' he wrote, 'is in fact a very good one,' and he went on to give details to justify his claim. No doubt the central government's concern was largely the possible loss of revenue, but from the point of view of the ordinary peasant the result of attention to this kind of detail was more tolerable working conditions.

Assyrian governors and provinces

An Assyrian governor (Akkadian *bel pihati*, meaning literally 'lord of the province'), appointed to administer a directly-ruled province, would, as the king's personal representative, hold a status combining civil, fiscal, military and religious duties. His official residence in the provincial capital was known as 'the Palace', and to this would be attached a staff including, amongst others, such officials as scribes, messengers, surveyors, accountants, diviners, astrologers, recruiting officers and irrigation controllers, as well as military aides and officers to command the armed forces at the governor's disposal. There must also have been interpreters in the governor's entourage, and certainly the Assyrian commander-in-chief at the siege of Jerusalem (2 Kings 18:26ff.) must have had a Hebrew-speaking herald on his staff.

Some of the more ancient provinces were customarily the responsibility of the great officers of state, who must frequently have left their provinces to government by deputy whilst they advised the king at the capital or led campaigns; other more recently constituted provinces were governed by officers of lesser prestige. There seems, however, to have been no generally maintained distinction between provinces based on seniority.

Within the provinces were smaller areas called *qannu*, centred on the large towns and under the control of an officer known as the *rab alani* ('chief of the townships'), who also had military forces at his disposal. In some cases, the municipal administrations of the great cities of both Assyria and Babylonia retained a measure of autonomy, derived ultimately from the social system of the early third millennium but more recently confirmed by royal charter in return for support at times of internal crisis, particularly rebellion or disputed succession (see page 106). But even in such cases, the presence in the area around the city of a representative of the central government, backed by troops, no doubt sometimes served to remind a truculent city administration of the wisdom of moderation in its demands upon the king.

One of the *rab alani*'s essential functions was to collect taxes, paid in kind, and to forward them to the central government depot; any shortfall would quickly set a royal inquiry under way. In a typical case an inspector, Ashipa, had been sent to examine suspicious circumstances in Babylonia and to report on deficiencies. He was apparently satisfied that the *rab alani* was not culpable. The missing grain, he wrote to tell the king, could not be transported to Sippar (where apparently the royal depot was) before the local canal had been opened: the writer gave his royal master an assurance that work on the canal was being carried out with all possible speed.

A *rab alani* would also obviously be responsible for safeguarding order within his area. On occasion, in a frontier region, it could happen that imperial security would depend upon his taking appropriate military action in the face of enemy troop movements. The royal archives contain several references to this situation. A typical example refers to a clash on the Urartian frontier to the northeast of Assyria, on which the local governor reported:

> I sent troops with the *rab alani*. . . . The *rab alani*'s lieutenant and nine men with him were wounded by bow-shot. Two of the enemy are dead and three are wounded.

Communications

An efficient communication system was vital to the security and smooth functioning of the empire, and extant letters show that provincial governors were in constant day-to-day touch with the central government. The *rab alani* officers in turn communicated regularly with the governors of their provinces and, where necessary, with the central government. Communication with the central government was by professional messengers of various classes, most commonly an officer called *mar shipri* ('son of the message'), who travelled along the 'royal roads'. These royal roads were the main arteries of the empire, and though they were probably cleared tracks rather than made-up roads in the modern, or the Roman, sense, they were certainly well enough defined to be used as boundaries between provinces, and level enough to permit the rapid passage of large armies accompanied by chariots. Along the roads across the empire, about a day's journey (twenty to thirty miles) apart, were posts permanently manned by government troops, containing a change of horses or mules for the use of the messengers on the next stage. A *mar shipri* would thus travel mounted, from stage to stage, with a small escort of troops, carrying round his neck in a bag[3] the tablets containing his governor's dispatches or the king's replies. The post-animals were restricted to particular routes, no doubt to ensure that each section should always have beasts available, and this sometimes led to friction. More than one letter is known containing a complaint to the king from the staff of a stage-post, to the effect that some high official had claimed the right to use the last remaining transport animal on an unofficial route. This could cause dislocation in the communication system, as one agitated official recognized when, caught in this dilemma, he explained to the king:

> The king my lord knows that there is no posting stage to Shabir-ishu; and (post animals) which go there do not return.

We thus see that the famous Persian system of post-roads operating throughout the Persian empire was not a Persian innovation but the development of a system already employed several centuries earlier by the Assyrians.

There were occasions when the regular imperial communication system was not adequate. For example, in the more remote and mountainous provinces, heavy falls of snow might impede mounted messengers, but the dispatches must still reach the court. We learn what happened in such cases from a letter by a certain Dur-ashur, probably the governor of a province in the mountains of what is now southeastern Turkey. He writes to the king:

> Perhaps the king will say, 'Why did you not send . . . by a *mar shipri*?' The snow is very heavy; I therefore sent a *dayalu* ['runner'] with a message.

The 'runner' must have been a skilled mountaineer who could find a way over terrain difficult for horses. Runners were employed for communications in the same area up to the nineteenth century AD; of them H. J. Ross, *Letters from the East* (1856), pages 239f., writes: 'They go at a steady trot, taking very little rest in the twenty-four hours, and carry the letters in a wallet on their back. . . . They cover 100 miles in twenty-four hours, that is to say 100 miles by road, but their knowledge of the short cuts over the mountains lessens the distance.'

Another circumstance in which an ordinary *mar shipri* could not be used was when news for the private ear of the king or a governor required to be communicated. Such a mission would be entrusted to a special envoy, carrying a letter of introduction attested by his principal's seal: his credentials having been presented, he could then pass on his confidential message with the requisite secrecy. The king had a number of such agents, called *Qurbuti* ('Intimates'), travelling on his business, and when a complaint was made against a senior official, it would normally be one of them who was dispatched to investigate and report to the king. Even a governor was liable to receive a visit of inspection from the king's confidential agent, for such an official was far from being left with a free hand in his territory: not only was the initiative permitted to him distinctly limited, since a governor often received instructions from the capital even on matters of seemingly trivial detail, but at times one governor might be subordinate to another, whilst not infrequently complaints lodged against governors were investigated by the king. But who dared to criticize his governor? It seems that such complaints could come either from another official who felt that the governor in question was encroaching on his privileges, or from a private citizen, even a non-Assyrian, who felt that he had been oppressively treated and who appealed to the king for justice. Thus we have the letter of a certain Marduk-shum-usur, probably of Babylonian origin, who appealed to the king for redress because a small estate granted him as a fief had been seized by his governor, although, Marduk-shum-usur claimed, he had never failed in the performance of his feudal duty:

> To the king my lord your servant Marduk-shum-usur. May it be well with the king my lord. May the gods Nabu and Marduk bless the king my lord.
>
> The father of the king my lord delivered to me a field of ten homers [about forty-five acres] in the land of Halahhi. For fourteen years I enjoyed the use of the field and no one disputed it with me. Now the governor has come . . . , mistreated the tenant, plundered his house, and taken away his field. The king my lord knows that I am a fief-holder and that I carry out the duties [literally 'keep the watch'] of the king my lord. . . . Now the king my lord may see that I am deprived of the land. Let the king my lord deal with my cause, that I may not die of hunger.

We do not know if Marduk-shum-usur succeeded in his suit. Nor do we know the conditions under which an appeal from a private citizen was likely to reach the king; no doubt officialdom could in many cases prevent a complaint from obtaining effective royal consideration, but the presence of such letters of complaint in the royal archives shows that in at least some cases they reached their destination.

Rights of cities

Even at the height of Assyrian royal power, some of the ancient cities still enjoyed a considerable measure of autonomy, which the king, whilst often seeking to curb it, was sometimes compelled to recognize. The manner in which such rights were maintained and developed is shown in some letters written to Tiglath-pileser III in 731 BC. The two writers, officials in Babylonia, found themselves in a difficult situation. They had a Chaldean rebellion on their hands, the capital, Babylon, was controlled by the rebels, and no adequate Assyrian forces were within reach. In one letter they reported to the king the measures they had taken. They had, they said, stood outside the city gate to attempt to negotiate with the people within. Their obvious attempt to drive a wedge between the rebel Chaldean leaders and the native Babylonians is curiously reminiscent of the situation at the siege of Jerusalem in 2 Kings 18:26ff., in which, to the alarm of the Jewish leaders, the Assyrian general, the Rab-shakeh, used Hebrew to offer terms direct to the populace. 'Why do you behave hostilely to us on their account?' cried the Assyrian officials; 'Should Babylon show favour to tribesmen?' And then they added, 'Your city's privileges are already set down in a charter', clearly implying that Assyria was, in return for their assistance, prepared to recognize all their traditional local rights. Another letter mentions that the writer had promised the people inside Babylon, 'I will free from forced labour and tribute any Aramaeans who desert'.

Within the ancient cities local government was usually still in the hands of the Elders, presided over by the *hazannu*, an official whose title is often loosely translated 'mayor'. The *hazannu* and the Council of Elders in a city such as Ashur could be a constant source of annoyance to the king, and this may account in part for several changes of capital in Assyria. It could also account for the existence in some of the great cities, alongside the *hazannu*, of another official whose title meant 'Man over the City'. This office seems by no means to have had the antiquity of that of *hazannu*, nor to have carried the religious significance which an ancient office usually involved, and it seems likely that the office of 'Man over the City' was deliberately created by the kings of Assyria as a counterbalance to the *hazannu* to safeguard the royal interests within the city. A comparable method of securing some royal control within powerful temple corporations was employed in Babylonia from before the middle of the first millennium.

Land ownership in first-millennium Assyria

The power of the Assyrian state ensured a considerable shift in the balance of control of land in favour of the king. None the less, temples and private persons still owned land, and if the king needed the land of a private landowner he had to buy it; we have a document giving an example of this when Sargon II (721–705 BC) wanted a site for his new capital of Dur-sharrukin. But by the eighth century much of the land of Assyria had come under the control of the king, and could be granted to army veterans as a reward for faithful service or to members of the civil service, or indeed to temples, in consideration of the performance of certain duties. Some favoured individuals might, along with their land grant, be given exemption from various customary dues upon land, and this would be specified in a charter. The following is an extract from such a document:

> I, Ashurbanipal, the great king, the mighty king, king of the civilized world, king of Assyria, king of the four regions, true

shepherd, worker of good, king of justice, lover of right, who makes his people prosper, who treats with favour the officials who stand in his presence and rewards the respectful who observe his royal commands,

As to Bulta, chief officer of the fodder supplies of Ashurbanipal king of Assyria, a good and well-disposed man, . . . whose heart is perfect towards his lord, who has stood before me in faithfulness, who has gone about in integrity within my palace, . . . who has guarded my kingship,

at the prompting of my own heart and by my own counsel I thought of doing him good. . . . I have declared exempt from taxation the fields, orchards and people that he has acquired under my protection . . . and I have written and sealed (this charter) with my royal seal and delivered it to Bulta, chief officer of the fodder supplies. From those fields and orchards no grain tax shall be levied, no straw tax shall be levied, the increase of their cattle and their sheep shall not be liable to be seized as taxes; they [the lands and their personnel] shall not be liable to corvée or militia service; they are clear of quay and ferry taxes. . . .

New Babylonian period, 605–539 BC

The collapse of Assyrian rule in the last quarter of the seventh century BC did not involve a general breakdown of government throughout the Near East: had it done so, it would have been impossible for the successor-state, Babylonia, to reorganize the region so rapidly that within thirty years, under Nebuchadnezzar, the empire was apparently as strong as it had ever been. The main change, from the point of view of administration, was that the imperial centre was now in an area where the temple estates had in recent centuries enjoyed far more economic and social power than in Assyria. The growing might of Assyria during the first millennium, and its frequent interventions in Babylonian internal affairs, had much diminished the political power of the Babylonian king, and the temples had taken advantage of this. There may also have been a directly religious factor. In Assyria the king was consecrated at the beginning of his reign once and for all, and so was the representative of the gods without limitation; but it was otherwise in Babylonia. To the very end, the king had to lay his royal insignia humbly before the god each year, submit to personal indignities at the hands of the high priest, make a declaration of good intentions, and only then receive re-investment with the royal authority for a further year. This meant that in Babylonia the king remained a tenant-at-will of the god, which, at a time when he could not counterbalance this by external political power, put him at a disadvantage relative to the temples. In consequence, an important factor in the domestic history of Babylonia in the New Babylonian period was a struggle for power between the dynasty and the temple corporations, in which the main measure of success lay with the corporations.

This trend is seen in the city of Uruk, the biblical Erech, about a hundred miles southeast of Babylon. Under the Assyrian empire this seems to have been fairly firmly under royal control; decisions about canals, about corn supplies, about action against troublesome Chaldean tribesmen encroaching on lands belonging to Erech, all originated from the Assyrian capital. But the documents from the New Babylonian period show the temple authorities to have been exercising a large measure of autonomy, which the Babylonian kings attempted, without much success, to check.

At the beginning of the New Babylonian empire, Eanna, the great temple at Erech, owned vast tracts of land in Babylonia, from Ur in the south to within sight of Babylon in the north. It was controlled by three principal administrators, the *Shatammu* ('Superintendent'), the *Qipu* ('Warden'), and the *Tupsharru* ('Scribe', 'Secretary'). Probably the *Qipu* was a royal nominee, but his diminishing importance in the documents of the period suggests that he was gradually being elbowed out of any real share in the control of temple affairs. It was therefore desirable for the king to take measures to reinforce his representative's waning influence in the temple administration. The king had certain privileges in connection with the temple, such as a share of particular revenues, and these gave him grounds for intervening. In 553 BC, the third year of his reign, Nabu-na'id installed two royal officers (with titles meaning 'Royal Inspector' and 'Royal Officer over the King's Coffer') ostensibly to safeguard such interests, in fact as a counterpoise to the power of the *Shatammu*. In the great temple in Babylon, indeed, it is known that Nabu-na'id actually had his own henchman as *Shatammu*, a highly unpopular state of affairs which helped to bring about his downfall, as we know from a poem which narrates the events of his reign from the viewpoint of his opponents:

> Zeria the *Shatammu* bows before him,
> Rimut the *Zazakku* stands at his side.
> They establish the instructions of the king, they make his word stand;
> They bare their heads, they take an oath,
> 'It is not until now that we understand, after the king has spoken.'

Temple administration in New Babylonian Erech

Goods produced on the temple estates were in the first place brought to a depot in Erech. The network of canals made transport a simple matter: we see an example in a letter which gives instructions for sending a consignment of sheep. The writer, probably the *Shatammu* of Erech, orders:

> If the terrain is suitable, let them come on the hoof; if not, let them come by ship.

Ships so employed were probably in most cases temple property, although sometimes they were hired from private shipmasters. As they neared Erech all ships destined for the temple came under the jurisdiction of the *Shatammu*. We find mention of quay-masters along the canals, apparently royal officers empowered to stop passing shipping and levy a toll, but ships plying for the temple were privileged, and the *Shatammu* could, by providing a ship with an emblem called a *hutaru*, a kind of sacred staff, obtain toll-free passage for it, as the following letter shows:

> Letter of Iddina and Shamash-eriba to the *Shatammu* our lord. Daily we pray to Bel, Nabu, the lady of Erech and Nana for the life, breath, happiness and health and length of days of our lord.
>
> We have brought up 200 *kur* of dates [about 30 tons] from the canal (called) 'Nadin-apli's cutting'. We are being detained by the quay-master in Bit-kasir. Let a missive come from my lord to Nuna the quay-master to let us pass the quay. . . . Half a shekel of silver as the hire of the ship and one shekel of silver as the hire of hired men (is accruing) against us per day. Our lord ought to know that we have been detained at the quay since the twentieth. Let a *hutaru* come with my lord's missive and let it stay on board.

Like monasteries much later, Eanna, the great temple of Erech, was more than a religious shrine; it was a thriving trading centre, and a substantial part of the goods collected there subsequently went out again to other parts of Babylonia and even abroad. Extant letters contain many references to trade by which the products of the temple estates, mainly agricultural, were exchanged for such goods as pottery, alum, metals, timber or cloth, some of which came from as far afield as Asia Minor. Erech also provided wine for the capital; one letter mentions an indignant complaint from some authorities in Babylon that wine had been sent to them in a ship which also contained pitch.

The temple administrators included amongst their duties responsibility for many thousands of people on the temple estates, who ranged in status from senior officers of the temple with ancient prescriptive rights, such as *mar-bani* (members of patrician families, noblemen with certain duties) down to the lowest type of slave. There was also a very large class of temple servants known as *shirke* (singular *shirku*). *Shirku* meant 'a person bestowed', and the *shirke* were people – of either sex – who had been dedicated to the goddess Ishtar of Erech and who were thus technically her slaves. This status was hereditary. At Erech, *shirke* were recognizable by a star – Ishtar's symbol – tattooed on the wrist, and this mark is frequently mentioned as the decisive evidence in the records of lawsuits dealing with personal status. Thus there is a lawsuit recorded in which a certain Shamash-shum-iddin was claimed in court as a *shirku* on the grounds that he was 'the son of Silim-ishtar, the daughter of Harshi-nana, a female *shirku* of the Lady of Erech [Ishtar]'. The crucial evidence was that given by an elderly woman who had known the grandmother of the man concerned. The old lady swore:

> I certainly saw the star and tattoo marks upon the back of the hand of Harshi-nana, the slave-woman of my uncle Nadina-ahu, the grandmother of Shamash-shum-iddin, whom – before she had a child – my uncle Nadina-ahu dedicated for *shirku*-ship to the Lady of Erech.

The status of a *shirku* could be very different from that of an ordinary slave, and some of these people held positions of high responsibility. Their services were not confined to any particular sort of duty, and temple correspondence shows them working in a great variety of crafts, trades and professions both inside the temple of Eanna and on the temple estates. On the estates they would come more directly under the control of the Royal Inspector, and it was probably by means of this that the king gradually acquired rights over the *shirke*. By the time the Persians took over Babylonia under Cyrus the Great (539–529 BC), ultimate control of the *shirke* lay with the central government, even though their duties were still in connection with the temples.

Letters and administrative documents show that in the New Babylonian period the king took a share of the temple revenues; and indeed, as we have seen, special royal officers came to be installed to regulate this. Amongst temple revenues at this time were tithes on date-crops and catches of fish, rents (payable in kind) on corn-land, a cattle tax, and offerings which farmers had to make at particular festivals. In addition, death duties were levied on rich private citizens, and although these, like the tolls in certain of the canals, went wholly to the king, the temple authorities may have been responsible for their assessment and collection.

10

Trade and Commerce

SOUTH Iraq lacks three commodities needed by most human societies – stone, hardwood timber, and metal ores. Shortage of stone and copper in the earliest culture of the region, *Ubaid*, is reflected in the extensive use, for sickles and other implements, of baked clay, made very hard by firing to a temperature almost high enough to vitrify it. But there was some use of stone, including flint and obsidian, and this must have been imported. Since the nearest source of obsidian was the Lake Van region in eastern Turkey, nearly six hundred miles away, this must have come in by trade, although we do not know whether it was obtained by long-distance expeditions or by transmission from settlement to settlement. Timber was needed for the *Ubaid* temples, and must have come from the mountain ranges – the Zagros, the Taurus, the Amanus and the Lebanon – which form a half-circle round the fertile crescent.

From the beginning of the third millennium there is evidence for Sumerian influence on Egypt (see plate 64), pointing to some kind of trading link; the obvious meeting-point was Syria, but it has alternatively been suggested that the two peoples met at the Horn of Africa, at the southern end of the Red Sea, when on sea voyages in quest of gum-resins for incense; this seems improbable, since there is no other indication of journeys in that direction by Mesopotamians, nor any proof that they used gum-resins at that time. But a few centuries later there is definite proof of trading voyages between Sumer and places reached by sea via the Persian Gulf. Three trading stations in particular are mentioned – Tilmun, Magan, and Meluhha. Tilmun was probably the island of Bahrein and part of the Arabian coastal area nearby. Magan is generally taken to have been either Oman or the region opposite it on the Iranian site of the mouth of the Persian Gulf. Finally, most scholars now accept that Meluhha represented the Indus valley, where a major civilization flourished from the middle of the third millennium, sometimes called Harappan after one of its best-known sites. There was substantial commerce between these places and south Iraq; and Sargon of Agade (early twenty-fourth century BC) was able to refer proudly to ships trading with Meluhha, Magan and Tilmun moored outside his capital (unidentified but somewhere near the later Babylon). Engraved seals of Harappan type have been found in Mesopotamia, and there is even mention of an interpreter of the Meluhhan language.[1]

We hear no more of direct contact with Meluhha from soon after the time of Sargon of Agade, but direct trading with Magan continued down to the end of the III Ur dynasty (about 2000 BC). Texts of this period tell us of the storehouse of the temple of Nanna, the Moon-god of Ur, issuing large quantities of garments, wool, oil and leather objects to be taken by ship to Magan to buy copper: clearly, this trading was operated on a system of barter. Lists of deliveries to the temple show us that, in addition to copper, the goods brought back from Magan included such commodities as beads of precious stones, ivory, and vegetables called Magan-onions.

Whether Magan was Oman or the Iranian coast opposite, it cannot have been a primary producer of ivory, since it had no elephants; its source of ivory could have been either Egypt (via the Red Sea) or India. Clearly, Magan served as an international emporium. Direct contact with Magan seems to have been lost after the collapse of the III Ur empire, and in the succeeding centuries it is Tilmun of which we hear as the principal trading station within the Persian Gulf area.

Texts from the third and early second millennia list as imports from Tilmun goods such as copper, precious stones and ivory, none of which the island itself produces. Tilmun had thus, by the late third millennium at latest, become an emporium for goods originating in more remote countries. Our most detailed knowledge of maritime trade with Tilmun comes from the Isin-Larsa period (*c.* 1900 BC). At this time the city of Ur, then on the lower Euphrates (the river changed its course later), was the principal port of entry into Mesopotamia, and it is Ur which provides us with the main group of tablets dealing with the Tilmun trade. The principal imports mentioned were copper (in ingots or as manufactured objects), lapis lazuli, pearls (if this is what the ideogram meaning literally 'fish-eyes' denotes), and certain kinds of wood. It is not necessary to suppose that all these goods originated in the same place, since Tilmun may well have constituted a neutral meeting-place for merchants from many lands, particularly since Sumerian tradition thought of it as a holy island characterized by lack of strife.

The principal exports from Sumer to Tilmun were textiles and oil, provided by private capitalists. In the absence of coined money (which was not invented until well into the first millennium BC), there was always the problem of paying for goods and of stating the relationship between the values of different commodities. One solution was to use a silver standard, even when payments were not actually made in silver. At the period we are considering, contracts gave the silver value of the exported goods and stated the agreed silver value for the copper to be brought back by the trader. Here is a typical document of this type:

> 2 minas of silver, (the value of) 5 *gur* of oil (and of) 30 garments, Lu-meshlam-ta-e and Nig-si-sa-nabsa have borrowed from Ur-ninmar-ka (as the) capital for a partnership for an expedition to Tilmun to buy copper. After safe termination of the voyage, he [the creditor] will not recognize (any responsibility for) commercial losses (which the debtors may incur); they [the debtors] have

> agreed to satisfy Ur-ninmar-ka with 4 minas of copper for each shekel of silver as a just (price).

This kind of use of a silver standard without actual payment in silver was a widespread commercial device before the invention of coinage. An Egyptian document of just after 1300 BC presents another good example of it. It is a record of a lawsuit relating how a merchant had gone from house to house, offering a Syrian slave-girl for sale, until finally the wife of an official bought her. The price was stated in terms of silver, but was actually paid in various cloths, garments and bronze vessels, each item being valued in silver separately.

The financing by private capitalists in the Isin-Larsa period is a point of difference from the maritime trade of two hundred years earlier, in which it was not an individual but the temple which financed the seafaring merchant. In the document quoted, the entrepreneur Ur-ninmar-ka received a fixed return for his outlay; there is no mention of any share in profits, and a share in any loss was explicitly excluded. A less common arrangement was for the investor to become a full partner in the venture, sharing both trading risks and any profits.

We know something of the scale of the trade in copper, since one text mentions thirteen thousand minas of the metal, which is rather more than six tons. It came in ingots of up to four talents (roughly 250 lb), that is, as one might expect, in blocks about as heavy as the average labourer could lift.

As to the technical side of ancient sea trade, Sumerian and Babylonian ships were, by modern standards, very small. Some of the ancient records give the size in terms of hold capacity, and with this converted to weight in terms of the specific gravity of grain, it has been calculated that Sumerian ships in the third millennium would hold up to about twenty-eight tons,[2] and Babylonian ships in the first millennium about forty tons. Loads of copper of comparable cubic capacity would have weighed considerably more. Such ships would, to judge by a model found at Ur (see plate 2B), be of the same basic shape as a type of boat called a *belem* still used in Iraq, and would be equipped with a mast, a sail and a steering oar as a primitive rudder. For river transport there were also rafts consisting of a wooden platform supported by inflated skins (*kelek* in Arabic, after their ancient name), still occasionally seen on the Tigris up to the 1950s AD, and flat-bottomed coracles called *quffas* in modern Iraq. For internal trade, shipping remained important throughout the whole of Babylonian history, and we have innumerable references to the transport by water from city to city of foodstuffs, wine, building materials, metals, wood, reeds, leather, and so on. At Calah, the Assyrian capital in the early first millennium (today the mound of Nimrud), there was a massive quay wall of great blocks of heavy limestone to serve shipping on the Tigris.

Overland trade

Geography dictated the main routes in the ancient Near East. There were deserts which it was not safe to attempt; there were mountain ranges which could only be crossed at passes; and there were great rivers which could be followed upstream from Sumer for hundreds of miles. By following either the Euphrates or the Tigris, one came eventually into Anatolia (eastern Turkey); or one could go from the elbow of the Euphrates in north Syria by an easy journey westwards to the Orontes and thence to the coast, or into Cilicia and Asia Minor or south to the ports on the Lebanese littoral.

The earliest Mesopotamian overland trade on which there is any written evidence is that of the *Early Dynastic* period, to which there are allusions in Sumerian epic literature, reflecting circumstances of about 2700 BC. One of these texts describes how a donkey caravan was equipped in Erech and dispatched carrying sacks of barley to a city-state, Aratta, somewhere over the mountains in Iran, to obtain lapis lazuli and carnelian. Since the only Near Eastern source of lapis lazuli was Badakhshan, north of the Hindu Kush in Afghanistan, whilst carnelian came from India, Aratta (perhaps in the Kerman area) must have served as an entrepôt for this trade in semi-precious stones. Another allusion to an ancient trading initiative comes in the *Gilgamesh Epic*. One of its themes is a journey of the hero to a forest protected by a monster, where he proceeds to cut down trees, and this probably reflects the beginning of the exploitation, also in the *Early Dynastic* period, of the forests of the Zagros. By the middle of the third millennium this had become a routine operation, and we frequently find Sumerian rulers referring to expeditions to the mountains for timber. Some of them speak of imposing tribute on peoples from the Persian Gulf to the Mediterranean, but in most cases this did not mean that the ruler had achieved political dominion over the whole of that area; it expressed the fact that he had gained the economic benefit of regular trading missions.

Sargon of Agade, who established the first Mesopotamian empire in the twenty-fourth century BC, presents us with a special problem. Contemporary inscriptions indicate that he himself claimed control as far as the Amanus range in north-west Syria, designated 'the silver mountains'. But there was a later literary tradition which accorded Sargon a more extensive commercial empire, reaching well into Asia Minor. It is not impossible that this wider claim had some grain of historical basis, in the form of Mesopotamian merchant colonies in Asia Minor before the end of the third millennium. Without question there were such merchants there from 1900 BC onwards, for the archives of a colony of Assyrian traders have been found at Kultepe (ancient Kanesh), near Kayseri in the centre of eastern Turkey. These prove the existence of a continuous and extensive caravan traffic between Kanesh and Ashur on the middle Tigris, and the documents have enabled scholars to work out the commercial and economic system in some detail. The trade was generally by donkey caravan, which might consist of up to two hundred beasts, travelling perhaps twelve to fifteen miles a day; but between certain towns in Asia Minor it might be by wagon, which points to the existence of some form of road system. The caravan-leaders were given an allowance on setting out, and kept diaries recording their expenses *en route*, rendering an account to their principals at the end of the journey. The chief export from Asia Minor was copper, in quantities of up to five tons. The goods sent from Assyria were chiefly textiles and tin ores, the latter needed to make bronze. The precise source of the tin ores is not known, but as there were no known deposits in either Asia Minor or Mesopotamia, it must have been imported into Mesopotamia for transhipment from somewhere in Iran. Other merchandise sent to Asia Minor included vegetable oil, hides, fleeces, and wool, the last in consignments of up to two tons.

We know very little about arrangements for security on these journeys. Traders were certainly liable to misadventures of various kinds, since the laws of Hammurabi legislate for such matters as loss by brigandage or act of god. Judging by evidence from Mari, a caravan going through foreign territory paid toll-charges to local officials and was then entitled to the use of wells and the protection of the local ruler. From a slightly later period we find a royal letter to a customs official, giving a certain man immunity from all transit dues for his asses. Later Hittite, Israelite and Greek laws make special provision for the protection of the foreign trader in the community, and this probably goes back much earlier.

Market economy or state-controlled economy?

Economic historians have paid much attention to the nature of the economy of ancient Mesopotamia. Some of them have concluded that it was not a market economy, that is to say, prices were not fixed directly by the interplay of supply and demand. As these economic historians see it, in ancient Mesopotamia prices were simply equivalences between commodities, established either by custom or by state decree. On this view, Babylonian and Assyrian merchants did not make their profit from a price differential, and so trading was (in its economic aspect) risk-free. It is pointed out that the documents of the Assyrian colony make no reference to business profit or loss or to default on debt. And so it is argued that the Assyrian merchants in Cappadocia were merely state agents, holding their positions by descent, apprenticeship or appointment, and responsible firstly for encouraging copper production by assuring the natives of Kanesh that appropriate goods would be forthcoming in agreed amounts, and secondly for the physical transport of copper and other goods from one place to another.

It is very likely that the Cappodocian trade and those engaged in it were indeed subject to the municipal or national authority in Ashur, but this does not require us to accept that trade in ancient Mesopotamia was exclusively state-controlled. In Babylonia insolvency and default on debt did occur, and this must have resulted from risk-bearing enterprises; financial mishaps of this sort were one of the main paths by which a free man or his dependants could fall into slavery. Moreover, there is positive evidence for price-fixing by the interplay of supply and demand in ancient Mesopotamia: there are instances of rocketing prices in times of war or famine; Assyrian kings sometimes mention low prices of staple products consequent upon a good harvest, and officials report on price levels; whilst when Ashurbanipal had conquered and looted the Arab tribes, he specifically stated that camels were so numerous that the price fell to a shekel and a half.

International trading centres

A region of great importance for international trade was Syria, where routes from Asia Minor, Egypt and Mesopotamia met. From the twenty-fourth century onwards there are intermittent references in Mesopotamian records to trade with Syria, but the most vivid representation of Syrian trade is provided by an Egyptian source of about 1400 BC. This is a painting from the tomb of a mayor of Thebes, showing ships manned by Syrian crews discharging cargo in an Egyptian town. The crew was subject to some kind of check, for a port official is seen recording names or other particulars of a group of sailors.

The main merchandise consisted of large jars of wine or oil, and vases of precious metal; the picture indicates that these were sold through a government official, presumably the owner of the tomb, who had charge of the municipal storehouses. There seems in addition to have been some small-scale private trading, for waterside shops are shown, where sandals, textiles and foodstuffs are being sold. On one of the ships are two lonely-looking women and a boy, possibly slaves brought as a *douceur* for the high Egyptian official himself.

To facilitate international trade, colonies of expatriate merchants were established in various centres of commerce: a well-known biblical instance is provided by 1 Kings 20:34 (see page 242). There were similar provisions at Ugarit in Syria at about 1400 BC, when, in addition to a thriving trading colony established by Mycenaean merchants, there were also Assyrian and Egyptian colonists, to judge by a document listing wine deliveries for peoples of these nationalities. The king of Ugarit encouraged foreign trade; we find a royal contract which gives a man exemption from customs duties on his ships returning from Crete. Another document showing royal supervision of trade at Ugarit is a kind of passport issued by the same king to a man and his son, authorizing them to use the routes to Egypt and the land of the Hittites.

At the end of the second and the beginning of the first millennium the old pattern of trade across Mesopotamia and Syria was seriously distorted by the pressure of nomadic Aramaeans forcing their way into Babylonia and Assyria (see pages 90ff.). The consequent economic difficulties were probably one of the factors which led to Assyria's attempts, finally successful, to gain military control of the routes to the Mediterranean littoral, where there were other important centres of international trade, notably the Phoenician ports of Tyre and Sidon.

Trade in the first millennium BC

Documents directly bearing on first-millennium trade in either Assyria or Babylonia are scanty. We can, however, deduce some general trends.

Most of our evidence about movements of commodities in Assyria comes from accounts of tribute paid by subject peoples. Mention of tribute can engender the reaction that it was nothing but barefaced imperialistic exploitation of subject peoples. Undoubtedly the net advantage from the tribute system lay with the imperialist Assyrians, but tribute, in the first-millennium Assyrian empire, was not mere plunder. Rather, it was a sort of tax on vassal or subject states, administered through a bureaucratic machine. The benefits from the system were not wholly one-sided in Assyria's favour; throughout its empire, Assyria provided the international infrastructure for policing routes, maintaining good communications, guaranteeing security, and even sometimes distribution of emergency supplies in the event of local famine.

Tribute payments were a mechanism for the international distribution of commodities; if this was not trade as generally understood, it did link up with genuine trade as the source of those commodities. For example, we find large quantities of iron being paid as tribute from the Damascus area; we know that Damascus was not a primary area of iron production, and for it to be a source of tribute in iron it must have been a centre of the iron trade. In fact, in the first millennium Damascus was a major centre of international trade, not only for iron; when, in the middle of the ninth century, the Israelites gained a military advantage over Syria, they recognized the international commercial importance of Damascus by establishing a merchant colony there (1 Kings 20:34).

Other important international trading centres in the Assyrian empire were Tyre and Carchemish. Even more important was Egypt, but here Assyria had no direct control, except for less than two decades just before the middle of the seventh century. But Assyrian recognition of the value of trade with

Egypt is shown in an inscription of Sargon II in 720 BC, in which he says: 'I opened the trading station [or 'quay'] of Egypt, (which had been) sealed up, and I mixed peoples of Assyria and Egypt together and caused them to engage in trade.' But at most times, Assyrian trade with Egypt was mainly indirect, many commodities of Egyptian origin, such as fine linen and rolls of papyrus, reaching Assyria via Phoenicia, whose ports had since the third millennium always engaged in sea trade with Egypt.

Babylonian trade in the first millennium

At the end of the second millennium and the beginning of the first, the trade of Babylonia, and likewise of Assyria, had been adversely affected by the nomadic Aramaeans across the routes from Syria and along the Euphrates. The subsequent political dominance of Assyria for most of the remainder of the first half of the millennium might have been expected to have had adverse effects upon Babylonia, but generally Assyria made no damaging interference. On the contrary, it represented the power able to keep trade routes open and to maintain the territorial rights of the cities against the pressure of those Aramaeans who had settled in north Babylonia and of the tribal Chaldeans in the south of the country. In general the economic interests of the Babylonian cities and of the Assyrian empire went hand in hand, so that even when Assyria was in its death throes after 626 BC, some of the Babylonian cities still continued to support it to within a few years of the final fall of Nineveh in 612 BC.

In first-millennium Babylonia, the great majority of written records point to internal trade having been largely in the hands of the great temple corporations, such as Eanna in Erech. It has to be remembered, however, that there could have been a great deal of small-scale private trade of which we have no record because it was never documented, and certainly we find occasional references to people who must have been pedlars in such commodities as salt or firewood.[3] Private trading is also proved by records of loans for trading journeys, such as the following:

> Three minas of silver of Shum-ukin . . . in the charge of Zababa-shum-iddin . . . for a (trading) journey. Zababa-shum-iddin shall share equally with Shum-ukin in the profit, as much as there may be in town or country . . .[4]

Another indication of the existence of trading outside the temple system is given by contracts in which the temple authorities hire boats from private persons. This implies that there were private boats plying between the cities of Babylonia, and the transport of temple goods can hardly have been the sole purpose for which they existed, or they would soon have come under direct temple control, like so many other sectors of New Babylonian life.

The mechanism by which temples in Babylonia financed imports is illustrated by a document recording that two persons received from the Eanna temple in Erech '15 minas of silver for a consignment of merchandise from Syria'.[5] The obligation upon the debtors was that 'they shall deliver to Eanna white wine, white honey, copper, iron, tin, purple-dyed wool and other necessities according to the consignment which they receive in Syria and bring to Babylon'. There is nothing in the contract to suggest that the two traders were temple servants, there is no mention of payment to the two men, and the amounts of commodities to be brought back are not specified. Almost certainly, then, it was accepted that they would make a profit by being able to buy the required commodities in Syria at less than they were worth to the temple in Erech.

However, most of what we know about New Babylonian commerce relates to that directly administered by temple corporations, arranged between officials of different temples. This is illustrated by such a letter as the following, written in 616 BC to the *Shatammu* of Erech by a man who, as he calls this administrator 'brother', must have held comparable rank in a temple further north:

Letter of Shuzubu to Marduk-shakin-shum [*Shatammu* of Eanna in Erech] and Nadin my brothers. May Bel and Nabu decree the wellbeing of my brothers.

I have sent Bel-na'id-shu to the Sealands [south Babylonia] for *shibeshu*-wood. He does not know the territory. Let my brothers send a man with him who knows the way. Give him provisions.

Let my brothers send gall-nuts (to the value) of one mina of silver, and let your messenger come to me, and I will send white linseed which is satisfactory to my brothers (to the value) of one mina of silver . . .

This letter also provides another instance of the use of silver as a standard of value without any silver actually changing hands (see page 236).

When Babylonia again became the leading power in Mesopotamia after the fall of Assyria, the country saw a conspicuous accession of wealth under Nebuchadnezzar, marked by grandiose schemes of public works, notably a magnificent rebuilding of Babylon. This did not, however, result from any significant renewal of economic activity in Babylonia, but rather from the diversion to Babylonia of imperial resources which had formerly mainly benefited Assyria. After Nebuchadnezzar, the effects of the economic realities began to work through. The Medes who had assisted in the overthrow of Assyria, and their associates and eventual successors the Persians, had firm control over trade routes not only through Iran but also in regions to the north of Assyria in Anatolia and Asia Minor. This had adverse economic consequences on Babylonia, where prices doubled between 560 and 540 BC. It seems that some of the New Babylonian kings were aware of the problem, and attempted to take remedial steps. King Neriglissar in 557 BC made an expedition to Cilicia to try to secure control of the rich route which passed through it between north Syria and Asia Minor and Greece. But the Persian ruler, Cyrus the Great, outmanoeuvred the Babylonians and himself quickly gained control of Asia Minor and its trade. The last New Babylonian king, Nabu-na'id, turned westwards, spending ten years at Teima in northwest Arabia (see page 136), establishing colonies as far south as Medina in an attempt to gain control of south Arabian trade to the benefit of his country's economy. He also attempted internal economic reforms, but these were too late, and in 539 BC the whole of the Babylonian empire fell into the hands of Cyrus.

Babylonian merchants

In the Old Babylonian period, trade was largely the professional concern of a class known as *tamkaru* (singular *tamkarum*); this term is commonly translated 'merchant', but the *tamkarum* might also act as a broker, a merchant banker, a money-lender, or a government agent. References to *tamkaru* in the laws of Hammurabi shed light upon their activities. Their operations were not confined to the homeland; one of their activities abroad was certainly the slave trade, for the laws of Hammurabi envisage the case in which a native Babylonian, captured on royal service, comes into the hands of a *tamkarum*. The slave trade was not, of course, restricted to foreign lands, and there are many tablets showing that men of the *tamkarum* class dealt in the buying and selling of slaves within Babylonia. Besides dealing in slaves, *tamkaru* also organized trade in such commodities as foodstuffs, wool, timber, garments, textiles, grain, wine and ale, metals, building materials such as reeds and bricks, and cattle and horses. Letters of the Old Babylonian period, referring to internal trade in such commodities, show that it was largely river-borne. The trading activity of the *tamkarum* is illustrated by such a letter as the following, in which Hammurabi is giving orders to an official:

> Ilushu-ibi the *tamkarum* . . . had notified me in these terms, saying thus: 'I delivered thirty *gur* of grain to the governor Sin-magir and I have his tablet (to this effect). For three years I have kept asking him but he will not repay the grain to me'. . . .
>
> I have seen his tablet. Let Sin-magir have grain delivered with the interest due on it; then pay it to Ilushu-ibi.

The following letter shows a *tamkarum* sending goods by river:

> The *tamkarum* Tamlatum son of Kish-nun hired the ship of the shipmaster Ibbatum and had it sailed downstream to Babylon. That ship, which he has moored, until now has carried bricks . . .

The letter goes on to deal with a dispute which had arisen between the *tamkarum* and the shipmaster.

In his capacity as merchant banker, a *tamkarum* might provide money for others to go on trading journeys for him. Here again the laws of Hammurabi take notice of the situation, laying down provisions regulating the relations between the *tamkarum* and his agents. It appears that on the normal type of loan made by a *tamkarum* to an agent for a trading journey, the *tamkarum* could reckon on a minimum profit of 100 per cent. We deduce this from paragraphs of Hammurabi's laws which read:

> If a *tamkarum* has delivered silver to an agent for selling and buying and has sent him off on a (trading) journey, . . . if he [the agent] sees a profit where he has gone, he shall register the interest of the silver, as much as he has received, and they shall count up his days and he shall pay his *tamkarum*.
>
> If, in the place where he went, he has not seen a profit, he shall double the silver which he received and the agent shall return it to the *tamkarum*.

There was another type of loan, called *tadmiqtum*, in which, if the agent made a loss on the enterprise, he simply returned the full capital sum to the *tamkarum*. It is likely that any profit was shared in a fixed proportion between the agent and the *tamkarum*.

Loan transactions

Loans were a common feature of Babylonian economic life at all periods. A proverb sums up the attitude to loan transactions thus:

The giving of a loan is like making love;
The returning of a loan is like having a son born.

This obviously refers to the interest added at repayment. The religious feeling against usury, so prominent in Hebrew and Islamic law, was entirely absent from the Sumero-Babylonian world, where the payment of interest upon a loan was regarded as normal and respectable and was presupposed in laws and contracts. Excessive rates of interest were, however, frowned upon, and the laws of Hammurabi provide that a *tamkarum* who attempted to charge more than the legal rate would forfeit his capital:

> If a man who has run up a debt has no silver (with which) to pay back but does have corn, according to the ordinance of the king the *tamkarum* shall take the interest on it in corn; but if the *tamkarum* raises the interest on it above 100 *qa* per *gur* (of corn) . . . he [the *tamkarum*] shall forfeit whatever he has loaned.

The rate of interest payable on loans varied from period to period and according to the commodity involved. In the Old Babylonian period it was commonly 33⅓ per cent on barley and 20 per cent on silver. In Old Babylonian contracts, it is often not very clear what the period of the loan was, nor is it explicitly stated whether payment of interest was monthly or annual. But the normal situation was that the loan would run until the harvest was in, or until the conclusion of the trading journey for which it had been made.

There was another type of loan, called *hubuttatu*, on which interest was paid in a different way. The amount received by the borrower was less than the sum entered in the contract, and the difference represented the interest payable. Such a loan would have a fixed term for repayment, and if it ran beyond that time, further interest would become due according to normal practice. Here is an example of such a transaction:

> Shamash-nasir the governor . . . has received from Ilushu-nasir and Nanna-ibni 133 *gur* 1 *pi* 4 *sutu* of grain as a *hubuttatu*-loan; for two years no interest shall accrue. If he has not returned the grain

by the third year, then he shall add interest. [The names of witnesses follow, together with the date.]

Since 1 *gur* = 5 *pi* = 30 *sutu*, the amount of grain mentioned is 133⅓ *gur*, which represents a real loan of 100 *gur* plus interest of 33⅓ per cent for the two years.

The primary condition for the validity of most commercial transactions was the presence of witnesses and a written record in the form of a contract. We have already quoted a letter (page 246) in which Hammurabi examined a creditor's tablet before giving judgement in his favour, and Hammurabi's laws specifically say that loans made without a contract and witnesses could not be recovered. An apparent exception to this general principle occurs in the Assyrian merchant colony in Cappadocia, where there was a type of interest-free loan called *ebuttu*, which required neither witnesses nor contract and had no fixed term. But this was a very specialized situation; the loans were between members of the same merchant colony, who could trust each other's credit.

Tablets recording contracts were usually validated with the impressions of the cylinder seals of those concerned, or in the later period with the mark of a finger-nail. Falsification or forgery was sometimes attempted, but, apart from this being a heinous crime, it was unlikely to succeed without the collusion of a competent scribe. In the earlier period the tablet was often enclosed in a clay envelope bearing a duplicate text (see plate 26A); this rendered falsification impossible, since the envelope would not be broken unless a dispute arose, when the protected inner text would be taken as the official version; this use of an envelope had disappeared by New Babylonian times. At some periods, tablets concerned with debts state that when the debt is paid the tablet is to be broken.

Because of the importance of cylinder seals for authentication of contracts, the disappearance of one was a serious matter. The loss had to be recorded in writing the same day, with details such as colour to help identify it, and proclaimed by the town crier.[6]

One problem in business transactions was that weights and measures might differ slightly from place to place. This obviously opened the way to roguery, for an unscrupulous dealer might lend or buy on one system of weights and receive repayment or resell on another. The prophet Amos denounces dealings of this kind:

> Hear this, O ye that would swallow up the needy, and cause the poor of the land to fail, . . . making the ephah small, and the shekel great, and dealing falsely with balances of deceit. (Amos 8:4–5)

Deuteronomy 25:13 and Proverbs 20:10 and 23 also mention the use of different sets of weights to the user's advantage. In Mesopotamia, roguery of this kind was often forestalled by writing into a contract the provision that payment should be made by a particular standard, for example, the mina of Shamash, that is, the weights used in the temple of Shamash. None the less, this kind of dishonesty was not unknown in commercial dealings in Babylonia; a magical text refers to releasing a man from the consequences of

> delivering by small measure, receiving by great measure;
> delivering by a small shekel, receiving by a great shekel;
> delivering by a small mina, receiving by a great mina.

Most transport of goods within Babylonia was by ship, and the Euphrates, along channels of which most of the great cities lay, must often have presented a busy scene. On the middle Euphrates Mari was an important centre for boat-building, and several letters to the sub-king Yasmah-adad from his father Shamshi-adad relate to this. Once, sixty boats at a time were to be built. The boatmen navigating these vessels formed a close-knit group, with – according to a literary text – their own Sumerian jargon. They took their wives with them, as we learn from a letter in which the ruler of Carchemish complained to the sub-king of Mari that they have detained at Tuttul thirty sheep, fifty jars of wine and the wife of a boatman.

Shipping faced hazards other than over-zealous officialdom. Weather was sometimes pleaded as an excuse for delay. Thus, we find one official explaining, in answer to a complaint,

> These vessels went off, but I detained all of them at Tuttul. From the day that these vessels came here, the heavens opened and it has been raining continuously.

Another letter mentions some accident that had occurred to a ship carrying grain for the palace: the vessel had had to be beached and the official wanted instructions about disposal of the grain now lying on the river bank. Collisions between boats on the river were not unknown, and §240 of the laws of Hammurabi deals with a particular case of this.

Real-estate transactions

Documents concerned with the sale of land and houses are very common from the III Ur Dynasty onwards. At the sale of real estate a written record was drawn up and given into the keeping of the purchaser. The following is a simple example:

> 1½ *sar* [just under 600 square feet] with a house built on it, next to the house of Kununu and next to the house of Irraya, Arad-zugal has bought from Arad-nanna. He has paid him 8½ shekels of silver as its full price.
>
> Arad-nanna has taken an oath by the king that he will not in the future say 'It is my house'.
>
> [The names of the witnesses, and the date, follow.]

The clause against reopening a former claim was very common, especially in contracts of real estate sales. Sometimes a specific penalty is mentioned in the event of such a claim, as in the following:

> 1 *sar* (of land) with a house built on it, next to the house of Shubisha and next to the house of Bur-sin, with one long side by the Ishkun-Sin canal and the other long side by the old house of Mishar-gamil, Ilushu-nasir the son of Bur-sin has bought from Mishar-gamil, the owner of the house. He has paid him silver as its full price. His [Mishar-gamil's] heart is content, the affair is settled.
>
> They have taken an oath by Ishtar and by Ibal-pi-El the king that neither will in future return against the other. He who makes a claim shall pay two minas of silver and his tongue shall be torn out.
>
> [Names of witnesses follow, with the name of the scribe.]

Sale of land was not always a straightforward matter; there could be legal impediments. The odd phrasing of the following contract from Mari was probably designed to get round such a problem:

> Ili-palahum has granted by division five *sar* (of land), with a house on it, to Yarim-adad. Yarim-adad of his own free will has granted by division half a shekel of silver to Ili-palahum. [Several lines of text are lost] . . . In the presence of [ten named witnesses]. They have eaten the bread, they have drunk the cup, they have anointed themselves with oil.

The final section refers to some ceremonial meal sealing the sale.

The verb translated 'granted by division' is not the ordinary word for 'to sell'; properly it refers to the sharing of tribal property amongst members of a tribe. The cognate Hebrew verb is used in the Bible for 'to divide for inheritance' in Numbers 34:17–18 and Joshua 19:49. The transaction in the contract was therefore apparently a sale under the fiction of a division of common property, and presumably had to be done in this way because the land was technically tribal property which could be shared out but not sold.

There is evidence elsewhere in the ancient Near East for land which could not legally be sold, notably in the Nuzi area, near the present city of Kirkuk. At about 1400 BC land in that area seems to have been inalienable as a general principle. None the less, wealthy men were managing to build up large estates. This was a two-step process. Firstly, the wealthy man had to get round the legal obstacle and acquire plots of land from poor peasants. Then he would consolidate the individual plots into an estate by exchange with other owners; there was no legal barrier to this. The initial purchase of plots was effected by the fiction of adoption. The capitalist would have a document drawn up in which he was 'adopted' by the poor man from whom he wished to buy the land. He would give his adoptive father a 'present' which really represented the price of the land, and he would then receive as his 'inheritance' from his adoptive father the piece of land he wished to buy. The following is an abridged extract from a typical document of this kind, with the names of the poor seller and the rich buyer represented respectively by X and Y:

> Tablet of adoption which X made for adoption of Y.
>
> X has given to Y as his (inheritance) portion 8 *awihari* of irrigated land in Nuzi . . . On the same day Y has given X 9 minas of tin as his gift.

11

Magic and Religion

What account of their religion can you suppose to be learnt from savages? Only consider, Sir, our own state: our religion is in a book: we have an order of men whose duty it is to teach it; we have one day in the week set apart for it, and this is in general pretty well observed: yet ask the first ten gross men you meet, and hear what they can tell you of their religion.

(Boswell's *Life of Johnson*, 29 April 1776)

THOUGH the Babylonians were by no means savages, one does well, in studying their religion, to bear Dr Johnson's warning in mind. Very different conclusions can be reached, depending upon whether we are trying to get at religion as it was practised and experienced by the common man and his family in the mud hut, or whether we are considering the systematized theology of priests and scholars. Here the emphasis will be upon trying to see how religion actually affected ordinary Babylonians.

Knowledge of Babylonian religion has never been completely dead, inasmuch as some details of it were preserved in classical writers and in the Old Testament. From these sources alone, enough remains for the definite assertion that Babylonian religion was polytheistic, and strongly marked by features associated with fertility cults. Classical sources amplify this with some details of Babylonian cosmogony. The principal material of the latter kind comes from the fragments quoted in other ancient authors of a work written in Greek by Berossus, a Babylonian priest of *c.* 340–275 BC.

These scanty and distorted details have been enormously augmented and much clarified by the mass of cuneiform material of religious significance which has come to light since the middle of the nineteenth century. This material includes epics, myths, hymns, prayers, incantations, exorcisms, ethical treatises and proverbs, omens, ritual instructions, lists of god-names, and so on. Even a prosaic business receipt may shed light on the cult when it refers to such matters as the delivery of beasts for sacrifice or equipment for rituals. The great majority of the documents are written in either Akkadian or Sumerian or bilingually in both; occasionally a Hittite or Hurrian text from Asia Minor or Syria sheds light on religious practice inside Mesopotamia. In all these languages there are texts of which the detailed meaning is open to dispute, and a writer unfamiliar with the original languages and working with inadequate translations is sometimes able to use such texts as apparent proof of very doubtful theories. It may not be out of place to point out that scholars with unquestioned expertise in Akkadian and Sumerian but lacking training in the history of religions are equally capable of arriving at invalid conclusions.

It is impossible to draw a clear line between Babylonian magic and religion, and the distinction between them is due to ourselves; the Babylonians did not make it. Magic reflected an older stratum than what we think of as religion: it did not focus upon personal gods; its concern was control of the impersonal unknown. It had a social and psychological function. The world was full of things mysterious, terrifying or dangerous, from eclipses to earthquakes to sunstroke to epidemics. Magic gave the Mesopotamian confidence that, come what may, he could handle it. As man grew in mastery of his environment, and learnt to control hostile phenomena directly, the role of magic began to wither, although so slowly that even in our own time it is not wholly dead.

It is very easy to hold any religion up to ridicule, if we look only at the external trappings without considering the inner attitudes and aspirations of the worshippers. Consider, for example, what we might think of Israelite religion at the time of Isaiah if we knew only its outer form. In front of the temple in Jerusalem were two bronze pillars, bearing personal names as though they were people (1 Kings 7:15–21), whilst inside there was a bronze snake supposed to cure snakebite (2 Kings 18:4; Numbers 21:6–9), and a special ornamental seat for the god himself (Exodus 25:17–22). There were bells on the priest's robes so that he jangled when he went into the god's private room, to avoid taking him by surprise (Exodus 28:31–35); and the people's sins could be physically transferred to a goat for removal to the desert (Leviticus 16:21–22). And, of course, there were all those bloody holocausts: the Israelite god just loved the smell of burning meat fat (Numbers 28:11–13, etc.).

We know that these things in Israel were only external trappings, retained from more ancient magical practices by the force of religious conservatism, and reinterpreted in a more spiritual sense by the enlightened. It is at least possible that in Babylonia and Assyria by the first millennium BC, and possibly much earlier, something similar was happening. Certainly the external forms of Babylonian religion sometimes lagged a long way behind advances in thought. For example, by the fourth century BC Babylonian astronomers were able to calculate lunar eclipses a year ahead; yet, when an eclipse of the moon actually took place, the Babylonian priests still banged on drums to drive away the supposed demons which, in more primitive belief, caused an eclipse by attacking the Moon-god (see page 258).

In discussing any of the great monotheistic religions, one is able to start from a fairly precise date. This is not possible with non-reformed religions, where changes of belief and modifications of practice have come about by gradual evolution from a system with roots in prehistory.

An issue on which a great deal of ink has been spilt is whether ancient Mesopotamian religion was Sumerian or Semitic. We can dispose of this very simply: the question is meaningless. Religion is a reflection of a culture as a whole; it is not an outcrop of a particular language or of a particular racial or ethnic stratum associated with a particular language. The stamp was put on Mesopotamian religion by the circumstances in which it took its framework at the beginning of the third millennium, and it was entirely irrelevant to this that the predominant language in the area at the time was Sumerian. Changes the religion underwent later were reflections of changes in society, and although they may have been accompanied by a new balance between language groups, the changes in religion were not the direct consequence of that new balance.

From early in the third millennium, the ordinary man in the Sumero-Babylonian world saw himself surrounded by supernatural forces ranging from gods to demons; but there was an earlier stage before clearly defined gods emerged. Imagine how primitive man in south Mesopotamia saw his world. There were many natural forces affecting him, and the same force might act for good or ill. For example, up to a point water was undoubtedly good; without it, the earth grew parched, and drought, famine and death ensued. With it, there were good harvests, and the cattle thrived. But too much water could be bad, causing floods which brought death and destruction. There was the same ambivalence for the sun, or the winds, or thunderstorms. Thunderstorms are terrifying: people and cattle can be struck by lightning, and buildings and forests set on fire. But thunderstorms can also bring rain to drench the earth after a drought, and cooler air after intense heat. To primitive man all natural forces are in themselves neither good nor bad. They are just there, powerful forces controlling human existence.

At a later stage, man begins to think of everything in personal terms. And so he begins to personify the waters, the winds, the thunderstorms. Gradually, what used to be seen as impersonal forces become thought of as personal supernatural beings. The change from one concept to another becomes reflected in terms of myth, as a superhuman personal being, that we could call a god, defeating the old non-personal representation of the same force. To rationalize this, primitive man splits the old concept of the supernatural force into its two opposing elements, its good side and its bad side. This is linked to the struggle between the god and the old non-personal force, and in this way the god comes to take on the beneficent qualities of (say) the waters, whilst the old concept in non-human form remains linked to their evil aspect.

We can actually see this process at work in some instances, as for example in the origin of Ninurta from the thunderstorm in the mountains (see pages 288f.), and the development of Ea/Enki from the primeval sweet waters of the *apsu* (see page 283).

Whilst the gods came to incorporate supernatural forces in fully personified form, there were other aspects of existence where the process was not complete, so that a more primitive stage of belief remained. This was reflected in the widespread belief in demons, who were so far from being personified that they might not have even a name or a shape. Unlike gods, the demons were irrational in their action, but their power was not necessarily less than that of the gods. They were everywhere. There was a raging demon who manifested himself in the sandstorm sweeping in from the desert, and the man who opposed this demon was likely to be smitten with a painful sinusitis. The shimmering light which appeared upon the eastern mountains just before sunrise was the glow from the haloes of the scorpion-men who guarded the sun at his ascent. A host of demons stood always ready to seize a man or a woman in particular circumstances, as, in lonely places, when eating or drinking, in sleep, and especially in childbirth. The gods themselves were not exempt from the attacks of demons; a myth narrates how the Moon-god Sin was temporarily vanquished by these beings:

> The Seven Evil Gods forced their way into the vault of heaven; they clustered angrily round the crescent of the Moon-god. . . . By night and day he was dark and did not sit in the seat of his dominion.

This myth forms the introduction to a ritual to be used at the time of an eclipse.

Protection against demons

For protection from demons, or for deliverance in the event of attack, the Babylonians had the consolations of official and popular religion in many forms. An amulet (examples in plates 56B and 57A) might be worn as a prophylactic, and the great gods themselves did not scorn such magical devices, for when Marduk went to combat with the primeval monster Tiamat,

> in his hand was clasped a plant to annul poison.

In its most elaborate form, an amulet bore a portrayal of the devil against whom protection was sought and a magical incantation invoking the great gods against the threatened evil. One such reads:

> *Incantation.* That one which has approached the house scares me from my bed, rends me, makes me see nightmares. May they consign him to the god Bine, gatekeeper of the Underworld, by the decree of Ninurta, prince of the Underworld, by the decree of Marduk who dwells in Esagila in Babylon. Let door and bolt know that I am under the protection of the two Lords. *Incantation.*

One common type of amulet seems to have originated as protection against the appalling discomfort and even danger of the hot west wind which in summer brings sandstorms into Babylonia from the desert. This amulet took the form of either a grotesque head of the demon carved in the round or, as in plate 57A, a bronze or stone plaque of the whole creature, with a bird-like chest, human arms and legs terminating in talons with one hand holding a thunderbolt aloft, four wings and a curled tail. In either form the inscription on the back of the amulet (see illustration on page 260) reads (with slight variations):

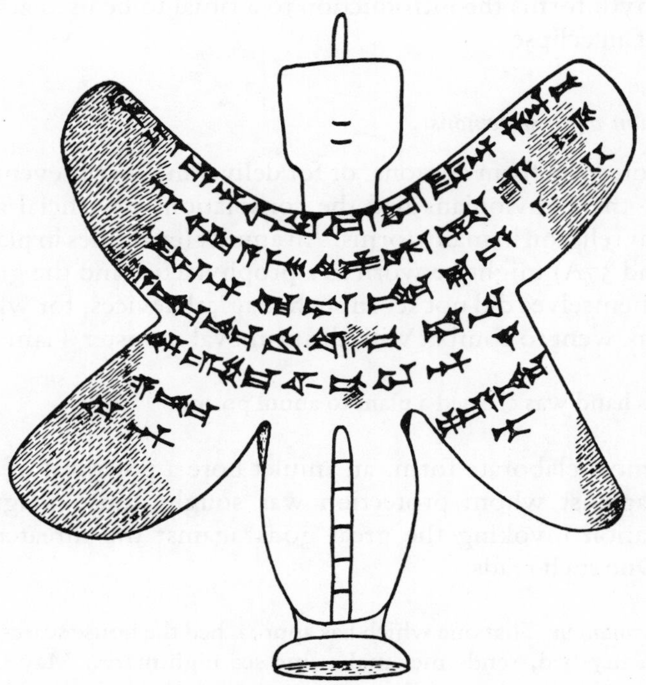

Inscription on Pazuzu amulet

> *Incantation.* I am the god Pazuzu, son of the god Hanbi, king of the evil wind-demons. It is I who rage mightily in the Mountain (of the Underworld) so that they come up. As to those winds which accompany them, the west wind is stationed at their front. The winds, their wings are broken.

The last phrase here is apparently the magical formula which rendered the demons powerless against the possessor of the amulet. Another type of amulet, to protect women in childbirth, was specifically directed against Lamashtu (see plate 54B), the she-demon who threatened pregnant women and nursing mothers; there was also a whole series of rituals against this dreaded being.

Magicians (exorcists or witchdoctors)

When a victim already showed symptoms of demonic possession, an exorcist was called in to diagnose the malady and to expel the evil spirit: after invoking a god, he or an assistant would recite the proper incantation, accompanied by the appropriate ritual. Most commonly the god invoked was Marduk, son of Ea, the god of magic. In some contexts long series of deities are named to help against the demons, but not all deities were equally willing or potent to assist suffering humanity. But Ea, one of the first triad, was a constant friend of mankind, always alert to assuage the anger of other gods or to frustrate the malevolence of demons; as god of wisdom, he was the supreme authority on magic, and he freely imparted his knowledge to his son Marduk. The usual procedure for a man in distress was for him to apply for help to Marduk, through an exorcist. The typical liturgy then depicts Marduk going to his father Ea, repeating the problem concerned, and receiving the courteous answer, 'My son, what do you not know . . . ?' followed by advice on the magical procedure for the case in hand.

Fire was a great power against magic and evil influences, and so the three Fire-gods, Gira, Gibil and Nusku, were potent against black magic (see page 291).

The exorcists who performed such incantations and rituals against evil influences were known in Akkadian as *ashipu* and *mashmashu*; it is possible that the two terms were alternative writings for the same functionary. Whether or not we call such people priests (I do so where their approach to the gods is uppermost, although elsewhere I use the terms 'magicians' or 'witchdoctors') depends upon what we understand by 'priest'. Illness was thought to be due to evil forces, and so such functionaries were also concerned with healing the sick; for this they might employ incantations and rituals either alone or in association with surgical or medical techniques. The following text shows a blend of magic and practical measures in the treatment for toothache:

> After Anu had made the heavens, the heavens made the earth, the earth made the rivers, the rivers made the canals, the canals made the mud, the mud made the worm. The worm came weeping before Shamash, shed tears before Ea: 'What will you give me for my food . . . ?' (Ea replied:) 'I will give you the ripe fig . . .' (The worm said:) 'What is the ripe fig to me? Let me drink among the teeth, and set me on the gums, that I may consume the blood of the teeth and destroy the marrow of the gums.'[1]
>
> *Fix the peg* [i.e. forceps] *and grip the root!*
>
> Because you said this, O worm, may Ea strike you with the might of his fist.

The sentence italicized obviously contains the instruction to the operator. The final sentence presumably accompanied the wrench that brought out the tooth beneath which the offending worm lurked. The text concludes with instructions for the preparation of a mouth-wash of beer, oil and herbs.

Sympathetic, symbolic and substitutional magic

The exorcists' techniques often rested upon less practical measures, particularly the use of sympathetic or symbolic magic. We find an illustration of this in a text which first states that

> An evil curse has been put on this man like a *gallu*-demon

and then mentions his symptoms.

> A dazed silence has been put on him,
> An unwholesome silence, an evil curse, a spell, a headache;
> His god has gone away from him . . .

Then, says the text, Marduk noticed the man, went to his father Ea, and outlined the situation. Ea, after his usual courteous disclaimer of superior knowledge, gave Marduk instructions for the cure:

Go, my son Marduk,
Take him to the pure ablution-house,
Loose his spell, loose his spell,
That the activating evil of his body,
Whether a curse (related to) his father, a curse (related to) his mother, a curse (related to) his elder brother, a curse (related to) the murder of a man he does not know,
By the conjuration of Ea,
Let the curse be peeled off like this onion,
Let it be wrenched apart like this date,
Let it be untwined like this wick.

Separate incantations now follow for the onion, the date, and the wick, to be recited whilst the exorcist performed symbolic actions:

Incantation. Like this onion which he peels and throws into the fire, which the fire consumes entirely, . . . whose roots will not take hold in the soil, whose shoots will not sprout, that will not be used for the meal of a god or a king, so may oath, curse, . . . sickness, weariness, guilt, sin, wickedness, transgression, the sickness that is in my body, my flesh or my limbs, be peeled off like this onion. May the fire consume it entirely today; may the curse be taken away that I may see the light.

The mention of 'the pure ablution-house' suggests that the ceremony in question was performed at the temple, but this was not invariable; in other cases the rites might take place in a private house, in a sickroom, in a reed hut alongside the river, or in the open country.

Another magical technique was substitution. A good example is provided by a text from Ashur, of which the following is an abridged edition:

For making exchange for a man wanted by the Goddess of Death. At sunset the sick man shall make a kid lie down with him on the bed. At dawn you [that is, the priest] shall get up and bow (to the Sun-god). The sick man shall carry the kid in his lap to a house where there is a tamarisk tree. You [the priest] shall make the sick man and the kid lie down on the ground. You shall touch the throat of the sick man with a wooden dagger, and you shall cut the throat of the kid with a bronze dagger. . . .

You shall then dress up the kid with clothes, put sandals on it, put eye-black on its eyes, put oil on its head. You shall take off the sick man's turban and tie it on the kid's head. You shall lay the kid out and treat it like a dead man.

The sick man shall then get up and stand in the doorway whilst the priest repeats a charm three times. The sick man shall remove his garment, give it to the priest, and go off. The priest shall then set up a howl for the sick man, saying, 'So-and-so has passed away!' The priest shall then give orders to institute mourning, . . . and shall bury the kid.

Magical procedures of the kinds quoted go back, in their simplest forms, at least to the third millennium, perhaps to prehistoric times, but it was not until a much later date that collections of such texts were made: the three principal collections are known as *Shurpu*, *Maqlu* and *Utukki Limnuti*. The two first titles both mean 'Burning', but the two kinds of 'Burning' were distinct in their functions. *Maqlu* incantations were mainly to counter the machinations of human wizards and witches: they were uttered whilst wax, wooden, bronze or tow images of the witch who had wrought the evil were destroyed by fire. *Shurpu* ritual, on the other hand, was a means of getting rid of sins: offences which had brought ill upon the sufferer, whether ethical misdeeds, ritual shortcomings or breaches of taboos, were transferred to some object which was then burnt. *Utukki Limnuti* means 'Evil Spirits', and it was to exorcise such beings that these incantations and rituals were used.

These three types of conjuration were far from being the only ones. There is a text which contains an extensive catalogue of titles, which according to its first line were 'Series which are prescribed for learning and study for the exorcist-priesthood'. This list contains, in addition to those already mentioned, such titles as 'Headaches', 'Toothaches', 'To loose a curse', 'Eye-ache', 'To cure snake-bite', 'To cure scorpion-sting', 'Magical rites for town, house, field, orchard, river'. King Ashurbanipal sought such magical works for his library, and we have a letter in which he gives an official a list of his desiderata.

Demons and ghosts

The hosts of evil spirits which threatened the Babylonians and Assyrians were of many kinds. There was Lamashtu, already mentioned, the dreaded she-spirit who threatened women in childbirth and stole infants from the breast. Equally dreaded was Namtaru, the plague-demon, the messenger of Nergal, god of the Underworld. Rabisu, the Croucher, was to be met with in doorways and dark corners. Lilitu, probably the Hebrew Lilith, was a succubus who visited men and disturbed their slumbers by lascivious suggestions: born from such unions were creatures such as the *alu* and *gallu*, faceless monsters who would rend those who came into their power, and who – to judge by the corresponding form in Jewish tradition – clustered round the bedside of a sick man to greet their father after death. There was also a particular type of malevolent spirit which haunted the open country, described as 'the evil *utukku*-demon which kills a fit man in the steppe'.

In addition to these there were the plain ghosts of dead humans. The wraiths of those who had died by violence or in consequence of infringement of a taboo –

> whether a ghost that was slain by a weapon or a ghost that died of a sin against a god or a crime against a king –

were particularly liable to wander, as was one neglected by its family in the matter of funerary and memorial rites,

> a forgotten ghost, or a ghost whose name is not uttered or a ghost who has no one to care for it.

Not only could such ghosts strike terror into the hearts of those they haunted, but they might do actual harm. The following is an example of the kind of procedure used to deal with this menace.

The officiant prepared unleavened bread from specified ingredients, whilst he recited the following incantation three times:

> Dead folk, why do you appear to me, you whose towns are the ruins. . . . I do not go to Cuthah, the assembly-place of the ghosts: why, then, do you come after me? Be ye exorcised by . . . [names of deities follow].

As the sun was setting, this magic bread was introduced into a newly dug hole through an ox-horn. A censer was set burning, and as a column of incense rose to the setting sun, the officiant recited another incantation calling upon Shamash, the Sun-god, to exorcise the offending spirit and

> whether it be an evil spook or an evil *alu* or an evil ghost or an evil *gallu* or a buried ghost or an unburied ghost, or a ghost without brother or sister, or a ghost with no one to mention its name, . . . or a ghost which was left in the desert, . . . appoint it to the keeping of the ghosts of its family.

Finally, a wax image of the sick man was placed in the family grave together with clay images of the ghosts. This had a two-fold intention: it laid the ghosts by token burial, and it deceived them into believing that their victim had died.

An alternative cure was available if a ghost could be definitely identified. A clay figure was made, and assimilated to the offending ghost by inscribing its name on its left hip: it was then rendered helpless by twisting its feet, throwing it down, and putting a dog's tooth in its mouth as a gag. After making a libation to the Sun-god, the officiant recited three times:

> I conjure you by Shamash at his setting, get clear of the body of so-and-so; depart, begone!

33A B Scenes from the bronze gates of Shalmaneser III (ninth century BC)

34 Assyrian forces and [bottom register] prisoners-of-war

Relief on an obelisk of Shalmaneser III showing [top section] Jehu of Israel offering tribute

36 Foreigners bringing tribute to Assyria (from an Assyrian bas-relief)

37 Esarhaddon with captive Egyptian kings

38 Wild ass hunt (from an Assyrian bas-relief)

39 Herd of gazelles (from an Assyrian bas-relief)

40 Lions released for the hunt (from an Assyrian bas-relief)

41 Hunting dogs, and man with nets (from an Assyrian bas-relief)

42 The deer hunt (from an Assyrian bas-relief)

43A Dying lion (from an Assyrian bas-relief)

43B Paralysed lioness (from an Assyrian bas-relief)

44A Hunting c
(from an
Assyrian
bas-relief)

44B Hunting s
(from an
Assyrian
basrelief)

45 Assyrian archer and squire (from an Assyrian bas-relief)

46A Assyrian tortures (from an Assyrian bas-relief)

46B (*below*) Assyrian siege craft, showing prototype of the military tank (from an Assyrian bas-relief)

47 (*opposite*) Battle scene (from an Assyrian bas-relief)

48 Assyrian slingers (from an Assyrian bas-

The rubric adds:

> You shall bury that image in a hole at sunset, and as long as he lives that man will not see the dead ghost.

Demons could be diverted from their attacks upon a man by the provision of a substitute, such as an animal, or even an inanimate object such as a reed of the man's height. Whatever it was would be brought alongside the sufferer and identified with him in detail. The text for one such ceremony, using a goat kid, explains:

> An evil *asakku*-demon dwells in the man's body. It covers the man like a garment as he walks about. It holds his hands and feet, it paralyses his limbs.

There is then an obscure mythological reference to Ea, god of magic. This introduces the text for the ritual:

> The kid is the substitute for mankind, the kid is given for his life. The kid's head is given for the man's head, the kid's neck is given for the man's neck, the breast of the kid is given for the breast of the man.

The belief that if a demon was exorcised from a man, it was necessary to provide an alternative home, underlies the New Testament story of the Gadarene swine (St Matthew 8:28–32, St Luke 8:26–33), in which pigs were taken possession of by the multitude of demons expelled from a single man. The desirability of providing an exorcised demon with an alternative home is reflected in a New Testament parable:

> . . . the unclean spirit, when he is gone out of the man, passeth through waterless places, seeking rest, and findeth it not. Then he saith, I will return into my house whence I came out; and when he is come, he findeth it empty, swept, and garnished. Then goeth he, and taketh with himself seven other spirits more evil than himself, and they enter in and dwell there: and the last state of that man becometh worse than the first. (St Matthew 12:43–45)

Not all demons were ill-disposed to mankind, for some incantations conclude:

> Let the evil *utukku* and the evil *alu* go away,
> Let a benevolent *utukku* and a benevolent genie be present.

Well-disposed counterparts of the malevolent powers included good *utukku*-spirits, good representatives of various other demonic species, and beings known as *shedu* and *lamassu*. The last two could take various forms, and to ensure their presence the Babylonians and Assyrians made several kinds of representations of them, amongst them the huge winged bulls and lions (see plate 53) which stood at the entrance of Assyrian palaces as protection against evil. A private house or bedroom might be similarly protected by figures standing at the doorway or buried under the threshold. At Ur, for example, the excavators found clay figurines in boxes of burnt brick under the floor against the walls: the figurines, which had been lime-washed and then painted in black and red, faced into the centre of the room to guard it. They were of various kinds. Some took the form of humans clad in a pointed hat and a long robe painted with scales: these were fish-men, creatures mentioned in mythology. Other figures had human bodies and the heads and wings of birds, and some represented a benevolent-looking, long-bearded, long-robed godling (similar to plate 30), with his closed hands folded across his breast as though grasping something. Yet others were clay representations of the *mushkhushshu* or dragon, a composite creature with the body of a dog, the head of a serpent, and a long tail.

We have the text of the ritual for setting up figurines of this kind to protect a house. It begins by enumerating possible causes of the misfortune which had afflicted the dwelling:

> Whether it be an evil ghost or an evil spirit or an evil spook or an evil ghoul or an evil god or an evil Croucher or a *Lamashtu* or . . . the Seizer, . . . or Lilith . . . or . . . Plague-demon . . . or Death or Heat or Fever, . . . whatever there may be . . . which does harm to a man, in a man's house . . .

Instructions are then given for the preparation of magical figures of wood and clay:

> You shall sprinkle holy water; set up a portable altar; offer lambs for sacrifice . . . set up a censer with juniper-wood; pour out a wine-libation; do obeisance, purify the censer, torch, holy-water vessel and tamarisk wood, and speak thus before Shamash:
>
> *Incantation*: O Shamash, great lord, exalted judge, the one who supervises the regions of heaven and earth, the one who directs aright the dead and the living, You are . . . the holy tamarisk, the pure wood for the form of the statues which I shall cause to stand in the house of so-and-so for the overthrow of evil beings . . .

The tamarisk, thereby assimilated to the Sun-god, now had to be cut up in the approved manner. The rubric directs:

> then nick the tamarisk with a golden axe and a silver saw, and carve it with a chisel.

Groups of figurines were then made from the wood, appropriately dressed and set up, to the accompaniment of further incantations.

At sunrise next morning, there came the procedure for making figurines of clay. First, the potter's clay was made ritually pure by censing, adding holy water and other sacred objects, and reciting an incantation beginning 'O potter's clay! O potter's clay!' The clay was then used to make statuettes. Since both terracotta and unbaked moulded clay long outlast carved wood in moist soil, it is figurines of this type which have been found at Ur and elsewhere. The texts indicate that many of these clay figures were originally inscribed with magical formulae. Clay figurines of dogs, for example, had their magical names written on them in the following way:

> Name of one dog coated with gypsum: 'Don't stop to think; open your mouth!' Name of the other one: 'Don't stop to think; bite!'

Name of one black dog: 'Consume his life!' Name of the other one: 'Loud of bark'.

Name of one red dog: 'Driver-away of the *asakku*-demon'. Name of the other one: 'Catcher of the enemy'.

There were more rituals to complete before such statuettes of wood and clay became operational. It was not until after further sacrifices and libations to the Sun-god, made at the river bank at sunrise, that the statuettes were finally taken to the house. There, key points of the house – corners, doorways, roofs and air vents – were touched with various purifying substances to sterilize it from evil influences. It was now up to the statuettes to keep it clean. So that they might take up their task, sacrifices were now made to them, accompanied by incantations informing them that

> on account of some evil things which stand and call with malignant purpose in the house of so-and-so the son of so-and-so, . . . I have made you stand at the gate, at right and left, to dispel them . . . Let anything malignant . . . be removed from you a distance of 3600 double-hour journey.

The foregoing ritual was a lengthy and no doubt expensive affair, but it was efficacious against all types of evil influences, presumably indefinitely. Simpler rituals could provide security with a shorter period of guarantee:

> To cut off the source of evil from a man's house, you shall pound up, bray and mix in mountain honey the seed of . . . [seven named plants] . . . , divide it into three parts, and bury it in the threshold of the gate and to the right side and to the left side. Then illness, headache, insomnia and pestilence shall not approach that man and his house for one year.

Witchcraft

The kind of evil influences against which such rituals were directed did not always seize upon a man by their own volition. Often they were directed by witchcraft. There were simple ways of doing this. Spittle, for example, had magical properties, and when one spat the decent thing was to rub it out with the foot, to save other people from risk. But a worker of black magic might deliberately flout this precaution, and we find listed as one possible source of trouble 'evil spittle not covered with dust'. Such a passage as the following, from an exorcism, shows how widespread and feared witchcraft was:

> *Incantation*: My witch, my bewitcher, sits in the shadow of a heap of bricks. She sits and works bewitchment on me, makes images of me. . . .
>
> [The witch is now addressed]. 'The bewitchment which you have wrought, let it be directed against you! The images you have made, let them apply to you! The water which you have drawn up, let it be used against yourself!'

The laws of Hammurabi made the practitioner of witchcraft liable to the death penalty. Legislation, however, was of no avail against the dire consequences of witchcraft; exorcism was needed to counter it, and many such texts are known. Such a text would begin with the diagnosis, for instance:

> The witch has wrought her evil bewitchment,
> She has made me eat her no-good spirit,
> She has made me drink her drink, to take away my life,
> She has washed me with filthy washing, to make me a dead man,
> She has anointed me with her bad oil for my destruction,
> She has made me catch a bad illness which is the grasp of a curse,
> She has appointed me to the ghost of a stranger who prowls around, who has no kin.

Treatment succeeded diagnosis. The god Asar-lu-hi (identified with Marduk) noted the sufferer's situation and reported the diagnosis to his father Ea, telling him that 'the witch has gone to tear away his life'. Ea then gave instructions for treatment:

Go, my son Marduk! Give him your pure drink of life, let him eat the plant of life. Let him anoint himself and wash. . . . Reach his witch with the wind of your mouth! . . . Let bewitchment, venom, filth, be far from him. . . . Let the curse go forth into the wilderness, let the ghost of the stranger disappear! . . . Let the man live, . . . Whatever his witch has done to kill him, may Marduk loose.

From the need of the illicit operators of witchcraft to practise secrecy, it is only to be expected that we should find little direct trace of their activity. But we know at least one document used in illicit black magic. It takes the form of a letter to a god asking the deity to wipe out the writer and the whole of his family and connections. It begins:

Incantation. Bau-ah-iddina . . . addresses the great lord Ninurta thus: 'O Ninurta, great lord! Tear out the heart, extinguish the life, kill the wife, annihilate the sons, the relations, the connections, the name, the seed, the offshoot, the descendants of Bau-ah-iddina. . . .',

and ends with an oath, allegedly by the unfortunate Bau-ah-iddina, assuring the doubtless rather puzzled deity that Bau-ah-iddina and his relations bore

the effect, the penalty, the guilt, the sin, the offence of this oath.

Not all afflictions befalling a man were the result of witchcraft or of ill-disposed demons. A man might bring trouble upon himself by violating a taboo. Certain foods and certain activities were interdicted on particular days, and in a hemerology (list of lucky and unlucky days) we read:

In the month of Tashrit, . . .

first day: . . . (a man) shall not eat garlic, or a scorpion will sting him; he shall not eat an onion, or there will be dysentery for him . . . ;

second day: he shall not eat garlic, or an important person in his family will die; . . . he shall not ascend to a roof, or the Handmaid of Lilu will espouse him;

third day: he shall not have intercourse with a woman, or that woman will take away his sexual powers;

fourth day: he shall not cross a river, or his virility will fail;

fifth day: he shall not eat pig-meat, or there will be a lawsuit for him; . . .

Therefore, when a man was oppressed by sickness or trouble, such matters had to be enquired into, to trace the cause. It was only a step from this to enquiring into a man's other activities, which we (but not the Babylonians) would call his ethical standards. Thus, in an incantation for someone who is 'sick, in danger, distraught, very troubled', we find a list of the man's possible offences. It is said that he may, *inter alia*, have

> eaten what is taboo to his god, eaten what is taboo to his goddess, . . . divided son from father, father from son, divided daughter from mother, mother from daughter, divided daughter-in-law from mother-in-law, mother-in-law from daughter-in-law, brother from brother, friend from friend,

or he may have failed in his duty in that

> he did not set the captive free, did not release the man who was bound, . . . (but) said with respect to the captive, 'Keep him captive!', and with respect to the man who was bound said, 'Bind him well!'

It may be that

> he treated a god with disrespect, neglected a goddess, . . . neglected his father and mother, treated his elder sister with disrespect, sold by a small measure and received by a large, said 'there is' when there was not, said 'there is not' when there was, . . . lay with his neighbour's wife, shed his neighbour's blood . . .

or that

> he ate something taboo to his city, . . . lay in the bed of a person under a curse, sat in the chair of a person under a curse, ate at the table of a person under a curse . . .

Some of the offences are plainly, from the modern point of view, ethical ones. But the distinction between ethical sins and the unwitting breaking of taboos did not exist for the ancient Babylonian, who saw his life controlled not by a moral law but by the arbitrary and usually unpredictable will of forces in the supernatural world.

Divination

Far back in their past, the Babylonians had developed a kind of specious logic in their view of the relationship between events. They came to believe that if a certain event succeeded another in time, there must be a causal connection, and the same result might be expected to succeed the same event on another occasion. Lists of unusual occurrences with the supposed consequences were collected, and from this arose a great pseudo-science directed to the interpretation of omens. References in literature show that third-millennium Sumerians already used omens. From the Old Babylonian period onwards, they form a large proportion – perhaps as much as 30 per cent – of that part of Akkadian literature which is not economic in content.

The types of phenomena from which omens could be drawn were virtually unlimited, but they may be divided into three main groups: (i) those which employed special techniques, such as liver-divination; (ii) those which divined from casual phenomena, such as dreams, the movements of animals, or freak births; and (iii) astrology.

Certain techniques were favoured at particular times and places. Hepatoscopy (liver-divination) is well attested from Old Babylonian times, but astrology became of high importance only in later Assyria. It was also in later Assyria that dream-omens enjoyed their greatest popularity, although they were not unknown earlier. Predictions in omens had two main areas of interest: astrology and liver-divination were mainly concerned with state affairs, whilst other types mostly related to private persons.

The following examples of omens come from an ancient compilation known as 'If a town is set on a hill', from the first line, which reads:

> If a town is set on a hill, it will not be good for the dweller within that town.

It is typical of the genre that this is followed by its antithesis:

> If a town is set in a depression, it will be good for the dweller within that town.

Other omens in this very large collection mention circumstances during the building of a house, for example:

> If black ants are seen on the foundations which have been laid, that house will get built; the owner of that house will (live to) grow old.
>
> If red ants are seen . . . , the owner of that house will die before his time.

Omens were also drawn from the chance behaviour of various creatures:

> If a snake is aggressive to a man, seizes him, bites him, hard times will reach his adversary.
>
> If a snake passes from right to left of a man, he will have a good name.
>
> If a snake passes from left to right of a man, he will have a bad name. [These two omens well illustrate the standard interpretation of right as lucky, left as unlucky.]
>
> If a snake appears in a place where a man and wife are standing and talking, the man and wife will divorce each other. [The

symbolism is obvious. We ourselves could use closely related imagery in speaking of 'a snake in the grass' coming between a man and his wife.]

If a scorpion kills a snake in a man's house, that man's sons will kill him; he will die. [The lesser creature unexpectedly destroys the greater.]

If a mongoose kills a snake in a man's house, (this means) the approach of barley and silver.

If a snake falls (from the ceiling) on a man and wife and scatters them, the man and wife will be divorced.

If a scorpion lurks in a man's bed, that man will have riches.

If ants kill each other, making a battle; approach of the enemy, there will be the downfall of a great army.

If there are black winged ants in the town, there will be pouring rain and floods.

If an ox has tears come into both its eyes, some evil will befall the owner of that ox.

If an ass mounts a man, that man will be sold for money, or (alternatively) hard times will seize him.

If an ass gives birth and (the creature has) two heads, there will be a change in the throne.

If a nobleman is riding in a chariot and falls behind the chariot, it is of unfavourable portent for him; the Government will recall him from his post [literally 'the palace will make him return'].

If a wild ox appears in front of the great gate, the enemy will invest the town.

If a wild ox goes in to a herd of cows and pastures with them daily, it is favourable. If it separates and goes off the same day, it is unfavourable.

If a fox runs into the public square, that town will be devastated. [An incident of this kind was considered important enough to be reported to the Assyrian king. We have a letter which reads: 'To the king my lord your servant Nabua. May Nabu and Marduk bless the king my lord. On the seventh day of the month Kislimu a fox came into the city Ashur into the park of the god Ashur. It fell into a well. They got it out and killed it.']

If a sow kindles and brings forth three and their heads are white and their tails black, the furniture of that man's house will be pledged for silver. [Corresponding omens continue through a series of numbers and colour combinations.]

If a dog lies on his (master's) bed, his [the master's] god is angry with him.

If a white dog urinates on a man, hard times will seize that man.

If a red dog urinates on a man, that man will have happiness.

If a flood comes in the month Nisan and the river is coloured like blood, there will be pestilence in the land. [Although severe floods in Iraq can bring epidemics in their wake, the omen is simply seeing a magical connection between water which looks like flowing blood, and death.]

If fish are numerous in a river (this portends) quiet dwelling for the land. [The shoals of fish suggest contented crowds in the city streets.]

Illogically, it was considered possible to prevent the consequences of a bad omen, and rituals were available to ward off the ill-fortune foretold by such events. For example, to cancel the evil warned of by a dog cocking its leg on a man the following was prescribed:

The ritual for it. You shall make a dog of clay. You shall put (a piece of) cedar-wood on its neck. You shall pour oil on its head. You shall clothe it in a goatskin. You shall put hairs from a horse's mane as its tail.

The model dog was then taken to the river bank. There a portable altar was set up before Shamash, on which were placed twelve loaves of emmer bread, a confection of dates, flour, honey and butter, and vessels of choice beer. With everything in place the officiant recited incantations calling upon Shamash to remove the threatening evil.

Such rituals were performed not by the person directly concerned but by the type of exorcist called the *ashipu* or *mashmashu* (see pages 261, 415), who received a fee for his services.

Prayer

Although magic played such a great part in ancient Mesopotamia, it did not constitute the whole of the Babylonian response to the adversities and problems of life. On the contrary, prayer, the expression of a sense of utter dependence on a personal deity, was also a common means by which the Babylonian sought solace and aid. He himself possibly did not recognize any essential distinction between the two forms of contact with the spiritual world, for he headed both his magical formulae and his prayers with the term we translate 'Incantation'. None the less, the difference of approach is, to any practising Christian, Jew or Muslim, unmistakable. A typical prayer begins thus:

> *Incantation*. O Lord, Strong One, Famous One, the Omniscient,
> Splendid One, Self-renewing One, Perfect One, First-begotten of Marduk,
> . . . .
> Counsellor of the gods, . . .

and continues in like vein through a series of titles and attributes, culminating in the phrases:

> . . . You watch over all men,
> You accept their supplication,
> You bestow upon them wellbeing;
> The whole of mankind makes prayer to you.

The worshipper then introduces his personal circumstances:

> I, Balasu, son of his god, whose god is Nabu, whose goddess is Tashmetum,
> On account of the evil of the outbreak of fire in my house
> I am afraid, I am troubled, I am very troubled.

The 'evil' referred to is not the damage done by an outbreak of fire but the disaster which such an event was believed to foretell. This is clear from the fact that parallel prayers, intended for use by the king on behalf of the nation, often refer to 'the evil of the eclipse of the moon'. The prayer continues:

I am (one liable to be) plundered (or) murdered, one whose punishment is great;
I am one who is weary, disturbed, whose body is very sick,
So that taboo (and) pain have met me: I bow before thee.
Sickness from magic, sorcery, witchcraft has covered me;
. . . .
O Lord, Wise One of the gods, by thy mouth command good for me;
O Nabu, Wise One of the gods, by thy mouth may I come forth alive.

The exalted conception of deity which a prayer of this kind implies is beyond doubt. Yet it becomes abundantly clear that the priests representing the mainstream of ancient Mesopotamian religion saw no essential difference between magic and prayer, for in a later part of the same compilation we find, after a prayer to the Moon-god Sin, the instructions:

The ritual for it. At night you shall sweep the roof before Sin; you shall sprinkle holy water. You shall pile up a pyre . . . You shall prepare three measures of flour which a male has milled, and one measure of salt. . . . You shall heap them up on the pyre . . .

and so on, in just the same way as for the kinds of approach to the supernatural world which we would consider purely magical.

The following prayer to a goddess provides another example of a more noble conception of the relationship between man and deity:

Incantation. O Heroic One, Ishtar; Immaculate One of the goddesses,
Torch of heaven and earth, Radiance of the continents,
Goddess Lady-of-Heaven, First-begotten of Sin, Firstborn of Ningal,
Twin-sister of . . . the hero Shamash [the Sun-god];
O Ishtar, you are Anu [the supreme god], you rule the heavens;
With Enlil the Counsellor you advise mankind; . . .

Where conversation takes place, you, like Shamash, are paying attention, . . .
You alter the Fates, and an ill event becomes good; . . .
Before you is a *shedu*, behind you a *lamassu* [protecting spirits];
At your right is Justice, at your left Goodness,
Fixed on your head are Audience, Favour, Peace,
Your sides are encompassed with Life and Wellbeing;
How good it is to pray to you, how blessed to be heard by you!
Your glance is Audience, your utterance is Light.
Have pity on me, Ishtar! Ordain my prospering! . . .
I have sought your brightness; may my face be bright.
I have turned to your dominion; may it be life and wellbeing for me. . . .
Lengthen my days, bestow life!
Let me live, let me be well, let me proclaim your divinity.
Let me achieve what I desire . . .

At the end of the prayer comes the instruction:

You shall set a censer with juniper-wood before Ishtar: you shall pour a gruel-libation, you shall recite the 'hand-raising' three times, you shall do obeisance.

The hymns and prayers quoted bear suggestions, if not of monotheism, at least of henotheism, that is, the worshipping of only one god without denying the existence of others. That this was a conscious trend in Assyro-Babylonian religion is shown by texts in which parts of the deity adored were identified with other gods, as in this hymn to Ninurta:

Your two eyes, O Lord, are Enlil and Ninlil . . .
Anum and Antum are your two lips . . .
Your teeth are the 'Seven', who overthrow evil,
The approach of your cheeks, O Lord, is the coming out of the stars,
Your two ears are Ea and Damkina [his spouse], princes of wisdom . . .
Your neck is Marduk, judge of heaven and earth . . .

This trend has to be viewed, however, in the light of the extensive polytheism which characterized ancient Mesopotamian religion. From the *Early Dynastic* period, four thousand gods are known by name, and although later theologians reduced this number by cross-identification, a vast pantheon always remained.

The pantheon

The Mesopotamian pantheon of historical times was of complex origin. The life of the communities in south Iraq before 3000 BC had a common background, with local ecological differences. The extreme south was an area of marshes, lagoons and lakes, whereas there were other areas dominated by date-palms, or with good pastures for cattle-raising, or large tracts of land well placed for irrigation and corn-growing. These differences were, of course, a matter of emphasis: to some degree all these ways of life would be found almost everywhere, but their relative importance would vary. This difference of emphasis had its reflection in religion. The communities saw the powers evident in the natural world around them as supernatural; they thought of them as beings which we might call divinities, if not at first fully gods. In a lake area, the main divine power would be associated with the waters, whereas in a region of orchards, divinities would be related to the powers felt to be present in the palm trees, the date harvest and the community's date store. Where cowherding predominated, the people might represent the supreme supernatural power in the guise of the most formidable creature they knew, a bull. Grain farmers would be likely to link the principal divine power to the corn. Each community would see lesser divine forces alongside their principal one. These divine forces eventually took human form, but probably not in the earliest stage; later descriptions or representations in art sometimes reveal vestiges of animal or plant aspects of deities which must have been much more prominent earlier.

As city-states developed from clusters of smaller communities, their divinities would come together into a local pantheon, with the principal divine power as the chief deity, now mainly in human form. The Mesopotamian pantheon of later times was the sum of these local city-state pantheons, plus new deities who arose to take charge of fresh human activities as they developed, such as brewing, brick-making and writing.

Because each local pantheon originally had its own head, we sometimes find discrepancies in the later Mesopotamian pantheon; there may be a conflict as to the headship of the pantheon or the family relationship between deities or the divine control of a particular activity. Thus, Anu and Enlil are both at times represented as King and Father of the gods. The form of the pantheon which we shall describe is mainly the schematized form produced by later Babylonian theologians, who largely resolved (although sometimes only superficially) the problems arising from conflicting local pantheons.

Across the whole of Sumero-Babylonian religion, the god Anu (Sumerian An) was nominally accepted as Father and King of the gods, although he was often a shadowy figure. It was from Anu that mankind and individual rulers received kingship and its insignia; according to the *Epic of Etana* (see pages 380ff.) there lay before Anu in heaven the sceptre, tiara, royal head-dress and shepherd's staff.

Alongside Anu was Enlil (or Ellil), literally 'Lord Wind', the tutelary deity of Nippur. From early in the third millennium he was more than a local god: he became effectively national god of Sumer, and the possession of the whole of Sumer by the ruler of any city-state depended upon recognition by him. A Sumerian text speaks of a time when Shubur (north Mesopotamia), Sumer and Akkad, and Martu (the western nomads) all dwelt in peace and all gave praise to Enlil. Just as Anu was king of heaven, so was Enlil king of the earth. Like Anu, Enlil could be called 'Father of the gods' or 'King of the gods'. The clash between the ancient pantheons was resolved by making Enlil Anu's son, but at the same time treating them jointly as leaders of the gods, with executive powers in the hands of Enlil. Nisan, the first month of the year, in which the 'destinies' for the year were decided, was sacred to both of them. To Enlil originally belonged the Tablet of Destinies, by which the fates of men and of gods were decreed. It was he who, as Lord of the earth, had planned and created the world and its plants, who had devised the mattock and plough for man's benefit, who gave prosperity and abundance, and who watched over the wellbeing of the people of Sumer. But (like Yahweh [Jehovah] in Israel) his own great majesty and righteousness meant that human wickedness brought down his anger, and it was through his urging that the Deluge was unleashed upon the world, whilst in another myth he created the monster Labbu to destroy mankind. Enlil's consort, Ninlil, a faint shadow of himself, was ultimately assimilated to an aspect of Ishtar.

The third of the great gods at the head of the pantheon was known under various designations, the two commonest being Enki, 'Lord of the *Ki*' (*Ki* meaning either 'earth' or 'subterranean region') and Ea '(god of) the house [domain] of water'. He was originally the head of the local pantheon of Eridu in the far south.[2] The theologians generally made him son of Enlil, although sometimes Anu was regarded as his father (see page 284). But these were simply devices to fix him into a theologically organized pantheon, and there was yet another conception of him, which was probably the earliest one. According to this, he was born to Nammu, the mother of all. Nammu existed before all things, and represented the primeval waters, the great deep, the *apsu*; it was she who gave birth to heaven and earth. In this stratum of belief, it was thus Enki, who himself later incorporated the powers of the primeval great deep, who was the first and greatest god. Enki-Ea was god of wisdom, and as such unfailingly displayed benevolence to the human race and indeed to fellow deities: when Inanna was preparing to face the perils of a descent into the Underworld she directed her vizier, should she not return, to appeal for succour, first to Enlil and then to the Moon-god Nanna: if these did not help her, then assuredly Enki would come to her aid. The connection between the god of wisdom and Eridu, the oldest of Sumerian cities, was that it was there that the earliest flowering of Sumerian culture took place. Ea also bore the name Nin-shi-ku, sometimes falsely taken as Sumerian meaning 'Lord of the intelligent eye', although its real origin was as a Semitic title denoting 'the Prince'. Under another aspect he was Nu-dim-mud, 'Begetter of mankind'. His spouse was variously Ninhursag or Damkina.

The term 'first triad' is often applied to the three gods Anu, Enlil and Enki, but this can be misleading if 'triad' is taken to mean anything more specific than three gods of roughly equal rank. There is certainly nothing here corresponding to the Christian doctrine of the Holy Trinity.

How did the three supreme gods come into being? Sumero-Babylonian mythology is not consistent about this. One form of theological speculation made Anu and Enlil the end-product of a chain of twenty-one pairs of shadowy ancestors. *Enuma Elish*, the myth of creation current in Babylon from the late second millennium although it incorporates earlier material, gives its own account of the origin of Anu and Ea. The primeval Apsu (the Deep) and Tiamat (Ocean) produced two monsters, Lahmu and Lahamu, and from them were engendered Anshar and Kishar, the universe above and below. Then

> The days stretched out, the years multiplied;
> Anu their son, the equal of his forefathers,
> Anshar made him – Anu his firstborn – like (unto himself).
> Anu begat his likeness, Nu-dim-mud, . . .
> All-hearing [literally 'wide-eared'], understanding, mighty in power,
> Far stronger than Anshar, the begetter of his father,
> Without equal amongst the gods his brethren.

Here Ea is son of Anu, not of Enlil. Enlil plays no part in *Enuma Elish*, but it is possible that in an earlier form of this mythology he filled the hero's role, which was later transferred to the Babylonian national god Marduk.

Deities representing the sun, moon and Venus formed a second group; they were known in Sumerian and Akkadian respectively as Utu or Shamash, Nanna or Sin (a form of Sumerian Su-en), and Inanna (Innin) or Ishtar.

The Moon-god Sin

Sin was controller of the night, of the month and of the lunar calendar. According to variant theologies he was the son of either Anu or Enlil: his wife was Nin-gal, 'Great Lady', whilst Shamash and Ishtar were their children. Like the three supreme gods, Sin had a long and complex prehistory. Besides his predominant astral form, he also had an animal aspect, bearing the title 'brilliant young bull', and a myth tells of him impregnating his consort in the form of a cow.

The city with which Nanna-Sin was principally connected was Ur, whilst Harran in the north was also a city of the Moon-god. As the Bible gives both cities connections with Abraham, there have been attempts to see in the henotheistic worship of the Moon-god the roots of the religion revealed through Abraham, but this is highly speculative. In the sixth century BC the last New Babylonian king, Nabu-na'id, attempted a religious reform based on a cult which placed Sin at the head of the pantheon. As one might expect, the crescent moon was one of the symbols of Sin; this was later taken over as the main religious symbol of Islam.

The Sun-god Shamash

Shamash, in his daily course across the heavens, dispelled all darkness and could see all the works of man: by being the 'one from whom no secrets are hid' he was the god of justice, and it is he who is portrayed on the stele of Hammurabi as handing over the just laws to that king (see plate 21B). He is commonly represented with the rod and ring, symbols denoting straightness and completeness, that is, right and justice. In Babylonia his symbol was a disk with a four-pointed star and rays, as in plate 49. The principal cities with which Shamash was associated were Sippar and Larsa.

The goddess Ishtar

Although, well before the end of the third millennium, Mesopotamian society had at the conscious level become male-dominated, Sumerians and Babylonians still gave subconscious recognition, through religion, to the primacy of the female principle; this was reflected in the goddess Inanna-Ishtar, and in her sister Ereshkigal, Lady of the Underworld, who gave form to the dark and terrible side of this overwhelming force.

Ishtar (in the Sumerian context Innin or Inanna) was of vast significance in Sumero-Babylonian religion. By assimilating the personality and functions of other goddesses, she eventually became virtually the only female deity, so that the word *ishtar* came to be used for 'goddess' in general. Her formidable power is reflected in the mythological fancy that she drove a team of seven harnessed lions, or, according to an alternative concept, of seven evil winds. A Sumerian religious text says of her:

With Enlil in his land she fixes destiny. . .
The gods of the land assemble before her;
The great Anunna [the major gods] do reverence to her,
My Lady pronounces the judgement of the land in their presence.

Ishtar was venerated under many local manifestations, felt by worshippers to be in some way distinct, so that in Assyria we find Ishtar of Nineveh, Ishtar of Arbela, and Ishtar of Bit-kitmuri mentioned together. Ishtar of Nineveh was highly honoured outside her homeland, and on one occasion, at about 1400 BC, and possibly on a second, she was sent as far afield as Egypt, for the benefit of the Pharaoh.

The astral form of Ishtar as visible in the planet Venus was neither her only nor her major aspect. More importantly she was goddess of war and goddess of sexual love and procreation. The paradoxical union in one deity of these two disparate conceptions probably crystallized the idea that whenever life was cut off in the violence of battle or created in the fervour of the sexual act, there Ishtar was manifest. As the mother principle, she had big breasts and four milk-yielding teats.[3]

Ishtar symbol

The earliest known symbol of this goddess, as Innin or Inanna, was from Erech before 3000 BC, in the form of what is sometimes called a 'gatepost with streamers' (see illustration). This originally represented the bundle of reeds which formed the doorpost of a reed hut, of a type still found in the marshes of south Iraq: the connection between the reed hut and Inanna was that a fertility cult to which Inanna was central took place in a building of this type. Under her aspect of a sky-deity, Ishtar was often represented by an eight-pointed star.

The Weather-god Adad

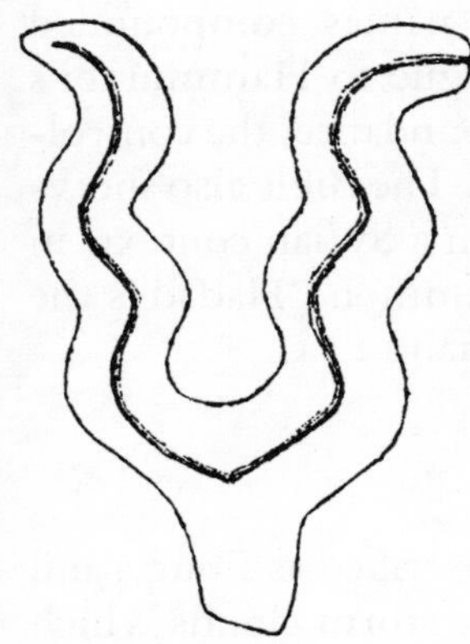
Adad symbol

The manifestations of this god, who was often associated with Shamash and Ishtar, were the lightning and thunder. His symbol was the forked lightning: the form shown here is from a Cassite boundary stone. Like Yahweh (Isaiah 19:1), Adad rode the clouds, and the thunder was his voice (compare 1 Samuel 2:10, 7:10, Job 37:4, 40:9, etc.).

The data for Adad present an excellent example of how religious differences linked to geography can come to be misrepresented as deriving from ethnic or racial differences. Speakers of Sumerian had a Weather-god Ishkur, but Ishkur was of little prominence. Semitic speakers called their Weather-god Adad and in some regions he was at the head of the pantheon. Ergo, the argument runs, there was a difference in the Weather-gods and this was a consequence of differences between Sumerian and Semitic religion.

The real explanation is quite otherwise. In Syria and Assyria, weather is variable and important, and agriculture depends heavily upon rain from storms; therefore one can expect that peoples deriving from those areas will have an important Weather-god. In Sumer, on the other hand, agriculture depends upon irrigation; there may be two or three rainstorms during the winter and a few light showers in the spring, but whilst these have their value in bringing a short flush of grass, they are not of crucial significance. Therefore, amongst agriculturalists living in south Iraq, interest in a local Weather-god will only be peripheral. This applied as much to Semitic speakers long settled there as to speakers of Sumerian. But from the end of the third millennium there were Semitic-speaking Amorites in the kingdom of Mari along the middle Euphrates, and in north Babylonia, who had come in fairly recently from Syria. Thus it is not surprising that in the documents from Mari, Adad is by far the most frequently occurring divine element in personal names compounded from god-names, and that in the epilogue to Hammurabi's laws, Adad is described as 'the lord of abundance, the controller of the floodgates of heaven and earth'. The Bible also shows the importance of Adad (spelt Hadad) in a Syrian context, in such names as Ben-hadad and Hadad-rimmon ('Hadad is the thunderer') in 1 Kings 15:18 and Zechariah 12:11.

The god Ninurta

Ninurta (whose name is sometimes transcribed as Enurta and in older books as Ninib) represented the storm clouds which drenched the mountains in the spring and brought the flooding of the rivers. What we know of him serves as a good example of how Mesopotamian deities developed.

Sumerian mythology knew of a supernatural being, Imdugud, which embodied the power of the thick storm clouds. Imdugud came to be represented in the form of a bird (see plate 10), and the divine Imdugud-bird was given the name of Anzu. An Akkadian myth (see page 376) tells how Ninurta defeated Anzu, who was now considered an evil being, and the text explicitly says:

> [Ninurta] drenched the midst of the mountains
> When he had slain the evil Anzu.

What had happened is that, with the development of deities in human form, the old powers earlier seen in Imdugud had become personified in the god Ninurta. But the old non-anthropomorphic powers lingered on, and an explanation was needed of the connection between the two. The myth offered this explanation: the power in the older form had been conquered by the god in human form. A similar process lay behind the development of some other gods. For example, in the myth *Enuma Elish*, Ea defeated the primeval being Apsu to gain the subterranean waters (the *apsu*) as his realm (see page 364). But allusions in other texts show that Ea and the *apsu* represented the same supernatural forces as comprehended at different stages of thought.

Ninurta was identified with several other gods, most notably in the third millennium with Ningirsu, deity of Girsu, the central part of the city-state of Lagash. He seems at an early period to have been associated with the pantheon of which Enlil was head, for he was son of Enlil and in some respects appears to have been virtually identified with him. Gods had numerical symbols, the number for Enlil being fifty, and Ningirsu's temple at Lagash bore the name E-ninnu, 'House of Fifty'. Also, one of the epithets of the wife of Ninurta was Nin-nibru, 'Lady of Nippur', and it was Enlil who was Lord of Nippur.

Several myths represent Ninurta as a champion of the gods in battle. This led to his being thought of as a warrior-god, and as such he was identified with the warrior-god Zababa of the city-state Kish. It was Ninurta who granted to such a king as Hammurabi 'the exalted weapon' which gave victory. He achieved special prominence in Assyria from the late second millennium onwards. In Assyria, Ninurta gave success to the kings in their religious duty of hunting, and it is interesting that ancient Calah (Genesis 10:11), the Assyrian capital during part of this time, is now known as Nimrud, the Arabic form of Nimrod, the name which Genesis 10:9 gives to the 'mighty hunter before the Lord'.

Nergal

A powerful and much feared deity was Nergal, the god of pestilence and of the Underworld; in magical texts his city, Cuthah (see 2 Kings 17:24, 30), is called 'the assembly-place of ghosts' (see page 266). As patron deity of Cuthah, Nergal had a consort of little significance called Laz, but as Lord of the Underworld his spouse was Ereshkigal ('Lady of the Great Place'). The goddess Ereshkigal, elder sister of Inanna, was the original mistress of the Underworld, and an Akkadian myth, *Nergal and Ereshkigal*, tells how Nergal became king in that realm. The gods made a banquet, and because Ereshkigal was unable to come up from the Underworld to partake, she was invited to send her messenger to receive her portion. When the messenger reached the divine Assembly, the gods stood up out of respect to his mistress. But one god – Nergal – withheld this courtesy, and so was ordered to go down to the Underworld. Before he went, Ea, god of wisdom, gave him advice on how to conduct himself, specially warning him not to accept food or drink, nor to succumb to the seductions of Ereshkigal. But the charms of Ereshkigal were too much for Nergal, and he lay with the Queen of the Underworld in her bedchamber for six days. On the seventh day she granted him a temporary return to the upper world. But when Nergal had gone, Ereshkigal felt a strong yearning for him, wanting him as her husband. She therefore sent up her messenger to demand the return of Nergal, employing, as her sanction to enforce compliance, her power to blight all earthly fecundity, fertility and life. Nergal returned, went up to Ereshkigal, seized her by the hair and pulled her from her throne. The pair then lay together for a further six days. Finally a message came from the gods above giving permission for Nergal to remain in the Underworld, where henceforth he reigned as king.

This myth probably reflects a stage of society in which leadership by a female had become unacceptable.

Minor deities

Almost every aspect of life was under the control of some deity or other, and hundreds of other gods could be named, who received mention in particular circumstances, but most of these were of only minor or occasional significance. There were so many minor deities that a Babylonian normally thought of himself as having a personal god who specially looked after him: the concept was rather that, held by some Christians, of the guardian angel. One of the tasks of the personal god was to make supplications to the great gods on behalf of the human being in his care. Wicked behaviour could drive away the personal god and leave the Babylonian with no protection against evil supernatural forces.

Amongst minor gods the Fire-gods Gibil and Gira are worth mentioning, since they were regularly invoked in magical texts as destroyers of witchcraft and black magic, as in the following text:

> *Incantation*. Flaring Gira, son of Anu, the hero, you are the fiercest amongst your brothers. You who judge cases like the gods Sin and Shamash, judge my case, make a decision concerning me! Burn my wizard and my witch! O Gira, consume my wizard and my witch! O Gira, burn them! O Gira, consume them! O Gira, bind them! O Gira, annihilate them! O Gira, send them away!

The Fire-god Nusku, whose symbol was the lamp, manifested himself in the sacrificial flame, consuming sacrifices and sending up incense to the great gods.

Marduk

In the latter part of the second millennium, Marduk of Babylon achieved a position of supremacy in the pantheon and became national god of Babylonia. In some respects Enlil had already been a national god in Sumer in the third millennium, and many of the functions and titles which now fell to Marduk were taken over from Enlil. This process had already begun at the time of Hammurabi, for in the Code of Hammurabi Enlil is said to have given Marduk *enlilutu kishshat nishe*, 'Enlil-ship over the whole of the people (of Babylonia)'. But this did not yet give Marduk supremacy, for in the prologue to the code, Marduk remained formally subordinated to Anu and Enlil, and in the reliefs at the top of Hammurabi's stele it is from Shamash and not from Marduk that he receives the rod and ring symbolizing justice. Building inscriptions of Hammurabi and his successors show the secondary importance of Marduk by naming him after Enlil and other deities.

By the time of the final recension of *Enuma Elish*, the Babylonian creation myth, the elevation of Marduk was complete. The reality was that this reflected the unquestioned dominance which Babylon had achieved, but the myth had to explain on the religious plane how a relatively minor god had finally reached supremacy in the pantheon. The answer was that he had served as champion of the gods in a cosmic battle. There were many old myths concerning primeval conflicts, reflecting the existence, behind the anthropomorphic pantheon of historical times, of the shadowy supernatural forces of prehistory, felt to be threatening the new order. These old myths were skilfully reworked to show Marduk as the great hero of primeval times. And so the myth represents the junior god Marduk, 'created in the pure Apsu', whose 'father Ea begat him', whose 'mother Damkina gave birth to him', whose 'form was inscrutable, transcendent, passing understanding', appearing before Anshar, the proto-deity, and offering his services to destroy the primeval monster Tiamat. But Marduk made a condition:

If I am to bind Tiamat and give you life,
Set an Assembly. Make my destiny surpassing and proclaim it.
Sit together in the assembly-chamber in gladness.
Let the utterance of my own mouth fix destinies, instead of you.

The gods duly assembled, and granted to Marduk the pre-eminence he had asked for. They proclaimed:

It is you who are the honoured one among the great gods,
Your destiny is unrivalled, your utterance is Anu;
O Marduk! You are the honoured one among the great gods . . .
We have given you kingship over everything.

At the end of the sixth tablet of *Enuma Elish* and in the seventh and final tablet, the gods in assembly proclaimed the 'fifty names' of the victorious Marduk. He was 'Son of the Sun-god'; 'Marukka – Verily of the gods, he is their creator'; 'Marutukku – Verily the support of the land, the city and its people'; 'Lugaldimmirankia', which was Sumerian for 'King of the gods of heaven and earth'; 'Asarri, who bestows agriculture, . . . who creates corn and plants and makes greenery come forth'; 'Tutu', of whom it is said that 'No one among the gods is like him'; and 'Shazu, the one who knows the hearts of the gods, who understands their mind'. In his visible manifestation he was Nibiru, the planet Jupiter. Ea even assimilated Marduk to himself:

Ea heard and his heart rejoiced;
He said: 'He whose name the gods have made splendid,
Let him be like me, let his name be Ea.'

Finally, in making the last of his fifty names 'Fifty', the assembly of the gods formally assimilated him to Enlil, to whom that numerical designation belonged, and Marduk is indeed called the 'Enlil of the gods'.

This deliberate assimilation of Marduk to many of the other major gods shows a movement in the direction of monotheism. But it is hardly necessary to emphasize the difference between this Babylonian theological trend and the emergence of monotheism in Israel. The religion of Israel, as revealed through the prophets, considered the Baalim (Baals) as differing from Yahweh (Jehovah, The Lord) not only in degree but also in essential nature. The assimilation of the supreme god to other deities, as was happening with Marduk in Babylonia, was one of the main trends against which the prophets in Israel were fighting.

As the 'Lord' *par excellence*, Marduk received the title Bel, 'Lord', just as Ishtar was often called simply Belit, 'Lady', and under this name he is mentioned in the Old Testament (Isaiah 46:1) and in the amusing book of *Bel and the Dragon* in the Apocrypha.

The spouse of Marduk was Sarpanitum, 'The shining one'; she had little independent importance, although by a pun on her name, taken as Zer-banitum, 'Creatress of Seed', she was assimilated to a creatress-goddess.

Nabu

Closely associated with Marduk was Nabu (Nebo), the god of Babylon's neighbouring city of Borsippa; Isaiah 46:1 refers to this connection. Theologically Nabu was the son of Marduk, and some scholars see indications that in the final stages of Babylonian civilization, just as Marduk had supplanted Enlil in supremacy in the pantheon, so Nabu was beginning to supplant Marduk.

Nabu was patron god of the scribal art. His spouse bore the name Tashmetum, which means 'Hearing', and was virtually a personification of a quality of this beneficent deity, who is described as 'wide of ear', that is to say, ever ready to hear prayer.

Dagan

We meet this god (spelt Dagon) in the Old Testament (Judges 16:23, 1 Samuel 5:2–5 and 7, 1 Chronicles 10:10), but he was known in both Babylonia and Assyria long before the earliest of the biblical passages. In Ugaritic myths – documents of the fourteenth century BC found at Ras Shamra on the Syrian coast and representing ancient Canaanite religious literature – Dagan was the father of Baal.

Dagan was of particular importance in the kingdom of Mari. A cuneiform letter from Mari shows how he once made a direct intervention in the politics of the kingdom. A certain man had had a dream, which was considered of sufficient importance to be reported to the king, Zimri-lim. This is what the man had dreamt. In the course of a journey, he arrived at Terqa and entered the temple of Dagan there. The god asked him if peace had yet been concluded between Zimri-lim and the sheikhs of the troublesome Benjamina tribes.[4] When told that this had not yet been achieved, Dagan commented:

> Why do the messengers of Zimri-lim not present themselves regularly to me and deposit his full reports before me? Were that done, I would long ago have delivered the sheikhs of the Benjamina tribes into the hands of Zimri-lim.

The dreamer was instructed in his dream to pass on the hint, and had dutifully done so. Clearly Dagan was considered to be a national god able to direct political events and the outcome of battle. On the other hand, he was far from omniscient, for he knew only what had been reported to him.

The service of the gods

As city-states began to develop in Mesopotamia, the idea arose that the gods were lords of the temple estates and cities, and that the human inhabitants were the gods' tenants, owing them rents and services. Service of the gods was not an optional extra: in ancient Mesopotamian theology, the very reason for which humans were created was to relieve the gods from the tedium of labour (see page 357). On this view of the world-order, it was necessary for the gods, in order to obtain their rights, as well as to mediate their beneficent powers to the people, to appoint human representatives.

In historical fact the earliest leaders of the community, and possibly the persons who took care of the cult and the god's house, were appointed by the community itself (see page 145), but the special position enjoyed by such leaders and functionaries, once appointed, led to their being considered, whether *En* (Lord), *Lugal* (King), *Ensi* (Governor) or *Sanga* (Priest), as the god's representatives. Both the royal household and the temple organization became thought of as divinely ordained.

Throughout the whole of Babylonian and Assyrian history, the king remained the direct representative of the god, and it was he who was responsible for ensuring the fertility of the land by participation in New Year rituals. Within the temples an elaborate administration developed on behalf of the gods, embracing both economic and sacerdotal activities; it is only the latter with which we are concerned here. Temples had a considerable staff, ranging from senior administrators to common labourers, but from Old Babylonian times they were divided into those who had the right of entry to all parts of the temple, and those to whom some areas were forbidden. Those who had full rights of entry, known as *erib biti*, may be considered as clergy – admittedly an anachronistic term, but one which has a measure of justification, in that it does cover a number of different types of functionary, all of whom had some sacerdotal aspect, even if they could not all be called priests. The *erib biti* personnel appear to have carried out the ordinary ceremonials for the regular offerings to the gods and to have assisted other classes of officials in special ceremonies, as when we read that

> the chief *erib biti* will lead the torch from the ziggurat, with the *mashmashu*-priests, the *kalu*-priests and singers . . .

or

the king and the *erib biti* go to the sanctuary, and the *erib biti* holds out the water basin for hand-washing to Ishtar.

Priests in the narrowest sense were the functionaries known as *shangu* (Sumerian *sanga*), headed by the *shangamahhu* ('supreme *sanga*'), who were concerned with the temple ritual generally. In the late period, the high priest who officiated in Babylon at the New Year Feast and bestowed upon the king his insignia was known as the *sheshgallu* (from Sumerian *shesh-gal*, 'Big Brother' or 'Great Guard') (see page 335).

Exorcists

There was another group who could be called priests more loosely. These were the exorcists, whom we might equally well call witchdoctors. There were two Akkadian terms for these people – *ashipu* and *mashmashu*; see further on page 261. A word related to *ashipu* is used in Daniel 2:10 and elsewhere for 'enchanter'. For the curriculum for their training and the kind of incantations they used, see pages 264f. They had regular tasks in the temple, such as performing the purification rites at the beginning of temple rituals. But their services were not limited to the temple, and many of the rituals and incantations performed by the exorcists took place in the home of an afflicted man who needed their ministrations as witchdoctors.

Musicians

From earliest times music was an important feature of the temple cult, and we know of two associated groups concerned with this.

The first was the *kalu*, whose title is conventionally translated 'lamentation-priest', although laments were by no means the whole of his professional activities. Besides laments, he might sing hymns, prayers and incantations, typically accompanying himself on a type of harp called *balaggu* (see plate 7 for one very early type of harp); in some of his rituals he might use drums of various kinds (*halhallatu*, *manzu*, and *lilissu*). We are very vague on the details of some of these instruments, but we do know that the *lilissu* was a bronze kettledrum which was set up in the temple courtyard at the time of a lunar eclipse for the rituals to drive away the demons attacking the Moon-god.

At least some *kalus* had a specifically priestly status, since they had their hair cut to a characteristic tonsure and wore special linen robes. Some of them were in the service of particular deities. Apart from their duties in the temple, where their primary task was 'to calm the heart' of the god by their music, they sometimes had to assist an *ashipu* by chanting the texts appropriate for his magical rituals. *Kalus* were of relatively high status, and they were certainly literate, as we hear of them copying out the religious texts they performed and even composing new ones. Some literate musically expert Sumerians, presumably *kalus*, had even devised a musical notation. This notation, which comprised a series of terms for musical intervals interspersed with numerals, has been recognized and interpreted in recent decades by the very few specialists who combine expertise in Assyriology and musicology; we have to thank them for giving us an approximate idea of how Sumerian music sounded.[5]

Closely associated with *kalus*, but of lower status, were *narus*, 'singers', who accompanied themselves on the lyre (see plate 52). They might be either male or female, the term for the latter being *nartu*. They were more numerous than *kalus*, and we sometimes hear of groups of them running into hundreds; whole families could engage in the profession. In the temple, their task was to assist the *kalu* in his rituals, but there were also choirs of them at royal courts. What these musicians sang in the latter setting we do not certainly know, but we have a text which gives the first lines of a number of songs, which they may have used. The songs in question seem to be love songs, typically beginning in some such way as 'I smile at the lusty shepherd boy', or 'When I lie in the arms of my lover'. Such songs probably originated in the cult of Ishtar, and the first lines have indisputable similarities to some of the lyrics in the biblical Song of Songs.

Other servants of the cult

There were many other classes of functionaries for specialist aspects of the cult, such as the *pashishu* ('anointer') and *ramku* ('washer') for rituals of anointing and washing; for the latter type of ritual a temple or palace would have a special room called the *bit rimki*, literally 'ablution house' – in effect, bathroom. Practical operations such as the making of images were the concern of the *mari ummani* ('craftsmen'). An officer called the *nash patri* ('swordbearer') was responsible for slaughtering sacrificial beasts, and also performed such duties in rituals as the symbolic decapitation of images of evil beings.

Diviners

The great pseudo-science of omen-interpretation required its own experts. Although diviners could operate in connection with the temple establishment, they were by no means limited to this, and they sometimes played an important part in state affairs. There would, for example, be one or more diviners accompanying any military campaign, and the king would at all times consult such functionaries before taking major decisions.

The Babylonians and Assyrians firmly believed that omens revealed the future, but their thinking about this was not consistent. There were traditions that already before the Flood some kings had employed divination, and this reflects the fact that this superstition went back to prehistoric times. We have already seen that it was not until the dawn of history that the Mesopotamian gods developed fully as personal beings in human form. Therefore, if divination already existed in prehistoric times, it preceded the existence of Mesopotamian gods, and must in origin have been non-deistic. That is to say, in earliest thinking the belief that one particular event presaged another was seen as an automatic consequence of the nature of things, not a decision made and revealed by divine beings.

But with the development of Babylonian theology, a

contrary view came in: now there arose the belief that the gods themselves directed future events, and that if suitably approached they would reveal their intentions to a suppliant. And so invocations of the gods were introduced into the rituals for divination. But in many cases the form of the texts makes it very clear that these references to the gods were not central and had merely been added to something much older.

The major type of officiant in this area was known as the *baru*; the term means literally 'observer', 'seer'. Originally the *baru* had a number of techniques at his disposal, but after the Old Babylonian period he concentrated on divination from the entrails of animals (extispicy or haruspicy), particularly from the liver (hepatoscopy).

Details of the *baru*'s procedure varied with period and place, but basically it was as follows. With the modification of the old pre-deistic approach, the official theory now was that the god Shamash, the Sun-god and god of divination, could be induced to write an oracle on the internal organs of a sacrificial animal. This is sometimes specifically stated, as when Shamash is told: 'You give decisions by writing upon the flesh inside the lamb.'

The diviner began by making himself ritually pure by putting cedar resin in and around his mouth, in his hair and in his crutch: this substance had magical properties. He was now in a state to approach the god Shamash. A question was written on a clay tablet and set before the god, who was asked to write his answer on the internal organs of the sacrificial animal. The animal was then sacrificed and the organs examined. The answer could be given in one of two ways. In one, certain abnormalities of the internal organs had specific meanings; the *baru* interpreted these either by consulting commentaries which listed the meaning of features of different organs, or by using clay models of internal organs (see plate 27B) marked with significant features with the meaning inscribed by them. The other technique was binary. The question was put in a form admitting the answer 'yes' or 'no', and certain features on the internal organs were regarded as being positive or negative. These were added up, and a preponderance of positives was interpreted as the answer 'yes'. If there were any doubt about the answer the first time (which generally meant, if the answer given was not the one wanted), the procedure could be repeated a second or even a third time as a check.

Such procedures were concerned with state affairs. The kind of matter to which they might apply is shown in the following example of a question by a first-millennium Assyrian king:

O Shamash, great lord, on the matter about which I question you, answer me a firm 'yes'.
From this day, the third of this month Ayyar [May] until the eleventh of the month Ab [August] of this year,
For these hundred days and hundred nights, the period stipulated in this extispicy, . . .
Will . . . the troops of either the Cimmerians, or the Medes, or the Mannaeans, or any enemy whatever,
Strive and plot (against me)?

There were other classes of omen interpreters. A type called *sha'ilu* (literally 'askers') are often mentioned beside *baru*-diviners, but the latter had higher status. One hymn described the *sha'ilu* as a solver of dreams, and this seems to have been his primary function. There were also female members of this class; the functions of such a person, a *sha'iltu*, seem to have been wider than those of her male counterpart. She was apparently outside the official religion centred on the temple, and the texts suggest that it was women in particular who made use of her services to ascertain the will of the gods.

The sexual dimension of religion

Two of the basic facts of human life, deny them though we may, are that there is an essential sexual difference between men and women, and that the most intimate way in which men and women can relate is by sexual union. Any religion which ignores these facts is sterile. Sumero-Babylonian religion recognized them and reflected this recognition particularly in the characteristics it bestowed upon the goddess Inanna-Ishtar.

Inanna-Ishtar was explicitly linked to sexual love. She was the divine harlot, and texts speak of her many lovers; one tells how she could take 120 men without tiring. A hymn addresses her as a harlot, soliciting for a lover.[6] One would expect this aspect of the goddess to be reflected by the presence of prostitutes amongst her cultic personnel. But some scholars argue that there cannot have been religious prostitution in Babylonia because the texts do not explicitly speak of prostitution in this context. This proves nothing. In any society, words meaning 'prostitution' are used only for forms of paid sexual relationships of which society disapproves; sexual licence which is not subject to general disapproval will not be referred to in opprobrious terms. For example, the loosening of standards in contemporary British society has brought a growing tendency to replace the term 'harlot' by 'call girl', although the factual situation has not changed one whit.

There is in Islamic society an ancient form of sexual relationship (*mut'a*) still practised by Shi'ah Muslims (though stoutly rejected by Sunnis), which westerners would call prostitution. A man making a stay in another city can, through and with the approval of the Muslim authorities, obtain a woman whom he agrees to marry for a specific limited time, which may run into months or be as little as an hour; at the end of the agreed period the 'marriage' automatically terminates.

We know of an Old Assyrian marriage contract (for genuine marriage) in which it is stipulated that the bridegroom may not marry another woman in his home area (Cappadocia) but may 'take' a *qadishtu*-woman in the city of Ashur (which he was accustomed to visit on trading journeys). The verb for 'take' is the same as the verb for 'marry', and so it looks as though the *qadishtu* was a woman of the same class as those available for temporary 'marriage' (*mut'a*) in Shi'ah Islam: in both cases they are women entering into temporary sexual relationships for money – what we westerners in our coarse way would call prostitutes. The exact Hebrew philological equivalent of *qadishtu* is *qadeshah*: it occurs in Deuteronomy 23:17 [Hebrew text 18], where AV translates it 'whore' and RSV 'cult prostitute', alongside the male counterpart *qadesh* ('sodomite' in AV), and both of them were prohibited in Israel. 2 Kings 23:7 shows that there were male cult prostitutes associated with the temple of Yahweh (RSV, 'the house of the Lord') up to the late seventh century BC, and that alongside them were women in the service of a goddess, doing things of which the prophetic movement disapproved. It looks as though the women called *qadishtu/qadeshah* played a religious sexual role in both Babylonia and Israel.

Classical tradition certainly believed that religious prostitution took place in association with Babylonian temples. The Greek traveller Herodotus in the fifth century BC reports that in Babylon

> every woman must once in her life go and sit in the temple of Aphrodite and there have intercourse with a stranger . . . Once a woman has taken her seat she may not return home until some stranger has cast a silver coin into her lap and taken her outside the temple to lie with her. As he throws the coin, the stranger has to say, 'In the name of the goddess Mylitta [= Akkadian *Mu'allitu*, 'the one who brings to birth', a title of Ishtar]. When she has surrendered herself, her duty to the goddess has been rendered and she may return home; from that time it will be impossible to seduce her, no matter how large a sum you offer her.[7]

Herodotus has certainly garbled the details, but his use of the genuine term 'Mylitta' shows that he had some basis for his statement.

There were two other curious types of temple personnel associated with the cult of Ishtar. We find mention of

> the *kurgarru* and the *assinnu* whose masculinity Ishtar has changed into feminity.

The authoritative *Chicago Assyrian Dictionary* comments that 'there is no evidence that they were eunuchs or homosexuals', and is inclined to see them as transvestites. But it is difficult to see what function transvestism could play in ancient religion if it were entirely separated from homosexuality, which is the most obvious way by which a man has his masculinity changed to femininity. They were certainly thought of as being neither male nor female, and they must have been a class of human being who seemed odd to the ordinary person and required some explanation for their existence, since there is a myth in which they were created out of dirt from the finger-nails of the god Enki. We know that such people also took part as actors and dancers wearing masks in various rituals.

The Entu

In quite a different category, although still with overtones of sexuality, was the high priestess known as the *Entu*. The Sumerian ideogram for her title can be interpreted either as 'the lady (who is) a deity' or 'the wife of the god'. She was of very high social standing, and a king might make his daughter the *Entu* of a god, as did Sargon of Agade in the third millennium and Nabu-na'id in the mid-first.

Omen texts and laws make it clear that the *Entu* was supposed to live in chastity. Why? There can hardly have been any other reason than that it was thought that the god had sexual rights over her. We know that in ancient Mesopotamia there was a periodic ceremony which we call the Sacred Marriage, in which, to ensure fertility, the sexual activities of the god were in some way represented. There is indisputable evidence that in certain times and places human participants played some part in this. It is not unreasonable, in view of the meaning of the *Entu*'s title, to conclude that such participation was her original function: this conclusion does not prejudge the question of whether the *Entu* had actual intercourse with the king playing the role of the god, or whether the intercourse was only on the mythical plane when the god made a supposed personal visit to her. The latter interpretation underlay a statement by Herodotus. He said that on top of the ziggurat at Babylon

> stands a great temple with a sumptuously-equipped couch in it. . . . No one spends the night there except one Assyrian woman, chosen by the god himself; or so say the Chaldeans who are the priests of Bel. These Chaldeans say – not that I believe them – that the god himself comes into the temple and takes his rest on the couch. The Egyptians tell a similar story about Thebes . . . Both women, we are told, are forbidden intercourse with men.[8]

The laws of Hammurabi show that under certain conditions an *Entu* could marry, although the general assumption in the texts is that any son she may have will be adopted. Presumably she was expected not to engage in normal sexual relations with her husband or anyone else. But nature often triumphs, and omens know of cases in which men had intercourse with an *Entu*; on one interpretation the mother of Sargon of Agade was a woman of this class, who disposed of her unwanted child by exposing him.

There was another class of temple woman called *naditu*, much lower in status than the *Entu*. Such women seem to have been comparable to nuns, and generally lived in a special part of the temple called *gagu*. They were usually unmarried, although they could marry, but as they were not allowed to have children it is questionable if their marriages, when they did occur, were concerned with anything more than social and economic status. It appears that such women were sometimes accompanied into marriage by a younger sister who had children by the husband as a surrogate for the *naditu*.[9] The precise function of *naditu*-women is not clear.

The feeding of the gods

Many early cylinder seals depict a worshipper bringing an offering of a goat to a deity, illustrating the conception that the gods required food no less than humans. In the temples they received regular meals, two or – at some places in the late period – four a day, a 'great' and a 'little' meal morning and evening placed on tables before the divine images. A text from the Seleucid period shows that provisions for the gods at Erech included a daily total of about half a ton of bread (made from flour of three-quarters barley and one-quarter wheat), fifty sheep, two oxen, one calf, eight lambs, and fifty-four containers of beer and wine. This recalls the story of *Bel and the Dragon* in the Apocrypha, in which

> the Babylonians had an idol, called Bel, and there were spent upon him every day twelve great measures of fine flour, and forty sheep, and six firkins of wine. (*Bel and the Dragon*, verse 3)

Other foodstuffs for the meals of the gods included honey, ghee, vegetable oil, milk, dates, figs, cakes, poultry, fish, vegetables, and 'golden fruit', perhaps some kind of citrus. All this food came in part from the temple estates and in part from customary dues upon cities and holders of land. From at least the end of the third millennium a ceaseless stream of cattle and other agricultural products flowed from the provinces to the great sanctuaries.

Not all gods ate all foods, as there were certain taboos: thus it was specified that mutton must not come near one god, beef near a second or poultry near a third.

The meal of the god was technically a banquet to which other deities were invited, and at which even the dead might be present. The gods ate behind curtains: this may have originated as a reflection of royal custom at some period, but on the practical level it enabled the priests to dispose of the uneaten food without the scandal of revealing that the gods never ate anything. Officially there were leftovers from the god's meal, which went either to the priests or to the king: it was a great honour to share in them.

In addition to the regular daily meals provided for the gods, there were offerings provided at particular festivals or made by worshippers who wished to bring themselves to the special notice of the gods. The commonest festivals were those known as *eshsheshu*, a term originally referring to the days of the new, half and full moon. Later the *eshsheshu* festivals were shifted and celebrated more frequently – up to eight days a month at Erech. We read in cuneiform tablets of meat 'which is served upon the table of Bel on the days of the *eshsheshu* festivals', and there is also mention of various cakes, recalling the passage in Jeremiah 7:18 in which 'the women knead the dough, to make cakes to the queen of heaven'. (See also Jeremiah 44:19.)

Animals offered to the gods were slaughtered on special altars or on the roofs of temples, the throat of the animal being cut by a *nash patri* ('swordbearer'). Unlike the typical sequel in Israelite religion, the meat was not then burned; presumably it was distributed.

The gods enjoyed the savour of sweet-smelling incense from the burning of cypress, cedar wood, myrtle and other aromatics. Herodotus states that about two and a half tons of frankincense were burnt annually in the temple of Bel in Babylon, but there is no evidence from the cuneiform texts of the specific use of frankincense, which would have had to be imported from south Arabia.

The temple complex

Archaeology shows that the earliest temples were simple one-roomed shrines, but later temples developed into a complex of buildings often covering many acres. The most conspicuous feature was the ziggurat, a great stepped tower of three to seven stages which dominated the city. Its base would be up to a hundred yards square and the whole structure perhaps as much as fifty yards high. On the top stood a small temple, probably covered in blue glazed tiles. The origin and function of these towers remain in dispute, but it can be said what they were not. They were not primarily observatories, and they were not (as the pyramids of Egypt were) tombs of kings.

Some scholars have seen the ziggurat as the throne of the

deity; others have suggested that it was regarded as an immense altar, an idea for which Ezekiel 43:13–17 – which describes an altar in the form of a miniature ziggurat – has been adduced in support.

The most commonly accepted explanation of the ziggurat is due to W. Andrae, with modifications from other scholars. Andrae pointed out that there were two temples associated with a ziggurat, one on its top and the other at its foot. Andrae saw the 'high temple' as the residence proper of the deity, who at appropriate times came down to the human level at the 'low temple'. There are two problems with this: firstly, some of the earliest ziggurats seem to have had only a high temple and no low temple. Secondly, in some texts it is the low temple which is regarded as the dwelling-place of the deity. It seems, then, that there was no single view on the matter. Probably there was a gradual evolution of view, the high temple being originally regarded as the proper dwelling-place of the god, but subsequently becoming an intermediate stage for the god on his way from heaven to his earthly residence, now the temple at the foot of the ziggurat. The ziggurat was thus a kind of ladder set up to heaven from earth. This idea links up with the story of the Tower of Babel in Genesis 11:3–5, which was certainly related to a Mesopotamian ziggurat, and also with the ladder mentioned in Jacob's dream in Genesis 27:12, of which we are told that it was 'set up on the earth, and the top of it reached to heaven: and behold the angels of God ascending and descending on it'.

The divine image

Inside the temple the most sacred area was a long chamber dominated by the statue of the god or goddess, on a podium. The image might be so placed that it was visible from the courtyard through several aligned doorways, or at other times and places, when there was a different attitude to the approach of the public to the divine powers, it might be deliberately hidden from view. It appears that in the kingdom of Mari a traveller passing through a city might without much ceremony go right into the temple to offer worship to the deity (see page 295), but such public access seems to have been quite contrary to the usual practice at most periods in Babylonia and Assyria.

The divine image itself would be carved from a block of wood, and ornamented with precious metals and jewels, a fact with which Isaiah 44:12–20 made merry play. In fact, despite Isaiah's satire, the more intelligent Babylonians did not for a moment think that such a god as Marduk was fully contained within his image. In their view, Marduk was so vast that he filled the universe, so that a Babylonian in his prayer to the god could say: 'The underworld is your basin, the sky of Anu is your censer.' Of another god it was said: 'He wears the heavens on his head like a turban; he is shod with the underworld as with sandals.'

The point about the divine image was that, with the proper rituals, the god would enter into such a relationship with it that it could serve as a point of contact between human beings and the deity. There was an elaborate ritual, known as the 'opening of the mouth', to ensure that the deity took up his dwelling within the idol. When the statue had been completed in the workshop, it was given a preliminary 'washing of the mouth' with holy water. After incantations, the god was led at night by torchlight to the river bank, where he was seated on a reed-mat facing east, with incantations and 'washing of the mouth' continuing all night. In the morning, after the sacrifice of a ram, came the crucial point of the ritual, when the idol became a sentient thing. To the accompaniment of an incantation, 'Holy image that is perfected by a great ritual', the priest 'opened the eyes' of the god by touching them with a twig of the magical tamarisk. The statue, now alive with the deity immanent within it, was led by the hand to his temple and, after further offerings, placed on his throne.

The divine images were not permanently confined to the temples. At particular festivals they came forth, richly clad and borne in honour on the shoulders of the priests to be displayed to the adorants. Chance movements of the image on such occasions, giving an apparent nod to a worshipper or a start away from him, were loaded with ominous significance. The gods might also pay ceremonial visits to other deities on the occasion of the great festivals: thus Nabu of Borsippa regularly visited his father Marduk at the New Year festival in Babylon, about ten miles away.

12

The Religious Role of the King

IN Mesopotamia kingship was one of the underlying concepts of civilization: it was one of the gifts won by Inanna from Enki to bestow upon the people of the Sumerian civilization centred at Erech (see pages 31f.). Kingship, the *Sumerian King List* tells us, was lowered from heaven; at the time of the Flood it must have returned there, for it was lowered again subsequently. Thus, for the Sumerians and their successors, kingship as an institution existed before, and independently of, the human king. This was even true of the insignia of royalty, for in the *Epic of Etana* we read:

> At that time no tiara had been worn, . . .
> Sceptre, headband, tiara and staff were deposited in heaven before Anu.

Originally the king was no more than *primus inter pares*, a temporary leader elected by the community of citizens in time of war, but this situation had been superseded before the end of the *Early Dynastic* period. The doctrine developed that the king was chosen by the gods and invested with the attributes of kingship by them.

Some authorities on comparative religion have argued that there was a single basic pattern in the ancient Near Eastern concept of kingship, and have drawn far-reaching conclusions for Israelite religion from Sumero-Babylonian evidence.

However, there were in fact significant divergences between the Sumero-Babylonian and Israelite attitudes to kingship. When kingship finally arose in Israel, it evoked severe religious disapproval in some quarters, where it was felt that Yahweh (the Lord) alone was king (1 Samuel 8:7). Moreover, Deuteronomy 17:14 and 1 Samuel 8:5 explicitly recognize that kingship was not a native Israelite institution at all but one introduced in imitation of foreign practice. Thus, in the mainstream of official religious thought, kingship in Israel was accepted as being a specifically human institution, even though the man appointed as king had to be chosen or at least approved by the Lord. Except in the sense that the Lord himself was king, kingship was certainly not one of the basic concepts of Israelite civilization.

Much has been written about 'divine kingship' in Mesopotamia and the rest of the ancient Near East, but it would be wrong to say baldly that the king in Mesopotamia was considered divine. It is true that certain kings, notably all but the first in the III Ur Dynasty, sometimes (but not invariably) had their names written preceded by the cuneiform sign DINGIR ('god'), which indicates that the following name belonged to the class of the divine. But in these cases the apparent divine status probably derived from the deity having chosen the king, in some way we do not know, to play a part in the Sacred Marriage. Even in the period of the III Ur Dynasty it was accepted that there were significant differences between so-called 'divine kings' and gods proper: for example, a supposedly divine king might build temples to the gods 'for the king's own life', a formula which accepted that the king was not immortal.

From the religious point of view, the king was primarily the link between the gods and the people whom they had created to do them service. He represented the people before the gods, and in turn was the pipeline through which the gods regulated the affairs of the state for the people.

As the welfare of the nation depended upon the welfare of the king, any danger threatening the king was a matter of grave import. When omens and portents warned of such impending dangers, special measures had to be taken. In some circumstances a man would be chosen as substitute for the king and even (according to one interpretation) put to death in his place. Most of our information on this institution comes from Assyrian letters of the reign of Esarhaddon. The earliest occurrence known is from the Old Babylonian period, when (*c.* 1860 BC) a king of Isin died whilst eating hot porridge at a time when a substitute king had been appointed temporarily: the substitute remained permanently on the throne.

On one occasion in first-millennium Assyria the procedure for appointing a royal substitute was set in motion by an eclipse, which was believed to threaten dire disaster to the king. The substitute, chosen through an inspired priestess, was enthroned for a hundred days, during which time he enjoyed all the privileges of royalty, whilst the real king and his sons were strictly confined to the palace. The role of the substitute was to take to himself all the evil forebodings that threatened the real king. Some scholars suppose that once the substitute had taken upon himself the threatening omens, he was put to death, since a letter says of such a person that 'he went to his fate', a common euphemism meaning 'he died'. It is possible, however, that the substitute merely placed himself in readiness for any possible death awaiting the king, and it was then in the hands of fate whether he died or not. But whatever misfortune was to befall, it would strike the substitute and not the real king.

Temple building

Prominent amongst the duties of the king was his responsibility towards the earthly dwellings of the gods. It was not only a mark of piety but an absolute obligation for the king to give attention to the building or restoration of temples, and there are many representations of kings and princes carrying out this pious duty: plate 18A shows an example. The idea that it was a duty of the king to provide a fitting house for his god is not unknown in the Old Testament, where it was a matter of concern to king David, who

> said unto Nathan the prophet, See now, I dwell in an house of cedar, but the ark of God dwelleth within curtains. (2 Samuel 7:2)

Attention to the restoration of temples had important practical consequences, for, if a temple fell into disrepair or was destroyed, the gods might leave it. Esarhaddon relates that when Marduk became angry with events in Babylonia, he allowed Babylon to be devastated, whereupon 'the gods who dwelt therein flew off like birds and went up to heaven'.

The restoration of a temple, or the building of a new one, involved the most complicated rituals, as well as the most precise investigations to ensure that the god's will was properly understood and carried out. It was the god himself who actually made the decision that a temple ought to be rebuilt, and he informed the king of what was required. One of the best-known instances of this is in a dream of the third-millennium ruler, Gudea of Lagash, where the chief god was Ningirsu. In the words of Gudea's inscription:

> In the dream there was a man, who was as huge as heaven, as huge as earth. As to his upper part he was a god, as to his wings he was the Imdugud bird,[1] as to his lower part he was the Flood. . . . He commanded me to build a temple, but I did not understand his intention. The sun rose before me from the horizon. A woman was there . . . She held a stylus of gleaming silver, and wrote on a tablet . . . Next, there was a hero. . . . He held a slab of lapis lazuli and drew on it the ground plan of the (intended) temple. He put before me the pure hod, arranged the pure brickmould for me, and fixed in the brickmould the 'brick of decision of fate'.

Nearly two millennia later the New Babylonian king Nabuna'id similarly received instructions through a dream, about the rebuilding of the temple of the Moon-god Sin at Harran. He records:

> [The great gods] made me see a dream. Marduk the Great Lord and Sin the Luminary of Heaven and Earth were standing together. Marduk said to me: 'Nabu-na'id, king of Babylon, bring bricks in your horse-drawn processional wagons and build Ehulhul [the temple of Sin in Harran], and let Sin, the Great Lord, set up his dwelling in its midst.'

Explicit instructions of this kind might be amplified or even entirely replaced by the revelation of the divine will through omens. This could be very direct in form, as when the winds blew away the accumulated sand from a ruined temple, indicating that

> they wanted the ground plan to become visible.

Most commonly, however, the omens would be drawn from the examination of the liver of a sacrificial animal, and indeed Nabu-na'id lists a whole series of such omens taken to ensure that the time was ripe for the rebuilding of Sin's temple.

Once it was beyond doubt that the gods had really ordained the rebuilding of a temple, the site had to be cleared. This was a solemn matter involving special rituals and lamentations, as prescribed in texts of the following type:

> When the walls of a temple fall into ruins, in order to demolish and rebuild that temple, . . . in a propitious month, on a good day (of the month), at night, a fire shall be lit for Ea and Marduk, and a sacrifice shall be made for Ea and Marduk. The *Kalu*-priest shall sing a lament, the Singer shall make lamentation. In the morning, on the roof of the temple, you shall set up three cult stands for Ea, Shamash and Marduk. The *Kalu*-priest shall make music with a flute before Marduk . . . The *Kalu*-priest shall raise his hands and do obeisance before the god, then he shall recite a penitential psalm . . .

Excavations had then to be made into the foundations to recover the original divinely-approved pattern of the temple and its brickwork. If this were not done with scrupulous care, the temple might well collapse in consequence. This happened with the Ebabbara temple of the Sun-god in Sippar, which, says Nabu-na'id,

> Nebuchadnezzar the former king made; he sought its ancient foundation platform but did not (manage to) see (it), and (none the less) made that House. Within forty-five years . . . its walls collapsed.

Nabu-na'id himself undertook a more thorough restoration:

> I sought out its ancient foundation platform and I went down into the soil (to a depth of) eighteen cubits [about twenty-seven feet], and the Sun-god, the Great Lord of Ebabbara, the Dwelling of his Heart's ease, showed me personally the foundation platform of Naram-sin son of Sargon, which for 3200 years no king preceding me has seen.

It was of the greatest importance for the building of a new temple that the site should be ritually pure. There were various ways of achieving this. One was to dig trenches and light fires in them. At one temple site there is archaeological evidence for a bonfire over the whole area. More commonly a great pit was dug out, to about the depth just mentioned by Nabu-na'id, and filled up with clean sand. In one such case, a temple was built at the bottom of the pit, filled up with clean sand, and the main temple then built over the buried one. When a temple was to be rebuilt, a layer of clean sand or clean earth was often spread over the foundations of the older building.[2]

The ceremonial purification for building or rebuilding was not limited to the foundation of the temple itself but affected the whole town, where a kind of saturnalia took place. Thus, when Gudea of Lagash was about to build a temple,

> The city-prince gave his town instructions as though it had been just one man; Lagash unanimously followed him like a child its mother. . . . The mother did not scold the child, the child said nothing to upset its mother; the master did not strike the head of

the slave who had offended him, the mistress did not slap the face of the slave-girl who had done something wrong. No one brought a lawsuit before the city-prince, Gudea, who was building the temple. The city-prince cleansed the town, purified it with fire, put away from the town all that was unclean . . .

Finally came the moulding of the first brick. This was the direct responsibility of the king. Like other solemn undertakings, it might only be performed on a lucky day in a favourable month: the suitability of the day was declared by *ad hoc* omens as well as traditional lists of lucky and unlucky days. One month, Siwan (approximately late May and early June) is actually described in a hemerology as 'the month of the king's brick mould'. Gudea describes at length what happened:

In the evening he [Gudea] went to the old House in prayer, . . .
(Nex morning) the Sun-god shone forth splendidly on him;
Gudea went . . . to the holy city,
He offered cattle and goats without blemish,
He went to the House, performed (the ritual gesture of) 'hand to the face'.
He took for E-ninnu [the name of the temple] the pure head-pad, (and) the true brick mould of 'decision of fate' . . .
He poured luck-bringing water into the frame of the mould;
Whilst he did so drums were beaten.
He smeared (the mould) with honey, best quality oil, fine best quality oil; . . .
He raised the holy hod (and) went to the mould,
Gudea worked the mud in the mould,
Performed completely the proper rites,
Splendidly brought into being the brick for the House. . . .
He struck on the mould, brought the brick out to the light. . . .
The Sun-god rejoiced over the brick that he [Gudea] had put into the mould.

The mould itself, which had to be made of specified woods, was a holy object and was afterwards preserved within the temple.

Nothing could be done about the actual building operations until the first brick had dried out (this was the meaning of the phrase 'the Sun-god rejoiced over the brick') and the others had been made. In one case known, the interval between the ceremonial brickmaking and the beginning of building was about two months. Gudea describes the scene when the first brick, now dried and hardened, was taken from its mould:

> Gudea prepared the brick, brought it to the House,
> He put it down (to establish) the ground plan of the House. . . .
> Gudea, who built the House,
> Took on his head the head-pad for the House, as though it had been a holy crown;
> He laid the foundation . . .

The 'head-pad' was a shallow-sided basket in which labourers carried their building material on their heads; the same device, employed in the same way, was still used in Iraq up to the 1950s. Ancient kings and city-princes had figurines made (like the one illustrated in plate 18A) showing them engaged in this pious work; these were buried in the temple foundations. Other members of the royal family also had to assist in the sacred task of temple building, and a number of rulers record that their sons did this. At various stages of the building work there were appropriate rituals, and the whole operation was a time of festivity and extra rations for the citizens.

With the temple finally completed and consecrated with appropriate rites, the statue of the deity to whom it belonged was brought from his or her temporary refuge (probably some other temple), and reinstated by the king in the sacred house now made ready for use as a divine residence. Once again, for this solemn occasion, all strife, ritual uncleanness and whatever might displease the god was set aside from the city. Gudea describes the occasion of bringing the god to his newly-adored earthly home. He informs the gods:

> I, the shepherd, have built the House; I want to introduce my King into his House.
> Anunna-gods [the great gods collectively], pray for me about this!

The narrative then goes on to describe how Gudea

> Goes to the Lord in E-ninnu and prays to him:
> 'My King, Ningirsu,
> Lord who restrains the wild flood-waters,
> Lord whose word is supreme beyond everything,
> Son of Enlil, the Hero, you have given me orders,
> I have truly fulfilled them for you,
> O Ningirsu, I have built your House for you,
> May you enter therein in joy.'

Gudea likewise informed Bau, Ningirsu's spouse, that her shrine was waiting to receive her:

> My (lady) Bau, I have established your chapel for you;
> Take up there (your) pleasant abode!

The narrative goes on to say that

> His [Gudea's] cry was heard;
> The Lord Ningirsu, his King, accepted the offerings and prayer of Gudea;
> The year was past, the months were complete,
> A new year had arrived in the heavens,
> The month of this House had arrived,
> Of this month three days had passed,
> (Then) Ningirsu came from Eridu. . . .
> (Gudea), having spent the day in offerings, the night in prayer, . . . introduced the hero Ningirsu into his House.
> The King [i.e. Ningirsu] went to the House;
> He was (like) an eagle, that casts its glance upon a wild bull;
> As the Hero entered the House,
> He was (like) a storm, that summons to battle.
> Ningirsu went into his House.

The King as the god's steward

The king was not only the representative of humankind to the god, and so responsible for the due maintenance of the god's abode: he was also the god's steward, and as such responsible to the god for the welfare of his land. Accordingly it was to the gods, and not to the people, that the king had to make his reports. The early foundation inscriptions of the Sumerians were inscribed upon clay cones (see plate 25) or bricks, which were buried out of sight of man. It was, indeed, from these simple dedications, bearing merely the statement that such-and-such a ruler built the temple for such a god, that the Assyrian historical inscriptions evolved. This came about by two steps. First, a note was prefixed, relating the building of the temple to some point of time, in the form: 'When so-and-so had done such-and-such, he built. . . .' Further historical matter was then introduced before the account of the building operation, until this preface could contain a complete account of the king's military campaigns. The technical purpose of such inscriptions remained, however, the same as that of the simple building inscription: they were intended for the eye of the god and were in the form either of foundation deposits buried under the building, or of reports placed before the divine statue. The foundation deposits would only be seen again by a man if some later prince, in restoring the temple, came upon them anew, and such a finder was instructed simply to anoint them and leave them in place.

The most notable royal inscription in the form of a report to the gods is the letter of Sargon II to the god Ashur, reporting a major military operation against enemies east and north of Assyria. It begins:

> To Ashur, father of the gods, the great lord, who dwells in his great temple Ehursaggal-kurkurra, may it be very very well!
> To the gods of Fates and the goddesses who dwell in their great temple Ehursaggal-kurkurra, may it be very very well!
> To the gods of Fates and the goddesses who dwell in their great temple of the city of Ashur, may it be very very well!
> To the city and its people may it be well! To the palace situated in its midst may it be well!
> It is very very well with Sargon, the pure priest, the slave who reverences your great god-head; and (likewise with) his camp.

The king had a recognized responsibility not only to report to the god about affairs of state, but also to consult him directly about them. Provisional decisions on all major matters of state, such as a foreign campaign or the appointment of senior officials, were submitted to the god for approval. The proposal would be inscribed on a tablet and placed before the god, Shamash (the Sun-god and god of justice) being particularly favoured for this purpose at certain periods. The documents would take some such form as 'O Shamash, shall I appoint the man whose name is inscribed on this tablet to the governorship of such-and-such a province?' An animal was then ceremonially slaughtered, and its internal organs examined. The Sun-god was believed, if the correct ritual for slaughter had been used, to inscribe his oracle on the liver; and examination by the priestly experts, using an inscribed clay model (see plate 27B) as a key, would show whether the decision of Shamash was favourable or unfavourable. (Here there was clearly the possibility of intervention by some of the most intelligent and well-informed members of the hierarchy to prevent the execution of an ill-advised or unpopular plan.)

Another responsibility of the king as god's steward was the maintenance of the irrigation work upon which the fertility of the land depended, and many rulers describe their concern for the pious work of excavating or clearing canals. Hammurabi mentions in the prologue to his laws that he was

> the lord who made Erech live, who established the waters of abundance for its people, . . . the one who set grazing-places and watering-places for Lagash and Girsu, . . . the one who caused there to be an abundant water supply for Cuthah.

Canals, like temples and all other major works, could only be begun on a favourable day, and work on them required to be accompanied at all stages by appropriate rituals.

As representative or steward of the god, the king was also the 'shepherd' of his people, and this title was very commonly used by kings, or of them. An official writing to an Assyrian king in the first millennium BC quotes a song as saying:

All the people rely on you, O Shepherd, in connection with the propitious (utterance of) your mouth.

The king's task as shepherd was to guide his people, and in one text the simile is used that king Lipit-ishtar (see page 66) may guide the people of his land 'as a ewe guides her lamb'. This guidance largely took the practical form of the king giving his people the benefits of just law, protecting the weak, and attempting to control prices. Many rulers from the third millennium onwards speak of their activities directed to the end 'that the strong may not oppress the weak', whilst the royal insignia granted to the king by the gods actually included 'a sceptre of justice'. The reforms of the Sumerian ruler Uru-inim-gina (see pages 43f.) are a good instance of concern for social justice; and Hammurabi in turn proclaims in the prologue to his laws that

When Marduk commissioned me to set right the people of the land and to cause them to have government, I set truth and justice throughout the land, and made the people prosperous.

The 'Royal Tombs' of Ur

Some controversial evidence on Sumerian religion, with a possible bearing on aspects of kingship, comes from the 'royal tombs' of Ur. Sir Leonard Woolley excavated these tombs in the years following 1927; he designated them 'royal' because of the elaborate rites which must have been associated with the burials, and the rich hoards of ornaments and vessels of lapis lazuli and gold in the tombs. Some objects are inscribed with names, a few of which relate to *Early Dynastic* kings of Ur, and so the description 'royal' may have some justification, even though most of the names have no known royal connection. In date, the tombs are archaeologically equated with the First Dynasty of Ur, mentioned in the *Sumerian King List* (see page 30), and so at about 2700 BC.[3]

The graves at Ur called 'royal' numbered only sixteen out of nearly two thousand excavated in the cemetery. They are distinguished by being solid stone or brick constructions of one to four chambers, by their elaborate burial rites, and by the presence of bodies of people, ranging from three to seventy-four, who seem to have been the victims of human sacrifice.

Woolley's excavations indicate that the 'royal tombs' were made in the following fashion. A rectangular shaft was dug down to a depth of thirty-three feet or more, producing a pit with a size at the bottom of up to forty feet by thirty. A second shaft was dug to lead down by a slope or steps into one side of the pit. Finally, the actual tomb was built in the bottom of the pit.

At the time of interment, a number of people, predominantly women, some carrying stringed musical instruments, filed down the sloping shaft into the pit. Ceremonial carts drawn by oxen were then backed down the entrance passage: presumably these bore the body of the principal burial and tomb furniture. The musical instruments suggest that some ritual took place, presumably whilst the principal body was being laid to rest in the tomb. Then came a mass suicide, when each of the people in the pit or along the access shaft drank poison, from a little cup of clay, stone or metal. This mass sacrifice must have been voluntary, for there is no trace of disturbance or the use of force. The bodies lay in neat rows and even the delicate headdresses of the women had not been disarranged, showing that the deaths had taken place in a scene of calm. After the suicides, the animals harnessed to the carts were slaughtered, falling on top of their grooms, where Woolley found them. The excavated earth was then thrown back into the pit over the victims. At a certain level in the refilling of the shaft, a ritual meal took place; the traces of this, as described by Woolley, look very much like the funerary meal for the dead, known elsewhere in the ancient Near East.

In most cases where the evidence is clear, someone subsequently dug down into the tomb – generally through the roof – and plundered the 'royal' coffin and its immediate surroundings: Woolley took this as the work of tomb robbers, although a quite different interpretation of the evidence has been proposed. One tomb which was found undisturbed has as its central figure a woman whose name is given by an inscription on a cylinder seal as Pu-abi; it has generally been assumed that she was a queen. In the floor of her tomb, concealed by a chest, there was a hole broken through into a tomb below. Woolley took this has having been made at the time of the preparation of Pu-abi's tomb by rogues who wanted to plunder the earlier tomb beneath. He points to the fact that the bones in the lower tomb were scattered, indicating that the bodies that had been there had already decayed to skeletons at the time of the plundering. According to Woolley, this proves that the burial of the 'king' in the lower tomb took place some years before that of the 'queen' in the upper, so that the two tombs did not form part of the same interment ceremony. No 'royal' body was found in the lower tomb, and this, although explained by Woolley as the consequence of the grave robbers scattering everything in their haste, has great significance for supporters of another theory.

There are two main lines of interpretation of the sixteen 'royal' tombs, with many variants in points of detail. The two basic theories are:

(1) The king (or queen), regarded as a deity, had died, and the interment of the courtiers represented a voluntary human sacrifice, whereby the rest of the court accompanied their divine master (or mistress) into the next world.
(2) The tombs were part of a primitive fertility cult. The chief male and female participants were cultic personnel, possibly but not necessarily royal, who were put to death after representing the god and goddess in the Sacred Marriage upon which the fertility of the land was thought to depend.

A serious objection to the first theory is that nowhere in ancient Mesopotamia does there seem to be any positive proof of human sacrifice: a Sumerian text dealing with the death of Gilgamesh has been taken as speaking of the sacrifice of his entourage, but this interpretation is not beyond dispute.

Woolley meets this objection by the argument that the king, being a god, was not considered to die: his apparent death was merely a transference of his place of abode to another world, and it was fitting that his whole court should accompany him.

A letter from first-millennium Assyria tells us something about the burial rites for a man who had served as substitute for the king and then died (whether by execution or in the course of nature being disputable). Because the substitute actually was king from the religious point of view, the funerary rites with which he was buried were those appropriate to a king. The relevant part of the letter mentioned refers to the rites in these terms:

> We have made a tomb. He and his palace-lady have been properly prepared and put in place. . . . They have been buried and lamentation has been made over them.[4]

The mention of the 'palace-lady' sharing the burial could well be taken to support the view that even as late as the first millennium it was not unknown for the king to be accompanied in death by certain people close to him. Even at a much later period, such a practice is attested, although not from a Mesopotamian context. From a traveller in the thirteenth century AD we have an eyewitness account of a burial amongst a people called the Comans in south Russia. A rich lord had died. A trench was dug, in which the dead knight, sumptuously arrayed, was placed, along with a living horse. Then a faithful officer prepared to accompany his lord. Noblemen entrusted him with gold and silver to hold for them until they arrived in the other world, and the king gave him a letter of commendation to the first king of the Comans. When the officer had made his farewells, he joined his dead master in the trench, and the trench was then sealed with planks and covered over with a great mound of earth and stones.[5]

We may consider the objections to the opposing theory, that the 'royal' tombs related to the ritual death of participants after the Sacred Marriage. One problem lies in the number of tombs. Where we have specific evidence for the Sacred Marriage taking place, even if we do not know the details, it seems that it was an annual event. Archaeologically, the 'royal' tombs cover more than a century, so that if these were related to a form of Sacred Marriage in which the participants were afterwards put to death, there should have been substantially more than sixteen tombs. A second point is, that if both god and goddess were represented by human participants in the Sacred Marriage ritual, both being put to death, we should expect to find two principal bodies in each tomb; or if only the woman (or indeed only the man) was put to death, all the bodies should have been of one sex.

Tammuz

The German scholar Anton Moortgat, basically accepting the Sacred Marriage theory to explain the 'royal' tombs of Ur, relates the data to a Tammuz cult.

With the mention of Tammuz (Sumerian Dumuzi) we come to one of the main cruxes of ancient Mesopotamian religion. A great deal has been written about gods in the ancient Near East who supposedly died and rose again, and Babylonia is generally treated as the source of most of the assured evidence. In fact, the evidence is more questionable than some writers would allow. There is certainly ample evidence for mention of slain gods, and some for gods imprisoned in the underworld, but proof of a belief in a god or gods who regularly died and rose again on a seasonal pattern, or even of a god who had done so once and whose victory over death was seasonally re-enacted, is less easily substantiated.

In the official theology, Tammuz was no more than one of the two doorkeepers guarding the entrance to the chamber of the great gods; but he held a place of special regard in popular religion as (it is commonly supposed) a dying god of fertility: this cult, originating in Sumer early in the third millennium, spread far beyond its homeland, and by the middle of the first millennium BC was even found in Jerusalem, where, according to Ezekiel, at the gate of Yahweh's temple, 'there sat women weeping for Tammuz' (Ezekiel 8:14).

Fertility features were widespread in the cults of the great gods. This has been explained in two opposing ways. According to one view, there was, in Mesopotamia as in Israel, an active opposition between official and popular religion; the Tammuz cult is taken to represent popular religion, and fertility elements in the cults of the great gods are supposed to derive from syncretism, in which, under popular pressure, some characteristics of Tammuz had been assimilated to gods of the official pantheon. The other view (which is the one I accept) is that many, if not all, of the major Sumerian deities had from their beginnings a chthonic [underworld] and fertility aspect.

Moortgat claims that Woolley did not adequately explain certain facts about the 'king's' tomb beneath that of Pu-abi. Firstly, the body of the principal burial was not simply scattered, as Woolley's description might suggest: it was completely lacking from the tomb. Tomb robbers might have stolen jewellery, but hardly a complete royal skeleton. Secondly, the supposed robbers had left behind certain conspicuous and valuable objects, such as a silver boat over two feet long and eight inches high (see plate 2B), which could hardly have been missed, however hurried the looting. Thirdly, the ornaments in the tomb are rich in examples of motifs which (according to Professor Moortgat) all belong specifically to the Tammuz cult. Finally, considering the immense ritual importance obviously attached to Pu-abi's interment, and recalling the scrupulous priestly control of every small detail in the preparations leading up to any major ceremony, it is scarcely reasonable to imagine workmen being left to their own devices, digging in the sacred necropolis, long enough to be able to locate and rifle a royal tomb. This is particularly so when (on Woolley's own theory) not only was the presence of the tomb well known but it was actually being deliberately uncovered with a view to putting the new tomb of Pu-abi in physical contact with it.

The very close association between Pu-abi's tomb and that of the 'king' did not escape Woolley: he explained it, however, as due to the sentimental desire of 'Queen' Pu-abi to be buried as close as possible to her late-lamented husband. Moortgat, however, regards the two tombs as having a more intimate connection.

Professor Moortgat points out the unlikelihood of tomb robbers going to the trouble of removing the king's body from his tomb whilst they left behind such treasure as the silver boat. The absence of the body requires explanation, however, and Moortgat concludes that the tomb was in fact not plundered but rather that the dead body was released from its chamber through the ceiling. He emphasizes the presence in the tomb of a golden saw and golden chisels. These, he points out, can have had no practical use (gold is too soft) and their presence must have been symbolic, in connection with some ritual, like the golden axe mentioned on page 269. Moortgat's specific suggestion is that here was a ritual to release the dead king, identified with the risen Tammuz, from the tomb. A motif common on Akkadian and Old Babylonian cylinder seals shows a god (generally taken as the Sun-god at his rising) emerging from a mountain, holding a saw (see plate 50A). Moortgat suggests that this motif actually represented the god (probably the Sun-god in a chthonic aspect, and so parallel to Tammuz) rising from the Mountain of the Underworld, which was his grave.

Moortgat therefore explains the evidence of the two tombs, that of Pu-abi and the one adjacent, as follows. The one where no principal body was found was indeed the tomb of a king – a king who at the New Year Feast had played the part of Tammuz, celebrating the Sacred Marriage upon which the fertility of the city depended. He was then put to death and buried as Tammuz, to rise again as that god, through the symbolic withdrawal of his body through the roof of his tomb. Pu-abi was the king's partner in the Sacred Marriage: she was either the high priestess or the queen, and had been identified with Inanna as counterpart to the king as Tammuz.

The part played in the ritual by the death of Pu-abi may have corresponded to the descent of Inanna into the Underworld in the later myth of that name (see pages 370ff.).

There are two of Woolley's objections to the 'Sacred Marriage' theory which do not appear to be specifically answered by Professor Moortgat. One is the fact that whilst the Sacred Marriage was an annual event in the periods for which we have it certainly attested, there was not one 'royal' tomb for each year. This is not a fatal objection. It is known from other ancient and primitive cultures that a divine king was put to death not at the end of a year but when he had passed his prime and his physical powers (upon which the fertility of his land depended) began to fail. Thus it is possible that normally the king was (as in later times) identified not with Tammuz but with the city-god proper; only when his powers began to fail was he identified either directly with Tammuz or with the city-god in the form in which his chthonic aspect was predominant.

The other point of Woolley's which remains to be answered is his observation that Pu-abi was a woman of about forty and his unfounded assumption that gods preferred young virgins. If the divine king and his female counterpart, the high priestess or queen, were put to death in the circumstances envisaged, a new couple in the prime of their vigour would have to be chosen to represent the god and goddess in the annual fertility ceremony. Bearing in mind the differing rates of sexual development in the human male and female, one would expect the man chosen to be about twenty and the woman about fifteen. Thus the male and female partners in the fertility ceremony would always be of the same age within a few years. Therefore, as one could expect the king to show signs of being past his prime before he was fifty, it should not be surprising that his female partner was at that time a woman of about forty.

At the beginning of the second millennium, there are indications that certain classes of priestess were forbidden normal sexual intercourse with men until after the age of childbearing (see page 304f.). This suggests that there was a tradition that such cultic women remained exclusively in the god's service for sexual purposes until the menopause, and this could be a relic of an earlier custom by which a high priestess left the god's service at the age of forty or so by a glorious death.

Moortgat's theory in turn has been criticized, the main points made against it being:

(1) the difficulty of understanding why the body had to be removed furtively through a hole in the roof rather than through the main entrance. [It is no less difficult to understand why in certain oriental Christian sects the greater part of the Mass is performed in secret behind curtains, but the difficulty does not cancel out the fact. In a lighter vein, but relevantly, one may point out that in modern mythology Father Christmas is believed to come down the chimney even though the front door is available. It is also worth noting that the use by Babylonian priests of a secret hole in the floor, hidden by a table as the hole in the floor of Pu-abi's tomb was hidden by a chest, is alleged in the apocryphal biblical book *Bel and the Dragon*, verse 13.]
(2) the possibility that some of the tombs containing a woman's body as the principal burial also had deliberately-made holes in the roof.
(3) a general non-acceptance of Moortgat's view of a widely-diffused cult of Tammuz as the dying god who rose again.

The last is the weightiest objection. The better understanding of relevant texts casts doubt upon the view that Tammuz was a god who died and was afterwards restored to life again by the Great Mother. Thus, although Inanna (Ishtar) certainly went down into the Underworld, it is now clear that, whatever her purpose in doing so was, it was not to release Tammuz.

The Sacred Marriage

That the 'royal' tombs of the First Dynasty of Ur are in some way connected with a very early form of the Sacred Marriage seems to me, despite a few difficulties, particularly doubts about the role of Tammuz, the best explanation of the facts.

The details of the Sacred Marriage in the form it took later in the third millennium are fairly well known from texts of Shulgi of the III Ur Dynasty. It was the central element of the New Year Festival, in the ritual of which the king played, under the name Ama-ushumgal-anna, the part of the god Tammuz (Dumuzi): Ama-ushumgal-anna, possibly meaning 'the one great source of the date-clusters' and representing the productivity of the date-palm, may originally have been the name of a real ruler of Sumer. A hymn sets the scene:

In the palace . . . of the king of the land. . . .
A chapel has been raised for the goddess Nin-egal ['Lady of the Palace'].
The king as god is present within it.

The whole New Year ceremony in the Sumerian period may be analysed into five elements; the introduction scene, the ritual bath, love songs, the Sacred Marriage, and the determination of destiny. The central part played by the king is proclaimed in a hymn of Shulgi referring to the activities of the New Year Festival:

> Goddess! I will perform perfectly for you the rites which constitute my royalty. I will accomplish for you the divine pattern. Whatever sacrifices appertain to the day of the New Moon and the day of the New Year, I will do them for you.

Another text of Shulgi shows this king actually performing the ritual. The king goes by boat to the temple, and leading a sheep and holding a kid makes his entry before Inanna in the sanctuary of Eanna. The king is received with acclamation, and great joy fills the city. On seeing the 'good shepherd Shulgi', clad in his magnificent ceremonial robe and splendid headgear, Inanna falls into ecstasy, and, in the person of the high priestess representing the goddess, sings a love song for the king representing the god:

For the king, for the lord,
When I shall have washed myself,
When I shall have washed myself for the shepherd, Dumuzi,
When I shall have adorned my body . . . ,
When I shall have put amber on my face,
When I shall have put mascara on my eyes, . . .
When the lord who sleeps with the pure Inanna,
. . . shall have made love to me on the bed,
Then I in turn shall show my love for the lord;
I shall fix for him a good destiny, . . .
I shall fix for him as destiny
To be the shepherd of the land.

Yet another text describes how these things took place, giving details of how Inanna had a ritual bath, and then dressed herself in her trinkets and finery in readiness for the god-king her lover. A text of the Old Babylonian period (*c.* 1850 BC) gives an extensive list of the dress and ornaments of Ishtar (the equivalent of third-millennium Inanna) in one city. It includes two finger-rings of gold, one vulva of gold, nineteen fruit-shaped beads of gold, two breast-ornaments of gold, two ear-rings of silver, six cylinder seals, six breast-ornaments of ivory, one great ring of carnelian, two skirts, three outer garments of linen, six woollen ribbons, a silver mother-figurine, and two loin-cloths. These particular objects were used for dressing a statue, but the priestess playing the part of the goddess must have been similarly equipped.

Sexual intercourse between the incarnate god and goddess then took part in the sacred chamber of the temple known as the *Egipar* (Akkadian *giparu*).

After the Sacred Marriage the goddess 'fixed the destiny' of the king for the coming year, investing him with divine power to ensure fertility and security to the land. This done, there followed great popular rejoicing, including a banquet and music. There were probably also games in which the king took part.

The Akitu-*festival*

As in many other societies, in Mesopotamia some festivals which were originally distinct finally became interfused; thus, the New Year Festival centred on the Sacred Marriage ultimately came to assimilate the rituals and even the name of the *Akitu*-festival.

The term *Akitu*, which is often applied to denote the whole New Year Festival, actually applies only to a part of it and in the third millennium was quite distinct. The *Akitu*-festival was known in the city of Ur in the pre-Sargonic period, and in Nippur, and possibly also in Lagash and Umma, by the end of the third millennium BC. By Old Babylonian times the *Akitu*-festival was widely disseminated amongst the principal shrines of Babylonia and Assyria.

Originally in Ur, as also in Nippur, the feast took place twice in the year, in the twelfth and in the sixth or fourth month, the two feasts being differentiated as 'the *A-ki-ti* of seed-time' and 'the *A-ki-ti* of barley-cutting'. The evidence points to the celebration of the feast being originally an event of autumn which was later, with a change in the calendar, transferred to the spring.

The finer details of the *Akitu*-festival elude us. We know that it centred around a visit to the *Akitu*-house, which was some kind of temple built on or near a canal in the open country outside the walls of the city. The god's statue went in procession from the city temple, and embarked on a ship for a journey to the *Akitu*-house, returning afterwards by the same means. The king's participation in the ceremony was essential, and it is clear that the populace joined in with great joy and feasting. We learn this from what Utanapishtim, the hero of the Babylonian Flood story, says in connection with the building of his ark:

> I slew bullocks for the people,
> I killed sheep every day,
> I gave the workmen . . . wine

As freely as though it were river water;
They made a feast as though it were the day of *Akitu*.

It is probable that the origin of the *Akitu*-festival was linked to a practice of the populace going out into the countryside at the end of summer, when the cooler air brought relief from the blazing heat which envelops Mesopotamia between May and September, and announced again the coming of the time for tilling and sowing the land. It seems certain that originally the *Akitu*-festival had nothing to do with the Sacred Marriage. However, by the first millennium BC the two had come together into one great feast revolving round the king.

In Babylon in the first millennium, the New Year Festival took place in the first eleven days of Nisan, the month which included the spring equinox, about 21 March. The ritual for the first day has not yet been found. On the second day a priest called the *sheshgallu*, having risen before daybreak and performed ceremonial ablutions, went in before the statue of the god Marduk, to whom he made a long prayer, referring to the god's triumphs over his enemies and asking his favour towards the city, the people and the temple. The temple doors were then opened, and the other priests were admitted to bring the daily food offerings before Marduk and his consort.

The ritual for the third day began in similar manner. Afterwards materials were given to craftsmen to make two wooden puppets for use on the sixth day. These figures were clothed in red and adorned with gold and precious stones. One grasped a snake in his left hand and held his right hand extended; the other held a scorpion in his right hand.

On the fourth day the *sheshgallu* rose three hours and twenty minutes before sunrise, and after praying before the god and goddess went out into the temple courtyard. There he awaited the rising of a constellation known as the 'Acre', sacred to Babylon, and greeted its appearance with an incantation. In the evening of the fourth day the whole of *Enuma Elish*, the form of the Creation myth current in Babylon (see pages 361ff.), was recited: some scholars think that a cult drama accompanied the recitation, rather like a mediaeval mystery-play.

On the fifth day, after the routine prayers and food offerings, there took place a purification ceremony from which the *sheshgallu* had to absent himself to avoid accidental contamination. After the temple had been sprinkled with holy water and holy oil, a sheep was used in a magical ceremony. The animal was beheaded, and an incantation priest went round rubbing the bleeding headless body against the walls of the temple to absorb all evil. This done, the incantation priest and the swordsman who had decapitated the sheep took the head and the body to the river and hurled them into the water. They themselves, now in a state of ritual impurity, had to remain in the open country until the whole New Year Festival was over.

The fifth day also saw the erection of a special canopy called the 'golden sky', in preparation for the coming of the god Nabu from Borsippa. The gods were asked to cast out all evil in readiness for his arrival.

It was now time for the king to make his appearance. A priest took him into the temple to the holy of holies where the statue of Marduk stood, and left him there alone. The *sheshgallu* then joined him, and taking from him his royal insignia, laid them before Marduk. Kneeling before the god, the king now recited a negative confession in which he claimed not to have offended against the god in certain specified ways:

> I have not sinned, O Lord of land, I have not been negligent in respect to your godhead;
> I have not destroyed Babylon, I have not ordained (anything) to disrupt it;
> I have not disturbed Esagila [the temple complex in Babylon], I have not been oblivious of its rites;
> I have not smitten the cheek of the people under (your) protection,
> I have not occasioned their humiliation;
> I have cared for Babylon, I have not destroyed its walls.

At this point the *sheshgallu* struck the king's face and pulled his ears: the more painful the treatment, the better for Babylon, for if tears came into the king's eyes, Marduk was considered to be well pleased with his land. The *sheshgallu* then restored to the king his insignia of kingship.

That evening at nightfall the king took part in another ritual. A trench was dug in the courtyard, and into it was placed a sheaf of forty reeds bound with a palm branch. Beside the trench a white bull was tethered. Then the king, in the company of the *sheshgallu*, set fire to the reeds and sacrificed the bull, whilst the king and *sheshgallu* joined together to chant an incantation beginning:

> Divine Bull, splendid light that illumines the darkness.

On the sixth day the principal event was the arrival of Marduk's son, Nabu, from his temple in the neighbouring city of Borsippa. The two puppets which had been made on the third day had been so placed that as Nabu approached they were pointing at him; at Nabu's arrival, they were decapitated by a swordsman and cast into a fire. Clearly the two figures represented some evil force or evil beings overcome by Nabu.

The direct account of the ritual for the remainder of the New Year Festival is lost, but other references to it give us a general idea of what took place. Firstly, it is clear that the presence of the king was indispensable: instances are mentioned when the inability of the king to officiate prevented the feast from being held at all. Secondly, we know that the events of the remaining days must have included the procession to the *Akitu*-house, the Sacred Marriage, the 'Fixing of Destinies' for the coming year, and dramatic representations of myths.

Something is known about the procession to the *Akitu*-house from excavations at Babylon itself. There the brilliant team of German archaeologists found remains of the Sacred Way used for this ceremony. Made of stone paving, it passed through a splendid gateway, called the Ishtar Gate (see plate 6), and along walls decorated in enamelled bricks showing the figures of bulls and dragons in relief. The king himself led the divine statue of Marduk by the hand from his shrine and along the Sacred Way to the *Akitu*-house; where necessary, there was a transfer to a ceremonial barge. The procession was gravid with ominous significance. It seems probable that when Marduk entered the *Akitu*-house, he fought a ritual combat with the primeval monsters whom, as *Enuma Elish* tells, he had anciently challenged and defeated.

The details of the celebration of the Sacred Marriage at Babylon in the first millennium BC are not known. It probably differed substantially from that already described for Shulgi in the third millennium, for the fifth-century account of Herodotus (see page 305) indicates that the high priestess spent the night not with the king, but in a lonely vigil in the sacred bridal-chamber, waiting for the god himself to come down to possess her.[6]

The Tree of Life

The king, at least in Assyria, was the primary participant in another fertility rite, quite distinct from the Sacred Marriage. This is the rite usually called 'cone-smearing', frequently represented on the monuments, especially Assyrian bas-reliefs of the first millennium BC. Plate 32 shows an example of the scene, with the king and a winged attendant represented symmetrically on both sides of a sacred tree. The rite is usually explained as relating to the pollination of the date-palm. But this will hardly stand, since the tree depicted is not usually a palm, whilst the cones, supposed to be the male date spathes, are applied not to the female flower but (as seen in plate 31) to the king and his weapons. Most probably the tree, which is frequently overspread with the winged disk, was the Tree of Life, and the purpose of the ceremony was magically to identify the king with the Tree of Life and so to invest him with the fertility and longevity of the tree. The Tree of Life was probably originally the grapevine; the two syllables of the Sumerian word for 'grapevine', GESHTIN, mean 'tree' and 'life'. For the grapevine as the Tree of Life in religious imagery, we may also recall Christ's words, 'I am the vine, ye are the branches' (St John 15:5).

Finally, we may resume what has been touched upon already (see page 312) and point out that there is very little, of what has been said or could be said about the place of the king in ancient Mesopotamian religion, that can be paralleled convincingly from the Israelite institution of kingship. Attempts have, indeed, been made to see parallels, but the arguments lack conviction. In particular, although at one period there were cult prostitutes in the temple at Jerusalem, there is no proof that the rite of the Sacred Marriage was ever officially practised in an Israelite New Year festival. We have seen that insofar as the king in Mesopotamia was divine, his divinity derived from his assimilation to the god in the Sacred Marriage. If there was no tradition in Israel of the king's participation in a Sacred Marriage, there is no reason why the Israelite king should ever have been considered (even in the limited Mesopotamian sense) as divine.

13

Literature

THE Babylonians themselves made catalogues of their literature, some items of which they believed to be 'from before the Flood'. Some of the texts are attributed to specific authors, either legendary humans or actual people encountered elsewhere in the scribal tradition. Other texts had a more unusual origin: thus, we find one ascribed directly to the god Ea and another is said to have been written 'at the mouth of a horse'.[1]

'Literature' in its widest sense embraces anything written, and modern discussions of Babylonian and Assyrian literature employ the term in this wide sense when they include in it not only such genres as hymns, royal annals and building inscriptions, but also omens and medical, chemical, mathematical, astronomical and philological texts. There is justification for this, since the people of ancient Mesopotamia did not make a formal distinction. However, in modern English, 'literature' is frequently used of written material marked out by the excellent of its form and style and the interest of its ideas, and it is convenient to apply this to ancient Mesopotamian written material. We therefore divide off myths, epics and Wisdom literature for separate consideration. It should be noticed that although from their interest such works are amongst the best-known of cuneiform texts, quantitatively they form only a small fraction of all extant cuneiform writing.

Myths and epics

At present we know of about thirty compositions in Sumerian which could be classified as myths or epics and about half that number as substantially complete works in Akkadian, although there are others known only from brief allusions or fragmentary lines.

The Epic of Gilgamesh

In the more limited sense of the word 'literature', the greatest and longest work in Akkadian is the *Epic of Gilgamesh*, called in Akkadian, from its first line, *ša naqba imuru*, 'who saw the deep'. Most of its extant text comes from Ashurbanipal's library at Nineveh (see plate 22), but enough fragments remain from other sites and earlier periods to show that as an Akkadian epic the work dates from not later than the early second millennium. The Russian Assyriologist I. M. Diakonoff argues that, at least in an oral form, it must date from as early as *c.* 2200 BC. It had wide circulation: a fragment was found in Palestine and fragments from Boghazkoi in Turkey show that it had even been translated into Hittite and Hurrian. It was based on earlier Sumerian traditions: behind the Akkadian *Epic of Gilgamesh* lie at least four separate Sumerian stories, which some anonymous Akkadian-speaking poet of genius wove into a unified narrative. The last of the twelve tablets of the Akkadian epic in its final form is no part of the original Akkadian composition but a clumsy later addition translated from yet another Sumerian poem.

We call the story an epic rather than a myth because its main participants are predominantly human rather than divine in their characteristics. Gilgamesh himself, who is perhaps represented in some cylinder seals (see plate 50B), is described as one-third human and two-thirds divine. Presumably this curious genetic make-up is attributed to him on the grounds that his divine mother, the goddess Ninsun, counted for twice as much as his human father, the *En* (priest-king) of Kulaba.

This mixed parentage reflects the Sacred Marriage, in which the priest or priestess of the city lay with the goddess or god to ensure the fertility of the soil, flocks and herds, and humans. Gilgamesh, himself an *En*, doubtless incorporates a shadowy memory of some real sacral ruler or series of rulers in the dawn of history.

The epic, after briefly summarizing the exploits of Gilgamesh, goes on to set the scene. Gilgamesh was oppressing Erech, taking the son from the father, the maiden from her lover, and the people of Erech complained. The gods heard them, and commissioned the goddess Aruru to make a rival to Gilgamesh. Using clay, Aruru created Enkidu, a wild man, a creature of the steppe:

His whole body is covered with hair . . .
The locks of hair on his head grow abundantly like barley,
He knows neither people nor country . . .
He eats grass with the gazelles, . . .
His heart is glad at water with the wild creatures.

A hunter discovered the existence of Enkidu. He was terrified, and reported to his father that the wild man was destroying his traps and preventing him from catching the wild beasts. His father recommended him to inform Gilgamesh, who should send a temple-harlot to ensnare the wild man with her charms:

Let her strip off her garment; let her lay open her comeliness;
He will see her, he will draw nigh to her.

His innocence lost, says the old man, Enkidu will find that the wild beasts will no longer accept him among them.

The plan was carried out with success:

The prostitute untied her loin-cloth and opened her legs, and he took possession of her comeliness;
She used no restraint but accepted his ardour,
She put aside her robe and he lay upon her.
She used on him, the savage, a woman's wiles,

His passion responded to her.
For six days and seven nights Enkidu approached and coupled with the prostitute.

The honeymoon over, Enkidu tired of his new plaything and turned again to his gazelles. But now they shunned him and fled. Enkidu, no longer able to pace them, returned to the harlot, who, as he sat at her feet, Delilah-wise said:

'O Enkidu, you are wise, you are godlike;
Why run with beasts of the field?
Let me conduct you to Erech . . .'

Enkidu accepted the advice of the courtesan. So she brought him to civilization, where for the first time he learnt to eat the normal food of mankind:

He was accustomed to suck the milk of wild animals;
When they placed bread before him, he was puzzled, he looked and stared.
Enkidu did not know about eating bread; he had not been taught about drinking strong drink.

However, he trusted his woman, and ate and drank until his heart was merry and his face glowed. Then he, formerly a naked savage, anointed himself and dressed like a man. From this time he helped the shepherds to protect the flocks.

One day a messenger came, summoning the people to Erech, apparently to the feast of the Sacred Marriage in which Gilgamesh would 'fertilize the woman of destiny'. As Enkidu arrived in the city, the assembled multitude recognized him as a match for Gilgamesh, and combat ensued between the two heroes. This theme may go back to a practice in which the priest-king, upon whom the fertility of the land depended, had to defend his ritual position against all comers. In *The Golden Bough* (abridged edition, page 1), Sir James Frazer graphically describes the priest in the sacred grove, prowling, sword in hand, awaiting the adversary who was sooner or later to murder him and succeed to the priesthood, as he himself had gained that office by slaying his predecessor.

At the encounter of Gilgamesh and Enkidu, the two heroes wrestled until the walls shook. Evidently wrestling had a ritual significance, since cylinder seals depict this activity, and there is a copper stand in the form of two wrestlers (see plate 51B). Apparently the aim of such wrestling was not to throw the opponent but to get his feet off the ground, for the line recording the defeat of Enkidu reads:

> It was Gilgamesh who leant over, with his foot (still) on the ground.

Gilgamesh bore his defeated rival no malice, and the two heroes became fast friends. They now undertook an expedition together against an ogre who was warden of the cedar forest in the mountains. This was Huwawa (or Humbaba): his voice was the hurricane; his mouth was the Fire-god; his breath was death; he was strong and never slept. (For a representation of his face, see plate 54A.) Gilgamesh placed himself under the protection of the Sun-god Shamash, and the two friends, equipped with great axes and daggers of two hundred pounds apiece, set out for the cedar forest, regardless of the dissuasion of the elders of Erech. On reaching the mountain, Gilgamesh was at first overcome with fear, but he was encouraged by his friend and by dreams which the gods sent him:

> Gilgamesh leant his chin on his knees;
> Sleep, which is poured out upon mankind, fell upon him;
> In the middle watch he ended his sleep,
> He rose and told his friend,
> 'My friend, you did not call me, yet I am roused,
> You did not touch me and yet I am bemused;
> A god did not pass by and yet my limbs are benumbed.
> My friend, I have seen a third dream,
> And the dream that I saw was very confused.'

The two former dreams had already been described. The first is lost to us. In the second a mountain toppled over and trapped Gilgamesh by the feet. But a man of great beauty appeared, to drag him out and to give him water to drink. In the yet more terrifying third dream, Gilgamesh saw a volcano. He related to his friend:

> The mountain stood stark and still; it became overcast with gloom;
> The lightning flashed, it caught fire,
> . . . it rained down death,
> . . . and that which fell turned to ashes.

Enkidu listened to his friend and then 'made him accept his dream', that is, made him view it as a good omen. And so they continued in the enterprise. Now Gilgamesh cut down a cedar, and by so doing brought his presence to the notice of Huwawa. Gilgamesh attacked the monster, who was rendered powerless by eight winds sent by the hero's patron, the Sun-god Shamash. Huwawa offered surrender, but Enkidu insisted that he must be put to death.

Gilgamesh returned victoriously to Erech, washed his flowing locks and donned clean raiment. Seeing him in his full virile beauty, Ishtar, goddess of love and fertility, offered herself to the hero:

> Bestow your fruit upon me as a gift;
> Be you my husband, and I will be your wife;
> I will have a chariot of lapis lazuli and gold harnessed for you,
> With wheels of gold and trappings of precious stone;
> You shall harness to it storm-winds as though they were giant mules; . . .
> Your goats shall bring forth triplets, your sheep shall bear twins;
> Your pack-ass shall be able to outpace the wild ass;
> Your chariot-horses shall be famed for their running.

Gilgamesh insolently rejected the honour offered by the goddess: he vilified her as:

A back-door which does not keep out the wind or draught, . . .
Pitch which fouls the man who carries it,
A water-skin which leaks over the man who carries it, . . .
A shoe which throws its owner down.

He pointed out her fickleness:

What lover did you ever love constantly? . . .
Come! I will enumerate your lovers. . . .
For Tammuz, the lover of your youth,
You have brought about repeated weeping year upon year;
You used to love the pied *allalu*-bird,
Yet you struck him and broke his wing,
And he stands in the woods and cries 'my wing!'
You used to love the lion, perfect in strength,
Yet you have dug innumerable pits for him.
You used to love the horse, renowned in battle,
Yet you have assigned to him the whip, the goad and the lash . . .
You used to love the herdsman,
Who . . . daily slaughtered kids for you,
Yet him you struck and turned into a wolf,
So that his own shepherd lads chase him,
And his dogs snap at his shanks,

and, says Gilgamesh,

You would love me too, and then make my fate like theirs.

The furious Ishtar went raging to her father Anu to enlist his help to avenge the insult. Under her pressure, Anu finally created the heavenly bull, which came down to earth to punish Gilgamesh. After destroying by the hundred the first humans it met, the bull made a rush at Enkidu, but

Enkidu sprang and seized the heavenly bull by its horns, . . .
He seized it by the thick of its tail, . . .

and Gilgamesh

Thrust his dagger between the neck and the horns.

Thereupon,

When they had killed the heavenly bull, they tore out its heart,
And set it before Shamash.

As a final insult to Ishtar, Gilgamesh tore out the bull's thigh-bone (possibly a euphemism for 'genitals') and hurled it at the goddess, taunting:

'And as for you, if I could get you,
I would do the same to you as to him.'

There followed popular rejoicing and feasting. But that night Enkidu had an alarming dream. He related it to Gilgamesh:

Anu, Enlil and Shamash took counsel together,
And Anu said to Enlil,
Because they have killed the heavenly bull and killed Huwawa,
One of the two must die . . .
Enlil said, 'Enkidu must die;
Gilgamesh is not to die.'
But Shamash retorted to Enlil the hero:
'Was it not at my command that they killed the heavenly bull and Huwawa?
And is the innocent Enkidu to die?'
But Enlil was enraged at Shamash . . . ,

and the decision of Anu and Enlil had to stand.

And so Enkidu became sick, even unto death. Gilgamesh was overwhelmed with grief:

Enkidu lay (dying) before Gilgamesh,
And as his tears streamed down,
(Gilgamesh lamented): 'My brother, my dear brother, why do they give me reprieve instead of you? . . .
Shall I never again see my dear brother with my eyes?'

Enkidu, regretting the fate to which leaving the wilds had brought him, cast curses upon the gate of Erech, the hunter and the courtesan. But when Shamash called to him from heaven and pointed out the benefits of civilized life and the splendid burial rites by which civilized society honoured its dead, Enkidu became calm, and cancelled his curses upon the courtesan with a blessing:

> Princes and nobles shall love you, . . .
> For love of you a wife, (though) a mother of seven, shall be forsaken.

Now there came to Enkidu a dream telling of the condition of the dwellers of the Underworld. Then, after twelve days on his sickbed, he died. Gilgamesh raised a lament over his lost friend:

> 'Now what is the sleep which has seized you?
> You have become an object of fearfulness, for you do not hear me!'
> . . . Yet he could not take [his eyes from him].
> He touched his heart, and since it did not beat, he veiled his friend like a bride.

The dread of death for himself then entered into Gilgamesh:

> Gilgamesh runs about in the steppe-land,
> Weeping bitterly for Enkidu his friend.
> 'I myself shall die; shall not I be like Enkidu too?
> Sadness has entered my bowels.
> I fear death, and I run about in the steppe-land.
> I propose taking the path to Utanapishtim son of Ubar-tutu,
> And I shall go there quickly.'

Gilgamesh therefore set out to consult the deathless Utanapishtim, who was his ancestor. He passed the mountain of Mashu at the edge of the world, behind which the sun rose at dawn and set at night. Here he came upon

The scorpion-people who keep watch at its gate,
Whose radiance inspires terror, a glance at whom is death,
Whose lambent halo spreads out over the cosmic mountain,
Who at sunrise and sunset stand guard over the sun.

But the scorpion-people recognized Gilgamesh as two-thirds divine and allowed him to pass through the gate of the mountain and to follow the path the sun takes when not visible on earth. Through the darkness he travelled for eleven leagues, till the first rays of the sun appeared. Presently it was fully light, and Gilgamesh found himself in a garden of shrubs bearing precious stones. Here he spoke with the sympathetic Sun-god, who warned him, however:

'To what purpose are you wandering around, Gilgamesh?
You will not find the Life you are yearning after.'

Proceeding on his way, Gilgamesh came to the abode of the lady Siduri, the innkeeper who lived by the edge of the Abyss. She looked out and saw Gilgamesh coming along. Siduri was alarmed at the appearance of the stranger, and

She locked her outer gate and shot the bolt.

Gilgamesh, however, threatened to break down the gate, and eventually, having received some explanation of her strange visitor, Siduri admitted him. Gilgamesh related his exploits, and Siduri asked him,

'Why is your face sad? Why are your features anguished?
Why is there grief in your bowels?'

Gilgamesh told her of the loss of his friend, of how he refused to face the fact of his death until the maggots were actually crawling on his face, of his dread at the thought of his own ineluctable death, and of his determination to consult Utanapishtim. 'Tell me,' he said, 'the way to Utanapishtim,' and

> 'If it is possible, I will even cross the Abyss.'

Siduri said to Gilgamesh:

> 'At no time, O Gilgamesh, has there been a crossing
> And whoever since olden times has reached this point has not been able to cross the Abyss;
> The valiant Sun-god does indeed cross the Abyss, but who but the Sun-god can cross it?
> The crossing is arduous; the way is very arduous
> And in the middle part the waters of death are channelled on its surface.'

Siduri tells Gilgamesh, however, of the existence of Urshanabi, Utanapishtim's ferryman, and of the whereabouts of some enigmatic objects called 'those-of-stone'. Precipitately Gilgamesh goes off and apparently smashes the latter. Then he finds Urshanabi and is again called upon to account for his unusual appearance and remarkable journey. Urshanabi tells him that because he has smashed 'those-of-stone' – which apparently had some magic power to enable their bearer to cross the waters of death – he has made attainment of his object more difficult. Nevertheless, said Urshanabi, he was to

> 'Go down to the forest, cut punting poles, each thirty yards long,
> Paint them with bitumen, put on a tip and bring them to me.'

Gilgamesh followed these instructions, and he and the ferryman, thus equipped, boarded the boat, which sped along at a miraculous pace, at fifteen times the normal speed. Thus they arrived at the waters of death, where Urshanabi instructed Gilgamesh to use his poles for punting. The purpose of the large number taken now becomes clear. Not a drop of the water of death might touch the hands of Gilgamesh, and each pole, when Gilgamesh had made his thrust with it, had to be dropped into the waters of death. Finally Gilgamesh had exhausted the hundred and twenty poles he had brought aboard. Now they were within sight of the further shore, where Utanapishtim watched in wonderment:

Utanapishtim gazes into the distance
He reflects within himself, he makes a comment
As he takes counsel within himself:
'Why are the "those-of-stone" of the ship smashed?
And why is someone other than its master riding on it?'

Finally Gilgamesh reached Utanapishtim and as in his previous encounters gave an explanation of his distraught appearance and strange mission. In reply Utanapishtim pointed out the transience of all human activity and all nature:

'Do we make a house (to last) for ever? Do we seal (a document that it may hold good) for ever?
Do brethren divide (paternal property that the division may last) for ever?
Does hatred continue in an enemy for ever?
Does the river raise a flood and bear it up for ever? . . .
The Anunnaki, the great gods, are assembled, . . .
They set out death and life,
But do not reveal the days of death.'

The Flood Story

Gilgamesh was not, however, satisfied. He pointed out to Utanapishtim that the latter appeared to be no different in nature from Gilgamesh himself, yet he could lie at ease, without the gnawing anxiety of thoughts of death. 'Tell me,' he asked, 'How is it that you have acquired eternal life?' In reply Utanapishtim related to Gilgamesh the celebrated story of the Deluge:

'I will reveal to you, O Gilgamesh, a secret matter;
Yes, I will tell you a secret of the gods.
Shuruppak, a city that you know yourself,
That was set on the bank of the Euphrates,

That city was ancient, and within it were the gods.
The great gods felt driven to make a Deluge.'

The principal deities are enumerated. Amongst them was the wise and benevolent god Ea, who recognized the folly of extinguishing all mankind. He devised a stratagem whereby, without breaking the confidence of the gods, he could warn one favoured mortal:

He repeats their words to a reed hut,
'O reed hut! reed hut! Wall! wall!
Reed hut, hear! Wall, pay attention!
Man of Shuruppak, son of Ubar-tutu,
Pull down your house, build a ship!
Leave your goods, seek life! . . .
Make every kind of living creature go up into the ship.'

When Utanapishtim understood his instructions, he promised to obey Ea, but was concerned as to how to explain his conduct to the other people of his city. The clever Ea taught him a punning answer which was to deceive those who heard without involving Utanapishtim in an actual lie. He was to say:

'I have become aware that Enlil hates me,
So that I cannot continue to live in your city . . .
I must go down to the Abyss and dwell with my lord Ea,'

'Then when I have gone,' he was to continue,

'Enlil will make showers of *kibati* rain down upon you,'

where *kibati* is ambiguous in that it can mean either 'wheat' or 'grave misfortune'.

The construction of the ship or ark is now described in detail. It was a remarkable vessel, built in seven decks, with the area of the base almost an acre, and the height of the vessel equal to the length of a side. Some scholars have concluded that this made it a perfect cube, but this does not necessarily follow, for the decks may have been stepped, in which case the ark would have looked, in dimensions as well as shape, like a floating ziggurat. The workmen were feasted without thought of expense until the vessel was completed. Then Utanapishtim loaded it with his silver and gold, with livestock, with his family, with wild creatures, and with craftsmen, and at a warning from the Sun-god, went aboard himself and battened down the ship. Then he handed over control of the vessel to Puzur-Amurri, the pilot.

In the morning the storm began:

There came up from the horizon a black cloud,
Adad [the storm-god] kept thundering within it,
The gods Shullat and Hanish go in front,
They go as throne-bearers over mountains and flat lands;
Irragal [Nergal, god of the Underworld] tears out the (retaining) posts (of the dam of the waters beneath the earth),
Ninurta comes, and makes the weirs overflow;
The Anunnaki raise their torches,
They set the land aglow with their flashing.

Darkness succeeded, and as the cataclysm continued it became so terrifying that

Even the gods became fearful of the deluge,
They retreated and went up to the heaven of Anu.
The gods crouched outside, curled up like dogs.
Ishtar cries out like a woman in travail,
The sweet-voiced Lady of the gods calls out:
'(Mankind of) olden times has, alas, turned to clay,
Because I myself decreed evil in the Divine Assembly;
How came I to decree evil in the Divine Assembly,
To destroy my people? . . .
(And now) they fill the sea like fish fry.'
The gods – that is, the Anunnaki – wept with her;
The gods were humbled, they sat in tears.

After seven days the storm abated, and Utanapishtim was able to look out upon the watery desolation. In every direction all was sea. Then there emerged a number of islands, which were the mountain peaks. On one of these – mount Nisir – the ark grounded. After seven days, as the waters declined, Utanapishtim sent forth a dove, but the dove found no resting-place and returned. Likewise a swallow was released, but that too found no resting-place and returned. Finally a raven was released. The raven found that the waters were now falling back into their accustomed bounds, and Utanapishtim saw that the raven

> Was eating, flying about, cawing – and did not return.

Thereupon Utanapishtim was able to release everything from the ark, and he himself prepared to make a sacrifice to the gods on the top of the mountain. The gods smelled the odour of the aromatic woods, and

> The gods clustered like flies round the lord of the sacrifice.

Ishtar arrived, still lamenting the folly of the universal destruction. She was followed by Enlil, who was furious to find that his decision had not been fully implemented:

> Enlil saw the ship and was furiously angry,
> He was full of wrath against the high gods:
> 'Who could come out (alive); no human was to survive the destruction.'

His son and counsellor Ninurta spoke to him:

> 'Who can perform anything without Ea?
> For Ea it is who understands every kind of business.'

Ea then addressed Enlil in propitiatory tones, pointing out both the injustice and the unreasonableness of indiscriminate destruction of mankind as a whole:

'On the sinner impose his sin, on the transgressor impose his transgression, . . .
Instead of causing a deluge, let a lion come and reduce mankind;
Instead of causing a deluge, let a wolf come and reduce mankind:
Instead of causing a deluge, let a famine be instituted and let it reduce the land;
Instead of causing a deluge, let plague come and smite the people.'

Enlil, appeased by the words of the wise god, went up into the ship and took the hand of Utanapishtim. He made Utanapishtim and his wife bow down in obeisance; he touched their foreheads, he stood between the pair and blessed them, announcing their apotheosis:

'Formerly Utanapishtim was human,
Now Utanapishtim and his wife shall indeed become gods like us,
Verily Utanapishtim shall dwell far away, at the mouth of the rivers!'

Thus concluded Utanapishtim's account of the deluge, which served only to emphasize the uniqueness of the happy lot of himself and his wife: Gilgamesh could expect no similar deliverance from the common fate of mortals, for, asked Utanapishtim,

'Who is going to assemble the gods on your particular account,
That you may find the Life that you seek?'

To emphasize how little Gilgamesh would be able to bear immortality, Utanapishtim challenged him to remain awake for six days and seven nights, but at once, as Gilgamesh squatted there,

Sleep wafts over him like a mist.

The wife of Utanapishtim had compassion on the weary hero, and urged her husband to awaken him, that he might return in peace on the road to Erech. But Utanapishtim had planned to bring fully home to Gilgamesh his frailty:

'Humanity is deceitful; he would seek to deceive you.
Come then! Bake his bread rations and keep setting them at his head,
And mark up on the wall the days that he sleeps!'

Day by day she did this, and had just set down the newly baked bread for the seventh day when Utanapishtim roused Gilgamesh. Gilgamesh quickly excused himself; he had been taking a nap:

'Scarcely had sleep poured over me,
When you quickly touched and roused me.'

Utanapishtim commanded him:

'Gilgamesh, count your bread-rations,
So that the days you have slept are known to you!'

Gilgamesh, dismayed, did so: he found bread-rations ranging from newly-baked bread, through bread that was sour and mouldy, to the dried-up remains of bread which had stood a week in the open sun. Perforce he acknowledged that he had utterly failed in his test, and accepted death as his lot:

'The "Snatcher" has hold of my flesh,
Death sits in my bedchamber,
And wherever I set my feet there is Death.'

Utanapishtim now prepared Gilgamesh for the return to his city. He instructed Urshanabi to wash him, to replace the filthy skins he had been wearing with a fair new garment, and to put a new turban upon his head. Just as Gilgamesh and Urshanabi had embarked and begun to move out to sea for the return journey, the wife of Utanapishtim prevailed upon her husband to give Gilgamesh some reward for his wearisome journey. Utanapishtim called out to Gilgamesh the secret of a magic plant, a plant with thorns, found beneath the sea, a wonderful plant called 'The old man becomes young', which would restore to an ageing man his youth and virility. Gilgamesh tied heavy stones to his feet and sank down into the sea, where despite the thorns he obtained the plant. Casting off the weights from his feet, he was thrown up by the sea upon a shore, where Urshanabi rejoined him. They walked on for fifty leagues, until they stopped for the night. There

Gilgamesh saw a pool whose waters were cool,
He went down into it and bathed in the waters.
A snake smelled the scent of the plant,
It came up . . . and took the plant,
And on its return sloughed its skin.

Gilgamesh, finding the loss of the plant to gain which he had so greatly wearied himself, sat down and wept. He had obtained nothing for himself: it was the snake, which he called the 'earth-lion', which had won the reward of renewing its youth, by its annual casting of its skin.

Empty-handed, Gilgamesh and Urshanabi reached Erech: Gilgamesh took his guide up upon the walls of Erech and pointed out to him the magnificent city. The brickwork was not mere sun-dried clay but burnt brick, and the city itself was in three equal parts, the built-up area, the orchard lands and the open fields, to say nothing of the lands belonging to the great temple of the patron goddess Ishtar. To show Urshanabi all this splendour, for fortifying which he himself was responsible, was the one consolation remaining to Gilgamesh.

Atrahasis

An Akkadian epic with some material in common with the *Epic of Gilgamesh* is that known to us as *Atrahasis* (the name of its hero) and to the Babylonians as *inuma ilu awilum*, probably meaning 'When the gods like man', although other interpretations have been proposed.

Atrahasis begins with a mythic account of the universe before the creation of man. The three great gods had divided the universe between them, Anu taking the heavens, Enki the ocean and Enlil the earth. There was work to be done on the earth, and the great gods compelled the junior gods to undertake the toil.

The junior gods wearied of this; they went on strike and made a violent demonstration against Enlil. The great gods convened to discuss the problem, and decided that man should be created to bear the toil, and instructed the Birth-goddess (variously named Belet-ili, Nintu or Mami) to undertake the necessary procedure. The Birth-goddess called for the assistance of the wise god Enki, who decreed

> Let them slaughter one god, . . .
> With his flesh and his blood
> Let Nintu mix clay;
> Let very god and man
> Be mixed together in the clay.
> In after days let us hear the drum,
> Let there be a wraith from the god's flesh.

The 'drum' probably meant the heartbeat, taken as evidence of the life from the god within man, and 'the wraith from the god's flesh' was the spirit which survived after death.[2]

The myth goes on to give details of how the goddess created man. To accompanying incantations, she nipped off fourteen pieces of clay, and placed them in relation to a brick and perhaps the knife for cutting a newborn baby's umbilical cord. This does not tell us much about Babylonian ideas of Creation as such, but it illustrates the kind of circumstances in which myths might be used. Here the myth has obviously become involved with the ritual used at a birth.

The text subsequently returns to Creation mythology. After twelve hundred years mankind had become so numerous and noisy that they disturbed Enlil. Enlil decided to take action, and directed the Plague-god, Namtara, to reduce mankind. Every Babylonian had a personal god to protect him; usually this was a very obscure divine being, but there was a hero Atrahasis, whose name meant 'Pre-eminent in Wisdom', who had as his personal deity the great god Enki. Enki advised Atrahasis how to deal with the catastrophe. Humans were to direct their worship to Namtara in person. When they did this, the flattered Namtara relaxed the plague.

Another twelve hundred years passed, and Enlil made a second attempt to reduce mankind, by directing Adad to withhold the rains and bring famine. (This part at least of the myth cannot have come from third-millennium Sumer, where rainfall was not of crucial significance; it reflects the ecological background of people further north and west, probably immigrating Amorites.) But again Enki intervened, advising that humans should pay particular homage to Adad; this they did, and thereupon he surreptitiously watered the earth.

It now becomes difficult to follow precisely what happened. This is probably a consequence of the nature of our sources. There are Old Babylonian, Assyrian and Late Babylonian pieces of text, none complete, and these may well have contained different emphases and perhaps different incidents. We have to piece the story together from several sources, which may have conflicted at some points, and this is bound to cause confusion.

One would expect the myth to proceed to a different type of natural disaster. Instead, it goes on to a second and more rigorous famine. I suggest that this is linked to a point already made – that rainfall is not crucial for crops in south Iraq. Specifically I suggest that when this myth began to circulate amongst people who only knew the ecology of south Iraq, it became necessary to introduce a second version of the famine disaster, covering the much more serious problem of the failure of the rivers to flood. The result was devastating, for the land completely ceased to yield corn. On the parched fields appeared salt crystals, as often happens still in Iraq. For six years the famine became progressively worse, until finally the unfortunate people sank to cannibalism:

When the sixth year arrived, they would prepare a daughter for a meal,
They would prepare a child for food.

This second famine does not fit the earlier patterns, since it is now Enki himself who frustrates its effects. Enlil, now suspicious that some god was acting against him, summoned a divine Assembly, in which he urged united action against mankind. Some god, whose name is lost but who was almost certainly Enki, saw the absurdity of this plan:

In the Assembly of the gods laughter overwhelmed him.

Enki represented man's developing control over his environment, and the divine laughter here is a figure in myth for man's brave defiance of the worst the hostile powers can do to him. But Enlil succeeded in persuading the gods that mankind must be totally destroyed:

The gods decreed total destruction;
Enlil made an evil plan for the people.

The evil plan was a universal flood. The story of the Deluge follows; it is so similar to the Flood story in the *Epic of Gilgamesh* that there must have been a common source.

It has been suggested that Enlil's concern was with what we today would call a population explosion. This seems anachronistic to me and very improbable; rather, I see the aetiology of this myth as an assurance, in the face of natural disasters, that whatever catastrophes may befall man, he has powers working in his favour which will overcome them.

The Epic of Adapa

This epic shares with *Gilgamesh* the theme of man's quest for immortality. It is known from first-millennium fragments from Ashurbanipal's library at Nineveh and from a piece found in the fourteenth-century cuneiform archives at El Amarna in Egypt.

Adapa was a votary of the cult at Eridu in the most ancient times. One day he was out in his boat fishing, when the south wind came and capsized him. Infuriated, Adapa gave vent to a curse: 'I'll break your wing!' So powerful was Adapa's magic that this utterance in itself was sufficient to break the wing of the south wind.

In consequence, the south wind ceased to blow. On the level of the physical world, this relates to the fact that it is the south wind which ripens the date crop, so that the failure of the south wind at the appropriate season is a serious matter, resulting in infertility for a major source of food. After seven days the high god Anu noticed the disturbing absence of the south wind and called his vizier for an explanation.

> His vizier Ilabrat answered him; 'My Lord!
> Adapa, son of Ea, has broken the wing of the south wind.'

Consequently, Adapa was summoned to appear before Anu. But Ea stood by Adapa, advising him how to ensure his safety. He was to go dressed as a mourner, with his hair dishevelled. At the gate of Anu he would find two gods, who would ask why he was in mourning. He was to reply:

> Two gods have disappeared from our land,
> For that reason am I thus.

And when the gods asked who the two gods were, he was to reply,

> Tammuz and Gizzida.

These were two fertility gods, whose disappearance from the land was the mythic expression of the loss of the date harvest, from the failure of the south wind to blow. Adapa's mourning for them would gain their goodwill and secure a favourable introduction to Anu. At the interview, Ea warned, Adapa would be offered food and drink, but he was not to accept, because it would be the bread of death and the water of death:

As you stand before Anu,
When they offer you bread of death, you shall not eat it.
When they offer you water of death, you shall not drink it.

Adapa went before Anu and explained the circumstances of his offence. Tammuz and Gizzida (the very gods who had been directly affected by it) spoke on his behalf, and the anger of Anu was appeased. Then said Anu:

Fetch bread of life for him that he may eat it.

But Adapa recalled Ea's advice: we do not know whether that advice was given in good faith, or whether Ea had foreknowledge of what Anu would do and intended to prevent Adapa from gaining immortality; but as a consequence of it

When they brought him the bread of life, (Adapa) would not eat it;
When they brought him the water of life, he would not drink it.

At Adapa's refusal, Anu looked at him and laughed:

Why would you neither eat nor drink?
You shall not therefore gain (eternal) life.

Adapa, his chance of immortality lost, was sent back to earth.

Enuma Elish

A Babylonian work which from our modern point of view is second only to *Gilgamesh* is the myth of Creation current in Babylon in the first millennium BC, known from its initial words as *Enuma Elish* ('When Above'). This work, consisting of seven tablets, was recited at Babylon on the fourth day of the New Year Festival (see pages 333ff.), and in Assyria was correspondingly employed with substitution of the name of the Assyrian national god, Ashur, for the Babylonian Marduk.

Formerly, many scholars attributed this myth to the Old Babylonian period. But since it honours as supreme the god Marduk, who did not achieve national pre-eminence until the late second millennium, it cannot be earlier than the thirteenth century and may be as late as 1100 BC.

The myth gives an account of the origin of a world order in which the universe was governed by a pantheon of deities amongst whom Marduk was supreme. Mankind existed only to serve the gods. In the beginning there were only the primordial beings, Apsu (the Sweet Waters or Abyss), and Tiamat (Ocean). These beings had many ramifications within mythological thinking, but amongst other things they represented male and female principles. A third term also occurs; this term is Mummu, which as an ordinary noun means 'craftsman' or 'creator'. Some writers have wanted to see Mummu as the third element in a primeval Father–Mother–Son triad, but this view is untenable. The term actually occurs in two different contexts. In one it is prefixed to the name Tiamat, whilst in the other it represents some being or principle with which Apsu took counsel. Theologically it probably connoted something like 'Creative Life-Force', the conception being rather like that of the Holy Spirit in Neoplatonism.

The state of affairs before Creation is described at the beginning of the myth:

When on high the heavens had not been named,
And below the land had not been called by name,
When only Apsu the primeval, who spawned them,
And Mummu-Tiamat, who gave birth to them all,
Mingled their waters as one;
When reed-thickets had not consolidated, canebrakes were not to be found,

49 The high-priest and goddess escort the king to the Sun-god sitting in his shrine behind the sun-disk (first millennium BC, probably copied from a more ancient monument)

50A The rising of the Sun-god; a cylinder seal impression

50B Mythical hero [Gilgamesh?] with lion; a cylinder seal impression

51A Boxing, possibly as a cult act (from a plaque)

51B Copper stand in the form of wrestlers (third millennium)

51C Sexual cult scene of questionable nature (from a plaque)

52 (*opposite*) Musicians (from an Assyrian bas-relief)

53 (*above*) Colossal human-headed lion, representing a good genie guarding an Assyrian palace

54A Face of Humbaba, an ogre mentioned in the *Epic of Gilgamesh*

54B Lamashtu, a dreaded female demon (from an amulet)

55 (*opposite*) A Babylonian devil

56A (*above*) Babylonian monster (*circa* 1900 BC)

56B (*left*) Amulet, showing gods associated with mythical beasts

The wind-demon Pazuzu, with [top register] exorist priests in animal head-dress (an alabaster amulet from Babylon, first millennium)

3 (*below*) Detail from reredos by Jacques de Baerze (*circa* 1300 AD) showing astral symbols and demons possibly deriving ultimately from ancient Mesopotamia

58A Rein-ring from Ur (third millennium)

58B Weight in form of a lion (first millennium BC)

59 Brazier (from Nuzi)

60A A carved ivory; a lady [perhaps a cult-woman] at her window

60B A carved ivory

61A Winged ibex (Achaemenid period)

61B Bronze dragon's head from Babylon (sixth century BC)

62 Ancient Near Eastern jewellery

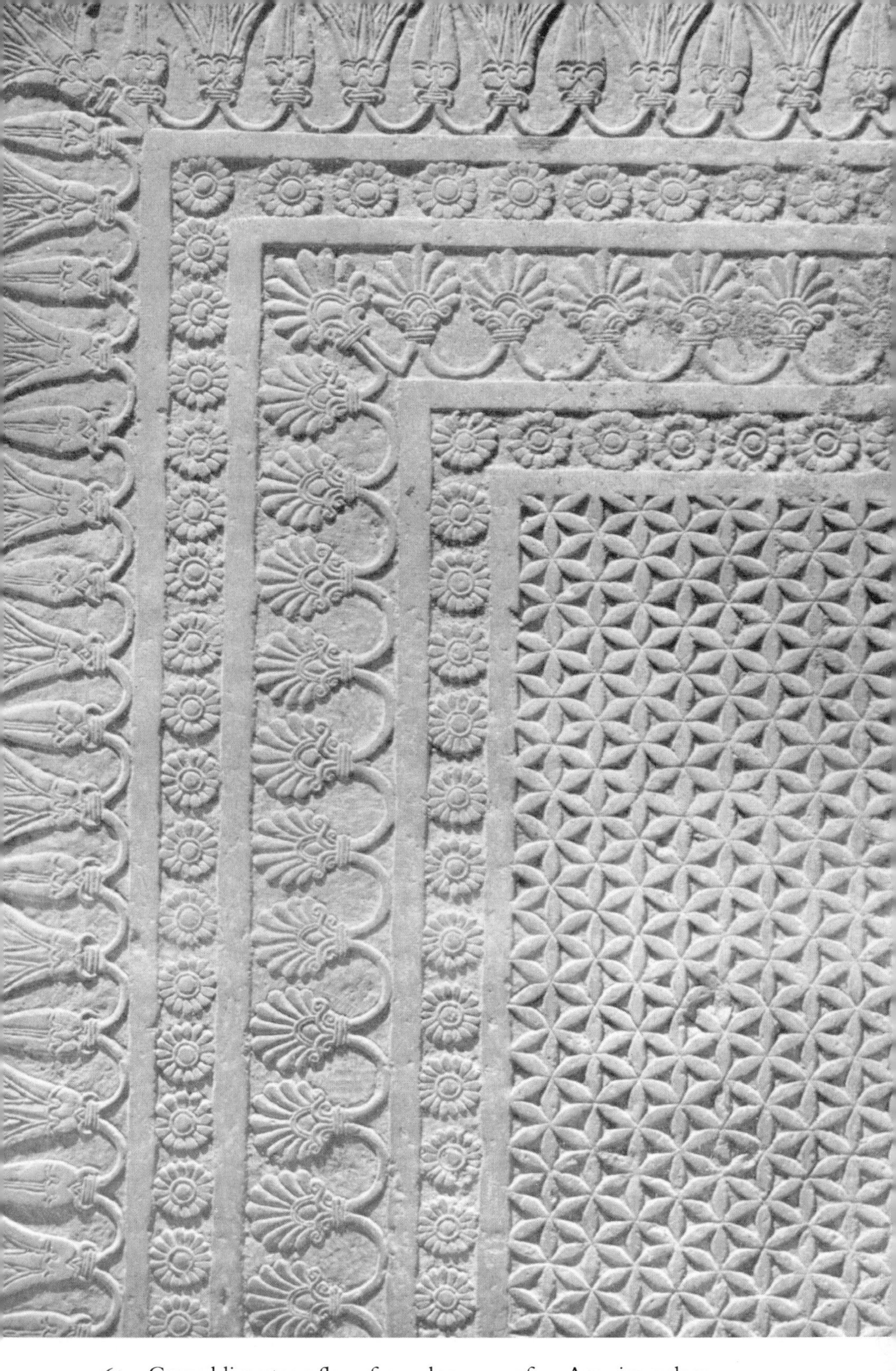

63 Carved limestone floor from doorway of an Assyrian palace

64 The Gebel el-Arak knife, with carved handle showing ship of Mesopotamian

When no god at all had been made manifest,
When they had not been given a name, when there had been no fixing of the(ir) destiny,
Then were the gods created inside them [i.e. inside the mingled waters of Apsu and Tiamat].
Lahmu and Lahamu were made manifest, they duly received names.
While they grew great and flourished,
Anshar and Kishar were created, who exceeded them.
The days stretched out to great length, the years added up.
Anshar made Anu his firstborn equal to him.
Anu begat as his likeness Nu-dim-mud [i.e. Ea].
Nu-dim-mud it was who was Creator [literally 'Begetter'][3] for his fathers;
Perceptive, wise, of outstanding intelligence,
Much more powerful than Anshar, his father's begetter,
He had no equal amongst the gods his brethren.

These new and junior gods now proceeded to give annoyance to the primeval beings by their tumultuous and noisy conduct.

Then Apsu who spawned the great gods,
Cried out and called to Mummu his vizier,
'O Mummu, my vizier, who gladdens my heart,
Come and let us go to Tiamat!'
They went and sat in front of Tiamat;
They took counsel together in the matter of the gods their firstborn.
Apsu opened his mouth
And said forcibly to Tiamat:
'Their behaviour is hurtful to me,
By day I cannot rest, by night I cannot sleep;
Let me destroy, yes, let me put an end to their behaviour,
That silence may be re-established and that we may rest.'

Tiamat, however, strongly dissented, and angrily asked:

'What! Should we destroy what we ourselves have created?
Their behaviour is certainly very hurtful, but let us have patience.'

On the other hand, Apsu's vizier Mummu – that is, theologically, the personification of the divine force of Apsu's utterance – favoured destroying the mutinous gods, and the two together plotted action. This came to the knowledge of the junior gods, and Ea, 'who understood everything', took action. He cunningly devised a powerful incantation, recited it and caused it to dwell in the waters. By this means he 'poured out sleep' over Apsu and paralysed Mummu. Apsu he slew, founding his dwelling-place and shrine over his slain body (wherefore Ea is lord of the Apsu, the cosmic waters), and Mummu he made his prisoner.

Within the Apsu Ea dwelt with his spouse Damkina, and there a god was begotten. It was Marduk, described as wisest and most powerful of the gods. The poem details the splendour of the new god:

> His dimensions were cunningly devised and incomprehensible,
> Impossible to understand, difficult even to see;
> His eyes were four, his ears were four,
> When his lips moved, fire blazed out . . .
> He was tall indeed; among the gods his stature was pre-eminent.

All this contributed to the disturbance wrought by the junior gods and consequently to the discomfort occasioned to Tiamat. Tiamat's advisers reminded her of the fate of Apsu and Mummu, and urged her to avenge them. Their words found favour in her sight, and she prepared a series of monsters to fight against the young gods:

> Mother Hubur [a title of Tiamat], who fashions everything,
> Added an irresistible weapon; she gave birth to dragons
> – Their teeth were sharp, their fangs unsparing –
> She filled their bodies with venom for blood;
> She clad raging monsters with fearsomeness,
> She arrayed them with supernatural radiance; she made them like gods . . .
> She brought into being the *Bashmu*-serpent, the dragon, and the *Lahamu*-monster,

The lion-demon, the mad dog and the scorpion-man,
Fierce storms, the fish-man, the bison,
Bearing unsparing weapons, not fearing battle.

Tiamat created eleven monsters of such kinds, and at their head she placed Kingu, her firstborn among the gods. In her Assembly she told Kingu:

'I have cast an incantation for you, I have made you great in the Assembly of the gods,
I have placed fully in your hand the power of ruling all the gods;
You are indeed very great; you alone are my consort!'

The younger gods learned that Tiamat was preparing for battle. Ea heard of it and for a while was struck dumb. Finally he went to his ancestor Anshar and told him what he had heard:

'My father, Tiamat who bore us now hates us,
She has put the Assembly into session, she is raging with anger;
The gods, all of them, have gone over to her;
Even those whom you yourselves created go at her side.'

Anshar was much troubled at the tidings, and proposed that Ea, who had dealt with Mummu and Apsu, should take action against Kingu. Ea's reply is broken, but it seems that he was unable to accept the challenge. Anshar then turned to Anu. Anu set out to deal with the enemy, but on coming within sight of Tiamat's mighty forces his heart failed him and he returned to Anshar. The gods sat in silent despair, and finally Anshar proposed that Marduk should be their champion. Marduk, who was apparently too young and junior to be at the divine Assembly, was called by his father Ea, and instructed to present himself before Anshar. This he did, to the great joy of Anshar. Marduk, however, made a condition:

'If indeed I, your avenger,
Am to bind Tiamat and give life to you,

Then put in session an Assembly, proclaim my destiny pre-eminent.
Sit joyfully together in the Hall of Assembly,
Let me determine destinies by the utterance of my mouth instead of you;
So that whatever I myself create shall be unalterable,
So that the word of my lips shall neither turn about nor be changed.'

Anshar thereupon sent his vizier Gaga to his own progenitors Lahmu and Lahamu, who with the other gods came to the Hall of Assembly:

The great gods, all of them who determine destinies,
Entered before Anshar; they filled the Hall of Assembly.
They embraced each other in the Assembly,
They held conversation, they sat down to a banquet,
They ate bread, they drank choice beer,
They made the sweet liquor flow through their drinking-tubes,[4]
As they drank the liquor, they became elated,
They were very carefree, their spirits rose,
For Marduk, their avenger, they determined his destiny.
They set for him a princely throne,
In front of his fathers he sat down for (the purpose of) exercising rule.

The Assembly of gods then proclaimed his pre-eminent status:

'You are the most honoured one among the great gods,
Your decree is unequalled, your utterance is Anu . . .
From this very day your command shall be unalterable,
To exalt or to bring low, this is verily in your hand,
What comes forth from your mouth shall come true, your utterance shall not prove false.
No one among the gods shall overstep your bounds . . .
We have given you kingship over the whole universe;
Sit in the Assembly and let your word be supreme!'

There followed a test of the power granted to Marduk. A star was chosen, and Marduk had to command it first to disappear and then to reappear. Astronomically this was a reference to the periodic disappearance and reappearance of some stars. When the test proved successful, the gods joyfully proclaimed:

'Marduk is king!',

and gave him the insignia of royalty. Then they armed him, and sent him off to destroy Tiamat.

He set the lightning in front of him,
His body he filled with blazing fire;
He made also a net to enmesh Tiamat within it,
He posted the four winds that nothing of her should get away,
The south wind, the north wind, the east wind, the west wind.
The net, the gift of his father Anu, he fastened at his side.
He created Bad-Wind, Whirlwind, Dust Storm,
Four-Wind, Seven-Wind, Cyclone, Irresistible-Wind;
Then he let the winds which he had created go forth, all seven of them;
They rose after him to disturb the inside of Tiamat.
Then the Lord took up the Deluge, his great weapon,
He rode the terrifying chariot, (drawn by) irresistible storm-demons,
Harnessing and attaching to it a team of four, (named)
Murderer, Unsparing, Trampler, Winged-one;
Sharp were their teeth, laden with poison.

Marduk, surrounded by the other gods, approached the raging Tiamat. As the hordes of Marduk and Tiamat met, the two threw taunts at each other, and Marduk challenged Tiamat to combat:

When Tiamat heard this,
She became like a mad person, she went out of her senses,
She cried out aloud in temper,
She trembled in her lower parts down to the roots,
She recited an incantation, she kept casting her spell.

Then Tiamat and Marduk joined in battle:

The Lord spread out his net to enmesh her,
He let loose Bad-Wind . . . at her face;
When Tiamat opened her mouth to swallow him up,
He made Bad-Wind go in so that she could not close her lips;
The furious winds inflated her belly,
Her inside was blown up, her mouth was agape.
He shot an arrow, thereby splitting open her belly,
He cut open her inside, he slit her in the middle.
He bound her and then extinguished her life.
He threw down her corpse, he stood upon it.

The victorious Marduk then proceeded to deal with the auxiliaries of Tiamat. He took them prisoner, amongst them their leader Kingu, from whom he took the Tablet of Destinies, fastening them upon his own breast. Marduk then returned to the body of Tiamat, and with it created heaven and earth:

The Lord rested and inspected her corpse,
He would divide the monster and bring clever works into existence;
He broke her into two parts like a split fish,
One half of her he set up and roofed the sky,
. . . he posted guards,
He commissioned them not to let her waters come out.

Thus the physical heaven and earth were created. The next section of the myth has reference to astronomical phenomena, mentioning the fixing of the constellations and the stations of certain heavenly bodies. With the heavens made perfect, Marduk now had the idea of creating a creature, to be known as Man, for the purpose of performing the service of the gods, that they themselves might be at ease. He put forward his scheme to his father Ea, who approved the scheme but considered it necessary for one god to perish in order that Man might be created:

Ea answered him, he spoke a word to him,
For the sake of the repose of the gods he detailed a plan to him,
'Let one of their brethren be handed over,
Let that one be destroyed and let mankind be formed.
Let the great gods assemble
So that the guilty one may be handed over and they themselves
may be secure.'

The Assembly was duly called, and Marduk asked for a decision upon who it was who had led Tiamat into hostilities against the gods. The great gods replied with an accusation against Kingu. Marduk thereupon bound the captive and led him before Ea:

They imposed on him the penalty of his guilt, they spilt his blood;
From his blood they created mankind;
He [Ea] imposed service (on mankind) and so set the gods free.

Marduk now divided six hundred Anunnaki (the principal gods of the pantheon) into groups based in heaven and on earth (or, the underworld).

In gratitude for their deliverance the Anunnaki now exerted themselves to make a worthy shrine for Marduk. For a full year they laboured, and by the second year they had created the great temple complex of Babylon, Esagila – 'House of the Exalted Head' – with its ziggurat, which was thought of as a mirror image of the Apsu which lay beneath the earth.

There follows a passage dealing with the dedication and cult of Esagila. The remainder of the passage, whilst containing many obscure mythological allusions, is in its present form primarily an elaborate theological work in which Marduk is proclaimed and exalted under his fifty names (see page 293).

Enuma Elish, though the longest and best preserved, is not the only myth of creation extant from Babylonia. We have already noted the motif of making mankind from the blood of a slain god, in the *Epic of Atrahasis* (see pages 356ff.).

Myths of the Underworld

The Underworld held a prominent place in Babylonian mythological thinking; texts such as omens, incantations and hymns are full of allusions to it. One myth in this area, *Nergal and Ereshkigal* (see page 290), must have been widely disseminated in the ancient world, for parts of it were found in the fourteenth-century cuneiform archives at El Amarna in Egypt, and at Sultantepe in the south of Asiatic Turkey.

The most important Mesopotamian myth concerned with the Underworld deals with a visit there by the goddess called Inanna in Sumerian and Ishtar in Akkadian. This myth, *The Descent of Inanna* (or, *Ishtar*) *to the Underworld*, is preserved in both Sumerian and Akkadian versions.[5]

Superficially, the basic plot of the myth, more fully preserved in the Sumerian version, seems easy to understand. Inanna (Ishtar) decided to visit her sister, Ereshkigal, Queen of the Underworld. To make her journey, Inanna dressed in her jewels and insignia and left the cities of Sumer and Akkad to go down to the Land of No Return. Before leaving, she instructed her handmaid, Ninshubur, that if she should fail to return, Ninshubur was to put on a mourning garment, and go to Ekur, the shrine of Enlil in Nippur, to explain the danger in which Inanna stood. If Enlil took no action, Ninshubur was to proceed to the Moon-god Nanna in Ur. If Nanna did nothing, Ninshubur was as a last resort to present herself to the god Enki in Eridu. Enki, 'who knows the food of life, who knows the water of life', would certainly render assistance.

Inanna presented herself at the first gate of the Underworld, saying that she had come for the funerary rites of Gugalanna, husband of her sister Ereshkigal, Queen of the Underworld. The gatekeeper reported to his mistress, and received instructions. Inanna was permitted to proceed upon surrendering her crown.

Neti, chief gatekeeper of the Underworld, obeyed the word of his queen;

He opened the seven gates of the Underworld. . . .
He said to the pure Inanna, 'Come, Inanna, enter!'
As she entered, her *sugarra*-crown was removed.
'What, now, is this?'
'Silence, Inanna! It is in keeping with the decrees of the Underworld;
O Inanna, do not question the customs of the Underworld.'

A like procedure followed at each of the six other gates, Inanna successively losing all her insignia and clothing, until finally she entered the Underworld naked. There she fought with Ereshkigal, but the seven divine judges of the Underworld cast upon Inanna the glance of death. Inanna became a corpse, and in the Sumerian version Ereshkigal hung her body from a peg like a joint of meat.

Then Ninshubur, true to her trust, set up mourning and applied herself to Enlil. But

Father Enlil stood not by her in this affair; she therefore went to Ur.

In Ur the Moon-god Nanna likewise failed to offer assistance, and so Ninshubur betook herself to Enki in Eridu. As Inanna had foreseen, Enki was disturbed at the news. He answered Ninshubur:

What has happened to my daughter? I am troubled.
What has happened to Inanna? I am troubled.

Enki then took steps to secure the release of Inanna (Ishtar) by means of a trick. The details differ in the two versions. In the Sumerian version, Enki scraped dirt out of his finger-nails and made from it two beings called *kurgarra* and *kalaturra*, who were probably thought of as being sexless, in the sense of being either eunuchs or homosexuals. Apparently such peculiar creatures were not subject to the normal rules and could enter and leave the Underworld unchecked. These beings reached the Underworld and found Ereshkigal lamenting for dead children. As Enki had instructed them, they sympathetically joined in her lamentations. This created a bond which led Ereshkigal to promise to give them whatever they asked. And so

> They said: 'Give us the corpse hanging from the peg!'
> Holy Ereshkigal made answer to the *kalaturra* and *kurgarra*
> That it was the corpse of their queen.

But the *kalaturra* and *kurgarra* insisted, and Ereshkigal gave it to them. They then sprinkled it with the food of life and the water of life with which Enki had provided them, and revived Inanna.

In the Akkadian version of the myth, there is no mention of instructions to a handmaid, but after the capture of Ishtar it is the vizier of the great gods who reports the problem to Ea; all animal and human breeding had ceased. Ea thereupon made a being called a *kulu'u*, named Asushu-namir, which means literally 'His appearance is fair', implying 'Prettyface', a good name for a male prostitute, as the class of people called *kulu'u* must have been. Like the two beings in the Sumerian version, Asushu-namir had no difficulty in getting through the seven gates of the Underworld, and Ereshkigal was glad to see him. He succeeded in getting her to swear by the great gods to give him whatever he asked. What he then asked was:

> O My Lady! Let them give me the waterskin; let me drink water therefrom.

Ereshkigal showed annoyance at this and said:

> You have requested of me a request not to be requested!

Clearly in the Akkadian form of the myth, Ishtar had been turned into a waterskin. Ereshkigal cursed Asushu-namir in terms appropriate to a male prostitute:

> May doorways be your dwellingplace,
> May drunkards [literally 'the drunk and the thirsty'] strike your face,

but the goddess was bound by her oath to grant the request, and duly delivered Ishtar to him. There was, however, a condition: if Ishtar returned to the upper world, another person must be sent down as her ransom.

The remaining lines of the Akkadian version are damaged and obscure, but they mention Tammuz and the goddess Belili, and appear to conclude:

> On the day that Tammuz comes up to me, when the lapis lazuli flute (and) the carnelian ring come up to me with him,
> When there come up with him the weeping men and weeping women,
> Let the dead come up and smell the incense.

This was formerly taken as proof that the purpose of Ishtar's visit was to rescue Tammuz from the Underworld, as a god who died and rose again. But the wording does not support this, and the fuller Sumerian version of the myth is directly against it.

In the Sumerian version, when Inanna had been revived, she ascended to the upper world accompanied by a crowd of demons, seeking a substitute for their erstwhile victim. When Ninshubur, the handmaid, came to meet Inanna, the demons wished to carry her off, but Inanna restrained them in gratitude for her loyalty. The party then proceeded to the temple of the city of Umma, where the tutelary deity Shara threw himself into the dust before Inanna, who thereupon kept the demons from seizing him. A similar thing happened at a second city, Bad-tibira. Inanna and her ghastly entourage then made their way to Inanna's own city, Erech, to the district Kulaba. Here they found the god Dumuzi (Tammuz), Inanna's husband, showing no signs of mourning but contentedly sitting on his throne. Inanna, enraged at his absence of show of feeling, handed Dumuzi over to the demons.

But Dumuzi was not so easily caught. He appealed for help to the Sun-god, Utu in Sumerian. Utu helped him to escape, and when he was recaptured, to escape again. The demons pressed his sister Geshtinanna to reveal his hiding-place, but she refused to betray him.

At this point the extant texts of the Sumerian *The Descent of Inanna* fail, but another Sumerian text, known as *Dumuzi's Dream*, continues with the tribulations of Dumuzi, and shows that he was finally caught in his own sheepfold and killed. Yet another text suggests that when Dumuzi went to the Underworld, his sister Geshtinanna was able to substitute for him there for half the year.

When we attempt to see what *The Descent of Inanna (Ishtar)* was really about, other than being an entertaining story, we find many problems. Firstly, what was the original motivation for Inanna (Ishtar) going down to the Underworld? The Akkadian version gives no reason, but the Sumerian seems to offer two. We deduce one from a phrase which says that Inanna 'desired the Great Above, desired the Great Below', which may mean that she was ambitiously seeking to control the Underworld as well as her own domain. The other is quite explicit: it is the explanation Inanna gave to the gatekeeper of the Underworld for her visit. She told him that she had come for the funerary rites of the recently dead Gugalanna, 'the Great Bull of Heaven', the husband of Ereshkigal.

The specific statement must have meant something to the ancients. When we remember that Inanna (Ishtar) was visible as the planet Venus, her visit to the Underworld becomes meaningful. As seen from the earth, Venus has a periodic motion ('synodic period') of about 584 days. After approximately a year from the beginning of that period, the brightness of the planet gradually declines, until finally it disappears from visibility entirely for about seventy-eight nights.[6] I suggest that on one level the myth represented this sequence of astronomical events: the successive stripping off of all Inanna's finery until she reached the Underworld naked was a mythological reflection of the gradual diminution of the planet's brightness until it vanished from sight altogether. The reason given for Inanna's visit to the Underworld may also have had an astronomical element, if Gugalanna, 'the Great Bull of Heaven', was a constellation which disappeared from the night sky shortly before Venus.

There were, however, other elements than astronomical in the myth. The Akkadian version is shorter than the Sumerian, and the final lines in the form in which we have it suggest that it was used in some ritual festival for the dead, a kind of primitive Feast of All Souls. We may therefore concentrate attention upon the Sumerian version.

The most illuminating insights into the Sumerian form of the story are due to Thorkild Jacobsen.[7] He points out that the story as we have it is a combination of three myths, about the deaths or departure to the Underworld of Inanna, Dumuzi and Geshtinanna in turn. He sees Dumuzi as representing the power in grain and in beer brewed from grain. The name of Dumuzi's faithful sister, Geshtinanna, is clearly compounded from the word *geshtin*, which is Sumerian for 'grape-vine'. Dumuzi and Geshtinanna then, according to Jacobsen, were the power in respectively the beer and the wine. In mythological thinking, they died at the time of the grain and vine harvests. They substituted for each other as wine can substitute for beer, and they died and rose at different points in the year, because the grain harvest was in the spring and the grape harvest in autumn.

Jacobsen has some equally interesting ideas about the Inanna element in the myth, although there is one aspect of this which I do not find convincing. He tentatively suggests that the fate of Inanna reflected the gradual depletion in late winter of the food stored in the storehouse, until only a joint of tainted meat (represented mythically by the corpse of Inanna) was left. I see certain difficulties in accepting this, namely that (1) the bulk of Sumerian stores of food would have been in the form of grain, not meat; (2) by the beginning of the third millennium the social infrastructure was so well developed that dramatic food shortage would not normally occur as a seasonal matter;

(failure of the rivers to flood could produce famine, but on the mythological level that would be entirely different); (3) the Akkadian version substitutes a waterskin for a corpse or joint of meat, and it is difficult to link the 'foodstore' hypothesis to this.

Inanna was revived in the Underworld by putting upon her corpse the food (or, as Jacobsen translates it, 'grass') of life and the water of life, which Enki, god of the sweet waters, had provided. Jacobsen sees this as referring to the replenishing of the storehouse, but this could well incorporate a more fundamental mythic concept; it suggests to me that at one level in this myth Inanna represented the surface of the earth itself, which was restored to life by water and the new growth of herbage. Ishtar as the empty waterskin in the Akkadian version, requiring water before it became the symbol of life, fits into this. This would make Inanna (Ishtar) at this level of the myth a form of the Earth-Mother, one of the most widely spread concepts in primitive and prehistoric religion.

The myth of Anzu[8]

The large number of extant fragments and incidental allusions indicate that this myth had wide currency. We will outline the myth first and then discuss what it may have meant.

The myth in its final first-millennium form begins with a hymn in honour of the god Ninurta. It then goes on, in a badly broken section, to describe the origin and functions of Anzu, who, as we know from this and other sources, was a supernatural being in the form of a lion-headed bird. The myth proper starts with Anzu thinking of stealing sovereignty from Enlil (otherwise Duranki), father of the gods. Enlil's powers resided in something called the Tablet of Destinies, whose magical powers gave the wearer control of the universe:

As Anzu kept glancing at the father of the gods, Duranki,
He conceived in his heart the idea of removing the sovereignty,
'Let me myself take the Tablet of Destinies of the gods, and let me gather the ordinances of the gods – all of them.

Let me gain the throne, let me be lord over the established order.
Let me control the whole pantheon.'

The opportunity for the theft came when Enlil was washing himself:

Whilst Enlil was washing with pure water,
Stripped, and his crown set on the throne,
(Anzu) reached out with his hand to the Tablet of Destinies.
He took away the sovereignty: the established order was abrogated.
Anzu flew off and made for his mountain.

The gods were distressed, and Anu called for a volunteer to go and slay Anzu. Whoever would slay Anzu should 'make his name great in all cities'. The Weather-god Adad (also named Gugal) was called upon, but he refused. A second and a third god were summoned, but they likewise declined. Finally Ea proposed that the gods should ask the great Creatress-goddess known variously as Mami, Ninhursag or Belet-ili ('Lady of the gods') (see page 357) to make her son Ninurta available. This was done and Ninurta was appointed champion of the gods. His divine mother told him:

Mount your total attack!
Make your tempests flash! Let them go against him.
Bind the winged Anzu!
Drench the earth which has been created! . . .
Let the sun not shine upon him,
Let the bright day be turned for him to darkness.
Destroy his life! Vanquish Anzu!
Let the winds carry his wings for good tidings
To the exalted one, your father Enlil, to his house Ekur.
Hurry and drench the midst of the mountains!
Cut the throat of evil Anzu!
Let the kingship re-enter Ekur. . . .
Make yourself glorious before the gods! Let your name be 'The Mighty One'.

The myth goes on to describe how Ninurta harnessed the seven tempests and went to confront Anzu in his mountain. Anzu was furious, and battle ensued:

> Darkness was imposed; the mountains, their faces were concealed. . . .
> Death clouds pour rain, arrows flash as lightning.
> There is deadlock between them; the battle thunders on.

Ninurta shot an arrow against Anzu, but Anzu used the power of the Tablet of Destinies to repulse the arrow by a spell:

> O reed-arrow that has come against me, return to your canebrake!
> Frame of the bow, to your forests!
> Return, O thong, to the sheep's rump, and feathering to the birds!
> This is He who bears the divine Tablet of Destinies in his hand!

Ninurta sent a messenger back to tell Ea (Ninshiku) of the problem. Ea sent new instructions:

> Tire him out, so that at the onslaught of the hurricane he droops his pinion.
> Take, O Lord, your arrow for a spear.
> Lop off his pinions. Dash them to right and left!
> When he catches sight of his two wings, let him produce his formula.
> 'Wing (come back) to wing!', he will cry.

Ninurta did as he was told. But Anzu knew that his powers prevented Ninurta doing him any irreversible harm, and when Ninurta cut off his wings he immediately restored himself by the magical formula 'Wing (come back) to wing!' But Ea's cleverness had outreached Anzu. The magic formula operated against all wings and feathers, and when Anzu uttered it, the feathers on the arrow, from the wings of a bird, pierced Anzu's own wings:

> Just as he cried: 'Wing (come back) to wing!', a dart sprang up at him,

A javelin passed through the front of his heart.
(Ninurta) made an arrow pass through pinion and wing. . . .
Ninurta slew the Mountains; he drenched their wild terrain;
In his wrath he drenched the wide world;
He drenched the midst of the Mountains, when he had slain the evil Anzu.
The Hero Ninurta restored the divine Tablet of Destinies to his hand.

The final part of the myth is another hymn in honour of Ninurta, identifying him with other gods.

To see what this myth was about, we need first to consider what Anzu represented. The Sumerian writing of his name is IM.DUGUD, which means literally 'heavy wind', or 'heavy raincloud'. Representations of him in art (see plate 10) show a being with outspread wings, suggesting a thundercloud. Taken together, these points show that Anzu must have represented the heavy clouds of the thunderstorm. We notice also that Anzu's home was in the mountains, and we see what happened when Anzu went into action there: darkness came down and the mountains were concealed, lightning flashed and thunder roared, and there was drenching rain. All this makes it clear that Anzu was the power in the torrential thunderstorms which occurred in the mountains.

When we look at the characteristics of Ninurta, we find that although he eventually became a god of war, this was secondary, and in early times he too, like Anzu, represented the power of the thunderstorm in the mountains. His close link with Anzu is shown in the account Gudea of Lagash gave of a dream (see page 314). He described the central figure of his dream, who must have represented Ningirsu, the local form of Ninurta, as part god, part Imdugud-bird and part Flood. In fact, the connection between Ninurta and Anzu was more than a close link: Ninurta actually was Anzu, but at another stage of religious thought. Anzu was the old prehistoric pre-anthropomorphic expression of the power in the mountain thunderstorms, but at the beginning of the third millennium the change in human society, with the development of organized city-states, brought a parallel change in religious thought. The supernatural powers now became conceived of in human form, and so the power of the mountain storms became seen in the anthropomorphic god Ninurta. But there was then the problem of the relationship between the old idea and the new: how did it happen that powers which had been seen as a lion-headed bird now belonged to a god? The myth supplied the answer: the new had overcome the old in a cosmic struggle. And Gudea in his dream saw the lower parts of Ningirsu as the Deluge, because it was Ninurta, in the form of torrential thunderstorms in the Zagros and Taurus mountains, who made the Tigris and Euphrates rise and flood.

There are subsidiary points in the myth. Adad proves unable to cope with Anzu of the mountains. Now Adad was a Weather-god who brought storms and rain, but what he specifically represented was the thunderstorms which brought rain directly to the desert and south Mesopotamia. Such rains were undoubtedly beneficent, and could bring a few weeks' growth of grass to pasture the sheep, but they were distinctly limited in their usefulness and certainly were not adequate to maintain a full programme of agriculture there. The refusal of Adad to face Anzu is the mythological reflection of this: local rainstorms could by no means replace the fructifying floods brought by the tempestuous storms in the mountains.

Etana

This is a myth in Akkadian, best known from a version found in the library of Ashurbanipal but also extant in Old Babylonian and Middle Assyrian fragments. Etana was a man who is referred to in the *Sumerian King List* as a post-diluvian king of Kish, the city which was the northern cultural centre corresponding to Erech in the south.

The opening of the myth concerns the sending of kingship to earth. Then comes an account of a friendship between an eagle and a serpent who used to hunt together and share their catch. But eventually the eagle ate the serpent's young. The serpent went weeping before Shamash, god of justice, asking to be avenged on the eagle. Shamash agreed to avenge the injured serpent, and gave him instructions to enable him to catch the eagle himself:

> Shamash opened his mouth and said to the serpent:
> Take the path, cross over the mountain.
> I will bind a wild bull for you.
> Open its inside, tear its belly,
> Make your dwelling in its belly.
> Every kind of bird of the heavens will come down to eat the meat;
> The eagle will eat the meat with them. . . .
> When he comes into the inside, you seize him by his wing.
> Tear off his wings, his pinions and his talons,
> Pluck him and throw him into a pit.

The serpent did as Shamash ordered and caught the eagle. The eagle begged for mercy, but the serpent followed the instructions of Shamash, and cast the eagle into a pit.

From the pit the eagle cried out for mercy to Shamash. Shamash replied that because of his grievous offence he himself would not directly intervene, but yet he would send a man who would come and help him.

The myth now introduces us to Etana. Daily Etana prayed to Shamash, asking that he should be given a son:

> O Lord, let (the command) come forth from your mouth; give me the plant of birth;
> Show me the plant of birth! Strip away my burden and establish a name [i.e. progeny] for me.

In reply to his prayers, Shamash directed Etana to the mountain pass leading to the pit where the eagle was trapped. The eagle would show Etana the plant of birth. Etana found his way to the pit and released the grateful eagle. Learning of Etana's quest, the eagle undertook to carry him up to the highest heaven, the heaven of Anu:

Come, I will bear you up to the heaven of Anu;
Place your breast upon my breast,
Place your palms against the feathers of my wings,
Place your arms upon my sides.

Etana did as he was instructed, and the eagle bore him upward. The poem comments on how small things looked from a great height:

The eagle spoke to Etana,
'Observe, my friend, how the land is.
The sea has turned (in appearance) into a gardener's ditch.'

But the flight was not immediately successful. At one stage the eagle, and Etana with it, crashed back to earth, but fortunately landed on brushwood which broke their fall. They tried again, apparently more than once. The end of the myth is still not clear, but the *Sumerian King List* indicates that Etana did receive the son and heir he sought.

Epics and legends

A useful rule of thumb for dividing off myths from epics is to say that the former concern gods whilst the latter recount the exploits of human heroes. But this distinction cannot always be rigidly maintained in the literature of ancient Mesopotamia, since such a protagonist as Dumuzi (Tammuz), who is usually regarded by both the ancients and ourselves as a god, may originally have represented a real historical personage. Gilgamesh, who was said to be two-thirds divine, was certainly in origin a real person.

There are some epics in a different category from the *Epic of Gilgamesh*, in that, whilst they are not to be taken as pure history, they grew up around fully historical people in a definite historical setting. The most celebrated story of this kind is the legend of Sargon of Agade, part of which is translated on pages 46f.

Another king of Sargon of Agade's dynasty around whom legends grew up was his grandson, Naram-sin. Some of the legends are reflected in very obscure allusions in omens. The principal extant legend of Naram-sin is best known from texts from Ashurbanipal's library at Nineveh, but there are also Old Babylonian fragments, a well-preserved section from Sultantepe in Turkey, and a piece in Hittite from Boghazkoi.

Legend of Naram-sin

Naram-sin introduces himself as a pious ruler. We then hear of an invasion by a great horde of warriors with ravens' faces:

> Warriors with bodies of birds-that-live-in-holes, people with ravens' faces,
> The great gods created them, and . . . Tiamat gave them suck . . .
> In the midst of the mountain they grew up, . . .
> 360,000 was the number of their troops.
> The king their father was Anubanini, the queen their mother was named Melili.

The names of seven brothers, acting as leaders, are now given. This horde, coming from the northern mountains, first overran Purushkhanda, an Akkadian trading station in what is now central Asiatic Turkey. They then thrust on into Subartu (Assyria), Gutium (central Kurdistan) and Elam (south-western Iran), finally reaching the Persian Gulf and going on to devastate Tilmun (Bahrein), Magan (Oman?) and Meluhha (perhaps Baluchistan or the Indus valley). Naram-sin did not know if these hordes were men or devils, but sent an officer to make an experiment:

> 'Touch them with a dagger, prick them with a pin!
> If blood comes out they are men like ourselves,
> If blood does not come out, they are devils, plague-demons,
> Ghosts, evil Croucher-fiends, the work of Enlil.'

The officer returned his report:

'I touched them with a dagger,
I pricked them with a pin, and blood came out.'

Naram-sin thereupon consulted the gods by omens to obtain permission to attack the invading hordes, but this was not forthcoming. Despite this he decided to take action on his own initiative. The result was disastrous. In three successive years he sent out large armies (120,000, 90,000 and 60,700 men), only to have them utterly annihilated. In addition there came upon his land all the horrors of drought, famine, plague and flood. In the fourth year, it seems, Ea persuaded the great gods to relent and to give Naram-sin a favourable omen at the New Year Festival, in consequence of which he was enabled to do something (possibly mount a successful offensive, but the passage is broken) which resulted in his taking twelve prisoners. He took omens as to whether these men should be executed, but the sentence of the gods was that they should be spared, for, as the planet Venus (that is, Ishtar) explained:

'In after days Enlil will take note of them for evil,
They are waiting for the angry heart of Enlil.
The city of those warriors will be destroyed,
Its dwellings will be set fire to and besieged;
The (men of the city) will pour out their blood,
The earth will diminish its yield of corn, the date-palm its crop,
The city of those warriors will die.
City will show hostility to city, house to house . . .'

The point seems to have been that if the twelve prisoners remained as a permanent memorial to Enlil, in due course he would ponder upon the evil that their race had done, and wipe out their cities by warfare, famine and civil strife.

Wisdom literature

Many readers are well acquainted with ancient Wisdom literature from the Old Testament books of Proverbs, Job and Ecclesiastes. Generally speaking, Wisdom literature tends to be cosmopolitan rather than national in character. This is clearly demonstrated in the Old Testament. There we find that the queen of Sheba (a kingdom in Arabia) visited Solomon on account of his 'wisdom', whilst Edom (Obadiah verse 8, Jeremiah 49:7), Egypt (Isaiah 19:11, 12) and the 'children of the East' (1 Kings 4:30) had a reputation for wisdom in Israel. Many examples of Wisdom literature are known from ancient Egypt, and works in this category were translated from one language to another across the ancient Near East.

The earliest Wisdom literature extant from Mesopotamia is a Sumerian text from the mid-third millennium known as *The Instructions of Šuruppak*, which, like other examples from both Mesopotamia and Egypt, is in the form of advice from a father to his son. Most Sumerian Wisdom literature comes in texts of the early second millennium.

The most common type of Wisdom literature in Sumerian is the proverb. From the hundreds known a few are quoted:

> Pleasure from liquor; weariness from a journey. [There is word-play in the Sumerian between *kash* 'liquor' and *kashkal* 'journey'.]

The value of alcohol in relaxing tension was well recognized:

> He who doesn't know liquor, doesn't know what is good; liquor makes the house pleasant. [A mark of the savagery of Enkidu, the being created to oppose the hero Gilgamesh (see page 341), was that he was unacquainted with bread and liquor.]

> Flatter a young man, he'll give you anything you want;
> Throw a scrap to a puppy, he'll wag his tail at you.

> The man who supports neither wife nor child,
> His nose has never borne a tether.

> To have wives is (a matter) for a man (himself),
> (For him) to have sons is (a matter) for the god.

The penis of the adulterer fits the vulva of the adulteress.

Conceiving is nice, pregnancy nasty.

It is the poor men who are the silent men in Sumer.

Resembling proverbs in spirit are what one may call precepts and maxims. 'Precepts' are pithy sentences bearing exhortations on moral behaviour, introduced as the advice of a parent to a son. This type of composition is well known from the Old Testament, for example from Proverbs 31, which is introduced as the precepts delivered to king Lemuel by his mother. The genre is also attested from Egyptian, whilst another good instance of it is an Aramaic composition called *Words of Ahiqar. The Instructions of Šuruppak*, already mentioned, is mainly a precept text. Some sections of other Sumerian precepts read:

Pay heed to the word of your mother as to the word of a god!

Where there is a quarrel, don't let your own face appear angry;
When quarrelling consumes someone like a fire, make sure you know how to extinguish (the flame) . . .
Should he say something unfriendly to you, don't say the like to him; this (involves) serious (consequences).

When you pronounce judgement, don't accompany it with censure.

Texts of the type which we call 'maxims' are better represented in Akkadian than in Sumerian; they differ from precepts in being general statements rather than direct advice. The following extracts are from the Sumerian version of a bilingual text, with Akkadian variants in square brackets:

He who sleeps with [impregnates] a man's wife, his guilt is grave.
He who casts unseemly words at his family [brothers],
He who oppresses a subordinate,
He who hands over the weak to the strong, . . .
Such a one incurs blame.

Contest texts

Another widely represented branch of Sumerian Wisdom literature is a category sometimes called 'Contest literature'. The Sumerian term for this was *adaman-duga*. *Duga* means 'speaking', and the logogram *adaman* is composed of the sign for 'man' written twice together, with the second 'man' upside down, thus: MAN.NAW. *Adaman-duga* therefore literally means 'speaking between two people opposed to each other'. The term is in fact used of the verbal contest between two parties who possess distinct characteristics, for example, Summer and Winter, Shepherd and Farmer, Copper and Precious Metal, Pickaxe and Plough. Such compositions may have been devised as entertainment at court festivals. They have a stereotyped form: first comes a mythological introduction, setting the scene at some particular point in creation or history, showing how the disputants fit into the world order, and giving the grounds for the argument. The contest proper follows: each party extols his own merits or runs down his adversary. Finally the two have recourse to a god, who pronounces the judgement between them; they accept the divine decision and become friends again.

The longest composition of this type is *Summer and Winter*. The following summary of it makes considerable use of the work of S. N. Kramer.

The god Enlil decided to establish agriculture and with it the blessings of plenty, and to this end created two brothers, Summer and Winter, assigning them certain duties. Winter brought about the birth of lambs, kids and calves; he gave abundance of milk; he brought greenness to gardens and caused the trees to come into bud; he made the fish spawn and he caused the grain to sprout. Summer, on the other hand, filled the farms with crops, brought on the harvest and loaded the granaries with corn; and caused houses, temples and cities to be built (an allusion to the fact that summer has always been the time of brickmaking in Iraq).

Their tasks performed, the two brothers made their way to

Enlil at his city, Nippur, bringing gifts connected with their functions. On the way the two became jealous of each other and began to quarrel:

> Summer shunned Winter like an enemy, wouldn't walk at his side;
> Winter . . . lost his temper and began to quarrel with Summer.

(There is an obvious parallel here to Genesis 4:2–8, where offerings brought by Cain and Abel became the grounds of a quarrel.)

This marks the beginning of the contest proper, and each contestant now proceeds to argue his own superiority. Winter points out the important part he plays in the cult:

> When the king, . . . the divine Ibbi-sin, . . .
> Is clad in his ceremonial garment and his royal robe,
> To officiate at the festival of the gods, . . .
> Then it is I who am concerned in preparing the sweet butter.

Summer makes a sharp retort on the discomforts that Winter brings:

> . . . Summer answered Winter,
> 'Winter, my brother, in your season the thick clouds roll up, . . .
> Within the town teeth are chattering,
> Even at midday no one ventures out into the streets.'

Finally the two contestants appeal to Enlil. Both state their case, Summer beginning by flattering Enlil, Winter speaking more directly. At last Enlil gives his decision:

> Enlil replied to Summer and Winter:
> 'Winter controls the waters which give life to the lands,
> He, the farmer of the gods, brings all the crops in abundance;
> O Summer, my son! How can you compare yourself with your brother Winter?'

The brothers accept the verdict, and reconciliation follows.

Texts on scribal education

Another important class of Sumerian Wisdom literature was concerned with the *edubba*, literally 'house of the tablet', in effect, 'scribal school'. These compositions, narrated in satirical vein, relate to the education of a scribe. Scribal schools were not specifically associated with temples, and most literary texts have been found not in temples but in private houses.

By the Old Babylonian period, Sumerian as a spoken language was rapidly dying. But it still dominated in literature and religion, and so scribes had to be taught to write it. This was the main function of the scribal schools. The *edubba* texts give us a glimpse of how they were organized. At the top was the headmaster or dean, called in Sumerian *ummia*, which literally means 'expert'. Next came the form-master, known as *adda edubba*, literally 'father of the tablet-house'. For particular subjects there were specialist teachers, such as the *dubshar nishid*, literally 'scribe of counting', that is, mathematics master, and the *dubshar ashaga* ('scribe of the field'), who taught geometry (see plates 23 and 24) and surveying. Scribal expertise in surveying is reflected in maps on clay tablets: plate 26B shows a late example; the earliest known, on a tablet now in Philadelphia, shows a map of Nippur not later than 1500 BC. Most prestigious of all the teachers was the *dubshar kengira*, the 'scribe of Sumerian' or classics master. Much of the actual teaching was carried out by a pupil-teacher or prefect known as 'Big Brother'. Administration was the responsibility of a school secretary, who also played a part in maintaining discipline.

This information comes mainly from a text first edited, like so many others, by S. N. Kramer. It begins with the student being asked:

> Son of the tablet-house, where did you go in your early days?

He replies:

I went to the tablet-house, . . .
I read my tablet, ate my meal,
Prepared my tablet, inscribed it, completed it.
When the tablet-house opened, I went home.
I went into the house; my father was sitting there.

The lad gave his father an account of his day and then prepared for an early supper and bed:

I'm thirsty. Give me some drink.
I'm hungry. Give me some food.
Wash my feet, make my bed, I want to sleep.
Wake me early in the morning;
I mustn't be late, or my headmaster will thrash me.

Next morning the boy's mother gave him two rolls, and off he hurried to school. But it was a bad day for him. He was late, and got into trouble. The form-master caned him for a bad exercise the previous afternoon, and he received further canings for other subjects and for his behaviour in general, which his superiors found unsatisfactory. The day proved so disastrous that the lad suggested that his father might do well to arrange to entertain the headmaster. His father responded, preparing a sumptuous entertainment for the headmaster, providing him with a fine new garment, making him a present, and feasting him. The boy was accordingly taken back into favour, the flattered headmaster prophesying a great future for him.

Another tablet from the same series of texts gives an account of the later history of the once timid schoolboy. He is now in his second year and has become a bold, conceited youth, asserting himself against 'Big Brother'. Invited to suggest what he should write, he arrogantly answers that he is not going to do mere routine exercises:

I am determined to write something of my own; I'll give the instructions.

Big Brother rebukes the conceited young man:

If you are to give the instructions, I am not your Big Brother;
Where does my Big Brother status come in then?
In the scribal art, conceit destroys a Big Brother relationship.
O Massive intelligence! . . .
Your hand may be skilful, but not with a stylus on a tablet.

He lists the student's inaptitudes in detail:

He inscribes a tablet – he doesn't manage it effectively;
He writes a letter – he gets the wrong form of address;
If he goes to divide an estate, he won't be able to do it.

There is more in the same vein, and the scornful Big Brother sums up:

O man without praise amongst the scribes,
What are you skilful at?

The student makes a spirited retort. After defending his own technical ability, he turns the attack upon the Big Brother's skill, criticizing his arithmetic, his geometry, and the accuracy of his copying of religious texts. The abuse and counter-abuse grow more heated until finally (to judge by the sequel, for the relevant passage is missing) the quarrel develops into a fight. Another tablet gives the conclusion to the affair. The headmaster appears and thunders at the delinquent student:

Why are you two behaving so? . . .
Why is it that your Big Brother exists?
(It is) because he is more learned than you in the scribal art. . . .
A person acting like you will come into conflict with his Big Brother.
There is a cudgel, . . . I will beat such a one with it;
I will put a copper chain on his foot;
. . . he shall not go outside the tablet-house for two months.

Then, says the text, the headmaster, having uttered his grim threat, took the two young men by the hand in token of reconcilation.

Texts of religious philosophy

There are also Mesopotamian examples of the type of Wisdom literature, well known to the Jewish and Christian world from the *Book of Job*, which examines the problem of evil and suffering. Sumerian is not without examples, but they are rare and difficult to interpret, and we therefore illustrate this genre from Akkadian texts.

The Poem of the Righteous Sufferer

One of the best-known works in this category is that known from its first line as *Ludlul bel nemeqi* ('I will praise the Lord of Wisdom'), or alternatively, from its subject matter, 'The Poem of the Righteous Sufferer'. It has also been referred to as 'The Babylonian Job', but this title is unmerited, for the biblical work by its spiritual insight and beauty of imagery soars so high above the Babylonian that the two can scarcely be compared. It is true that the basic theme of the work is the problem explored in *Job*, that is, that a righteous man can undergo undeserved suffering, but it does not go into the matter in any depth, and is mostly taken up with showing how the god Marduk restores his pious worshipper to prosperity.

The literary characteristics of this poem, which probably originally consisted of about 500 lines in four tablets, indicate that it originated in the Cassite period (late second millennium). It begins with a hymn emphasizing the ambivalence of the deity, with one line speaking of the consequences of his anger or punishments and the next of the blessings of his kindness; for example:

His lashes are barbed, they tear the body;
His bandaging soothes, it brings life to the doomed.

The remainder is a monologue put into the mouth of a pious Babylonian nobleman, who tells how he was deserted by all the gods, so that the king became angry with him, the courtiers plotted against him, and he became an outcast. The diviners and magicians were unable to help him. He recalls his former exemplary piety and sadly concludes that man does not know what satisfies the gods:

> I instructed my land to keep the divine ordinances,
> I urged my people to hold the name of Ishtar in esteem.
> I made praise for the king to be like that for a god,
> I taught the populace reverence for the palace.
> O that I knew that these things found favour with the god.
> What is good to oneself is an insult to the god;
> What is disgusting in a man's own heart is good to the god.
> Who knows the will of the gods in the midst of the heavens?

A whole series of devils then came up from the Underworld to seize upon the unfortunate man, leaving him incapacitated with symptoms ranging from headache and cough to fever, paralysis, and impotence.

This is as far as the work goes in exploring the problem. The remainder is concerned with restoration to prosperity. It tells of three dreams sent to the sufferer. We lack the text of the first, but in the second a young man appeared to perform rites over the sufferer on the instructions of the god. In the third dream there entered first a goddess-like queen bringing a favourable message, and then a bearded incantation priest who bore a tablet from the god Marduk with a promise of prosperity. With Marduk once more favourably disposed to the sufferer, his miseries quickly departed. The devils were sent back to the Underworld and the man recovered his health and his place in society and proceeded to the temple of Marduk to give praise.

The Babylonian theodicy

This work, possibly a little later in its date of composition than the foregoing, takes the form of a dialogue between a sufferer and his friend. From the point of view of construction it is an elaborate composition, consisting originally of twenty-seven stanzas, each of them containing eleven lines all beginning with the same syllable. The twenty-seven syllables make up an acrostic which yields a sentence meaning, 'I am Saggil-kinam-ubbib the incantation priest, worshipper of the god and king.' This is thus one of the few ancient Babylonian literary works which is not anonymous.

The argument of part of the work may be summarized as follows, the sufferer and his friend speaking in alternate stanzas:

Sufferer: I was a posthumous child and my mother died in child-bed, leaving me an orphan.
Friend: Death is the lot of all people.
Sufferer: I am in bad health, miserable and not well off.
Friend: The gods finally reward the pious.
Sufferer: But some people prosper without piety; I have been pious without prospering.
Friend: We do not understand the ways of the gods. The impious who prosper temporarily will finally get their deserts.
Sufferer: In my experience that does not happen.
Friend: It is blasphemy to dispute the decisions of the gods.

So the dialogue continues, setting the theory of divine retribution against the conflicting experience of actual life. The two speakers finally agree that men are unjust, and that they are so because the gods made them so.

To give some flavour of the original, a translation of one stanza is offered: the elaborate courteous introduction is a characteristic of the whole composition.

My friend, your mind is a reservoir whose source is unfailing,
(It is) the mass of the mighty sea of which there is no lessening.

I will pose a question to you; heed my saying!
Pay attention for a moment! Listen to my words!
My bodily grace is hidden, distress overclouds me.
My good fortune has gone by, my abundance has passed;
My vigour has turned to weakness; my prosperity has come to an end;
Lamentation and grief have disfigured my face.
Supplies from my farm are far from adequate for me;
Wine, the life of mankind, is far from sufficient.
Is there a time of favour assigned for me? I would like to know the way to it.

The Dialogue of Pessimism

This is another work in dialogue form, but of a very different character. It recounts a series of exchanges between a master and his slave, the master each time proposing some course of action, to the propriety of which the slave at once offers glowing testimony. The master immediately makes a volte-face, matched by the succeeding speech of the slave, who is equally ready to recommend the opposite course. Only at the end does the slave offer an independent opinion, when, directly asked what course of action really is worthwhile, he answers:

To have my neck and your neck broken
And us thrown into the river – that is good!

It can hardly be denied that the work is satire. This is not, however, to deny that, underlying the humorous treatment, there was serious consideration of a philosophical problem, namely, What is the purpose of life? A section will give some idea of the tone of the work:

[*Master*]: 'Slave, make yourself agreeable!'
[*Slave*]: 'Yes, sir, yes!'
[*Master*]: 'Fetch water for my hands straightaway and give it to me,

So that I may make sacrifice to my god.'
[*Slave*]: 'Do that, sir, do that!
Anyone who makes sacrifice to his god is a happy man,
He makes investment upon investment.'
[*Master*]: 'No, slave, I will by no means make a sacrifice to my god.'
[*Slave*]: 'Don't, sir, don't!
You can train a god so that he trots after you like a dog,
When he wants rites from you, or anything else.'

The cynical final speech of the slave came near to blasphemy, from the point of view of official religion.

Akkadian proverbs and related categories

We have already noted proverbs and associated genres in Sumerian, but there are also examples in Akkadian. Most Akkadian proverbs occur alongside a Sumerian equivalent, indicating their ultimate source, but there are a few instances of collections of proverbs written solely in Akkadian.

Some examples of the various categories are offered.

Proverbs

A hungry man will dig into a brick-built house.
Would you hand a lump of mud to someone throwing things around?
At the gate of the judge's house the mouth of a sinful woman is mightier than her husband's.

Akkadian proverbs are sometimes appositely quoted in letters. For example, king Shamshi-adad of Assyria (early second millennium) wrote to his son Yasmah-adad telling him not to mix in political intrigues; to drive home his point he quoted an old saying: 'A bitch that mated with more than one dog had lame pups.'

Precepts

These usually take the same form in Akkadian as in Sumerian, that is, advice from a father to a son. A typical example is a text known as the *Counsel of Wisdom*, which comes from the second millennium. Like Lord Chesterfield, this father gave his son good, practical, down-to-earth advice, based not on ethical principles but on pragmatic considerations. The son is exhorted to shun bad companions; lest

> (Turning) from good habits you become associated in their attitude;
> You will diminish the value of your service, forsake your path;
> You will allow your opinion, which was profound and sensible, to become distorted.

The son is also advised to speak guardedly; to avoid blasphemy, falsehood and slander; and not to get mixed up in lawsuits. He should not make a slave-girl mistress of his household, nor marry a temple-prostitute. If put in charge of his prince's treasure-house he must shun the opportunity of embezzlement, not, be it noted, for moral reasons but because of the risk of being found out. Above all, he should worship the gods regularly and give them their due offerings and worship, which would bring their automatic reward:

> Sacrifice prolongs life,
> And prayer absolves guilt.

Maxims

A typical Akkadian example is the following:

> When you are provident, your god is for you;
> When you are improvident, your god is not for you.

The spirit is that of 'Trust in God and keep your powder dry.'

Anecdotes

The Babylonian sense of humour is illustrated by pithy stories, such as the following:

When a stallion came up and mounted a she-mule,
As he was riding her he whispered in her ear;
'The foal which you bear, let it be a courser like me;
Don't make it like an ass that has to carry a pannier.'

The joke is, of course, that a she-mule is sterile. Here is another example:

A little bird,[9] as it sat on an elephant,
Said, 'Brother, do I bother you? I'll be off to the watering-place.'
The elephant answered the little bird:
'I didn't know you were sitting there – What are you, anyway? –
And I shan't know when you get off.'

14

Mathematics and Astronomy; Medicine

> What, amongst other fine discourse, pleased me most, was Sir G. Ent [President of the College of Physicians], about respiration; that it is not to this day known, or concluded on, among physicians, nor to be done either, how the action is managed by nature, or for what use it is. (Samuel Pepys, *Diary*, 22 January 1665–6)

Numeration and mathematics

ONE of the surprises which met Assyriologists when cuneiform texts other than the common run of historical, ritual and economic material began to become available and intelligible, was the advanced stage of development which Babylonian mathematics had reached at an early period.

The origin of writing was related to the practical need of keeping records of temple property and produce. For this purpose number symbols were also required, and these are found from the beginning of writing in Mesopotamia. The cuneiform signs for the numerals were basically very simple. The single vertical wedge (in the earliest period , an elliptical impression produced by a slanting thrust with the rounded end of the stylus) denoted the numeral 1, and for the higher units groups of wedges were used, thus:

10 was denoted by a broad diagonal wedge (in the earlier period a circular impression) and multiples of 10 up to 50 by groups of broad diagonal wedges, thus:

Numbers up to 59 which were not exact multiples of 10 were represented by a group of broad wedges for the tens followed by a group of vertical wedges for the units, thus:

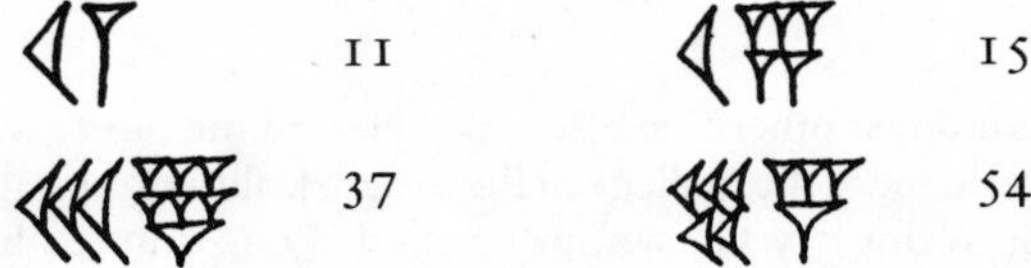

A less common procedure was to use a minus sign, , to assist in representing numbers just under a round number. Thus 19 was sometimes written as , i.e. 20 − 1.

At 60 complications arose. From the very beginning of Sumerian civilization two systems of numeration, a decimal and a sexagesimal, were in use. The decimal system, employing powers of 10, requires no explanation. The sexagesimal system used powers of 60 (that is, multiples of 1, 60, and 3600, corresponding to the units, tens and hundreds of the decimal system). This had the advantage of facilitating calculations involving fractions, since 60 has a large number of divisors (1, 2, 3, 4, 5, 6, 10, 12, 15, 20, 30), so that it was easy to represent, for example, $\frac{1}{2}$ ($\frac{30}{60}$), $\frac{1}{3}$ ($\frac{20}{60}$), $\frac{1}{4}$ ($\frac{15}{60}$), $\frac{1}{5}$ ($\frac{12}{60}$), and so on. It was seldom that either system was used with complete consistency, the only cases of consistent and exclusive usage of the sexagesimal system being in mathematical or astronomical calculations. Elsewhere the two systems occurred side by side, just as in Great Britain a decimal system is used alongside a system based on powers of 12, whilst the sexagesimal system continues in use for geometry and for the measurement of time.

As 60 was itself a unit in the sexagesimal system, it could be denoted by a vertical wedge, originally distinguished by its greater size from the wedge representing 1, though the distinction in size later disappeared. Correspondingly we find for numbers between 60 and 99 such groups as

70 80

90 94

On this system 100 would be , and indeed was often written in that way. Alternatively, however, 100 could be represented either (in the early period) by a specially big circle (implying a purely decimal system, in which 100, the large circle, is considered as a higher power of 10, the small circle), or by a special sign (pronounced ME), which in origin represents the actual pronunciation in Semitic of the word for 100. There are further modifications and combinations available to denote higher numbers. Thus 120 could be represented as

= 2 × 60 (the wedges originally being larger than the wedge for 1)

or (in the early Sumerian period) = 100 + 10 + 10

or = one ME + twenty.

1000, significant in the decimal system, had the special sign , compounded of and , and thus denoting 10 × 100. In the sexagesimal system the significant high number was 3600, the square of 60. This was denoted originally by a very big circle (also used, as already noted, for the square of 10 in the decimal system), and finally by the sign

It will be seen from the examples given that the germ of a

place-value notation (a system in which the value of a number-symbol depends upon its position relative to other symbols) was already present in the numerals used in Babylonia from an early period. For the less mathematically-minded, it may be pointed out that our own system is a place-value notation: thus in the numbers written 15 and 51, in the former the '5' symbol means 'five' whilst in the latter the identical symbol means 'fifty'. The use of Roman numerals illustrates a system which is not a place-value notation: thus although the groups iv and vi have different values, the symbol 'v' in whatever position it occurs means 'five' and nothing else. In cuneiform writing 𒁹𒌋 is quite distinct from 𒌋𒁹, since in the former the 𒁹 means 'sixty', whilst in the latter it means 'one', so that the two groups of which it is a part denote respectively 'seventy' and 'eleven'. King Esarhaddon made ingenious political use of the fact that these two numbers differ in cuneiform only in the position of the two constituent symbols; for the details see above, page 117.

This place-value system was developed and extensively employed by Babylonian mathematicians, initially under the influence of the scale of weights which occurs in economic documents from Sumerian times onwards. The basis of the Sumerian and Babylonian weight system was the mina: this weight, in the region of one to two pounds, was sub-divided into 60 shekels, whilst 60 minas made a larger unit, the talent. Thus the Babylonians were familiar with a numeration of X-Y-Z in which the units of X were 60 times those of Y and the units of Y 60 times those of Z. From this conception arose the possibility of an elaborated place-value notation, based on a sexagesimal system, in which X-Y-Z could mean either

$$(X \times 60 \times 60) + (Y \times 60) + Z$$

$$\text{or } (X \times 60) \quad + (Y) \quad + \left(\frac{Z}{60}\right)$$

$$\text{or even } (X) \quad + \left(\frac{Y}{60}\right) \quad + \left(\frac{Z}{60 \times 60}\right)$$

Such a system has two obvious disadvantages, both of which arise from the absence of a zero sign or a symbol corresponding to a decimal (or rather one should say here 'sexagesimal') point. In our own decimal system a number like 538.4 is unambiguous because of the convention that the first symbol to the left of the point represents units, the second to the left tens, and the third hundreds, whilst the first symbol to the right of the point represents tenths. The mathematically-minded will perhaps excuse elaboration of something which to them is obvious; but there may be readers for whom it will be useful or even surprising to emphasize that this decimal system of ours is no part of the nature of number itself but a mere (even if a very useful) convention. In the writing 538, 'three tens' is in fact simply represented by a 3 and 'five hundreds' simply by a 5, in each case made unambiguous by its position. Ambiguity could arise if there were either no tens or no units in the number: in such an instance this ambiguity is removed in our system by placing a zero sign in the appropriate position. If there are respectively no tens or no units, then to represent five hundred and eight or five hundred and thirty, we generally do not write 5 8, or 53 , which could be ambiguous, but use the symbols 508, 530.

Applied to Babylonian numerals, ambiguities of the two types referred to could appear in the following forms. In a writing like the vertical wedges could be intended to represent either the 'units' or the 'sixties' column, and the four broad wedges either the 'sixtieths' or the 'units' column. Thus such a writing (generally transcribed in the form 2,40) could denote in our terms either

$$(2 \times 60) + 40, \text{ that is, } 160$$

$$\text{or} \qquad 2 + \frac{40}{60}, \text{ that is, } 2\tfrac{2}{3}$$

The second ambiguity is that the two groups of wedges might not denote consecutive powers of the sexagesimal system; that is, in the cuneiform writing instanced above, if the four broad wedges represented simply forty units, the two vertical wedges might have represented not 'two sixties' but 'two' in the next higher power, namely, 'two times sixty squared', that is, 2×3600; 𒈫𒐏 would then represent $7200 + 40 = 7240$. In the earlier period this ambiguity was sometimes avoided by writing a number with the two elements spaced widely apart when they did not represent successive powers of 60. Thus 7240, which equals

$$(2 \times 60 \times 60) + (0 \times 60) + (40 \times 1)$$

might have been written as 𒈫 𒐏 very widely spaced: this was not, however, consistently applied. In the Seleucid period a special sign for zero (𒑱) was used in such cases.

It is obvious that errors could arise in such a system, and quite certainly occasionally they did. It is worthy of mention, however, that Neugebauer, the greatest modern authority on Babylonian mathematics, confessed that he made more errors in checking ancient computations than did the scribes in the original documents.

The mathematical texts with which we are acquainted belong to two distinct periods separated by well over a millennium. The earlier and larger group comes from the Old Babylonian period, the remainder from the Seleucid period, after 300 BC.

It has generally been assumed that behind the relatively advanced Old Babylonian mathematics there lay a long period of gradual development. There is, however, no concrete evidence in favour of such a supposition, and Neugebauer points out that in all instances of periods of mathematical advance of which we actually know the antecedents, the fact has been a century or so of rapid progress set as an island between two long periods of stagnation.

It may be well to re-emphasize at this point that the vast majority of the hundreds of thousands of cuneiform tablets so far known are economic in content, dealing with prosaic matters such as receipts, loans and ration issues. The number of purely mathematical cuneiform texts known amounts only to hundreds, comprising about a hundred 'problem texts' and two hundred 'table texts'. The problem texts are concerned with algebraical or geometrical problems, whilst the table texts contain tables for multiplication and division and the calculation of reciprocals, squares, square roots, cubes, cube roots and so on. Many of these table texts, coming largely from the city of Nippur, were evidently school exercises. This is clear from the fact that on some tablets the same table is repeated in different hands, whilst on others one finds mathematical tables written on one side and vocabularies (one of the items much used in the training of scribes) on the other. Nippur is now known to have been a flourishing centre of scribal education in Old Babylonian times, and mathematics was obviously a part of the scribal curriculum.

As to the actual level of mathematical achievement in Babylonia in the Old Babylonian period (about 1800 BC), Neugebauer compares it with that of the early Renaissance. It was basically algebraical, but the properties of elementary sequences, such as arithmetic and geometric progressions, were known, as well as a certain number of geometrical relationships. It is now clear that the substance of what is known to us as the Pythagoras theorem – that in a right-angled triangle the sum of the squares of the sides about the right-angle equals the square of the hypotenuse – was known to the Babylonians as a practical fact: there is, however, no evidence that the Babylonians could formally prove such a theorem, and though some authorities have supposed one Old Babylonian tablet covered with geometrical diagrams (see plates 23 and 24) to be concerned with theoretical proofs of the relationship between areas of different figures, Babylonian mathematical procedures (like all Babylonian science) generally rested on empirical knowledge rather than formal proof. The value of π was fairly accurately known as 3⅛, which is correct to about 0.6 per cent: this may be contrasted with the situation in Israel in the time of Solomon nearly a millennium later when, as 1 Kings 7:23 shows, π was inaccurately taken as exactly 3. Quadratic equations involving terms up to the eighth degree are known, and, as already mentioned, there are tablets of square roots and cube roots.

A brief account of two simple examples of Old Babylonian problems follows. The first is an example of a quadratic equation. It is set down initially in a literal translation, then with (it is hoped) sufficient explanation to make it intelligible to the reader who has at some time mastered elementary algebra.

> I have added the surface-area and the side of the square: 45′
> You shall put down 1, the unit.
> You shall break (it) in halves: 30′
> You shall cross-multiply 30′ and 30′: 15′
> You shall add 15′ to 45′: 1
> That is the square of 1
> You shall take away the 30′, which you have multiplied by itself, from 1: 30′, the side of the square.

When one takes into account that the sexagesimal system was in use in mathematical problems, this becomes much clearer. 45′ then represents $\frac{45}{60}$ = ¾, 30′ represents $\frac{30}{60}$ = ½, and 15′ represents $\frac{15}{60}$ = ¼. The sum may then be stated as follows:

Area of square plus side of square = ¾
Take coefficient (of the linear measurement) as unity.

Half of coefficient	= ½
Square of ½	= ¼
¼ plus ¾	= 1
Square root of 1	= 1
1 minus ½	= ½

Finally, set out in modern symbols, the processes may be expressed as follows:

$$x^2 + x = 3/4$$
$$x^2 + x + (1/2)^2 = 3/4 + 1/4$$
$$(x + 1/2)^2 = 1$$
$$x + 1/2 = \sqrt{1} = 1$$
$$x = 1 - 1/2 = 1/2$$

(The Babylonian mathematician did not, it will be observed, concern himself with the negative value of x.)

An Old Babylonian tablet dealing with geometrical relationships is illustrated in plates 23 and 24. The text is divided into sections, each of which consists of a figure with beneath it a note of the construction. The student was apparently required to calculate the area of the various shapes constructed. One section goes as follows:

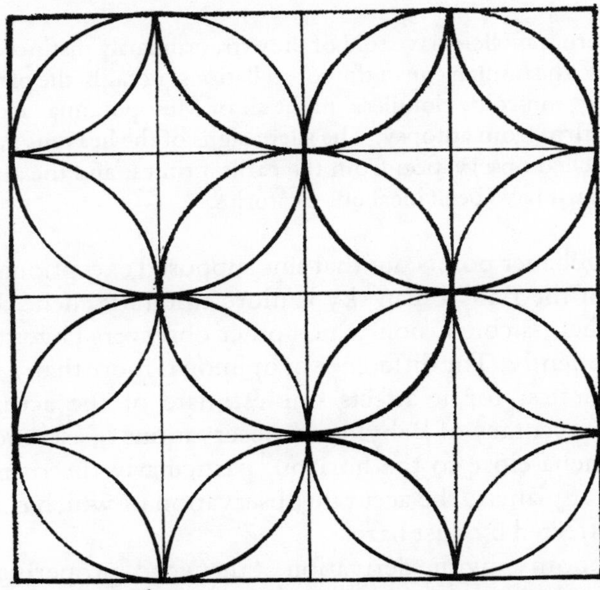

A square, the side is 1. Inside it (are) 4 quadrants, (and) 16 boat-shapes. I have drawn 5 regular concave-sided tetragons. This area, what is it?

Astronomy

Comparatively few Western Europeans with any pretensions to culture are able to live far from a city, with all that that involves in atmospheric pollution and bright street-lighting, both of them factors which seriously obscure the clarity of the night sky. In much of Iraq, however, these two factors are largely absent, whilst furthermore for much of the year it is very pleasant to sit outside after dark to enjoy the cool of the evening after the heat of the day. Thus it often happens that the European tourist or archaeologist, transported to Iraq and changing his habits accordingly, virtually sees the night sky for the first time, and is amazed by what he sees. As an interesting consequence of this, books by Assyriologists and others tend to contain extravagant statements about the brilliance of the night sky in Babylonia. As an instance, a Danish scholar states:

> Modern travellers have told of the extraordinarily distinct appearance to the human eye of the constellations, notably the planets, in the dry and cold, cloudless, night air of Mesopotamia, accounts I can affirm from autopsy. The silent signs of the heavens naturally compelled observation from the earliest times, and the ziggurats . . . must have been ideal observatories.

Neugebauer points out that this supposed exceptional 'brilliance of the Babylonian sky is more a literary cliché than an actual fact', a conclusion which other observers have reached independently. The difference of opinion is more than a matter of aesthetics, for it affects our estimate of the actual and possible accuracy of Babylonian observations of astronomical phenomena close to the horizon, particularly the rising and setting of planets, the accurate observation of which could be much affected by dust haze.

Astronomy, by the derivation of the word, properly means studying the laws governing the stars: it is essentially a mathematical discipline, and idle stargazing is not astronomy. It has usually been assumed that astronomy arose out of astrology, and whilst this remains a strong possibility, it has not been conclusively proved.

To discuss the relationship in ancient Babylonia between astrology and astronomy, we need first to clarify what we understand by astrology. In modern times astrology generally means horoscopic astrology, which involves the absurd belief that the fortunes of an individual throughout his life are related in a definable manner to the position of celestial bodies at the moment of his birth. This kind of astrology was not of ancient origin in Mesopotamia, and only arose in the second half of the first millennium BC. But long before this, the Babylonians were observing celestial phenomena and using them as omens to predict specific events. Traditional meanings were attached to particular incidents, sometimes on the basis of symbolism, sometimes from the precedent that such-and-such an event in the heavens on an earlier occasion was followed by such-and-such an event on earth. Some of the events noted in this way were not limited to sun, moon, stars and planets but concerned meteorological data or even geophysical happenings such as earthquakes; but the Babylonians and Assyrians lumped these all together without distinction of category, and to attain an accurate picture of their thinking we need to do the same. Such forecasts never concerned ordinary individuals: they referred either to the king, as embodying the state, or directly to the state, in relation to such matters as harvest, floods, epidemics, rebellions, invasions and the like. Some writers have attempted to reintroduce an archaic term, 'judicial astrology', for this application of events observed in the sky, but in view of the common current sense of the word 'judicial' this is confusing, and I propose to call this 'omen astrology'. The following are examples of the practical application of this procedure:

> If the sun stands in the station of the moon, the king of the land will be secure on the throne.
>
> If the sun stands above or below the moon, the foundation of the throne will be secure, the king of the land will stand in his justice [meaning of final phrase is obscure].
>
> If the sun and the moon are invisible, the king of the land will

show wisdom [literally, will make broad the ear].

In the night Saturn came near to the moon. Saturn is the star of the sun. This is the interpretation: it is favourable to the king, (for) the sun is the king's star.

If there is an earthquake in the month Nisan, the king's land will rebel against him.

If the heavens rain down in the month Ab, there will be a defeat of people. If a whirlwind comes from the west, there will be a defeat of the people of the west. If it thunders twice, the land which sent you a message of hostility will send you a message of peace.

The foregoing reports come from Assyria in the first half of the first millennium, but there are astrological omens which go back at least to the beginning of the second millennium and possibly to the period of Sargon of Agade (twenty-fourth century BC). These early omens were subsequently grouped in collections, known as 'series', which reached their final form in the late second or early first millennium BC. The most important is called *Enuma Anu Enlil*. Here is an extract:

If an eclipse occurs in the month of Siwan on the fourteenth day, and the (Moon-)god in his darkening darkens at the east side above and brightens on the west side below, a north wind gets up in the first night-watch and subsides in the middle night-watch, the (Moon-)god . . . is giving thereby a decision for Ur and the king of Ur: the king of Ur will see famine, the dead will be numerous. The king of Ur, his son will do violence to him, but Shamash [the god of justice] will catch the son who does violence to his father, and he will die for the impiety towards his father. A son of the king, who has not been proclaimed for kingship, shall take the throne.

The first text which appears to be purely astronomical goes back to the seventeenth century BC, although we only have it in the form of first-millennium copies. It is a list of heliacal risings and settings of Venus for the twenty-one years of the reign of king Ammisaduga of Babylon (1646–1626 BC). Despite some errors of transmission, these records are sufficiently accurate to enable modern astronomers to calculate the groups of year dates to which they could refer, and in consequence they have become the main basis for fixing the chronology of early second-millennium history. We do not know the purpose for which these records were originally made. In the form in which they have been preserved, incorporated into the series *Enuma Anu Enlil*, omens are attached to them, but the existing omens are certainly secondary. There is no proof that the observations were originally made to serve as the basis of omens, although this possibility cannot be excluded. But there is the alternative possibility that the observations were the work of some Babylonian genius, moved by scientific curiosity to see if he could establish the basis for the periodic disappearance and reappearance of the planet Venus.

Apart from these records of the heliacal rising and setting of Venus, the oldest astronomical documents extant from Mesopotamia are the so-called astrolabes. These are clay tablets inscribed with three concentric circles divided by twelve radii. In each of the thirty-six divisions thus made is the name of a constellation together with some numbers. The purpose of these astrolabes is not altogether clear, but it is evident that they formed a kind of celestial map and that they were probably related to the origin of the zodiac. The numbers mentioned in the astrolabes are related to each other in an arithmetical progression.

In copies themselves dating from about 700 BC but based on older material, we have two texts called ^{mul}APIN. In these the fixed stars are classified in three 'roads', and these texts in fact constitute a simple descriptive account of basic astronomical conceptions, divorced from mythology.

Astronomical observations

By 700 BC we also find the systematic reports of observations of astronomical events, supposed to bear on state affairs, already mentioned. These reports were certainly related primarily to omen astrology, and not only do they lack any mathematical treatment of astronomical phenomena, but they even fail to distinguish between astronomical and meteorological phenomena. None the less they do show that it was already recognized that solar eclipses could only occur at the new moon, and lunar at the full, which indicates the systematic recording of such events. Consistent with this is the report of the Greek astronomer Ptolemy (who lived in Alexandria in the second century AD) that records of eclipses were available to him from 747 BC onwards. Thus although the original purpose of observations of this type was astrological, such systematic observations from 700 BC onwards provided data from which values for the various periodic phenomena could be derived. In other words, on the basis of such series of observations extending over centuries, it was possible to calculate average apparent movements of the sun, moon and planets. Neugebauer argues that this knowledge did not develop into a systematic mathematical theory before 500 BC, since there was only haphazard intercalation up to 480 BC. Throughout Babylonian history the calendar was lunar, the month beginning (as still in Judaism and Islam) with sunset on the evening upon which the new moon was visible shortly after sunset: twelve lunar months amount only to approximately 354 days, which is 11¼ days short of the solar year. Thus an additional month was required roughly once in three years to bring the lunar calendar into step with the solar year. By some time between 500 and 400 BC, this was being done on a mathematical basis, the rule of seven intercalations in nineteen years being apparently in use. The actual order of intercalation in the nineteen-year cycle was as follows, the asterisks denoting a year containing an intercalary month:

1*	2	
3*	4	5
6*	7	8
9*	10	
11*	12	13
14*	15	16
17*	18	19

In the first year of this cycle the intercalation was in the middle of the year, in other cases at the end.

Once values for the principal periodic phenomena had been worked out, the next major development, applied originally and principally to the moon, was to consider the complicated movement of celestial bodies as compounded of a number of simpler periodic effects, and to apply the periodic deviations as corrections to the average movement. That is to say, if the sun and moon moved in the sky with apparently constant velocity, it would be simple to calculate their relative positions at any time and hence to arrive at the moment of new or full moon. In fact the actual apparent movement of the moon varies from the ideal (or average) apparent movement: such variations were recorded, found to be amenable to treatment as periodic phenomena and applied in this form as corrections to the ideal (or average) movement of the moon. Neugebauer concludes, from the details of the manner in which this method was applied in astronomical texts, that it was invented by a single individual in the fourth or third century BC: it was certainly in existence by 250 BC. The method was applied not only to the moon but also to the movements of the planets. Cuneiform texts from the last two or three centuries BC make it clear that the methods used by the Babylonians for calculating the movements of the moon were – as Neugebauer puts it – 'among the finest achievements of ancient science, comparable only to the works of Hipparchus and Ptolemy'. The Babylonians had only very crude equipment for observation – there is certainly no trace from texts or archaeology of such a thing as a telescope, although lenses of rock-crystal have been found – and individual observations were undoubtedly of no high order of accuracy. Thus the high achievements of late Babylonian astronomy were the result of the application of the relatively advanced mathematical techniques, developed over a millennium earlier, to a long series of fairly rough observations, to give results more accurate than could be obtained from any single observation.

The texts referred to, containing tables of the positions of the sun, moon and planets calculated for regular time intervals, are known as ephemerides; closely related to the ephemerides are 'procedure texts' giving the rules for calculating an ephemeris. About three hundred texts of these two types are known, a hundred from Erech and the remainder from Babylon. The periods covered by these computations extend altogether from about 230 BC to AD 49. Some of these texts are provided with a colophon giving the date of writing, and this shows that the tablets were usually written at a date near the beginning of the period covered by the computation. Thus the latest text in this class, of which the period of fifty-six years covered ends with AD 49, was probably written early in the first decade BC. The latest astronomical text of all – and the latest of all known cuneiform texts – has a date of AD 75.

There is another large group of astronomical texts, distinct from the ephemerides and procedure texts. Dating mainly from the sixth century onwards, some of these texts list, and others predict, lunar and planetary phenomena. Amongst this group is a minority, concerned with data on eclipses, going back to the eighth century.

Medicine

In Iraq before the revolution of 1958, the capital, Baghdad, contained only one-fifth of the population of the country but about three-quarters of the physicians. The situation between the capital and the rest of the country may well have been similar in ancient Babylonia, where the apparent non-availability of physicians to the ordinary man led Herodotus in the fifth century BC to write of the Babylonians:

> They bring out all their sick into the streets, for they have no regular doctors. People that come along offer the sick man advice, either from what they personally have found to cure such a complaint, or from what they have known someone else to be cured by. No one is allowed to pass by a sick person without asking him what ails him.

Herodotus was wrong in saying that there were no regular doctors, for the profession of the physician (*asu*) was attested from the middle of the third millennium, and medical practitioners and aspects of the profession are referred to in such categories of texts as legal codes, literary works, and letters. One literary text, *The Poor Man of Nippur*, tells us that the *asu* had a distinctive tonsure and carried his equipment in a bag.

Although it is the *asu* whose title we translate as 'physician', he was not the only functionary treating illness and disease, and at some periods and places not the principal one. Of at least equal importance in this area was the *ashipu*, whom we have already met on page 261. There, where we were speaking of him as someone who was expert at driving out evil influences in general, we rendered his title as 'exorcist'. But Babylonians saw disease as one particular aspect of demonic activity, and so the *ashipu* included this amongst his many functions, and in such contexts we are justified in calling him a witchdoctor.

The witchdoctor seems to have been held in higher esteem than the plain physician, as is still the case in parts of Africa and Asia. In Babylonia this was perhaps because to Babylonian thinking he was a greater expert, since his skill was not limited merely to healing a sick man: he could also do such things as drive evil influences out of a house or away from crops, and he even had the power to counter the evil influences at work in earthquakes and eclipses.

People of the two professions often worked closely together in the treatment of the sick. Both *asu* and *ashipu* are sometimes listed in a group with lamentation-priests and diviners, indicating that the *asu* was not thought of as essentially different in kind from these other functionaries, and that his expertise was regarded as part of the system for handling the supernatural.

Attempts have been made to define how the physician (*asu*) differed from the witchdoctor (*ashipu*) in treating sickness, but it is not easy to tie this down. It would be a comfortable solution to say that the *asu* used rational methods of treatment, and the *ashipu* magic, but in fact the distinction was by no means so clear-cut. It is certain that alongside methods of healing that were rational, the *asu* also employed a certain amount of magical humbug, and on the other hand the *ashipu* sometimes made use of medical materials. The difference was probably rather a matter of emphasis, coupled with the feeling that the *ashipu* covered a wider field with his expertise.

The Babylonians and Assyrians regarded disease as being of supernatural origin, and magical texts and omens are full of references to diseases reflecting this belief. Our main knowledge of Babylonian medicine is from diagnostic texts, which mainly give lists of symptoms, and from texts which contain prescriptions for the treatment of various complaints. The two classes are not completely separate, and one may find prescriptions in the diagnostic texts, or diagnoses amongst the prescriptions.

The diagnostic texts shed light on the basic notions behind the medical theories of the ancient Babylonians, and confirm, as one could equally deduce from magical and religious texts, that illness was generally thought to be due either to the 'hand' of a deity or to possession by a devil. In accordance with this view, a sick man might be treated either by rational medicine (or possibly surgery) to reduce the symptoms, or by magical procedures (efficacious then as now with cases of hysterical illness) to expel the supposed evil influence.

Diagnostic texts

These texts, dealing with symptoms and maladies, were edited in antiquity, probably in the Cassite period (late second millennium) into what Assyriologists call a canonical form, meaning a final standard wording. There is a good modern edition of this by a French scholar, R. Labat, under the title *Traité Akkadien de Diagnostics et Pronostics Médicaux*, I (1951).

The work originally contained forty chapters, and was divided into five sections. The first section, comprising two tablets or chapters, is not strictly medical at all, although the ancient scribes regarded it as part of the series. It actually contains omen texts concerning the interpretation of signs seen by the witchdoctor or some other person on his way to the patient's house, thus:

> If the door of someone's house, where the sick man is lying, cries out [i.e. creaks] like a lion, he has eaten something which is taboo to his god; he will drag out and then die.
>
> If [the exorcist] sees either a black dog or a black pig, that sick man will die.
>
> If [the exorcist] sees a white pig, that sick man will live . . .
>
> If [the exorcist] sees pigs which keep lifting up their tails, (as to) that sick man, anxiety will not come near him . . .
>
> If a snake falls on the sick man's bed, that sick man will get well.

The second section consists of twelve tablets which go through symptoms visible in the body, grouping them according to different organs and parts of the body; it is the symptoms themselves rather than the disease which are the interest of these tablets.

> If (the sick man) keeps crying out 'My skull! My skull!', (it) is the hand of a god.
>
> If he is beaten in his head [i.e. if his head throbs] on the right side, it is the hand of Adad . . .
>
> If he is beaten in his head and if the muscles of his brow, his hands and his feet are affected together, being red and burning, it is the hand of a god; he will live.
>
> If from his head to his feet he is full of red pustules, and his body is white, he has been attacked when in bed with a woman; hand of the god Sin . . .
>
> If he is puffy as to the temples, and his ears do not hear, the hands of his god are put upon him; he will die.
>
> If his brow is white and his tongue is white, his illness will be long, but he will recover.
>
> If he grinds his teeth, and his hands and feet shake, it is the hand of the god Sin; he will die.
>
> If the sick man's right ear throbs, his illness is serious but he will

live. If his left ear throbs, (cause for) anxiety. If both his ears throb, he will die . . .

If his face is white and overcast with yellow, and his mouth and lips are full of ulcers, and his left eye twitches, he will die.

If his neck keeps turning to the left, his hands and feet are stretched out, his eyes are wide open to the sky, spittle runs out of his mouth, he makes a croaking noise, he is delirious [literally 'doesn't know himself'], . . . it is epilepsy (?); hand of the god Sin.

If his neck throbs and his head keeps falling, and his hands and feet keep swelling up and he rubs (them) against the ground; the demon Handmaid of Lilu has seized him.

The treatise continues in like vein through symptoms of the throat, gullet, arms, hands, fingers, chest, breasts, loins, back, abdomen (in various sub-divisions), hips, anus, penis, urine, testicles, thighs, feet and other parts of the body. Thus:

If blood flows out of his penis, (it is) the hand of Shamash; sign of Land-of-no-return [i.e. the Underworld].

If his penis and testicles are inflamed, the hand of the goddess Dilbat [Venus] has reached him in his bed.

If his testicles are inflamed, if his penis is covered with sores, he has gone in to the high-priestess of his god.

In the third section (containing ten tablets) the prognoses are grouped according to the progress of the disease from day to day; at the end of this section groups of symptoms are listed as indicating specific diseases. The texts in this section have contents typically of the form 'If, when a man has been ill so many days, such-and-such a symptom is (*or* is not) visible, then his fate will be so-and-so', the period referred to increasing from one day up to a month or so. The following are examples:

If, having been ill three days, he gets up; in the night, easing [literally 'loosing'] of the illness. . . .

If, having been ill four days, he keeps putting his hand on his belly and his face is overcast with yellow, he will die.

If, having been ill for four or five days, sweat keeps coming over him, easing of the illness: if he has been ill for four or five days, hand of Ahhazu [name of a demon, literally 'the Seizer'].

If, having been ill for five days, blood comes out of his mouth on the sixth day, his illness will be eased; it is *setu*-fever.

If, having been ill for five days, his flesh is overcast with yellow (and) his eyes are full of blood, he will die. . . .

If, having been ill for five or ten days continuously, he suffers from chronic difficulty in breathing (?), he will die . . .

If, having been ill with a severe illness for five or ten days continuously, a steady (trickle of) blood comes out of his mouth for five days [or possibly 'on the fifth day'] and (then) stops, his illness will be eased; it is the *setu*-fever; he is cured; there is no 'hit' . . .

If, for five, ten, fifteen or twenty days the fingers of his hands and (the toes of) his feet stay contracted and he cannot open (them) nor separate (them), it is the Hand of Ishtar; she will, however, set (him) free; he will get on all right and will live.

If his illness keeps coming upon him in the middle watch (of the night), he has had sexual relations with someone's wife; hand of the deity Urash.

If, when he is ill, his body is very cold, his illness will be prolonged and he will die. If, when he is ill, he cannot keep in his stomach the food which he eats and cannot keep sustenance in his mouth but casts (it) out of his mouth, he will die.

If he is ill in the morning, and his illness leaves him in the afternoon, but returns to him quickly, abatement of his illness; he will get up and be well on

the second day some time before midday,
the third day at some time in the afternoon,
the fourth day before twilight,
the fifth day before the end of the day,
the sixth day before the (first) watch,
the seventh day before the middle watch,
the eighth day before the dawn (watch),
the ninth day before day-break,
or the tenth day.

As examples of the type of text at the end of the third section, in which specific syndromes are described, one may instance the following:

If a man's body is yellow, his face is yellow, and his eyes are yellow, and the flesh is flabby, it is jaundice.

If grief falls upon him, his throat is tight, when he eats food or drinks water it doesn't agree with him, he says 'Oh, my heart!' and keeps on sighing, he is sick with love-sickness; it is the same (diagnosis) for a man or a woman.

If a man's penis and the top of his stomach are burning, if he has a glowing fever, the bottom of his stomach troubles him and his stomach is disturbed, if he is burning in his arms, feet and belly, that man is suffering from a venereal disease; hand of the goddess Ishtar.

The fourth section of the work, originally comprising ten tablets, is very badly damaged and little of it remains. Amongst other things the remaining fragments refer to treatment in specific cases, as well as giving the description of various syndromes:

If something like sleep keeps taking him, if his limbs are unsteady, his ears sing, his mouth is gripped and he cannot speak; it is the hand of a malevolent *alu*-demon. If, after washing with water, as he comes up from the river he is taken with convulsions and falls down, the Croucher-demon of the river has struck him.

If grief falls upon him, and he begs for everything he sees, if he is burning, has sweating (fits) daily, keeps having furies of desire (for things) and coughs up (his) stomach until they bring (them) to him, and then when they bring (them) to him he sees but doesn't comprehend; it is the hand of a ghost which struck him in the water.

If the 'hand of Ishtar' turns (in) him to epilepsy(?), (this indicates) hand of the god Sin – (alternative diagnosis) hand of Ishtar. To save him: human semen, sea fruit, a hulu-mouse of the canebrake which is sparsely covered with hair, the tip of the ear of a black dog, hair of a black riding-ass, tail of a black dog, with the hair of a virgin kid, white and black, ditto. [Apparently, in view of the preceding paragraphs, 'ditto' here indicates 'you shall put at his neck and he will get well'.]

The final section, consisting of six tablets, relates to women and small children. The following extracts are typical of the part dealing with pregnant women:

If the top of a pregnant woman's forehead glows white; that which is within her womb is a daughter; she will be rich. If it is red, that which is within her womb is a man-child; he will die.

If the nipples of a pregnant woman are yellow, that which is within her womb will be miscarried.

If the womb of a pregnant woman lies on her stomach, she will bear a deaf child.

If the womb of a pregnant woman is thrown down upon the right side of her stomach, she has conceived a man-child.

If the pregnant woman keeps vomiting, she will not bring to completion.

If the pregnant woman discharges matter from her mouth, she will die together with that which is within her womb.

If blood comes out of the mouth of the pregnant woman, she will not survive her confinement.

Other prognoses foretell the birth of twins, and various other details of the wellbeing of mother and child. Other sections refer to the woman having sexual intercourse at various times during her pregnancy: thus, for intercourse between five months and three days and five months and ten days the prognosis is 'Life' except at five months and eight or nine days, when (respectively) the lady will be seized by *mamitu* (a word often meaning 'a curse resulting from a broken oath' but here perhaps a specific disease) or will die.

The other part of this section concerns babies:

If a baby takes the breast but is not satisfied and screams a lot, it is injured internally [literally 'its inside is broken'].

If a baby has its stomach inflamed and when the breast is offered to it it does not feed, a witch has picked that baby out.

If the baby keeps being cold and grinds his teeth, his illness will be long; it is a seizure of the god Kubu.

It will be seen from these diagnostic and prognostic texts that whilst some sections might be considered purely rational and others purely superstitious, the general approach of these texts to sickness was a tangle of crude superstition and acute practical observation. Supposed magical cures were, as one might gather from the chapter on Magic and Religion (see pages 254ff.), common in Babylonia, and frequently messy. As an instance, the ritual might require the priest to tear the heart out of a kid and thrust the still quivering organ into the hand of a sick man whilst a spell was recited. None the less, rational methods employing drugs were also in use; these are known principally from the prescription texts, which are numerically the most important group of medical texts.

Prescription texts

The earliest of these comes from the period of the III Ur Dynasty (just before 2000 BC). It is completely rational and, unlike many later counterparts, contains no mention of spells to accompany the procedures. Prescription texts in the Akkadian languages usually comprise a note of the symptoms, a list of pharmaceutical materials, and instructions for the preparation and application of the remedy, but in this Sumerian text the first element appears to be lacking. There are fifteen prescriptions on the tablet, classified according to the manner of application, which might involve poultices, potions, or bathing with hot infusions. An example of each type of prescription follows:

POULTICES:

> Having ground up the roots of [such-and-such plants] with dried river bitumen, and having poured beer over it, and having massaged (the affected place) with oil, you shall put (the preparation) on as a poultice.

POTIONS:

> When you have ground up the seed of [such-and-such plants] and put (the mixture) into beer, the patient shall drink (it).

BATHING WITH HOT INFUSIONS:

In our example of the third type of prescription, the practitioner is instructed to take various ingredients, including dried figs and some kind of salt, and is told

> having heated (them), you shall wash (the affected place) with the liquid. [There is a further instruction which is not clear. It may have referred to the administration of an enema through a tube.]

Apart from this Sumerian text, the oldest prescription texts are fragments from the Old Babylonian period. After this come some Cassite pieces and an important group from Boghazkoi in eastern Turkey. The great bulk, however, are from first-millennium Assyria, although the dialect used shows that the texts were Babylonian in origin, not Assyrian. These include whole series of texts classifying prescriptions according to the parts of the body. The following is an extract from a group prescribing for afflictions of the stomach:

> If a man's stomach is hot, and will not accept food or drink, you shall take the seed of tamarisk, and mix (it) with honey and curds.
>
> To remove heat in the stomach, you shall grind up together [seven named medicinal materials, of which only sweet cane and dates are certainly identified]. You shall strain, steep in beer, heat in an oven, take out, strain and cool. You shall add [further ingredients]. You shall put this into his anus and he will recover.

In another prescription, twenty-four drugs (mostly woods and wood resins) were mixed in beer, left to infuse, boiled up and strained. The practitioner was then instructed to add honey and pure oil, after which

> whilst it is still warm, you shall pour it into his anus. He will evacuate and recover.

Since none of these texts can be later than the seventh century BC, and the originals from which they were copied are likely to have been several centuries earlier, the enema must have been in use for medical purposes by the beginning of the first millennium at latest.

As one might suppose, medicaments were most commonly taken by mouth, but there were other methods of administration. For example, for a certain preparation from various plants, it is prescribed:

> [the patient] shall swallow it with his mouth and he shall suck it up into his nostrils, and he shall recover.

Another prescription reads:

> If pain seizes on a man, you shall put [various aromatics] on the fire and you shall fumigate his nostrils (therewith); you shall fill your mouth with oil and shall blow into his nostrils, and he will recover.

Inhalation of vapour was another form of treatment. The method was to infuse vegetable ingredients in oil and beer and then, the instructions say,

> you shall prepare a great . . . pot, stop up its sides with wheaten dough, boil the brew (therein) over a fire, put a reed tube into it, let him draw the steam up so that it strikes against his lungs, and he will recover.

As in modern times, it was sometimes specified whether the patient should take his medicine with or without food. We see this in the following extract from a group of tablets dealing with treatment for lung and chest troubles:

> If a man is sick of a cough, you shall beat up styrax(?) in strong beer, honey, and refined oil. You shall let his tongue take it without a meal; let him drink it steaming hot in beer and honey. You shall make him vomit with a feather. Afterwards he should

> eat a mixture of honey and curds and drink sweet wine, and he will recover.

As we saw in the earliest prescription of all, medicaments could also be applied in the form of poultices. Hammurabi refers to this in the epilogue to his Code, where he invokes upon any future ruler who attempts to cancel his work the curse:

> May the goddess Ninkarrak . . . bring upon his limbs a grievous disease, . . . a nasty wound that does not heal, of which the *asu* does not know its nature, which cannot be relieved with poultices.

It must be emphasized that treatments mentioned in the prescription texts were not necessarily purely rational; quite often the details of the practical measures to be taken were accompanied by the text of a charm which had to be recited during the treatment.

Anatomical knowledge; surgery

The diagnostic texts show that the Babylonians had no very advanced knowledge of anatomy or physiology. They were interested in organs mainly as the supposed seat of various aspects of human behaviour, rather than for their actual functions. Thus, although they obviously knew that the ears are for hearing, their main interest in the ear was as the seat of the understanding, and the heart was for the Babylonians the centre of creative intelligence. Variations in the pulse rate were known, as was the fact that blood flowed through the veins, but the Babylonians did not go further and deduce the circulation of the blood. Knowledge of anatomy and physiology was certainly hindered by the religious taboo upon dissection of a dead human body, but, if this had been the only impediment, it could have been overcome by the intelligent observation of animal anatomy. But although certain internal organs of animals were carefully observed, this was done only for the purposes of the pseudo-science of divination, and the interest was not in the function of the organs, but in any slight variations in their appearance. Moreover, as only beasts in good condition would be sacrificed, the Babylonian officiants were prevented by the very means of selection of sacrificial animals from gaining experience of animal organs in heavily diseased condition, which would have opened the possibility of connecting this with externally visible symptoms of sickness. An even greater hindrance than the taboo upon dissection was the belief that illness was due to demonic possession. Holding such a view, a Babylonian would have considered it foolish curiosity to attempt to learn more of the functioning of particular organs in sickness and in health; the only points of concern in illness were the demon who lay at the bottom of the trouble and the external symptoms.

In such a state of affairs one does not expect an advanced stage of surgery. But surgeons there certainly were, as early as the early second millennium, for the Code of Hammurabi lays down the fees payable in the event of successful treatment, together with penalties to which the operator rendered himself liable by failure; the relevant laws (§§215, 218) are translated on page 188. Fees payable to the surgeon were proportionately less if the patient was of a lower social class. The surgeon's profession was not without risk, for if he caused the death or blindness of a patient of the freeman class, his hand was cut off. Other sections of the laws of Hammurabi refer to the *asu* mending broken limbs.

Despite these relatively early references to surgery, there is no text amongst the hundreds of later medical texts which deals specifically and systematically with the subject. This might suggest that surgical procedures ceased to be used in the later period, but there is another possible explanation. Surgery is pre-eminently a matter in which techniques have to be learned by observation and practice: there is no place for the correspondence course in surgery. Thus it is probable that the apprentice surgeon in Babylonia acquired his knowledge and skill by watching a master of the profession at work, and there was nothing to be gained by attempting to commit the details of the techniques to writing.

Amongst minor surgical procedures which certainly took place were the lancing of abscesses and bleeding. We learn the latter from an instruction which reads:

> You shall incise [the man's] forehead with an obsidian knife and let his blood flow.

There are one or two broken texts in which there *may* be a reference to surgical operations. In the early second millennium there was a term of rare occurrence, *šilip remim*, which meant literally 'extracted from the womb', and this was formerly understood as referring to a caesarian birth. It has since been argued that the phrase was simply a term of brief and local currency for 'newborn baby'. Against the weight of current opinion, I am not entirely convinced that the earlier view was wrong: there were so many newborn babies that I would have expected that a term with that meaning, even if it was current only for a short time, would have had more occurrences than *šilip remim* actually does.

Eye disease, possibly cataract, is not infrequently referred to in phrases which speak of a man's eye being covered with a shadow, and one damaged text says:

> If a man's eye is covered with a shadow, with a lancet . . .

Did the remainder of the sentence refer to a surgical operation? At present we cannot tell. There is another text which is equally doubtful in its implications, since it mentions a cutting instrument and later seems to say

> If the sickness has reached the inside of the bone, you shall scrape and remove.

This has been taken to refer to a deep incision, but the text is not complete and clear enough for a definite conclusion.

15

Legacy and Survival

> Were the traveller to cross the Euphrates to seek for such ruins in Mesopotamia and Chaldaea as he had left behind him in Asia Minor or Syria, his search would be vain. The graceful column rising above the thick foliage of the myrtle, the ilex, and the oleander; the gradines of the amphitheatre covering the gentle slope, and overlooking the dark blue waters of a lake-like bay; the richly carved cornice or capital half hidden by the luxuriant herbage; are replaced by the stern shapeless mound rising like a hill from the scorched plain, the fragments of pottery, and the stupendous mass of brickwork occasionally laid bare by the winter rains. . . . He is now at a loss to give any form to the rude heaps upon which he is gazing. Those of whose works they are the remains . . . have left no visible traces of their civilisation, or their arts: their influence has long since passed away. The more he conjectures, the more vague the results appear. The scene around is worthy of the ruin he is contemplating; desolation meets desolation: a feeling of awe succeeds to wonder.
>
> (A. H. Layard, *Nineveh and its remains*, 1849, pp. 6f.)

The physical remains of Babylonian civilization

WHAT, physically, is left of ancient Babylonian civilization? As the Bible tells us (Genesis 11:3), the typical building material in the plain of Shinar – south Iraq, Babylonia – was not stone but brick. Brick weathers, and bricks can be dug out and easily transported for re-use by later inhabitants. In consequence, after the two and a half millennia which separate us from Nebuchadnezzar, only the most massive works of man remain visible from ancient Babylonia.

Architectural features

Most prominent are the ziggurats. Originally with a base of up to 300 feet square and up to 300 feet high, these great stepped towers, at least one in each city, must have dominated the Babylonian plain. Such of them as have outfaced the ravages of time to remain in recognizable form can still fill the viewer with awe at the achievements of ancient man. There are four in particular which still dominate the landscape: at Ur, at Birs Nimrud (ancient Borsippa) near Babylon, at Aqarquf (ancient Dur-Kurigalzu) near Baghdad, and at Nimrud south of Mosul in Assyria. Unhappily one of them, Ur, is no longer visible in the rugged weathered form in which the ages left it, since in recent decades it has suffered massive reconstruction, so that now the original lies invisible beneath a modern shell simulating its appearance of four thousand years ago. The others also are under sentence of the like living death of total restoration.

Ziggurats may, however, have left some further legacy than their own remains. According to the late K. A. C. Creswell, a leading authority on Islamic architecture, a few early Muslim minarets and other towers show the influence of ancient Mesopotamian architecture. The most striking example is the spiral minaret at Samarra, built between AD 849 and 852 and still standing: the sketch gives an idea of its appearance before the reconstruction of the top section in recent years.

Minaret at Samarra

According to Creswell (*Early Muslim Architecture*, II, page 261), the form of this minaret is directly based on the ziggurat, even though the tower is circular instead of square. The use of this spiral type of tower subsequently spread from the

Islamic world to China, where the same architectural form was employed between the eleventh and thirteenth centuries.

After ziggurats, the principal easily identifiable visible remains are ancient defensive walls, which can be seen around some cities, particularly Babylon, as long mounds, with occasional larger mounds marking the sites of towers. At Nineveh in Assyria (modern Mosul), both the inner and outer walls are still very evident. At Babylon, there are, or until recent decades were, other prominent mounds, marking the sites of ancient palaces, citadels, temples or in one case possibly the base of the famous Hanging Gardens. Excavation has sometimes given a clearer glimpse of the ancient world by revealing more extensive remains of buildings, but unfortunately a restoration is planned for Babylon, and is actually under way, on so massive a scale that all that is left from Babylonian antiquity will eventually be concealed for ever beneath a total modern rebuilding. It is, however, possible to give a permanent glimpse of the ancient world by excavation without massive self-defeating reconstruction. At the ruins of Sippar, Dr Farouk Al-Rawi has excavated whole streets in such a way that one can walk between the remaining lower parts of walls of buildings, and with a little imagination visualize the busy scene of citizens at the shops. There has also been some pleasingly restrained conservation of excavated structures at Nineveh.

Whilst ziggurats and defensive walls are the most prominent of identifiable remains, these are far outnumbered by the vast numbers of mounds in which ancient settlements, mostly of unknown name, lie buried. These can range in area from the size of a house up to hundreds of acres, and in height above the plain from almost nothing to forty or fifty feet. Some of them are littered with ancient brickwork or fragments of pottery or sculpture in stone, usually a signal that excavation will reveal more complete examples, and perhaps also clay tablets inscribed in cuneiform. There are places in Mesopotamia where it is possible to stand on one of these mounds and see over a hundred others scattered around the plain.

It is from excavation in these mounds, sometimes by organized archaeological expeditions, sometimes by illegal digging by natives, that the great mass of the physical remains of ancient Babylonian civilization has been recovered. When A. H. Layard, the first and still the greatest of Assyriologists, wrote the introduction to his *Nineveh and its Remains* in 1849, he was able to say with almost no departure from the literal truth that before his finds 'a case [in the British Museum] scarcely three feet square enclosed all that remained, not only of the great city, Nineveh, but of Babylon itself!' The position now is that every major museum, and many smaller ones, have considerable collections of material from ancient Babylonia and Assyria, amounting in some instances to hundreds of thousands of items.

Remains of Babylonian art

The objects best represented overall in museums are cuneiform tablets, the source of most of our detailed information about Babylonian history and society. But the museum collections also contain many objects which from the modern point of view fall into the category of art. Of the many articles and books which have been written to analyse and explain ancient Mesopotamian art, two books which can be especially recommended are H. Frankfort, *The Art and Architecture of the ancient Orient* (1954) and A. Moortgat, *The Art of ancient Mesopotamia* (1969).

The impact of ancient Mesopotamian art upon later civilizations has been limited. One factor in this is that almost all of what we think of as art in ancient Mesopotamia served the purposes of religion, either directly, or in relation to the king, who was the religious embodiment of the state. With so much Mesopotamian art expressing concepts with little relevance to subsequent civilizations, it is not surprising that much of it died. But some motifs were taken over into later civilizations.

A further factor is that at all times much of what we regard as works of art were never intended for human view. Much sculpture in the round comes into this category. The most numerous objects in this class, across the whole period from the third millennium to the first, were statues of rulers. In most cases, these were created not to perpetuate the person represented in the memory of his fellow men, but rather to stand in the temple near the image of the god, to give the ruler magically, by the proxy of his statue, permanent access to the god. An example of sculpture in the round which the ordinary Babylonian did regularly see was the images of the gods. In some instances they stood in their shrines in the temple in a position where they could be seen from the temple courtyard, and in any case they were carried in public procession at festivals. But the very different character of the religions which superseded Babylonian polytheism – Judaism, Zoroastrianism, Christianity and Islam – killed the tradition of the divine image, and the magnificence of existing statues of deities, made of precious metals and adorned with jewels, ensured that all of them were broken up for the wealth they represented, and that no major divine statue was left for posterity.

Other sculptures certainly intended to be seen by the ordinary man in the ancient world, and preserved for the modern, include such monuments as the stele bearing Hammurabi's laws (see plate 21B) and bas-reliefs set up on rock faces to celebrate victories. The earliest of the latter category still surviving is a relief cut in the twenty-third century BC high up in a rock in a pass in the Kurdish mountains not far from Sulaimania (see plate 16A): it depicts warriors ascending a mountain in pursuit of the enemy, with their king, Naram-sin, represented half as large again as his men and wearing the head-dress of a god, going at their head.

Our museums contain only a modest number of good examples of metalwork from ancient Mesopotamia, but this does not require us to conclude that metalwork was rare in the ancient Near East. Metals can be recycled, and therefore, when any metal object went out of fashion or became broken, it was likely to be melted down and used again. This factor would considerably reduce the number of examples of metalwork remaining from ancient Mesopotamia, and the number would be further diminished by the fact that metal objects left in the soil would, except in the case of gold, be very likely to corrode. But despite these factors, some fine examples of Mesopotamian metalwork remain. The finest is from the period of the Dynasty of Agade, in the form of a bronze mask (see plate 14), which some scholars think represented Sargon of Agade himself. It is of three-quarter size and of a vigour and dignity unsurpassed in all later examples of Mesopotamian art. The eyes must originally have been inlaid with precious stones, for the mask shows the scar where one has been gouged out.

Metalwork of the later period is known chiefly from vessels of various kinds, weights in the form of animals or ducks (see plate 58B), images a few inches high representing demons or monsters, and bronze bands (see plates 33A, 33B) decorated with scenes in *repoussé*, i.e. raised in relief by hammering from the back.

These *repoussé* bronze bands, of which the principal examples are in the British Museum, although Assyrian and not Babylonian, are relevant here as a stage in the development of narrative art. Narrative art was very ancient in Mesopotamia, for it is already found in the middle of the third millennium in the famous Standard of Ur (see plate 12), a work in inlay. It is in six registers, comprising a war panel and a peace panel, which show the story of a battle and the triumphal feast which followed it. In the war panel, which is to be read from the bottom upwards, the action of the battle is represented in its successive stages, by the 'strip cartoon' method. From left to right the bottom register shows first a war-chariot with the draught animals walking and the chariot crew not yet engaged, and then the animals breaking into a trot with the squire handing his charioteer a javelin for action. In the third section the charioteer has discharged his weapon, and the draught animals are in furious motion. Later we see naked prisoners being driven along under guard, and finally being brought before the city ruler, represented as bigger than anyone else present.

The finest ancient examples of narrative art are bas-reliefs on limestone slabs, of which the British Museum has the world's finest collection. Like the *repoussé* bronze bands with which they are artistically linked, they come from first-millennium Assyria. Relief carving was employed as early as the third millennium, but with the limitations imposed by restriction to a single stele. The Assyrians developed the old technique and brought it to the service of narrative. A whole wall or chamber would be lined with stone slabs and the whole covered with a series of scenes related in such a way that a narrative was built up. The scenes are of two main types: some show incidents in the royal campaigns (see plates 45–48) and others depict hunting scenes (see plates 40–44B). Traces of colour originally used to emphasize the figure of the king and his courtiers still survive.

In these reliefs the most noted mastery is found in the rendering of animals (see plates 38, 39). In the frieze of the wild ass[1] hunt, the asses seem really in motion, whilst the dying lion and lioness (plates 43A, 43B) in the famous lion-hunt scenes in the British Museum are amongst the most vivid examples of sculpture of all time. The fact that there is no developed conception of perspective and little attempt to represent spatial depth does not hinder the modern appreciation of these powerful reliefs.

The most widely represented specimens of what are treated as ancient Mesopotamian art are cylinder seals, stone cylinders typically the size of a thumb or less, engraved with a design incorporating religious motifs. Herodotus, writing in the fifth century, said that every Babylonian owned one. Such a seal would be rolled over an uninscribed area of a cuneiform tablet to authenticate its contents. The religious motifs engraved on the seal originally gave it magical power; at what stage – if ever – they became thought of as no more than conventional designs we do not know. But what is clear is that, for the ancients, cylinder seals were not *objets d'art*; they were purely things with a practical use, possibly incorporating some magical virtue. They were particularly convenient for rolling over clay tablets, but less so for use with documents on parchment or papyrus, and as alphabetic writing on such materials superseded cuneiform on clay tablets, cylinder seals became replaced with stamp seals, leaving no direct legacy.

Something which people in ancient Mesopotamia consciously valued for its aesthetic aspect, and thought of as art, was carving in ivory (see plates 60A, 60B); much of what remains of this is as pleasing to modern taste as it seems to have been to ancient. Carved ivory, often overlaid with gold, was employed widely in the ancient Near East, and a throne of ivory overlaid with gold is mentioned as a possession of Solomon (1 Kings 10:18), whilst king Ahab built an 'ivory house' (1 Kings 22:39). One of the main find-places of ancient carved ivory, some of it now in the British Museum, was Calah (modern Nimrud) in Assyria, south of Mosul. The ancient appreciation of them is proved by the fact that some of the most striking pieces had been thrown down a well to preserve them when the city was being looted by attackers; those who so hid the ivories were presumably killed themselves, for the objects remained in the well until it was excavated in AD 1952.

The legacy of knowledge and ideas

But far outweighing the tangible physical remains from ancient Mesopotamia is its persisting influence on aspects of our own civilization. Ancient Sumerian and Babylonian ideas and techniques have come down to us through a number of sources. Transmitted and often transmuted through the Bible come ancient myths, whilst other myths have become part of our own literature through the Greek tradition. Through Greece and Rome, Byzantium and the Arabs, there have come to us Mesopotamian elements in our calendar. Astrology has been transmitted through the same channels, as has knowledge of various food and medicinal plants and chemical processes. The science of astronomy itself and many astronomical concepts are a legacy from ancient Mesopotamia (see pages 410ff.). Ancient Mesopotamian elements probably lie at the bottom of some of our law and commerce, whilst long-distance overland communication systems can be traced back to ancient Mesopotamia (see pages 222f.). The superiority of the literate man – not always accepted in the Middle Ages but now so widely accepted in the modern world that literacy and the numbers of students receiving higher education are frequently used as criteria by which to judge a nation's progress – is an idea taken over at the Renaissance from the classical tradition, and linked there with the honour in which literacy was held in Mesopotamia (see page 389). The concept of international law is also in part a debt to the ancient Near East, for it comes to us from Rome, and Rome in turn developed it in its contact with Greece and Persia, and the latter certainly took over a great deal in connection with international order and administration from Assyrian and Babylonian practice. And although most of that part of ancient Mesopotamian religion which was essentially linked to polytheism withered, there were religious concepts which expressed ideas equally felt in the great monotheisms; and so some motifs in Christian art come by an unbroken tradition through Byzantium from Sumer, whilst more controversially one might argue that certain features of Christian ritual, such as the mystical significance of the East in worship and burial, had antecedents in Babylonian paganism.

The persistence of ancient religious motifs

It cannot be assumed without specific proof that every symbol or motif common to ancient and more recent religions necessarily represents a direct borrowing. If a symbol is of a very simple form, its occurrence in two different places or periods does not necessarily prove a connection. But when one finds that the symbol is a part of a wider complex of ideas held in common, this begins to point to direct borrowing. The crescent moon, used as a religious symbol both in Islam and in ancient Mesopotamia, is a case in point. Without further parallels, this could be a coincidence, but further parallels certainly exist: ancient Babylonia had a wholly lunar calendar, fixed monthly by the new moon, and to this day in Islam the determination of the beginning of a month is a matter for the religious authorities, and all months begin with the visual observation of the new moon.[2] Moreover, in pre-Islamic times it was the Moon-god who was lord of the Kaʿbah in Mecca, which subsequently became the most sacred structure in Islam.[3]

Another motif in Islamic art linked to ancient Mesopotamia is intertwined serpents: the example in the drawing, which is from an Islamic basin of the eleventh century AD, strikingly recalls the serpents of plate 11A, which represents a lamp cover from the end of the third millennium. The same symbol,

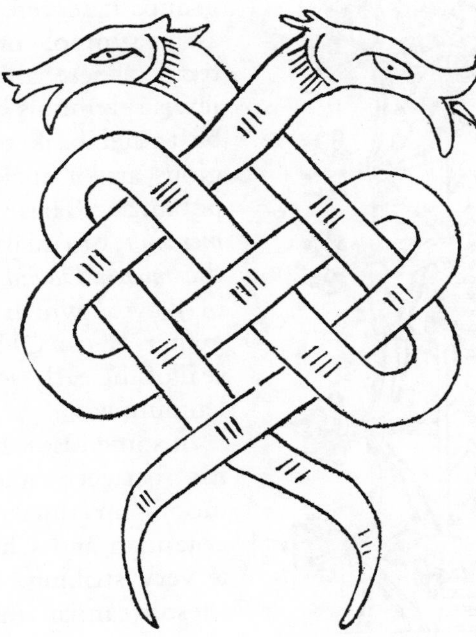

Intertwined serpents in Islamic art

which in Babylonia was associated with the son of the divine patron of healing, has been transmitted through Greece to the modern world as a symbol of healing.

Another instance is the cross, which is attested as a religious symbol, although not a common one, in ancient Mesopotamia. However, the simple Greek cross might have arisen independently as a symbol in two different religious settings. But with the more elaborate Maltese cross the case is different, and the fact that it already occurs as a religious symbol in the *Jemdet Nasr* period (*c.* 2900 BC) in the form (see plate 27A) in which it is met with in oriental Christian art can hardly be an accident. There is of course no suggestion that the Maltese cross meant the same thing to people in Mesopotamia in 2900 BC as it does to oriental Christians; but to both groups it served, or serves, as a symbol of religious truth. There are also two Jewish symbols which can be traced back to the religious art of ancient Mesopotamia. These are the *menorah*, or ritual lamp, and the *magen Dawid*, or shield of David, which occur together on an Old Assyrian seal of the early second millennium BC.

Assyrian sacred tree

In some cases the similarity between complicated motifs in ancient Mesopotamian and Christian art is very striking, and some Mesopotamian influence is generally accepted by historians of Christian art: the main point of contention is not the existence of the influence but the channels through which it flowed from ancient Mesopotamia to Byzantium and mediaeval Europe.

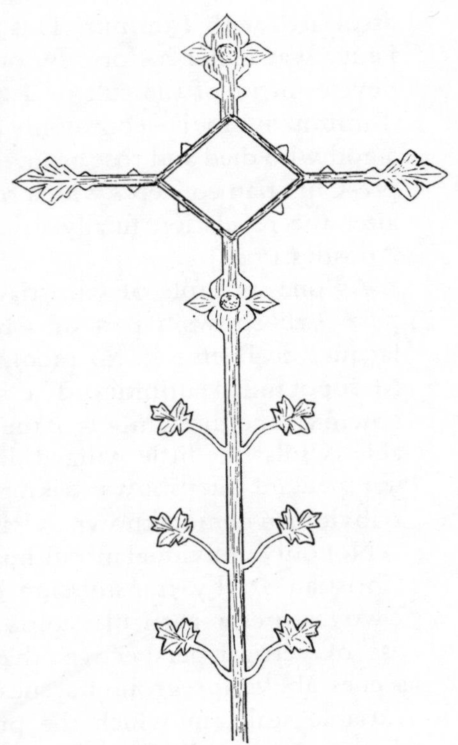

Cross in form of sacred tree, after a brass in an English cathedral

A religious symbol which undoubtedly comes by unbroken tradition from the ancient Near East is the Tree of Life. This is found in some of the earliest Sumerian art, and continues throughout Mesopotamian history, being very prominent in Assyrian friezes of the first millennium BC (see plate 32). The mythological concept of the Tree of Life is also found in Genesis 3:22, where it has been an important influence on Christian theology. This symbol is represented in oriental rugs, and occurs throughout Christian art from the earliest times to the present day.

There are a number of other motifs which art historians commonly accept as occurring in Christian art by transmission from ancient Mesopotamia: they may have come either through Parthian mediation or through the monks of Edessa and Nisibis (the north-eastern extension of Assyria, and the region of the earliest eastern church), who, according to O. M. Dalton (*East Christian Art*, 1925, page 9), 'from the fifth century . . . determined Christian iconography, and imparted to its artistic expression the un-Hellenic qualities'.

A number of these symbols were in ancient Mesopotamia

associated with Tammuz. This in no way implies that Christianity was either historically or doctrinally or emotionally a development of the cult of Tammuz. Christianity accepted Tammuz symbols – commonly presumed to be the symbols of a god who died and rose again – as it has always accepted any pre-Christian concepts which represent a striving in the dark after the revelation finally given in Christ (see Acts of the Apostles 17:23).

As one example of Christian re-use of ancient symbols, plate 57B shows a part of a reredos of the crucifixion by Jacques de Baerze (*c.* AD 1300), which is full of motifs with Mesopotamian affinities. The sun symbol (the rays on the crucifix), and the symbols of the moon and a star are indisputable, whilst the little winged devil snatching the soul of the unrepentant thief shows striking points of similarity with the Babylonian demon known as Pazuzu[4] (see page 260).

Not only individual motifs but also points of style appear in Christian art by transmission from ancient Mesopotamia. Two features in particular come into this category. One is the use of vertical perspective, that is, of placing background scenes above foreground scenes. The other is the device of variable scale, in which the principal figure in a scene is disproportionately large compared with the other figures. Even the manner in which Christ is represented in Christian art sometimes shows Mesopotamian influence. D. Talbot Rice points out (*Byzantine Art*, revised edition, 1954, page 81) that in Byzantine art there are two traditions: under Hellenic influence Christ is depicted as charming and youthful, but in the oriental presentation he is bearded and mysterious, with the numinous majesty characteristic of the old Mesopotamian deities.

Mesopotamian elements in the Bible

Any attempt to apply literary criticism to the Bible, or to suggest that the human instruments through whom the divine message reached us may have introduced elements from their own cultural environment, is likely to arouse strong passions in the hearts of more conservative Christians and Jews. To these I make a preliminary apology, and point out that I myself accept the spiritual value of the Old Testament as the message of God. It is beyond doubt, however, that certain of the stories in Genesis have some relationship to Babylonian or Sumerian myths. The Flood story has a very close relationship, with so many details in common, such as the sending out of birds from the Ark, that there can be no doubt that the accounts of the Flood in Genesis and in the *Gilgamesh Epic* have ultimately a common source: fundamentalists are at liberty to conclude that both are reporting an actual event, although they need to explain how Noah managed singlehanded to build a ship of about the tonnage of the *QE2*. No Mesopotamian original has plausibly been postulated for the actual story of the garden of Eden, but the late E. A. Speiser persuasively argued that the geographical details given in Genesis 2:6–14 require it to be conveived of as a part of the Near East closely connected with Mesopotamia.[5] Genesis 10:9–12 explicitly incorporates Mesopotamian historical geography, and the story of the tower of Babel (= Babylon) in Genesis 11:1–9 is directly linked by the Bible itself with Mesopotamia (= the plain of Shinar).

Less commonly recognized than the Mesopotamian elements in Genesis is the presence in the Old Testament, especially in Psalms, of references to magic and witchcraft. It is true that even if their presence is admitted in the Old Testament, it is not necessary to conclude at once that these ideas came from Mesopotamia, for witchcraft is a monopoly of no one section of mankind. Yet the details of such references do point strongly to direct Mesopotamian influence.

In Isaiah 34:14 there occurs a phrase, in the curse upon Edom, translated in RV as

> the night-monster shall settle there, and shall find her a place of rest.

The Hebrew word rendered 'night-monster' is *Lilith*, which can hardly be separated from the Akkadian *Lilitu*, a well-known and much-feared female demon. The late Professor Sir Godfrey Driver objected to this identification, on the grounds that all the other creatures mentioned in the passage are either real 'or may be such'.[6] However, the qualification 'may be such' admits the possibility 'may be otherwise', and robs the argument of its main force. Even apart from this, there is no reason to suppose that in a non-scientific society demons were considered as less real members of the fauna than what we accept as real beasts. I recall the nervous anxiety of the police escort when, on a visit I made to the site of Erech in the desert, night began to fall: it was clear that there was no well-marked distinction in the minds of the peasant policemen between the danger from prowling wild beasts which may have had their lairs amid the ruins and that from lurking jinn (hobgoblins). Both stood together as hazards from which those in their charge should be removed as soon as possible. So likewise there is no reason to assume that a rigid distinction was maintained in the Isaiah passage between fauna and fauns.

Although the Old Testament makes very little reference to demonic possession, there are probably in the original Hebrew text more allusions to witchcraft than has commonly been recognized. This does not imply deliberate concealment on the part of earlier translators, but merely unfamiliarity with rare Hebrew words or usages which have since become clearer in the light of comparative studies. Thus, it has been suggested that the first half of Psalms 94:20 is to be translated:

> Can he that binds spells charm Thee?

Likewise it has been suggested that the Hebrew of Proverbs 10:3 really means:

> The Lord will not allow the soul of the righteous to be bound by a spell,
> And the binding curse of the wicked He shall thrust away,

whilst Proverbs 10:11 is to be translated:

A fountain of life is (the product of) the mouth of the righteous,
But the mouth of the wicked utters baneful spells.

Two whole books of the Bible, Nahum and The Song of Songs, have been related by certain modern scholars to specifically Mesopotamian religious ideas. A. Haldar argues, for instance, that Nahum 2:3–4 refers to ceremonial races at the New Year Festival. Whilst this seems to me excessively speculative, there are clear references in Nahum and elsewhere in the Old Testament to a fertility cult with Mesopotamian associations.[7] The Song of Songs is a much clearer case than Nahum, and whilst some theologians have shown uneasiness over the matter, no one has been able substantially to refute the case, first made out by T. J. Meek,[8] that this was originally part of a fertility cult. (This need not prevent the Christian from finding a spiritual value in The Song of Songs; see Acts of the Apostles 17:23.)

The belief in demonic possession, and means of treating it, which ultimately goes back to the Babylonian view of the world-order, still persists amongst some educated and intelligent people.[9] As late as 1960 a rural dean in the Church of England stated the view, as reported in a local newspaper, that people can be possessed by evil spirits which can then be removed by exorcism:

> Fewer people were possessed by demons in this country than in Africa, because of the existence in every parish of a Christian community . . . When doctors could not discover the cause of a disorder, a priest might seek the consent of his bishop . . . [and] if the consent was given the evil spirit might be exorcised. It might enter into the priest, for which reason two priests were always posted.

I have also heard of a case in the 1970s in which young people who had been playing with black magic came in the middle of the night, in a state of terror, to beg a priest to come and exorcize the evil spirit they believed they had called up.

The doctrinal basis for such beliefs is certain passages in the New Testament referring to devils, such as the incident of the Gadarene swine (see page 267), and the story of the exorcized devil who returned with seven others worse than himself (see page 267). Such ideas reflect the current of thought of later Judaism, in which demons loom large as a result of the strong Babylonian influence to which it was subjected during the Exile. The idea of demons played little part in pre-exilic Israelite religion. Most of the pre-exilic references to supernatural beings not described as gods refer to ancient gods who had been reduced, under the pressure of Mosaic religion, to demons: such demoted gods still had a cult amongst the ignorant (Leviticus 17:7, Deuteronomy 32:17) but are never mentioned as threatening to possess a man.

A religious conception which has come down to us by unbroken tradition from the ancient Near East, mediated through the Bible, is the idea of coronation. As the late C. J. Gadd put it, in the ancient Near East 'the Crown was not merely a symbol but an amulet with its own magical powers, and so was the oil with which kings were anointed'.[10] These conceptions remain clearly visible in the coronation service used for English monarchs in the twentieth century.

Astrology, astronomy, numeration and time division

The folly of horoscopic astrology is still very much with us, and this has Babylonian roots. Omen astrology, giving general predictions about the king and state, was ancient in Babylonia (see page 410), but horoscopic astrology could not develop until some technique was devised to make a specious link between celestial phenomena and a particular individual. The link was through the zodiac. The zodiac was not invented for astrological purposes, but once it had been invented it was only a step from the idea of making general predictions about the future on the basis of the heavenly bodies, to making predictions about an individual, on the basis of the position of the planets in the zodiac at his birth. There is much dispute as to whether this development came about in Greece, Egypt or Babylonia, but two considerations combine to give priority to Babylonia. There is the theoretical consideration that the idea can only have arisen in a milieu where celestial bodies were regarded as divinities affecting the life of mankind, and there is the fact that much earlier examples of horoscopes are known from Babylonia than from Greece (where the earliest is from 62 BC) or Egypt (where they began in the first century AD). There is a cuneiform text in which a horoscope is cast for a child born on 29 April, 410 BC, and there are four further examples from the third century BC. The following is an example from 263 BC, translated by A. Sachs:[11]

> The child was born (in) year 48 [of the Seleucid era], (the month of) Adar, night of the twenty-third. At that time
> the sun was in 13½° Aries,
> the moon was in 10° Aquarius,
> Jupiter was at the beginning of Leo,
> Venus was with the sun,
> Mercury was with the sun,
> Saturn was in Cancer,
> Mars was at the end of Cancer. . . .
> He will be lacking in wealth. . . . His food will not satisfy his hunger. The wealth which he has in his youth will not remain, (although) for thirty-six years he will have wealth. His days will be long. [There are five more lines, of difficult and doubtful interpretation.]

Not only in the calendar but in numerical method, particularly in connection with the measurement of time, Mesopotamian procedures have left traces which are still evident in our own civilization. The old Sumerian sexagesimal system is still plainly seen in the division of the circle into 360 degrees and the division of the hour into 60 minutes and 3600 seconds: this represents an unbroken tradition handed on through ancient and mediaeval astronomers. The most important feature of the Babylonian numeral system, its place-value notation, has also probably reached our own civilization by an unbroken tradition. In this place-value notation, which has already been described in more detail (see pages 402ff.), a number written as

i.e. 3,2

would mean three times sixty [the sexagesimal unit] plus two. It seems likely that the principle of the Babylonian place-value notation was never entirely lost and that it was transmitted into early Hindu astronomy, through which intermediary it came in the first millennium AD into Islamic civilization and then into our own, in the so-called Arabic numerals, in which, analogously with the Babylonian system, 32 means three times ten [the decimal unit] plus two.

The division of the day into hours also goes back in part to Mesopotamia, the final result being the consequence of the crossing of Egyptian and Babylonian influence. The Egyptian astronomers devised a system for dividing the night into twelve time divisions by observations of the stars, but these divisions varied in length according to the time of year. Babylonians divided the night into three watches, and their astronomers developed this into divisions of equal and constant length covering the whole day and night. Hellenistic astronomers combined Egyptian and Babylonian systems to give the twenty-four-hour day which we still use.

Direct Babylonian influence can still be seen in the ecclesiastical calendar. The date of Easter is fixed on a nineteen-year cycle, as witness the *Book of Common Prayer*, 'A Table to find Easter-Day', which begins by explaining that one must first find the Golden Number for the year, and then instructs: 'To find the Golden Number, or Prime, add 1 to the Year of our Lord, and then divide by 19'. The principle is clearly to find where the year stands in a nineteen-year cycle, and this nineteen-year cycle was devised by the Babylonians; see page 412.

Not only these by-products of astronomy, but astronomy itself – defined by O. Neugebauer as 'those parts of human interest in celestial phenomena which are amenable to mathematical treatment' – is a legacy from Babylonia. Indeed, it is the most direct legacy of all, being, as Neugebauer points out, 'the only branch of the ancient sciences which survived almost intact after the collapse of the Roman Empire'. For some aspects of Babylonian astronomy see pages 408ff.

Vocabulary

The evidence of classical authors indicates that Greek medical practice, and so its modern descendants, owed more to Egypt than to Babylonia. But Greek use of some medicaments of vegetable and mineral origin must have derived ultimately from Mesopotamia, since some Greek nomenclature has evident links with Akkadian names of plants and minerals. It is not of course necessary that the name in Greek referred to the same plant or mineral as the related Akkadian name; anyone interested in plant names knows that in different places a particular plant may have different names, or a particular name may be applied to different plants. Names in this category which have reached our language include the following:

English	*Greek*	*Akkadian*
carob	charrouba	kharubu
crocus	krokos	kurkanu
gypsum	gypsos	gaṣṣu
hyssop	hussopos	zupu
laudanum	ledanon	ladinnu
myrrh	murra	murru
naphtha	naphthos	napṭu
saffron	———	azupiranu [through Arabic za'faran]
sesame	———	šamaššammu

Other words in European languages which either certainly or probably have some connection with ancient Mesopotamia include the following:

'Alcohol', through Arabic *koḥl* from Akkadian *guhlu*. According to R. J. Forbes (*Studies in Ancient Technology* III (1955), page 18) the term *koḥl* came to mean first 'a finely divided powder' and was subsequently applied to volatile substances and then specifically to what in consequence we call alcohol.

'Alkali' comes through Arabic from Akkadian *ḳalati*, 'burnt things' (with reference to the ashes of plants which were burnt to make potash).

'Cane', through Greek from Akkadian ḳanu, 'reed'. 'Canon' comes from the same word in its derived sense of 'measuring rod', 'standard'.

Greek *chrusos*, 'gold', and its modern derivatives beginning with 'chrys-' (such as 'chrysalis', originally 'golden thing'; 'chrysanthemum', 'golden flower') are probably related to Akkadian *khuraṣu*, 'gold'; possibly both the Akkadian and the Greek word have a common origin which is neither Semitic nor Indo-European.

'Dragoman' comes through Arabic and Aramaic from Akkadian *targumanu*.

'Horn' (Latin *cornu*, Greek *keras*) is possibly connected distantly with Akkadian *ḳarnu*, which has the same meaning; this may be another word of which the prehistoric original was neither Semitic nor Indo-European.

'Jasper' derives through Greek *'iaspis* from Akkadian *iashpu*.

French 'mesquin', Italian 'meschino', denoting 'poor, mean', are forms of an Arabic word considered to derive ultimately from the Akkadian *mushkinu*, meaning 'a lower-class freeman'.

'Mina' comes ultimately from Sumerian MA.NA, or if (as seems likely) the latter is a false ideogram representing a genuine Semitic word based on the verb *manû*, 'to count', from Akkadian. Not only was the name 'mina' taken over into Greek, but the actual unit was adopted into the Greek weight system, sixty minas making, as in Babylonia, one talent.

'Plinth' comes from the Greek *plinthos*, 'a tile or brick', which may perhaps derive from Akkadian *libittu* (etymologically *libintu*), meaning 'a moulded (i.e. sun-dried) brick'.

The name 'Rachel' comes from Hebrew *raḥel*, 'ewe-lamb', which, with two consonants transposed, ultimately goes back to the Sumerian LAḪRA, the name of a deity concerned with sheep.

'Shekel' comes through Hebrew from the Akkadian *shiḳlu*.

Architecture

An instance of an architectural legacy from ancient Mesopotamia, transmitted through Greece, is the Ionian column. This is the type of column which has deep fluting and is surmounted by a capital with lateral volutes. The basic shape, of which this can be recognized as a development, was used as a religious symbol in the art of the *Protoliterate* period. It was clearly originally a bundle of tall reeds tied together with the heads tied over, used as a post in the building of a cult-hut. The original device is still employed in hut-making amongst the marsh-Arabs of south Iraq.

Ionian column [right] *and its ancestor*

The legacy of writing, literature and thought

But ancient Mesopotamia's most important gift to the world was the idea of writing, invented before 3000 BC. As a consequence of trading contacts, the Egyptians took over this idea soon afterwards and developed it into their own hieroglyphic system. In the second millennium, the existence of the cuneiform and hieroglyphic systems led, at various places between Sinai and Syria, to experiments at simplified ways of writing, and it was one of those which by about 1100 BC had developed into the Phoenician alphabet. By 800 BC the Greeks had adapted that alphabet to form their own, and it is from this Greek alphabet that all subsequent European alphabets derive.

But it was not the idea of writing alone which we owe to Mesopotamia. Many specific applications of writing were first developed there. Although it was invented and originally used for nothing more than simple records of the delivery of goods, the Sumerians quickly adapted it as a means of transmitting information across space and time. The *Enmerkar Epic* (see page 35) records that it was a ruler of Erech, in the first quarter of the third millennium, who first thought of sending a communication in writing in the form which we know as a letter. By the middle of the third millennium the Sumerians were using writing to record compositions of the type we call Wisdom literature (see page 385) and before the end of that millennium writing was being used for myths and epics, which earlier had had to rely on oral transmission for their preservation. Written law likewise goes back to third-millennium south Mesopotamia.

Ancient Mesopotamia may also take some of the credit for the attitude of its successor civilizations to history, although precisely how we see this depends upon what we understand by history. If we think of history as basically an interest in the origins and development of human society, then we can trace it back to early myths. But most people would see history as meaning something more specific, namely the conscious bringing of the present into connection with the past, and on this view we do not see the first historical writing until towards the end of the second millennium, and then in Assyria rather than Babylonia, with comparable developments taking place in the Hittite area further north.

The Assyrian development came about in this way. In Mesopotamia, royal inscriptions had originally been building inscriptions; in Babylonia they continued in that form until the end. Typically the king recorded his names and titles, and followed these with a hymn of praise to the god and a brief reference to the time and circumstances in which the building work was put in hand; finally he gave an account of the building operation itself. In Assyria at about 1300 BC, the kings began to elaborate the note of time and circumstances to include a summary of all the king's military exploits to date. This eventually came to be arranged systematically according to yearly campaigns, and from this developed an elaborate form of annals. In many cases such annals were not limited to the recountal of raw facts, but offered statements of motive, criticisms of courses of action, appraisals of character, notes of political changes, generalizations about the history of a region or the characteristics of a race, as well as matters which though not essentially history are generally associated with history – such as geographical, topographical, strategical and tactical aspects of campaigns. Thus there are good grounds for regarding the Assyrians as the first true historians, perhaps jointly with the Hittites who had also developed historical records.

But the most immediate, if not the most significant, impact of ancient Babylonia still comes indirectly through the Bible. Throughout Old Testament times, from Abraham (who came from Ur of the Chaldees), to the Exile in Babylonia in the sixth century BC and the subsequent Return, the little land of Palestine, the homeland of the Israelites, lay in the shadow of the two cultural giants, Egypt and Babylonia. In these circumstances the wonder is not that there is so much in the Old Testament which shows Egyptian or Babylonian influence, but that there is so much that is original and independent of those influences. But the Egyptian and Babylonian influences are undoubtedly there, and still colour modern Bible-based thinking about the world and about the divine purpose for the world. We are not concerned here with Egypt, but we may point out some of the aspects of Babylonian culture and history which touch upon modern culture through the Bible. Jewish and Christian teaching holds that the evil which befalls a person may not be direct divine punishment for what that person has done, and this teaching is spelt out at length in the Book of Job. But the Book of Job had a Babylonian antecedent, *The Righteous Sufferer*, giving the same message (see pages 392ff.). Many of the best-known Old Testament stories have a Mesopotamian background: the Garden of Eden, the Tower of Babel, the migration of Abraham, the Assyrian who came down like a wolf on the fold, Jonah travelling by whalemouth to preach to Nineveh, Nebuchadnezzar, Daniel in the burning fiery furnace, Belshazzar's feast. Most of these have found a place in European art or music or poetry. To mention only a tiny random selection, the Tower of Babel was a theme of paintings by several of the old masters; one of Verdi's greatest musical compositions was his *Nabucodonosor*, written in 1842, based on the story of the Babylonian king Nebuchadnezzar, and from Sibelius we have *Belshazzar's Feast* (Opus 51), which reflects the biblical memory of Bel-shar-usur, son and regent of the last Babylonian king, Nabu-na'id. And the 'wolf on the fold' is Lord Byron's poetic evocation of the biblical story of Sennacherib's attack upon Palestine in 701 BC.

Perhaps the most conspicuous Mesopotamian element in western consciousness is the story of Noah's Ark, still the basis of a popular toy for children, and a staple of fundamentalist Christian belief. As recently as 1986–7 an East Anglian newspaper ran Noah's Ark and the Flood in its correspondence columns for months, with not a single letter (at least amongst those which the editor selected for publication) openly denying its literal truth. Now without question the biblical story of Noah and the Flood rests on a Babylonian prototype from the beginning of the second millennium BC. The Israelite writer lightly reworked the composition of the Babylonian poet, removing its polytheism and reducing the size of the Ark; from having the displacement of a giant oil tanker (as required by the Babylonian figures), it was cut down to the mere tonnage of the *QE2*, which, wrote an indignant East Anglian fundamentalist when this was challenged, Noah could easily have built with the help of his family, given time. But otherwise the Israelite writer left the whole of the Babylonian Flood story in substance and in many of its details, and it is a Babylonian story which our fundamentalists are defending. Why? The story of Noah's Ark and the Flood has absolutely nothing to do with the Christian message of the incarnation of God in Jesus Christ, and it in no way impinges upon religion's ethical or cultic demands upon man. What, then, makes it such essential believing for so many Christians? It is surely because the story brings a message of reassurance to a threatened world: whatever happens, it tells us, God will not permit a full end of the human race. But that message in the biblical Noah's Ark story comes unchanged from the central theme of the Babylonian original from which the story derives. And so, mediated through the Bible, the Babylonian poet of 2000 BC still gives a message of hope to our troubled world four thousand years after his time.

CHRONOLOGICAL TABLE I

From the rise of the Dynasty of Agade to the fall of the Third Dynasty of Ur

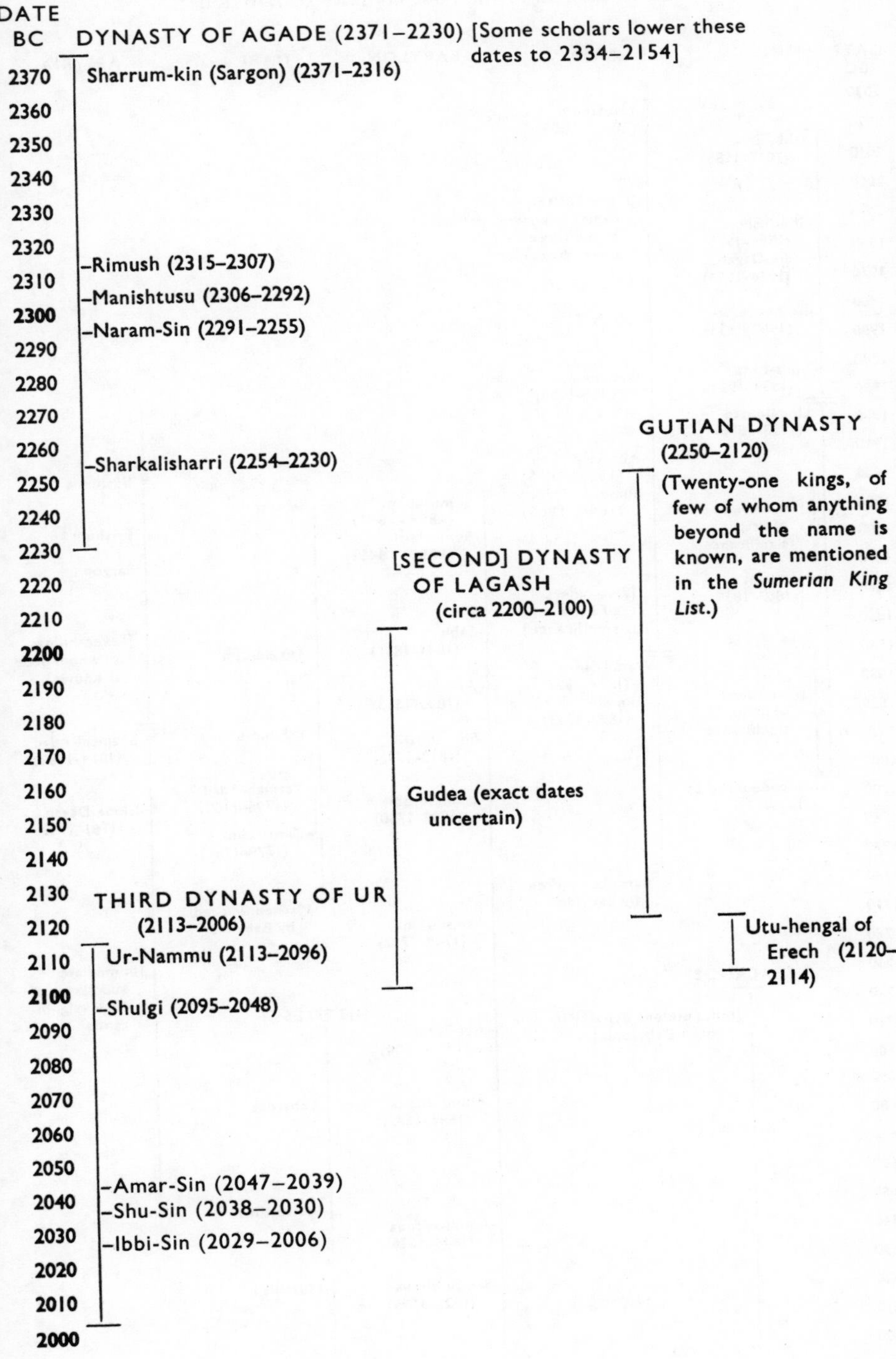

CHRONOLOGICAL TABLE II

Principal Dynasties of Babylonia and Assyria from the fall of the Third Dynasty of Ur to the end of the First Dynasty of Babylon

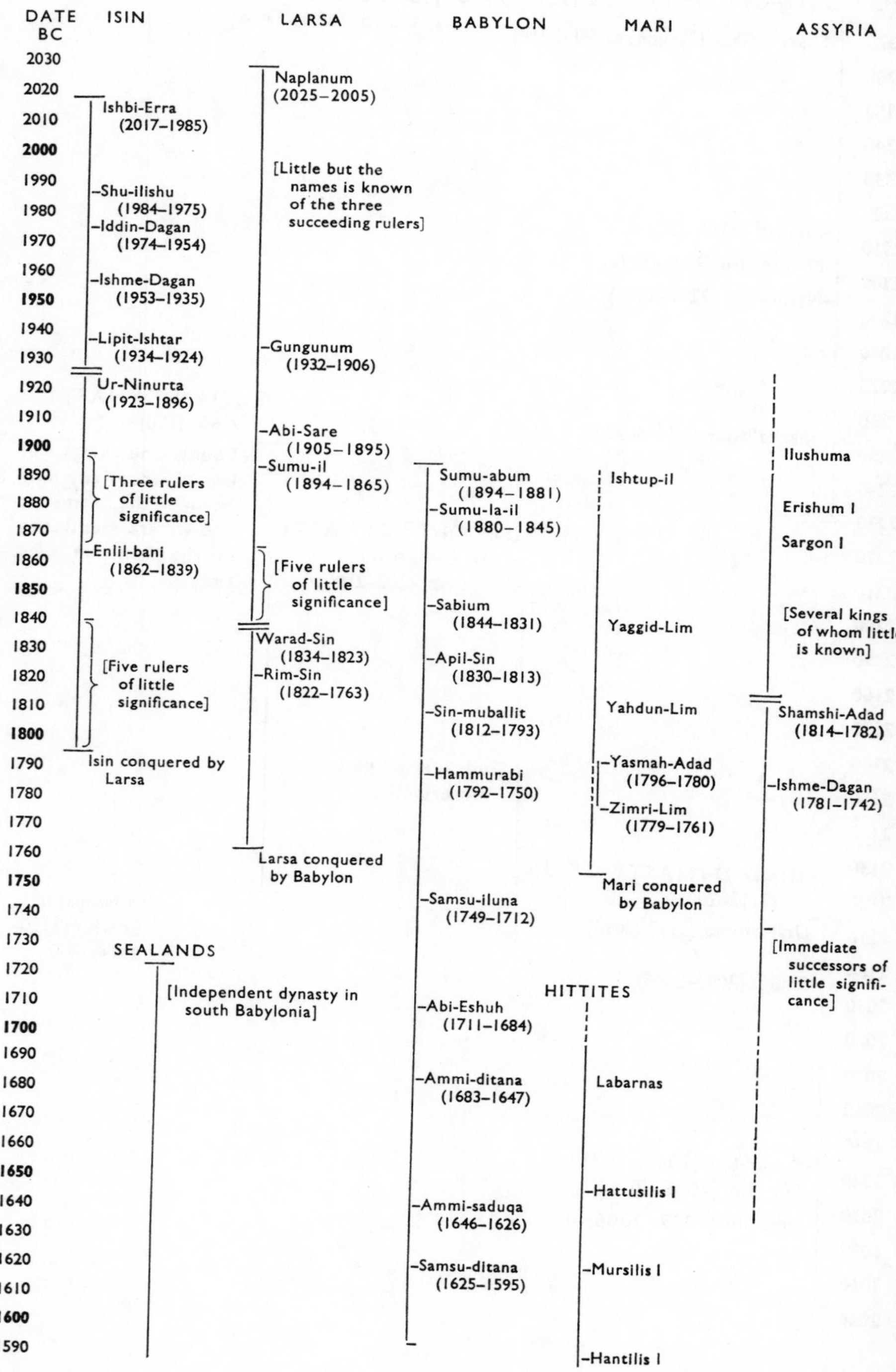

CHRONOLOGICAL TABLE III

Principal Kingdoms of the Near East from 1595 to 1250 BC

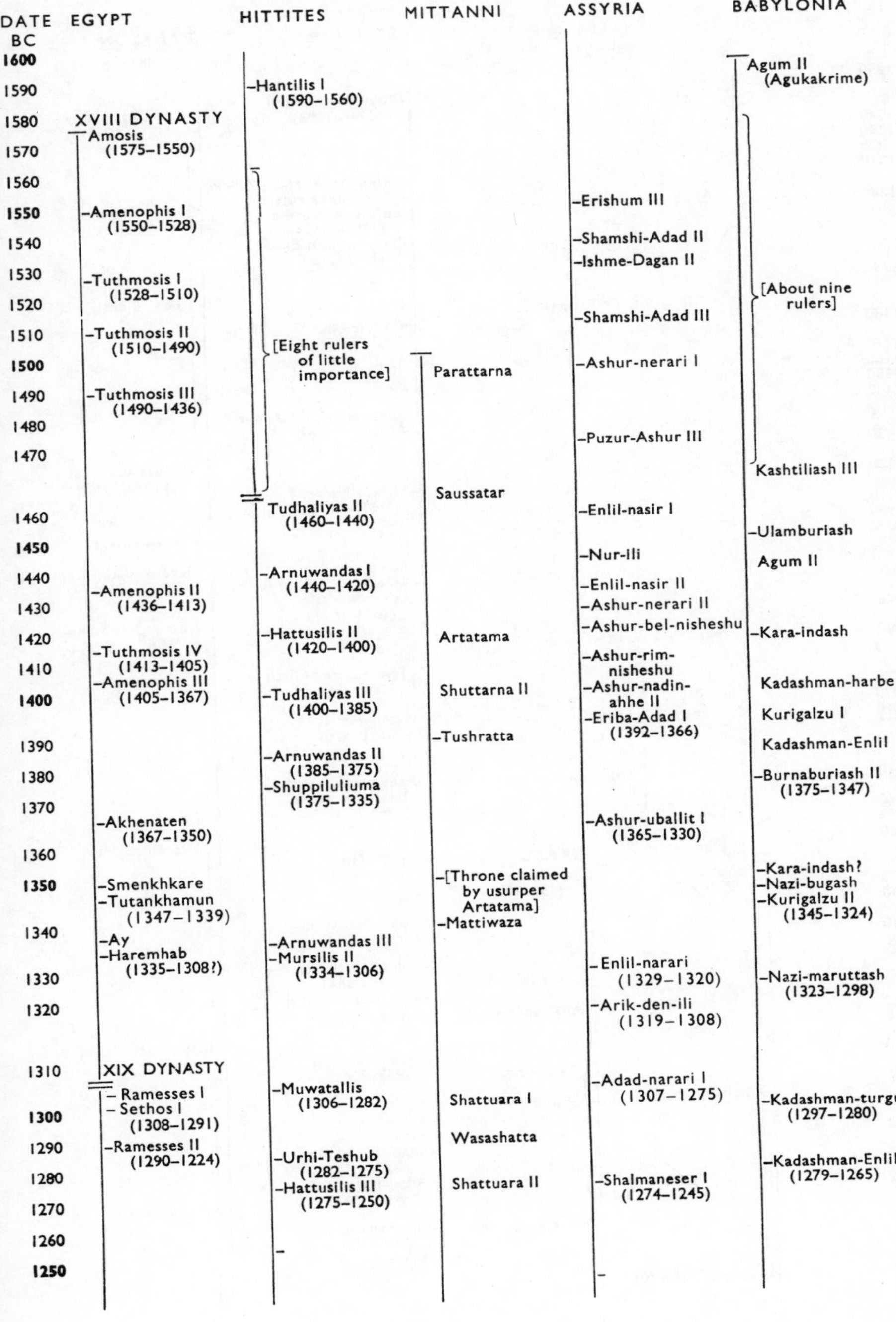

DATE BC	EGYPT	HITTITES	MITTANNI	ASSYRIA	BABYLONIA
1600					Agum II (Agukakrime)
1590		–Hantilis I (1590–1560)			
1580	XVIII DYNASTY				
1570	Amosis (1575–1550)				
1560					
1550	–Amenophis I (1550–1528)			–Erishum III	
1540				–Shamshi-Adad II –Ishme-Dagan II	
1530	–Tuthmosis I (1528–1510)				
1520				–Shamshi-Adad III	[About nine rulers]
1510	–Tuthmosis II (1510–1490)				
1500		[Eight rulers of little importance]	Parattarna	–Ashur-nerari I	
1490	–Tuthmosis III (1490–1436)				
1480				–Puzur-Ashur III	
1470			Saussatar		Kashtiliash III
1460		Tudhaliyas II (1460–1440)		–Enlil-nasir I	–Ulamburiash
1450				–Nur-ili	Agum II
1440	–Amenophis II (1436–1413)	–Arnuwandas I (1440–1420)		–Enlil-nasir II	
1430				–Ashur-nerari II	
1420	–Tuthmosis IV (1413–1405)	–Hattusilis II (1420–1400)	Artatama	–Ashur-bel-nisheshu	–Kara-indash
1410	–Amenophis III (1405–1367)			–Ashur-rim-nisheshu	
1400		–Tudhaliyas III (1400–1385)	Shuttarna II	–Ashur-nadin-ahhe II –Eriba-Adad I (1392–1366)	Kadashman-harbe Kurigalzu I
1390			–Tushratta		Kadashman-Enlil
1380		–Arnuwandas II (1385–1375) –Shuppiluliuma (1375–1335)			–Burnaburiash II (1375–1347)
1370	–Akhenaten (1367–1350)			–Ashur-uballit I (1365–1330)	
1360					–Kara-indash?
1350	–Smenkhkare –Tutankhamun (1347–1339)		–[Throne claimed by usurper Artatama] –Mattiwaza		–Nazi-bugash –Kurigalzu II (1345–1324)
1340	–Ay –Haremhab (1335–1308?)	–Arnuwandas III –Mursilis II (1334–1306)			
1330				–Enlil-narari (1329–1320)	–Nazi-maruttash (1323–1298)
1320				–Arik-den-ili (1319–1308)	
1310	XIX DYNASTY			–Adad-narari I (1307–1275)	
1300	–Ramesses I –Sethos I (1308–1291)	–Muwatallis (1306–1282)	Shattuara I		–Kadashman-turgu (1297–1280)
1290	–Ramesses II (1290–1224)		Wasashatta		
1280		–Urhi-Teshub (1282–1275) –Hattusilis III (1275–1250)	Shattuara II	–Shalmaneser I (1274–1245)	–Kadashman-Enlil II (1279–1265)
1270					
1260					
1250					

CHRONOLOGICAL TABLE IV

Babylonia and Assyria 1250–746 BC, with some biblical contemporaries

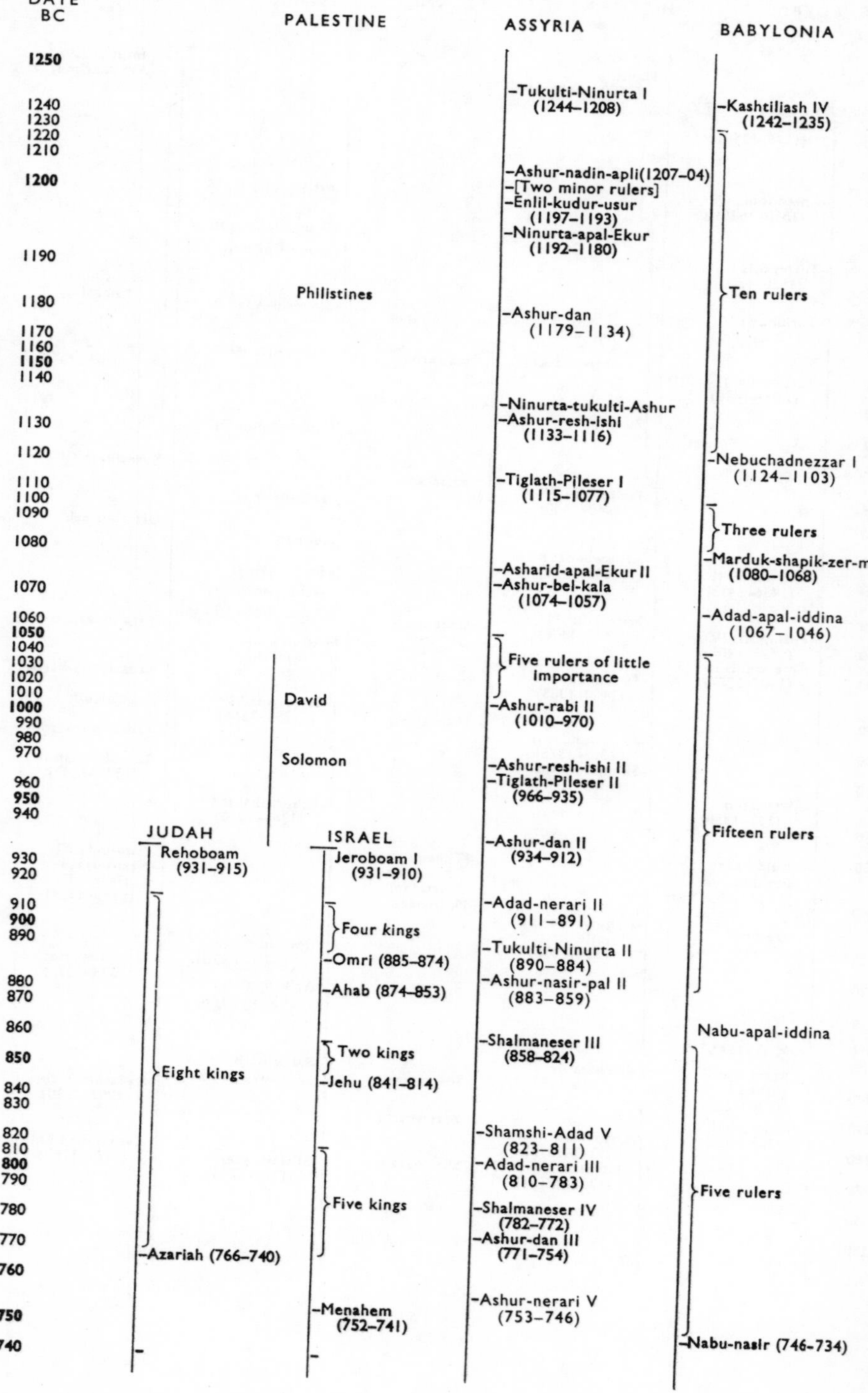

DATE BC	PALESTINE / JUDAH	PALESTINE / ISRAEL	ASSYRIA	BABYLONIA
1250				
1240			Tukulti-Ninurta I (1244–1208)	Kashtiliash IV (1242–1235)
1230				
1220				
1210				
1200			Ashur-nadin-apli (1207–04); [Two minor rulers]; Enlil-kudur-usur (1197–1193)	
1190			Ninurta-apal-Ekur (1192–1180)	
1180	Philistines			Ten rulers
1170			Ashur-dan (1179–1134)	
1160				
1150				
1140				
1130			Ninurta-tukulti-Ashur; Ashur-resh-ishi (1133–1116)	
1120				Nebuchadnezzar I (1124–1103)
1110			Tiglath-Pileser I (1115–1077)	
1100				
1090				Three rulers
1080				Marduk-shapik-zer-ma (1080–1068)
1070			Asharid-apal-Ekur II; Ashur-bel-kala (1074–1057)	
1060				Adad-apal-iddina (1067–1046)
1050				
1040				
1030			Five rulers of little importance	
1020				
1010				
1000	David		Ashur-rabi II (1010–970)	
990				
980				
970	Solomon			
960			Ashur-resh-ishi II; Tiglath-Pileser II (966–935)	
950				
940				Fifteen rulers
	JUDAH	ISRAEL		
930	Rehoboam (931–915)	Jeroboam I (931–910)	Ashur-dan II (934–912)	
920				
910			Adad-nerari II (911–891)	
900		Four kings		
890		Omri (885–874)	Tukulti-Ninurta II (890–884)	
880			Ashur-nasir-pal II (883–859)	
870		Ahab (874–853)		
860				Nabu-apal-iddina
850	Eight kings	Two kings	Shalmaneser III (858–824)	
840		Jehu (841–814)		
830				
820			Shamshi-Adad V (823–811)	
810				
800			Adad-nerari III (810–783)	
790				Five rulers
780		Five kings	Shalmaneser IV (782–772)	
770			Ashur-dan III (771–754)	
760	Azariah (766–740)			
750		Menahem (752–741)	Ashur-nerari V (753–746)	
740				Nabu-nasir (746–734)

CHRONOLOGICAL TABLE V

Assyria and Babylonia 745–539 BC, with principal contemporaries

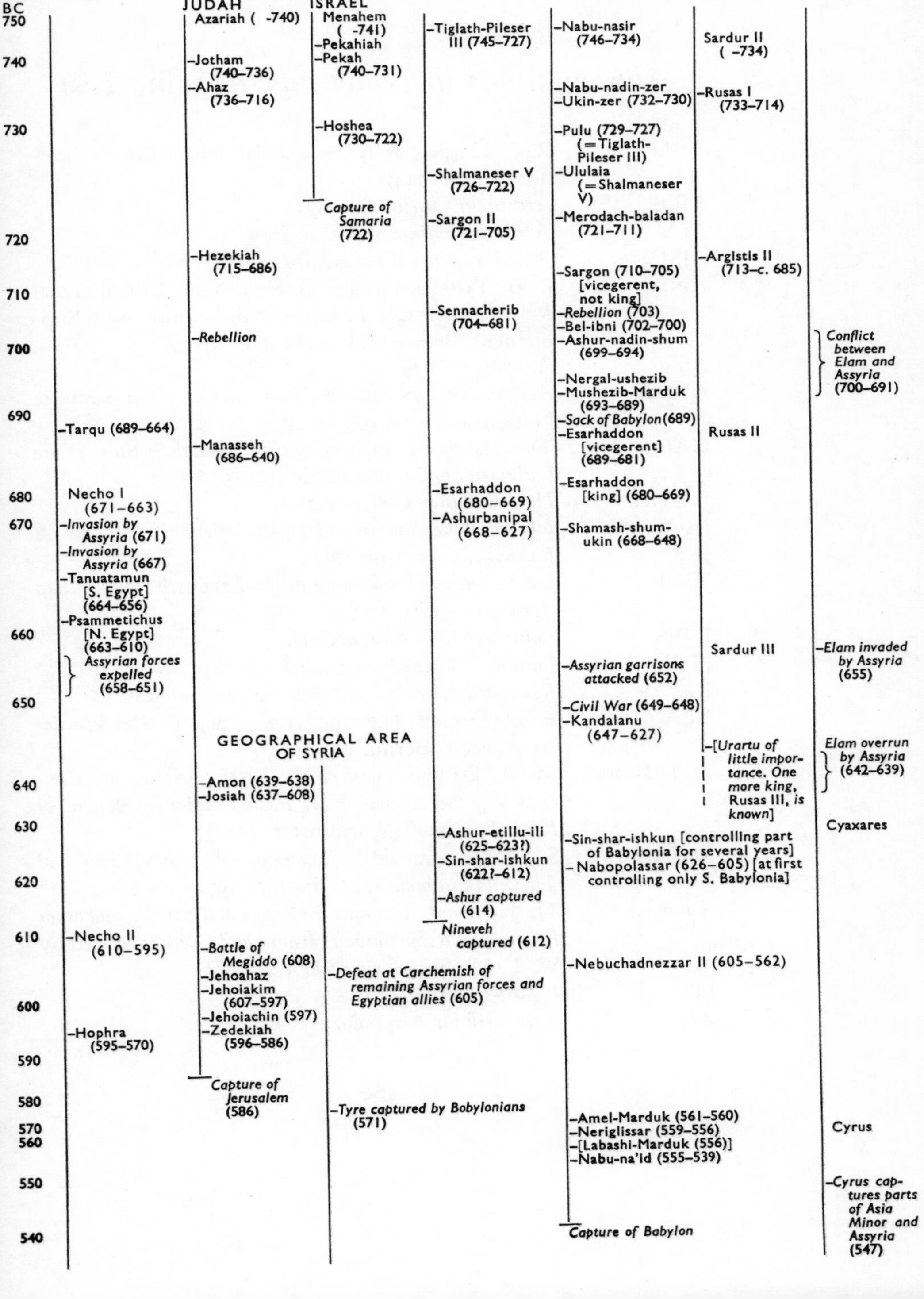

DATE BC	EGYPT	PALESTINE: JUDAH	PALESTINE: ISRAEL	ASSYRIA	BABYLONIA	URARTU	IRAN
750		Azariah (-740)	Menahem (-741) –Pekahiah	–Tiglath-Pileser III (745–727)	–Nabu-nasir (746–734)	Sardur II (-734)	
740		–Jotham (740–736) –Ahaz (736–716)	–Pekah (740–731)		–Nabu-nadin-zer –Ukin-zer (732–730)	–Rusas I (733–714)	
730			–Hoshea (730–722) *Capture of Samaria* (722)	–Shalmaneser V (726–722) –Sargon II (721–705)	–Pulu (729–727) (=Tiglath-Pileser III) –Ululaia (=Shalmaneser V) –Merodach-baladan (721–711)		
720		–Hezekiah (715–686)			–Sargon (710–705) [vicegerent, not king]	–Argistis II (713–c. 685)	
710				–Sennacherib (704–681)	–*Rebellion* (703) –Bel-ibni (702–700)		
700		–*Rebellion*			–Ashur-nadin-shum (699–694) –Nergal-ushezib –Mushezib-Marduk (693–689)		*Conflict between Elam and Assyria* (700–691)
690	–Tarqu (689–664)	–Manasseh (686–640)			–*Sack of Babylon* (689) –Esarhaddon [vicegerent] (689–681)	Rusas II	
680	Necho I (671–663)			–Esarhaddon (680–669)	–Esarhaddon [king] (680–669)		
670	–*Invasion by Assyria* (671) –*Invasion by Assyria* (667) –Tanuatamun [S. Egypt] (664–656) –Psammetichus [N. Egypt] (663–610)			–Ashurbanipal (668–627)	–Shamash-shum-ukin (668–648)		
660	*Assyrian forces expelled* (658–651)				–*Assyrian garrisons attacked* (652)	Sardur III	–*Elam invaded by Assyria* (655)
650			GEOGRAPHICAL AREA OF SYRIA		–*Civil War* (649–648) –Kandalanu (647–627)	–[*Urartu of little importance. One more king,* Rusas III, *is known*]	*Elam overrun by Assyria* (642–639)
640		–Amon (639–638) –Josiah (637–608)					
630				–Ashur-etillu-ili (625–623?) –Sin-shar-ishkun (622?–612)	–Sin-shar-ishkun [controlling part of Babylonia for several years] –Nabopolassar (626–605) [at first controlling only S. Babylonia]		Cyaxares
620				–*Ashur captured* (614) *Nineveh captured* (612)			
610	–Necho II (610–595)	–*Battle of Megiddo* (608) –Jehoahaz –Jehoiakim (607–597)	–*Defeat at Carchemish of remaining Assyrian forces and Egyptian allies* (605)		–Nebuchadnezzar II (605–562)		
600	–Hophra (595–570)	–Jehoiachin (597) –Zedekiah (596–586)					
590							
580		*Capture of Jerusalem* (586)	–*Tyre captured by Bobylonians* (571)				
570					–Amel-Marduk (561–560)		Cyrus
560					–Neriglissar (559–556) –[Labashi-Marduk (556)] –Nabu-na'id (555–539)		
550							–*Cyrus captures parts of Asia Minor and Assyria* (547)
540					*Capture of Babylon*		

Abbreviations in Notes and Reading List

ABL	R. F. Harper, *Assyrian and Babylonian Letters* (London, 1892–1914)
AfO	*Archiv für Orientforschung*
AJA	*American Journal of Archaeology*
AJSL	*American Journal of Semitic Languages*
ANET	J. B. Pritchard (ed.), *Ancient Near Eastern Texts Relating to the Old Testament* (third edition with Supplement, Princeton U.P., 1969)
AnSt	*Anatolian Studies*
ARMT	*Archives royales de Mari, transcrites . . .* (Imprimerie Nationale, Paris, 1950–)
CAD	*The Assyrian Dictionary of the Oriental Institute of the University of Chicago* (Chicago, 1956–)
HUCA	*Hebrew Union College Annual*
JAOS	*Journal of the American Oriental Society*
JCS	*Journal of Cuneiform Studies*
JEOL	*Jaarbericht van het Vooraziatisch-Egyptisch Genootschap 'Ex Oriente Lux'*
JNES	*Journal of Near Eastern Studies*
JTS	*Journal of Theological Studies*
RA	*Revue d'assyriologie et d'archéologie orientale*
RLA	E. Ebeling, B. Meissner *et al.* (eds), *Reallexikon der Assyriologie* (Berlin, 1932–)
St. Diakonoff	M. A. Dandamayev *et al.* (eds), *Societies and Languages of the Ancient Near East. Studies in Honour of I. M. Diakonoff* (Warminster, 1982).
St. Jacobsen	S. J. Lieberman (ed.), *Sumerological Studies in Honor of Thorkild Jacobsen . . .* (Chicago, 1976)
Tammuz	Th. Jacobsen, *Towards the Image of Tammuz and other Essays on Mesopotamian History and Culture*, edited by W. L. Moran (Harvard U.P., 1970)
UF	*Ugarit-Forschungen*
ZA	*Zeitschrift für Assyriologie*

Notes

Chapter 1

1. Paul Popenoe, *The Date Palm* (Miami, 1973), p. 4, note 5 mentions a place where untended palms 'form an almost impenetrable jungle'.
2. P. E. L. Smith and T. Cuyler Young, p. 31 in Brian Spooner (ed.), *Population Growth: Anthropological Implications* (Massachusetts, 1972).
3. M. N. Cohen, *The Food Crisis in Prehistory* (Yale University Press, 1977).
4. C. J. Rich, *Narrative of a Residence in Koordistan* (London, 1836), vol. 1, pp. 106f.
5. The dates given depend on a procedure known as carbon-14 analysis. Briefly the principle is this. The atmosphere contains carbon dioxide. Radiation from space ensures that a small proportion of the carbon atoms of this carbon dioxide are always radioactive. All living matter contains carbon, in constant interchange by breathing or transpiration with carbon atoms in the atmosphere. When an animal or plant dies, this interchange ceases. Any radioactive element loses its radioactivity at a constant rate unaffected by temperature or pressure, and therefore measurement of the residual proportion of radioactive carbon atoms will tell how long has elapsed since the animal or plant died. Such dating may be subject to a margin of error of several centuries. Revised calculations by physicists can necessitate a revision of these datings, and current indications are that dates given in the present book before the middle of the third millennium may need to be placed earlier.
6. The cylinder seal was a small cylinder of semi-precious stone usually not bigger than a man's thumb, engraved with a religious design which could be transferred to clay by rolling. Invented by the *Uruk* people, it quickly replaced the stamp seal, known since *Halaf* times, and became of wide application in later Mesopotamia. Its original purpose may have been to transfer the magic in the seal's religious scene to any object sealed with it,

and so to protect property. Later its function changed. It then often bore its owner's name in addition to the essential religious scene or symbols, and its primary use was now for rolling upon clay tablets of business or legal content to validate the name of the owner mentioned as either a principal or a witness.

7. G. Komoróczy, 'Das Rätsel der sumerischen Sprache als Problem der Frühgeschichte Vorderasiens', pp. 225–52 in B. Hruška and G. Komoróczy (eds), *Festschrift Lubor Matouš* (Budapest, 1978).
8. D. O. Edzard, *Die zweite Zwischenzeit Babyloniens* (Wiesbaden, 1957), pp. 31f.
9. There were two different gods who bore the name Enki. The Enki associated with Eridu was the one who was the great god of the waters. See Th. Jacobsen, *The Treasures of Darkness* (Yale University Press, 1976), p. 252, note 173.
10. There have been claims for earlier inscribed tablets from Tartaria in eastern Europe. But the very early date claimed has not been confirmed, and it has not been proved that the marks on the tablets really are a form of writing.
11. An example is a tablet from Nimrud, ND 2371.

Chapter 2

1. A. Moortgat, *The Art of Ancient Mesopotamia* (London, 1969), p. 8.
2. Th. Jacobsen, JNES, 2 (1943), pp. 159–72.
3. For full translation of the epic, with bibliography, see ANET, pp. 44ff. See also W. H. Ph. Römer, *Das Sumerische Kurzepos 'Bilgameš und Akka'* (Kevelaer, 1980).
4. S. N. Kramer, *Enmerkar and the Lord of Aratta* (Philadelphia, 1952), pp. 38–41, lines 502–7, 525f., 540.
5. ibid, p. 33, lines 421–32. The text contains the words (as translated by the first editor) 'He . . . crushed the . . . -stone, . . . brought it forth from the light to the shade, brought it forth from the shade to the light; after five, after ten years had passed, he crushed the . . . -reed . . . The lord looked with joyous eye upon it.' 'Light' and 'shade' might well refer to colour changes which occur when some chemicals are heated, and the reference to five or ten 'years' may relate to repeated heating in the fire. The passage could therefore refer to a process in which some mineral or mixture of minerals was heated five or ten times to a

temperature at which colour changes occurred. In fact, lapis lazuli can be prepared artificially by heating three ingredients together in the presence of air, but there must be repeated heating and cooling, by which the colour of the product is gradually changed from green to the desired shade of deep blue. It looks very much as if it was a technological process of this kind that the Sumerian text was describing.

6. R. D. Biggs, JCS, 20 (1966), p. 75, note 19.
7. A. A. Vaiman, p. 15 in J. Harmatta and G. Komoróczy (eds), *Wirtschaft und Gesellschaft im Alten Vorderasien* (Budapest, 1976).
8. R. D. Biggs, pp. 125–7 in L. Cagni (ed.), *La Lingua di Ebla* (Naples, 1981).
9. J. S. Cooper, *Reconstructing History from Ancient Inscriptions: the Lagash–Umma Border Conflict* (Undena, 1983), p. 46.
10. I. M. Diakonoff, *Structure of Society and State in Early Dynastic Sumer* (Undena, 1974, abridged translation of Russian article of 1959), pp. 12f.
11. J. S. Cooper, op. cit., p. 48.
12. ibid, p. 46.
13. Th. Jacobsen, AfO, 26, p. 1, note 2.
14. C. L. Woolley, *Ur Excavations*, Vol. 4 (London and Philadelphia, 1955), plate 41d.
15. Th. Jacobsen, op. cit., p. 6, note 27.
16. ibid, p. 8, note 36.
17. JCS, 23 (1970), pp. 106f., numbers 32 and 35; *Annual Review of Royal Inscriptions of Mesopotamia Project*, 4 (1986), pp. 6f., number 20.
18. S. N. Kramer, JCS, 21 (1967), pp. 104–22.
19. J. Klein, *Royal Hymns of Shulgi* (1981), p. 19.
20. ibid, pp. 20f.
21. ibid, p. 9, note 18.
22. C. J. Gadd, *Cambridge Ancient History*, Vol. I/2 (third edition, 1971), pp. 601ff.
23. A year-formula was a means of dating documents. Each year a short sentence was promulgated, relating to some current event, and the year would subsequently be identified by this. Some typical formulae are 'The town Simurru was destroyed', 'He made the ritual drum called Nin-igizi-barra for the goddess Inanna'.

Chapter 3

1. Extract from lines 211–29. For a translation by S. N. Kramer of the complete composition, with bibliography, see ANET, pp. 455ff.
2. S. D. Walters, *Water for Larsa* (Yale University Press, 1970), p. 144.
3. I. J. Gelb, *Journal of the Institute of Asian Studies*, 1 (1955), pp. 1–4.
4. ARMT, 2, number 72.
5. ARMT, 2, number 33.
6. ARMT, 2, number 76.
7. RLA, 2, p. 181, number 140.

Chapter 4

1. J. A. Brinkman, *A Political History of post-Kassite Babylonia, 1158–722 B.C.* (Rome, 1968), p. 86.
2. L. W. King, *Babylonian Boundary-Stones . . . in the British Museum* (London, 1912), vol. of plates, plate LXXXIV, lines 17–21.
3. J. Seidmann, *Die Inschriften Adadniraris II* (Leipzig, 1935), p. 32, lines 129f.
4. An argument that the Israelite king concerned was not Jehu is based on a misunderstanding of the way in which Hebrew names were transcribed into cuneiform.

Chapter 7

1. Th. Jacobsen, JNES, 2 (1943), pp. 159–72.
2. Th. Jacobsen, AfO, 26, p. 2, note 4.
3. A. Finet (ed.), *La voix de l'opposition en Mésopotamie* (Brussels, 1973), a work specifically concerned with opposition, identifies none with such an origin.
4. J. Van Dijk, *LUGAL UD ME-LÁM-bi NIR-G̃ÁL* (1983), p. 93, lines 334, 336f.
5. W. G. Lambert and A. R. Millard, *Atra-hasis; the Babylonian Story of the Flood* (Oxford, 1969), p. 46, lines 64–66.
6. J. Bottéro, p. 24 in *St. Diakonoff* (Warminster, 1982).
7. Akkadian *šamaššammu*, which by etymology means simply 'oil-plant', frequently occurs and was formerly translated 'sesame'; but according to palaeobotanists the plant which we now know as sesame did not reach Mesopotamia until the first millennium BC, when it took over both the role and the name of

the earlier oil-producing plant, linseed. Some Assyriologists are still fighting a rearguard action to retain their sesame, but we defer to the palaeobotanists' expertise and translate *šamaššammu* as 'linseed' in this edition.

8. A. Berlin, *Enmerkar and Ensuhkešdanna* (1979), p. 44, lines 97, 99.
9. See reference in CAD, I/J, p. 230a, 2.1′.
10. D. I. Owen, pp. 189–202 in G. Rendsburg *et al.* (eds), *The Bible World. Essays in Honor of Cyrus H. Gordon* (Ktav, New York, 1980).
11. It has been suggested that this may incorporate a literary embellishment of the actual procedure, but even if it does, it seems improbable that a Babylonian writer would have invented an incident completely outside known practice. See S. Greengus, HUCA, 40–41 (1969–70), pp. 35–44.
12. E. M. Yamauchi, p. 214 in H. A. Hoffner (ed.), *Orient and Occident* (Kevelaer, 1973).
13. J. and A. Westenholz, *Orientalia*, 46 (1977), pp. 198–215.
14. M. Civil, *Iraq*, 23 (1961), pp. 154–75.

Chapter 8

1. Akkadian *nakkapti . . . ipte*. The meaning has been much discussed, and proposals have ranged from doing something to the eye-socket or the tear-ducts to making cuts in the temple area to relieve pain, or lancing an abscess. However, in the most recent discussion (P. Naster and L. Missotten, AfO, Beiheft 19 (1982), pp. 317–241) an ophthalmic surgeon gives reasons for concluding that the expression referred to an operation for cataract.

Chapter 9

1. I. M. Diakonoff, *Structure of Society and State in Early Dynastic Sumer*, pp. 12f.
2. Verse 3 in the Hebrew text begins 'Behold Assyria, a cedar in Lebanon'. Some authorities, e.g. RSV, emend 'Assyria' out of existence, and take the whole passage as referring to Egypt, on the basis of the reference in verse 2 to Pharaoh king of Egypt. But there are statements in the passage which never applied to Egypt; e.g. Egypt had never been an imperial power since the middle of the second millennium, so that it would not have been true for a first-millennium prophet to say that (see verse 6) all great nations dwelt under the shadow of Egypt. We take the

poetic verses 3–9 as the original prophecy, referring to Assyria, and verse 2 as a secondary prose introduction, added later to apply the prophecy to Egypt.

3. Sir Alan Gardiner, *Egypt of the Pharaohs* (Oxford, 1961), p. 202.

Chapter 10

1. A. L. Oppenheim, *Ancient Mesopotamia* (Chicago, 1964), pp. 355f., note 24.
2. L. Casson, *Ships and Seamanship in the Ancient World* (Princeton, 1976), p. 24.
3. A. L. Oppenheim, JCS, 21 (1967), p. 244, note 35.
4. *Textes cunéiformes, Musée du Louvre*, 12, number 40.
5. A. L. Oppenheim, JCS, 21 (1967), p. 240.
6. H. Klengel, *Orientalia*, 37 (1968), pp. 216–19 and F. A. Ali, *Sumer*, 20 (1964), pp. 66–68.

Chapter 11

1. The idea that toothache was caused by a worm is still found in Shakespeare, *Much Ado About Nothing*, Act III, Scene 2, 'What! sigh for the tooth-ache? Where is but a humour or a worm.'
2. See note 9 to Chapter 1.
3. E. Reiner, JNES, 33 (1974), p. 224, line 3; J. A. Craig, *Assyrian and Babylonian Religious Texts*, Vol. 1 (Leipzig, 1895), plate 6, K.1285, reverse line 8.
4. There is nothing beyond the similarity of name to link these tribes with the biblical tribe of Benjamin. Jamin (*yamin*) implies 'on the right hand', i.e. 'south' for peoples orientating themselves by the rising sun. Benjamin (and any similar form) was thus a name given to the most southerly of a group of tribes, in Israel the tribe with the most southerly territory in the northern kingdom.
5. A record of the music has been published, with an accompanying explanatory booklet: Anne Draffkorn Kilmer *et al.*, *Sounds from Silence* (Bit Enki Records, California, 1976).
6. Th. Jacobsen, *The Treasures of Darkness*, p. 140.
7. Herodotus, *Histories*, I, 199.
8. ibid, I, 181f.
9. R. Harris, *Ancient Sippar* (Leiden, 1975), pp. 317ff.

Chapter 12

1. For a representation of Imdugud see plate 10.
2. R. S. Ellis, *Foundation Deposits in Ancient Mesopotamia* (Yale University Press, 1968), pp. 10–15.
3. On dating see H. J. Nissen, *Zur Datierung des Königsfriedhofes von Ur* (Bonn, 1966).
4. ABL, number 437; W. von Soden, pp. 103f. in K. Schubert *et al.* (eds), *Festschrift . . . Viktor Christian* (Vienna, 1956).
5. C. J. Gadd, *Iraq*, 22 (1960), p. 57. The Huns also had the companions of a dead warrior leader placed alive in his tomb; Procopius, *History*, I.iii.2–7.
6. A parallel to the idea of the intercourse of a god with a human bride occurs in Jewish tradition. The Jewish scholar Rashi (eleventh century AD), commenting on the ancient myth preserved in Genesis 6:1–2, writes: Rabbi Yudan said, '. . . when they had made (a bride) look good as she was adorned to enter the bridal chamber, a *Gadol* [a 'Great One', used of a supernatural being] used to go in and possess her first'. It is in no anti-Christian spirit (I accept the theological doctrine of the Virgin Birth) that I point out the possibility that the same cultural thinking underlies the form in which the annunciation of the Blessed Virgin Mary has been transmitted to us. Furthermore, St Paul's ordinance that a woman ought 'to have a sign of authority on her head, because of the angels' (1 Corinthians 11:10) may relate to the same idea.

Chapter 13

1. JCS, 16, pp. 59ff.
2. See J. Bottéro, pp. 25ff. in *St. Diakonoff*.
3. A variant reading gives the sense 'ruler of his fathers'.
4. See above, page 165.
5. The most useful discussions are in Th. Jacobsen, *The Treasures of Darkness*, pp. 55ff.; S. N. Kramer, *The Sacred Marriage Rite* (Bloomington, 1969), pp. 108ff.; A. D. Kilmer, UF, 3 (1971), pp. 299–309; W. von Soden, ZA, 58 (1967), pp. 192–5.
6. For a more detailed account see B. L. van der Waerden, *Science Awakening*, II (Leiden and New York, 1974), p. 51.
7. Th. Jacobsen, *The Treasures of Darkness*, pp. 55ff.
8. For the latest edition see H. W. F. Saggs, AfO, 33 (1987).
9. For translation see R. Borger, *Orientalia*, 33 (1964), p. 462.

Chapter 15

1. The animals shown are generally taken as wild asses, but one authority on equids kindly informed me that they look to him like typical wild Przewalski horses.
2. In some parts of the Islamic world, the requirement to have the sighting of the new moon reported by eyewitnesses has been modified in recent years. This does not affect the argument.
3. C. Brockelmann, *History of the Islamic Peoples* (Routledge & Kegan Paul, paperback, London, 1980), p. 9. Although the Moon-god of the pre-Islamic Kaʿbah was not specifically the Babylonian Moon-god, it was part of the same ancient Near Eastern religious development.
4. H. W. F. Saggs, AfO, 19 (1960), pp. 123–7.
5. E. A. Speiser, pp. 23–34 in J. J. Finkelstein and M. Greenberg (eds), *Oriental and Biblical Studies: Collected works of E. A. Speiser* (University of Pennsylvania, 1967).
6. Palestine Exploration Quarterly, 1959, pp. 55–8.
7. H. W. F. Saggs, JTS, 11 (1960), pp. 318–29.
8. AJSL, 38 (1922), pp. 1–14. See also S. N. Kramer, *The Sacred Marriage Rite*.
9. These people and the Babylonians may of course be in the right, even though current twentieth-century opinion is against them.
10. C. J. Gadd, *Ideas of Divine Rule in the Ancient East* (London, 1948), pp. 48f.
11. JCS, 6 (1952), p. 57.

Further Reading

Very detailed bibliographies of Assyriological publications are provided annually in the periodicals *Orientalia* and *Archiv für Orientforschung*. The following list is intended mainly to serve the needs of readers wishing to follow up topics discussed or touched upon in the present book.

General

ALBRIGHT, W. F., *From the Stone Age to Christianity* (Doubleday Anchor Books, New York, 1957).

BURROWS, M., *What mean these Stones?* (New Haven, 1941).

CHIERA, E., *They Wrote on Clay* (Chicago University Press, 1959).

EBELING, E., MEISSNER, B., *et al.* (eds), *Reallexikon der Assyriologie* (in progress, Berlin 1932–present).

KRAMER, S. N., *The Sumerians: Their History, Culture and Character* (Chicago University Press, 1963).

KRAMER, S. N., *History begins at Sumer. Thirty-nine Firsts in Man's recorded history* (third revised edition, University of Pennsylvania, 1981).

OATES, J., *Babylon* (Thames & Hudson, 1979).

OPPENHEIM, A. L., *Ancient Mesopotamia; Portrait of a Dead Civilization* (Chicago University Press, 1964 and posthumous revised edition).

PRITCHARD, J. B. (ed.), *Ancient Near Eastern Texts Relating to the Old Testament* (Third Edition, Princeton University Press, 1969).

ROUX, G., *La Mésopotamie* (Seuil, Paris, 1985).

SAGGS, H. W. F., *Everyday Life in Babylonia and Assyria* (revised edition, Batsford, London, 1987).

SODEN, W. VON, *Einführung in die Altorientalistik* (Wissenschaftliche Buchgesellschaft, Darmstadt, 1985).

Excavation

CURTIS, J. (ed.), *Fifty Years of Mesopotamian Discovery* (British School of Archaeology in Iraq, London, 1982).

Lloyd, S., *The Archaeology of Mesopotamia from the Old Stone Age to the Persian Conquest* (Thames & Hudson, 1978).

Mallowan, M. E. L., *Twenty-five Years of Mesopotamian Discovery* (British School of Archaeology in Iraq, London, 1956).

Parrot, A., *Archéologie mésopotamienne; les étapes* (Albin Michel, Paris, 1946).

Related to Chapter 1

Adams, R. McC., *Heartlands of Cities. Surveys of ancient settlement . . . on . . . the Euphrates* (Chicago, 1981).

Falkenstein, A., *Archäische Texte aus Uruk* (Harrassowitz, Leipzig, 1936).

Kraeling, C. H., and Adams, R. M., *City Invincible. A Symposium on Urbanization and Cultural Development in the Ancient Near East* (Chicago University Press, 1960).

Oates, D. and J., *The Rise of Civilization* (Elsevier-Phaidon, 1976).

Ucko, P. J., *et al.* (eds), *Man, Settlement and Urbanism* (Duckworth, 1972).

Related to Chapter 2

Diakonoff, I. M., *Structure of Society and State in Early Dynastic Sumer* (= *Monographs on the Ancient Near East*, 1/3, Undena, 1974).

Jacobsen, Th., *The Sumerian King List* (Chicago University Press, 1939).

Jacobsen, Th., 'The assumed conflict between Sumerians and Semites in early Mesopotamian history', *Tammuz*, pp. 187–92.

Jacobsen, Th., 'Primitive Democracy in ancient Mesopotamia', *Tammuz*, pp. 157–70.

Jacobsen, Th., 'Early Political Development in Mesopotamia', *Tammuz*, pp. 132–56.

Klein, J., *The Royal Hymns of Shulgi King of Ur* (= Transactions of the American Philosophical Society, 71/7, 1981).

Kramer, S. N., *Lamentation over the Destruction of Ur* (Chicago University Press, 1940).

Lewis, B., *The Sargon Legend* (American Schools of Oriental Research, 1980).

Sollberger, E., and Kupper, J. R., *Inscriptions royales sumériennes et akkadiennes* (Éditions du Cerf, Paris, 1971).

Related to Chapter 3

Dossin, G., *Correspondance de Iasmah-addu transcrite et traduite* (= *Archives Royales de Mari*, V; Imprimerie Nationale, Paris, 1952).

Gelb, I. J., 'The Name of Babylon', *Journal of the Institute of Asian Studies*, 1 (1955), pp. 1–4.

Jean, C.-F., *Lettres Diverses transcrites et traduites* (= *Archives Royales de Mari*, II; Imprimerie Nationale, Paris, 1950).

Kupper, J. R., 'Un gouvernement provincial dans le royaume de Mari', RA, 41 (1947), pp. 149–83.

Kupper, J. R., *Les nomades en Mésopotamie au temps des rois de Mari* (Paris, 1957, reprint 1968).

Walters, S. D., *Water for Larsa: an Old Babylonian Archive dealing with irrigation* (Yale University Press, 1970).

Related to Chapters 4, 5 and 6

Brinkman, J. A., *A Political History of post-Kassite Babylonia 1158–722 B.C.* (Pontificium Institutum Biblicum, Rome, 1968).

Dubberstein, W. H., 'Comparative Prices in later Babylonia', AJSL, 56 (1939), pp. 20–43.

Gadd, C. J., 'The Harran inscriptions of Nabonidus', AnSt, 8 (1958), pp. 35–92.

Grayson, A. K., *Assyrian Royal Inscriptions*, 2 vols (Harrassowitz, Wiesbaden, 1972, 1976). (More up-to-date and reliable translations than those in the work by D. D. Luckenbill, but unlike Luckenbill does not cover the final two centuries of the Assyrian empire.)

Knudtzon, J. A., *Die el-Amarna-Tafeln*, 2 vols (Hinrichs, Leipzig, 1915).

Luckenbill, D. D., *Ancient Records of Assyria and Babylonia*, 2 vols (Chicago University Press, 1924, 1926).

Saggs, H. W. F., *The Might that was Assyria* (Sidgwick & Jackson, 1984).

Smith, S., *Babylonian Historical Texts* (Methuen, London, 1924).

Weidner, E., 'Jojachin, König von Juda, in babylonischen Keilschrifttexten, pp. 923–35 in *Mélanges Syriens offerts à Monsieur René Dussaud* (Geuthner, Paris, 1939).

Wertime, T., and Muhly, J. D. (eds), *The Coming of the Age of Iron* (Yale University Press, 1980).

Related to Chapter 7

HARRIS, R., *Ancient Sippar; A Demographic Study of an Old Babylonian City (1894–1595 BC)* (Leiden, 1975).

KRAUS, F. R., 'Altmesopotamisches Lebensgefühl', JNES, 19 (1960), pp. 117–32.

SPYCKET, A., 'La coiffure féminine en Mésopotamie', RA, 48 (1954), pp. 113–29 and 169–77, and 49 (1955), pp. 113–28.

Related to Chapter 8

DRIVER, G. R., and MILES, J. C., *The Babylonian Laws*, 2 vols (Clarendon Press, 1952, 1955).

FIGULLA, H., 'Lawsuit concerning a sacrilegious theft at Erech', *Iraq*, 13 (1951), pp. 95–101.

FINET, A., *Le code de Hammurapi* (Les Éditions du Cerf, Paris, 1973; revised edition, 1983).

KRAUS, F. R., 'Ein Zentrales Problem des altmesopotamischen Rechtes: Was ist der Codex Hammu-rabi', *Genava*, n.s. 8 (1960), pp. 283–96.

OWEN, D. I., 'Widows' Rights in Ur III Sumer', ZA, 70 (1980), pp. 170–84.

YARON, R., *The Laws of Eshnunna* (Jerusalem, 1969).

Related to Chapters 9 and 10

DIAKONOFF, I. M. (ed.), *Ancient Mesopotamia, Socio-Economic History: A Collection of Studies by Soviet Scholars* (Moscow, 1969).

DOSSIN, G., 'Signaux lumineux au pays de Mari', RA, 35 (1938), pp. 174–86.

HARMATTA, J. and KOMORÓCZY, G. (eds), *Wirtschaft und Gessellschaft im alten Vorderasien* (Budapest, 1976).

HEICHELHEIM, F. M., *An Ancient Economic History*, Vol. 1 (Sijthoff, Leiden, 1958).

JACOBSEN, TH., 'On the textile industry at Ur under Ibbi-Sin', *Tammuz*, pp. 216–29.

KOMORÓCZY, G., 'Landed Property in Ancient Mesopotamia and the Theory of the so-called Asiatic Mode of Production', *Oikumene*, 2 (1978), pp. 145–53.

LEEMANS, W. F., *The Old Babylonian Merchant* (Brill, Leiden, 1950).

LEEMANS, W. F., *Foreign Trade in the Old Babylonian Period* (Brill, Leiden, 1960).

LIPIŃSKI, E. (ed.), *State and Temple Economy in the Ancient Near East*, 2 vols (Leuven, 1979).

MUHLY, J. D., *Copper and Tin. The Distribution of Mineral Resources and the Nature of the Metals Trade in the Bronze Age* (Connecticut, 1973).

MUNN-RANKIN, J. M., 'Diplomacy in Western Asia in the early Second Millennium B.C.', *Iraq*, 18 (1956), pp. 68–110.

OPPENHEIM, A. L., 'The Seafaring Merchants of Ur', JAOS, 74 (1954), pp. 6–17.

Related to Chapters 11 and 12

BOTTÉRO, J., La religion babylonienne (Paris, 1952).

CASTELLINO, G., 'Rituals and Prayers against "Appearing Ghosts"', *Orientalia*, 24 (1955), pp. 240–74.

DIJK, J. J. A. VAN, *LUGAL UD ME-LÁM-bi NIR-G̃ÁL* (Leiden, 1983).

DOSSIN, G., 'Une révélation du dieu Dagan à Terqa', RA, 42 (1948), pp. 125–34.

EBELING, E., 'Ein babylonisches Beispiel schwarzer Magie', *Orientalia*, 20 (1951), pp. 167–70.

FALKENSTEIN, A., and SODEN, W. VON, *Sumerische und akkadische Hymnen und Gebete* (Artemis-Verlag, Zürich/Stuttgart, 1953).

GADD, C. J., *Ideas of Divine Rule in the Ancient Near East* (British Academy, London 1948).

GURNEY, O. R., 'Babylonian Prophylactic Figures and their Ritual', *Annals of Archaeology and Anthropology*, 22 (1935), pp. 31–96.

JACOBSEN, TH., 'Mesopotamia', pp. 137–234 in H. Frankfort *et al.*, *Before Philosophy* (Penguin, 1949).

JACOBSEN, TH., *The Treasures of Darkness* (Yale University Press, 1976).

KILMER, A. D., CROCKER, R. L., and BROWN, R. R., *Sounds from Silence* (Bit Enki Records, Berkeley, California, 1976).

KRAMER, S. N., *The Sacred Marriage Rite* (Bloomington, 1969).

MEIER, G., *Die assyrische Beschwörungssammlung Maqlu* (= AfO Beiheft 2, Berlin 1937).

OPPENHEIM, A. L., 'A New Prayer to the "Gods of the Night"', pp. 282–301 in *Studia Biblica et Orientalia*, Vol. III, *Oriens Antiquus* (Rome, 1959).

PALLIS, S. A., *The Babylonian Akitu Festival* (Copenhagen, 1926). (In many respects antiquated and unreliable, but still interesting.)

REINER, E., *Šurpu. A collection of Sumerian and Akkadian Incantations* (= AfO Beiheft 11, Graz, 1958).

SAGGS, H. W. F., 'Pazuzu', AfO, 19 (1960), pp. 123–7.

SAGGS, H. W. F., *The Encounter with the Divine in Mesopotamia and Israel* (Athlone Press, London, 1978).

SODEN, W. VON, 'Gibt es ein Zeugnis dafür, dass die Babylonier an die Wiederaufstehungs Marduk geglaubt haben?', ZA, 46 (1955), pp. 130–66.

THOMPSON, R. C., *The Reports of the Magicians and Astrologers of Nineveh and Babylon*, 2 vols (Luzac, London, 1900).

THOMPSON, R. C., *The Devils and Evil Spirits of Babylonia*, 2 vols (Luzac, London, 1903).

Related to Chapter 13

ALSTER, B., *The Instructions of Suruppak: A Sumerian Proverb Collection* (Akademisk Forlag, Copenhagen, 1974).

DIJK, J. J. A. VAN, *La sagesse suméro-accadienne* (Leiden, 1953).

GADD, C. J., *Teachers and Students in the Oldest Schools* (London, 1956).

JESTIN, R., 'Übungen im Edubba', ZA, 46 (1955), pp. 37–44.

KRAMER, S. N., 'The Epic of Gilgameš and its Sumerian sources', JAOS, 64 (1944), pp. 7–23 and 83.

KRAMER, S. N., 'Schooldays: a Sumerian Composition relating to the Education of a Scribe', JAOS, 69 (1949), pp. 199–215.

KRAMER, S. N., *Enmerkar and the Lord of Aratta* (University of Pennsylvania, 1952).

LAMBERT, W. G., and MILLARD, A. R., *Atra-ḫasīs: The Babylonian Story of the Flood* (Oxford, 1969).

LAMBERT, W. G., *Babylonian Wisdom Literature* (Oxford, 1960). (There is a small addition to the most important Wisdom text in this volume, *The Righteous Sufferer*, in D. J. Wiseman, AnSt, 30 (1980), pp. 101–7.)

SAGGS, H. W. F., 'Additions to Anzu', AfO, 33 (1987), pp. 1–29.

SJÖBERG, A. W., 'The Old Babylonian Eduba', in *St. Jacobsen*, pp. 159–79.

THOMPSON, R. C., *The Epic of Gilgamesh. Text, transliteration and notes* (Oxford, 1930).

WILSON, J. V. KINNIER, *The legend of Etana: A New Edition* (Warminster, 1985).

Related to Chapter 14

(a) *Astronomy, Mathematics, Astrology*

NEUGEBAUER, O., 'The history of Ancient Astronomy; Problems and Methods', JNES, 4 (1945), pp. 1–38.

NEUGEBAUER, O., *The Exact Sciences in Antiquity* (Brown University Press, Providence, Rhode Island, second edition, 1957).

NEUGEBAUER, O., and SACHS, A., *Mathematical Cuneiform Texts* (New Haven, 1945).

SACHS, A., 'Babylonian Horoscopes', JCS, 6 (1952), 49–75.

SAGGS, H. W. F., 'A Babylonian Geometrical text', RA, 54 (1960), pp. 131–46.

THUREAU-DANGIN, F., *Textes mathématiques babyloniens* (Brill, Leiden, 1938).

WAERDEN, B. L. VAN DER, 'History of the Zodiac', I, in JEOL, 3 (1944–8), pp. 414–24; II, in JNES, 8 (1949), pp. 6–26.

WAERDEN, B. L. VAN DER, *Science Awakening: II, The Birth of Astronomy* (Noordhoff, Leiden, and Oxford University Press, New York, 1974).

(b) *Medicine*

BIGGS, R. D., 'Medicine in ancient Mesopotamia', *History of Science*, 8 (1969), pp. 94–105.

LABAT, R., *Traité akkadien de diagnostics et pronostics médicaux* (Paris, 1951).

OPPENHEIM, A. L., 'On the Observation of the pulse in Mesopotamian medicine', *Orientalia*, 31 (1962), pp. 27–33.

REINER, E., 'Medicine in ancient Mesopotamia', *Journal of International College of Surgeons*, 41 (1964), pp. 544–50.

Related to Chapter 15

AMIET, P., *L'Art antique du Proche-Orient* (Paris, 1977). (Also in English and German translation.)

FRANKFORT, H., *The Art and Architecture of the Ancient Orient* (Penguin, 1954).

MOORTGAT, A., *The Art of Ancient Mesopotamia* (Phaidon, London, 1969).

PERKINS, A., 'Narration in Babylonian Art', AJA, 61 (1957), pp. 54–62.

SPEISER, E. A., 'Ancient Mesopotamia, a Light that did not Fail', *National Geographical Magazine*, 49 (1951), pp. 41–105.

Selective Index

Index of Biblical References